NORWAY
NORWEGEN

THE WHITEWATER GUIDE · DER WILDWASSERFÜHRER

Olaf Obsommer found his place on earth: the eddy of the lake-to-lake drop, Eksingedalen.

Kayaking feeds the human body and spirit. Taking you on a voyage of personal discovery, this sport promises to be a spellbinding experience.
For every rapid noted in this book there are more just waiting to be found. Your discoveries are steppingstones to greater horizons. Be smart in your quest for adventure!

Olaf Obsommer going for an afternoon walk, Tordalen.

CONTENTS INHALT

THE RIVERS DIE FLÜSSE

FOREWORD

The simple facts make every whitewater kayaker tingle with excitement! Norway, slightly bigger than Germany, has just five per cent of the inhabitants. There are 18 national parks where you are allowed to camp. Whether you choose one of the numerous inexpensive campsites, pitch your tent at remote lakes or on high plateaux with breathtaking views, you are allowed to stay where you want as long as you do not disturb anybody else; every individual has this basic right in Norway. Because the sun takes a season ticket in summer, you have hours of daylight to spend on countless rivers of which only one third have so far been explored. And the water! You just can't ignore it! When in July and August the Alps dry up and the Pyrenees turn into a desert, in Norway water is gushing and rushing everywhere. Glaciers and snow left over from the winter – not to mention the odd rainstorms too – guarantee ultimate kayaking fun well into September. Without exaggeration, Norway in summer has the best whitewater kayaking on offer in Europe by a long way. It's a fact!

VORWORT

Schon die nüchternen Fakten begeistern jeden Wildwasserfan: Norwegen ist ein Stück größer als Deutschland, hat aber nur ein Zwanzigstel der Einwohner. Es gibt 18 Nationalparks mit der Lizenz zum Campen. Ob auf einem der vielen preisgünstigen Zeltplätze oder im Rahmen des Jedermannsrecht an einsamen Seen oder auf Hochebenen mit phänomenalem Weitblick – erlaubt ist was niemanden stört. Die unzähligen Flüsse, von denen bisher erst ein Drittel komplett erkundet ist, sind im Sommer bestens ausgeleuchtet, da die Sonne ein Dauerticket gelöst hat. Tja, und dann wäre da noch ein nicht zu vernachlässigender Faktor: Wasser! Während im Juli und August die Alpen ausdörren und die Pyrenäen zur Wanderdüne werden, rauscht es in Norwegen an allen Ecken und Enden. Gletscher, Restschnee und einige Regenschauer sichern vollendeten Paddelspaß bis in den September hinein. Es sei mit aller Bescheidenheit gesagt, dass Norwegen im Sommer das beste Wildwasserrevier in Europa ist. Und zwar mit Abstand. Basta!

Michael Neumann - KANUmagazin

Tungestølen, Jostedalsbreen Nasjonalpark.

How to use this river guidebook

What this book aims to do

This river guidebook provides information to make kayaking in Norway much easier. In order to find the right information as quickly as possible, you need to know where to look and that is what this chapter is all about.

This book seeks to be your travel companion through Norway and will give you an insight into the Norwegian culture whilst also providing helpful tips for an inspiring journey. Numerous pictures hopefully get you even more enthusiastic about kayaking: if not, maybe one of the anecdotes from our guest authors will.

Let us remind you however of the dangers lurking in every river and latent in each and every one of us. Overestimation of one's abilities and pure ignorance are probably the most frequent causes of accidents. Have a great time on the river, share experiences with your friends which you will remember a lifetime, but never forget: you are responsible for your own actions and you act for yourself and for nobody else!

Why English/German?

This book was published on a shoe-string budget. Low-volume publications inevitably mean high print costs and we were therefore forced to publish in two languages in order to address an adequately sized market. German readers need just a basic knowledge of English in order to understand captions and info boxes. We trust you will understand.

Zum Umgang mit dem Flussführer

Was dieses Buch will

Dieser Flussführer soll Informationen liefern, die Kajak fahren in Norwegen erleichtern. Um schnellstmöglich die richtige Information zu finden, solltest du wissen, wo sie geschrieben steht. Davon handelt dieses Kapitel.

Aber dieses Buch soll dir auch Gesellschaft leisten auf deiner Reise durch Norwegen, dir die norwegische Kultur näher bringen und hilfreiche Tipps für einen abgerundeten Urlaub geben. Die vielen Bilder machen hoffentlich noch mehr Lust aufs paddeln – und wenn nicht, dann vielleicht eine der Kurzgeschichten unserer Gastautoren.

Doch wir wollen auch an Gefahren erinnern, die auf jedem Fluss lauern – und in jedem von uns selbst. Selbstüberschätzung und Unwissenheit zählen wohl zu den häufigsten Unfallursachen. Genieße die Zeit auf dem Wasser, teile unvergessliche Erlebnisse mit deinen Freunden, doch vergiss nie: Du machst das nur für dich, und sonst für niemanden!

Warum soviel Englisch?

Dieses Buch wurde am finanziellen Limit produziert. Geringe Stückzahlen sind Grund für hohe Druckkosten, und zwangen uns zu einer englisch-deutschen Version, da der Markt für eine rein deutschsprachige Version nicht groß genug ist. Demnach werden von allen deutschsprachigen Lesern geringe Englischkenntnisse verlangt, zumindest um Bildunterschriften und Infokästen zu verstehen. Wir bitten um Verständnis.

How do I get my information as quickly as possible?

The maps

The maps give you an initial topographical overview: the *map of Norway* on the last page shows the different areas described in this book, the *area maps* (on the first page of every chapter) give you an overview of the area's rivers and a *sketch of each river* can be found at the end of every river description.

The info box

If you want to have a closer look at a river you should have a look at the info box which is always at the beginning of each description.

Classification: This describes the difficulties of a river according to the white water scale explained on page 50. WW III-IV (V, X) for example stands for difficulties between class three and four, but there is at least one rapid of class V and even one which is impassable. The difficulties relate to the water level specified. With higher levels a river usually becomes more difficult.

Level: This is designed to give you an overview of the approximate volume of water required in cubic metres per second (m^3/s). Here are a few figures for comparison: Normally 9 m^3/s of water flow into the Eiskanal in Augsburg, Germany. For the Oker in Germany's Harz region the figure is 7 m^3/s, for the Vøringsfossen in Hordaland, Norway, approx. 25 m^3/s. The Huka Falls in New Zealand are good to kayak when the volume of water is between 70-90 m^3/s.

Length: Represents the distance between put in and take out and is measured in kilometres.

Time: Approximate time taken to paddle from put in to take out. It is a mean value which can vary greatly from one group to the next. A smaller well-harmonised group which knows the river will be much faster than a bigger one which needs a lot of time to physically check the route and take appropriate safety measures.

Season: This section names the best month when the chance of finding an optimum water level is high. Of course, water levels can rise to an optimum level at other times too, particularly after heavy rainfall. Similarly, they can sink to a manageable level after a cold and dry period. »Water levels in Norway« on page 55 provides background information on this and an overview of all rivers can be found on page 236.

Put in: get on the river
Take out: get off the river
Good to go: How much water is necessary, when is it too much? When is the best time to go, where do you find the water-level indicator? All information about the water level can be found here.
Tip: A tip is always just a tip!

Wie bekomme ich am schnellsten meine Information?

Die Karten

Einen ersten räumlichen Überblick erhältst du auf den Landkarten: die *Norwegenkarte* auf der letzten Seite gibt Aufschluss über die im Buch beschriebenen Reviere; die *Revierkarten* (auf der ersten Seite eines jeden Kapitels) geben eine Übersicht über die Flüsse eines Reviers, eine *Skizze vom Fluss* findest du am Ende einer jeden Flussbeschreibung.

Der Infokasten

Willst du einen genauen Blick auf den Fluss werfen, solltest du den Infokasten ins Auge fassen, der sich immer am Anfang einer Flussbeschreibung befindet:

Class: Beschreibt die Einstufung in die Wildwasserskala, die auf Seite 50 erläutert wird. Ein Beispiel: WW III-IV (V,X) – die Schwierigkeiten liegen vorwiegend im dritten und vierten Grad, doch gibt es mindestens eine fünfer Stelle, ja sogar einen unfahrbaren Abschnitt. Die Schwierigkeiten beziehen sich auf den angegebenen Wasserstand, bei höheren Wasserständen steigen meist auch die Schwierigkeiten.

Level: Formt ein Bild über die in etwa benötigte Wassermenge, angegeben in Kubikmeter pro Sekunde (m^3/s). Zum Vergleich: Der Eiskanal in Augsburg führt bei normalem Durchlass 9 m^3/s, die Oker im Harz 7 m^3/s, der Vøringsfossen im Hordaland etwa 25 m^3/s. Huka Falls in Neuseeland werden bei 70-90 m^3/s befahren.

Length: Repräsentiert die Länge der Strecke vom Einstieg zum Ausstieg, vom Put in zum Take out; in Kilometern angegeben.

Time: Die Zeit die man ungefähr benötigt um vom Einstieg zum Ausstieg zu paddeln. Dies ist ein Mittelwert, der von Gruppe zu Gruppe um mehrere Stunden schwanken kann. Eine kleine und gut eingespielte Gruppe, die den Fluss kennt, wird es in der Hälfte der Zeit schaffen als eine große Gruppe, die viel Zeit zum besichtigen und sichern benötigt.

Season: Zeigt die Monate in denen die Wahrscheinlichkeit am höchsten ist, den optimalen Wasserstand vorzufinden ist. Natürlich können auch in der Nebensaison, insbesondere nach starken Regenfällen, die Wasserstände auf ein Optimum ansteigen, oder, aufgrund von Kälte und Trockenheit, auf ein vertretbares Level sinken. Hintergrundinformationen dazu gibt's im Kapitel »Wasserstände in Norwegen« auf Seite 55, eine Übersicht über alle Flüsse findet man auf Seite 236.

Put in: Einstieg
Take out: Ausstieg
Good to go: Wie viel Wasser brauche ich, wann ist es zuviel? Wann ist die beste Zeit, wo ist der Pegel? Alle Informationen zum Wasserstand findest du hier.
Tipp: Ein Tipp ist immer nur ein Tipp!

A COUNTRY OF CONTRASTS

The Norddalsfjorden near Sylte.

Feelings for Norway

You feel somewhat excited when driving to Norway to go paddling. It is the height of the holiday season and the motorways are full of frustrated holidaymakers. But you turn your back on chaos when you leave the rest of Europe behind.

What is it that sets Norway apart from other paddle regions and entices me and many others back to this magical country year after year? Our planet is covered in beautiful unknown rivers, but despite this, many of our dreams are about the fjells and fjords of Norway.

The kayaking experience in Norway is absolutely phenomenal. The rivers are not just simply wonderful, elegant and spectacular – they are like works of art in a gallery of physical and mental boundaries. It is here that whitewater sports are tested to the limits and new boundaries set.

Paddlers come with high hopes expecting to run everything, time permitting. But even after four weeks you only gain a rough impression. The gorges and rivers of Norway provide the modern whitewater paddler with absolutely limitless options. Let the power and beauty of Norway enchant you on your journey. Enjoy the ride!

Gefühle für Norwegen

Man fühlt eine gewisse Aufregung, wenn man Richtung Norwegen interwegs ist. Der Höhepunkt der Ferien ist erreicht, die Straßen sind mit frustrierten Urlaubern verstopft. Doch man entflieht dem Chaos, wenn man den Rest Europas hinter sich lässt.

Was ist es, das Norwegen abhebt von anderen Paddelrevieren, und mich und viele Andere immer und immer wieder in dieses magische Land zieht? Unser Planet ist übersät von wunderschönen unerforschten Flüssen, und trotzdem liegen viele unserer Träume in den Fjells und Fjorden von Norwegen.

Ein tief verwurzeltes Phänomen ist allgegenwärtig in dem einzigartigen Erlebnis Norwegen. Die Flüsse sind nicht einfach nur großartig, elegant und spektakulär – sie sind wie Kunstwerke in einer Galerie von körperlichen und mentalen Grenzen. Hier werden die Grenzen des Wildwasser ausgetestet und Messlatten gelegt.

Paddler kommen mit hohen Erwartungen, bereit soviel zu paddeln wie es die Zeit erlaubt. Doch selbst in vier Wochen erhält man nur einen groben Überblick. Für den modernen Wildwasserpaddler sind die Möglichkeiten, die in den Schluchten und Flüssen Norwegens liegen, schier unbegrenzt. Lass dich auf deiner Reise durch die Kraft und Schönheit Norwegens verzaubern. Enjoy the ride!

Deb Pinniger

»Immortal objects put you in your place!«
»Dinge die ewig sind, zeigen dir wo du stehst!«

The Voringsfossen close to Eidfjord.

A traffic jam

Discovering tranquillity

There are surprisingly many facets to Norway, a country full of contrasts. Barren and blooming, flat and rugged, grey and colourful. Norway is characterised by fjords cutting deep into the earth, huge mountain ranges and remote plateaux, glaciers, roaring rivers and innumerable lakes. Almost two thirds of the country are covered with rocks and ice between which precious meltwater roars endlessly down into the valleys.

When looking at the globe you will discover that the southern ice-covered tip of Greenland lies at the same latitude as Norway's capital Oslo; a good third of the country lies north of the arctic circle. Since Norway is one of the most northern countries in Europe, it is perhaps hard to believe that it is the ultimate destination for paddlers. We owe this to the Gulf Stream, a warm ocean current from the Gulf of Mexico, which has a moderating effect on the climatic conditions. It promotes vegetation and a more favourable climate which prevents the northern Atlantic coastline of Norway from being permanently covered by ice.

Norway is also characterised by remote farmsteads, cosy little towns and only a few big cities. Whereas other countries proclaim their zest for life, Norway only hums – quietly but constantly. Norwegians are typically somewhat reserved, but very friendly. In terms of size, Norway and Germany are almost identical, but whereas statistically 218 people share one square kilometre of land in Germany, in Norway it is only 12.

Initially only an insider's tip, the past few years have seen Norway take off to become the non-plus ultra whitewater region in Europe. Canoeists travel to Norway from all corners of the globe just to paddle in the land of the Vikings. The following pages take a closer look at Norway and introduce you to the country and people.

Die Entdeckung der Gelassenheit

Norwegen hat überraschend viele Gesichter, es ist ein Land voller Kontraste. Karg und blühend, flach und steil, grau und doch farbenfroh. Norwegen ist geprägt von tief ins Land einschneidenden Fjorden, von riesigen Bergketten und einsamen Hochebenen, von Gletschern, reißenden Flüssen und unendlich vielen Seen. Fast zwei Drittel des Landes sind von Stein und Eis überzogen, und dazwischen rauscht schier endlos das kostbare Schmelzwasser zu Tale.

Bei einem Blick auf den Globus stellt man fest, dass die eisbedeckte Südspitze Grönlands auf gleicher Höhe wie Norwegens Hauptstadt Oslo liegt; gut ein Drittel des Landes erstreckt sich nördlich des Polarkreises. Norwegen ist eines der nördlichsten Länder in Europa – so fällt es schwer zu glauben, dass gerade Norwegen das ultimative Ziel für Paddler ist. Danken können wir dem Golfstrom, einer warmen Meeresströmung aus dem Golf von Mexiko. Dieser begünstigt Klima und Vegetation und bewahrt die nord-norwegische Atlantikküste vor Dauereis.

Abgelegene Gehöfte, gemütliche Kleinstädtchen, und nur wenige Großstädte: Wo andere Länder vor Lebenslust singen, summt Norwegen nur – leise, aber unaufhörlich. Norweger sind meist etwas zurückhaltend, doch sehr freundlich. Flächenmäßig unterscheiden sich Norwegen und Deutschland nicht sehr, jedoch leben in Deutschland rein statistisch gesehen 218 Menschen auf einem Quadratkilometer – in Norwegen lediglich 12.

Norwegen hat sich in den letzten Jahren vom Geheimtipp zu einem viel besuchten Wildwasserrevier gemausert. Paddler reisen vom anderen Ende der Erdkugel an, um im Land der Wikinger zu paddeln. Wir möchten dir auf den folgenden Seiten Norwegen etwas näher bringen, und Land und Leute vorstellen.

The put in on the Sumelvi - Jostedalsbreen Nasjonalpark.

The country of contrasts

Norway has been shaped by thousands of years of cold, changeable weather and the warm hearts of its citizens. The country is precipitous and yet beautifully gentle – like fire and ice. Mighty mountain ranges and storm-swept plateaux take up large parts of the country with green valleys hiding in between. The Skanden, a Scandinavian mountain range which makes its way from the south to the north, has peaks which are an average of approx. 500 metres above sea level.

The Norwegians call a mountain range *Fjell*, plateaux which stretch between peaks are *Vidda*. It is here where the world takes a rest – nestled between rocks covered with red and green lichen, moss, hardy undergrowth, eternal snow fields and ice-cold lakes (*Vatn*). Here too, the routine of our everyday life dissolves into tranquillity and slowly vanishes before our eyes.

Fjords are huge inlets which can mainly be found along the west coast of Norway. Here the sea traverses the mainland like veins in a body and its powerful natural force has a huge influence on people's lives. In some areas, the fjords make such efficient use of the mountain ranges that there is almost no space left for man.

Das Land der Kontraste

Mit kaltem Händchen und warmem Herz wurde Norwegen in vielen Jahrtausenden geformt. Das Land ist schroff und doch butterweich, es ist wie Feuer und Eis. Mächtige Gebirgsmassive und windgepeitschte Hochebenen füllen weite Teile des Landes, grüne Täler verstecken sich dazwischen. Das Skandinavische Gebirge, die *Skanden*, erstreckt sich von Süden gen Norden und hebt die Durchschnittshöhe der Oberfläche auf etwa 500 Metern über den Meeresspiegel.

Norweger bezeichnen das Gebirge mit *Fjell* und die Hochebenen, die sich zwischen den Gipfeln erstrecken, mit *Vidda*. Hier oben ruht die Welt – eingebettet von Steinen mit rotgrünen Flechten, von Moos und hartem Gestrüpp, von ewigen Schneefeldern und eiskalten Seen (*Vatn*). Hier schwebt unser Alltag dahin, mit Ruhe und Gelassenheit, und verschwimmt langsam vor den Augen.

Fjorde nennt man die riesigen Meereseinbuchtungen, die in Norwegen vor allem entlang der Westküste zu finden sind. Dort durchzieht das Meer das Land wie Adern unseren Körper, und beeinflusst das Leben der Menschen mit all seiner Kraft. Denn teilweise füllen die Fjorde so gründlich das Gebirge aus, dass zum Leben nur wenig Platz bleibt.

Millions of years ago Norway was a vast expanse of undulating countryside. High and relatively flat, it was traversed by gentle river valleys. During the last Ice Age, the surface froze and became gradually encrusted with ice; huge glaciers formed. When the earth's surface warmed up again, the ice began to melt and move downhill. Single solid blocks of ice carved deep grooves in the rock to form valleys stretching from the interior of the country to the sea and which, today, lie up to 1,300 metres below sea level.

Ice and snow decorate the country in greatly varying amounts providing paddlers with the lifeblood they need in summer: water in the river bed. A large proportion of the snow is locked away in massive glaciers called *Bre*, which are permanently on the move and amongst the biggest in Europe. Because average temperatures in Norway are lower than in the Alps, the Norwegian glaciers push down into much lower regions. According to official statistics, there are 1,627 glaciers covering an area of 2,609 square kilometres. This corresponds to an area roughly three times the size of Greater Berlin.

Vor ein paar Millionen Jahren war Norwegen eine gemütlich gewellte Landschaft: hoch, platt und von sanften Flusstälern durchzogen. Mit der letzten Eiszeit vereiste und verkrustete die Oberfläche, riesige Gletscher entstanden. Als sich die Erdoberfläche wieder erwärmte, schmolz das Eis langsam und begab sich auf Wanderschaft. Einzelne, massive Eisblöcke gerieten in Bewegung und frästen tiefe Rinnen ins Gestein – Täler entstanden, die sich vom Landesinnere bis ins Meer hinein erstreckten, und heute bis zu 1300 Meter tief unter dem Meeresspiegel liegen.

Eis und Schnee verzieren in kleinen und großen Flecken das Land, und spenden uns Paddlern im Sommer was wir zum Leben brauchen: Wasser im Flussbett. Ein großer Teil dieser Schneemassen versteckt sich in den massiven, stetig wandernden Gletschern (*Bre*), die zu den Größten in Europa zählen. Da die Durchschnittstemperaturen in Norwegen im Vergleich zu den Alpen geringer sind, dringen die norwegischen Gletscher in wesentlich tiefere Lagen vor. Nach offizieller Zählung sind es 1627 Gletscher, die eine Fläche von 2609 Quadratkilometern bedecken. Das entspricht etwa der dreifachen Fläche Berlins.

Lake Gjende - Jotunheimen

Traffic has worn tracks in the winter road of ice.

Animals and plants

The effects of the Gulf Stream and the fact that the north and south of Norway are longitudinally so far apart mean that there is a broad range of vegetation: it is lush in coastal regions and barren in high altitudes. Whilst coniferous and mixed forests are to be found in this boreal region, the further north one travels, the more coniferous trees such as spruce and pine gain the upper hand. Plants which prefer warm conditions are mainly to be found at lower levels and close to the coast. Above the treeline – which is at a lower level than in the Alps – mosses and lichens are the winners of the biological battle to survive.

Could be useful: Autan mosquito spray.

The very extensive wooded areas provide habitat to innumerable animals, the most of which we have no chance of seeing, at least not in the wild. It is only on stickers or road signs that we see Norwegian national symbols like the elk. You will be lucky to sight a real elk (*Elg*) and get a picture of it; best chances to do so are in the evening. A fully grown bull elk weighs up to half a ton, its antlers span up to three metres in width. The elk belongs to the genus of deer, as does its smaller brother the reindeer (*Reinsdyr*). The reindeer can be seen more often: in myths, harnessed to sleighs and in butchers shops as »ham«. Being roughly the same size as the red deer of Central Europe, it is considerably smaller than the elk and in contrast to the elk it is a gregarious animal. Hardangervidda (Telemark) is home to the last remaining wild reindeer tribe; they can otherwise only be seen in small groups.

The animal most feared by tourists to Norway is actually an insect; the mosquito (*Mygg*). It is (unfortunately) neither on the verge of extinction, nor will you find it all alone. When swarms of mosquitoes are on your trail, they will plague and massacre you to death, fray your nerves and cause sleepless nights. The wolf (*Ulf*) goes hunting at night too, but this is more a problem for the locals because from time to time the farmer's sheep and goats are on its menu. The national smear campaign against the wolf, which was initiated by farmers and shepherds, even caught the attention of animal protectionists abroad.

The Norwegians are not without their problems with the salmon (*Laks*) either, but only because it is so popular. 30 years ago, in the face of rising demand, they started breeding salmon professionally in huge farms in the sea. Badly polluted by fish excrement, the enclosures in which the fish are kept are an ideal breeding ground for one disease after the other. How even paddlers are affected by problems with salmon can be found on page 53.

Tiere und Pflanzen

Trotz der geographischen Gegebenheiten ist die Vegetation recht vielfältig, denn wir befinden uns in der Zone der borealen Nadel- und Mischwälder. Je nördlicher man kommt, desto mehr setzen sich Nädelhölzer wie Kiefern und Fichten durch. Wärme liebende Pflanzen sieht man größtenteils in den tieferen Lagen und in Meeresnähe. Oberhalb der Baumgrenze, die in Norwegen wesentlich niedriger liegt als beispielsweise in den Alpen, sind Moose und Flechten die Gewinner des biologischen Überlebenskampfes.

In den weiten Landstrichen leben unzählige Tiere, die meisten von ihnen bekommen wir nicht zu Gesicht, zumindest nicht in freier Wildbahn. Lediglich auf Aufklebern und Straßenschildern sehen wir norwegische Wahrzeichen wie den Elch. Wer einen echten Elch (*Elg*) vor die Linse bekommt, kann sich glücklich schätzen. Die besten Chancen dazu hat man wohl in den Abendstunden. Ein ausgewachsener Bulle kann bis zu einer halben Tonne schwer werden, die Spannweite seiner Schaufelgeweihe beträgt bis zu drei Meter. Der Elch gehört zu der Gattung der Hirsche, ebenso wie sein kleiner Bruder das Rentier (*Reinsdyr*). Dem Ren begegnet man hingegen öfter: in Mythen, vorm Schlitten – und als Schinken. Sie sind wesentlich kleiner als der Elch, ungefähr so groß wie unser mitteleuropäisches Rotwild, und im Gegensatz zum Elch ein Herdentier. In der Hardangervidda (Telemark) lebt der letzte wilde Rentierstamm Europas, nur in kleinen Gruppen trifft man sie sonst noch an.

Das meist gefürchtete Tier der Norwegenurlauber ist ein Insekt: Doch die Mücke (*Mygg*) ist weder vom Aussterben bedroht, noch begegnet man ihr allein. Ist eine Horde Mücken auf der Jagd nach dir, rauben sie den letzten Nerv, plagen und massakrieren dich, und bereiten schlaflose Nächte. Auch der Wolf (*Ulf*) jagt nachts, doch damit haben eher die Einheimischen ihre Probleme, denn des Bauers Schaf und Ziege stehen hin und wieder auf seinem Speiseplan. Die nationalen Hetzkampagnen gegen den Wolf, initiiert von Bauern und Hirten, erregten sogar bei Tierschützern im Ausland Aufsehen.

Mit dem Lachs (*Laks*) haben die Norweger ebenso ihre Probleme – aber nur deshalb, weil er so beliebt ist: Aufgrund der steigenden Nachfrage begann man vor rund 30 Jahren mit der ertragsorientierten Züchtung von Lachsen. Sie werden in Massen in so genannten Lachsfarmen im Meer gehalten, die durchsetzt sind von den Exkrementen der Tiere. Diese wirken wie frischer Dünger für immer neue Krankheiten. Warum auch wir Paddler vom Lachsproblem betroffen sind, erfährst du auf Seite 53.

Whaling and sealing
Norway in the crossfire

Sketches of whales and collections of bones along the Norwegian coast imply that even the native inhabitants hunted whales. At that time whaling was laborious and dangerous which meant that only sick and slow-moving whales could be hunted. Technology has of course progressed relentlessly and today times are bad for the giant of the oceans with numbers culled to a minimum. A Norwegian's invention of the harpoon gun in 1864 ensured that Norway played a leading role in exterminating whales. An explosive harpoon bores its way into the mammal and in doing so releases a barb which prevents extraction. Modern steamships at that time did the rest.

By the beginning of the 1900s, whales along the coasts had been almost systematically exterminated and so whaling took to the high seas. New factory ships enabled whales to be processed out at sea and it was no longer necessary to tow them ashore. Soon a glut market caused the whaling fleet to go bankrupt. In 1946 the International Whaling Commission (IWC) was founded and whaling quotas were introduced. However, this was not intended to protect the whales – it was purely for economic reasons. It was not until the sixties that the protection of whales became an issue when it became clear that with no whales at all, the whaling fleet would be grounded. Norwegians often do things their own way however and in 1990 they decided to go harpooning minke whales even though the IWC had ruled against this.

Man's relentless technological improvements were also the reason why seal populations reduced to a minimum too. Animal activists drew the public's attention to the brutality of sealing and Norway came under fire from all sides. Fishermen always claim that seals consume an immense amount of fish and thereby disturb the balance of the Arctic Ocean. How fishing quotas disturb the balance is naturally never mentioned.

Tip: If you want to help improve the situation, please refrain from bringing home seal fur as a souvenir and from eating whale and seal meat.

Wal- und Robbenfang
Norwegen im Kreuzfeuer

Walzeichnungen und Knochenfunde entlang der norwegischen Küste lassen vermuten, dass bereits die Ureinwohner auf Waljagd gingen. Damals war der Fang mühsam und gefährlich, und so kamen nur kranke und langsam schwimmende Tiere in Betracht. Durch den technischen Fortschritt steht es heute schlecht um die Giganten der Meere, ihr Bestand ist auf ein Minimum reduziert. Norwegen trug wesentlich zur Ausrottung bei, Grundstein legte die Erfindung der Harpunenkanone 1864 durch einen Norweger. Hierbei bohrt sich ein Sprengkörper in das Tier, der bei der Explosion einen Widerhaken freisetzt. Die neu entwickelten Dampfschiffe taten ihr übriges.

Bis zum Beginn des zwanzigsten Jahrhunderts wurden die Wale an den Küsten fast systematisch ausgerottet, danach zog man hinaus in die Weltmeere. Neue Fabrikschiffe erlaubten dabei sogar die Verarbeitung auf offener See, der Wal musste nicht mal mehr an Land geschleppt werden. Doch bald sorgte eine Übersättigung des Marktes für eine Pleite der Walfangflotte. 1946 wurde die Internationale Walfangkommission (IWC) gegründet, Walfangquoten wurden eingeführt. Doch nicht um die Tiere zu schützen, sondern aus rein wirtschaftlichen Gründen. Erst in den sechziger Jahren ging es auch um Fragen des Artenschutzes, als man realisierte, dass ohne Wale die Walfangindustrie noch blasser aussehen würde. Doch die Norweger kochen gern ihr eigenes Süppchen: 1990 entschied man Zwergwale zu schießen, obwohl sich die IWC gegen diesen Entschluss ausgesprochen hatte.

Beim Robbenfang war es ebenfalls der technische Fortschritt, der die Bestände auf ein Minimum reduzierte. Tierschützer machten die breite Öffentlichkeit über die Grausamkeit der Fangmethoden aufmerksam – Norwegen geriet ins Kreuzfeuer. Argumentiert wird von Seiten der Fischer immer wieder mit dem gewaltigen Fischkonsum der Robben und Seehunde, der das Gleichgewicht im Nordmeer störe. Wie sich die Fangquoten der Fischer auf die Bestände auswirken, bleibt dabei natürlich im Dunkeln.

Tipp: Wer helfen will, sollte auf Robbenfelle als Urlaubsandenken verzichten und Seehund- und Walfleisch vom Teller bannen.

»Dude, let's go whale-fishing!«

Drawing: FicSch

A salmon farm in Norddalsfjorden close to Sylte.

War in salmon's paradise
by Antje Kahlheber

Northern tranquillity vanishes in a flash in Norway when salmon are the subject of conversation because these fish are a cornerstone of the country's identity just as much as cuckoo clocks are in staunchly traditional Bavaria. With more than 600 salmon rivers and one of the biggest wild salmon populations anywhere on earth, the land of the fjords is a leading salmon nation. However, the population has been decreasing for decades and now only half the country's rivers are habitat to a large healthy population.

The most recent scapegoat for this is about half a millimetre big and apparently not Norwegian at all. *Gyrodactylus salaris*, a parasitic worm, was first discovered amongst fish stocks in the seventies, shortly after a shipment of young fish had arrived from Sweden. The worm has wreaked havoc ever since and as many as 41 rivers and 37 salmon farms have been contaminated. Wherever *Gyrodactylus* shows up it devastates the salmon population. One single salmon can carry around up to 10,000 parasites which dine on their host's skin. Resulting wounds become infected and are inevitably a death sentence to most young fish.

As salmon always return to the rivers where they were born, each river has developed its own genetic line. In order to save strains of fish which have adapted to »their« river, drastic government action saw the setting up of the Wild Salmon Committee. This organisation has since had 25 watercourses poisoned with *rotenone*. This is a natural substance derived from tropical and subtropical leguminous[1] plants which is highly toxic to fish and many other water-borne life forms. It is quickly absorbed via gills or the trachea[2]. The functions of enzymes essential for

Mit dem Holzhammer
von Antje Kahlheber

Wenn es um Lachs geht, verliert Norwegen leicht seine nordische Gelassenheit. Denn der Lachs gehört zu Norwegens Identität, wie der Kuckuck in die Schwarzwalduhr. Mit über 600 Lachsflüssen und einigen der weltweit größten Wildlachspopulationen liegt das Land der Fjorde unter den Lachsländern weit vorn. Doch seit Jahrzehnten schrumpfen die Bestände – nur noch die Hälfte der Flüsse weist gesunde und große Lachspopulationen auf.

Der jüngste Sündenbock ist etwa einen halben Millimeter groß und anscheinend kein Norweger: *Gyrodactylus salaris*, ein parasitischer Saugwurm, wurde erstmals in den Siebziger Jahren nachgewiesen, kurz nachdem eine Lieferung schwedischer Jungfische in Norwegen eingetroffen war. Das Unheil nahm seinen Lauf, bis heute wurden insgesamt 41 Flüsse und 37 Aufzuchtsfarmen infiziert. Wo immer *Gyrodactylus* auftaucht, schädigt er die Lachspopulationen enorm. Auf einem einzigen Lachs können sich bis zu 10.000 Parasiten entwickeln. Sie fressen die Haut der Fische und verursachen große entzündete Wunden, die für Jungfische meistens tödlich sind.

Da Lachse immer wieder in ihre Geburtsflüsse zurückkehren, hat sich in jedem Fluss eine eigene genetische Linie entwickelt. Um diese an »ihren« Fluss angepassten Stämme zu retten, entschied sich die Regierung zu drastischen Maßnahmen. Das von ihr gegründete Wildlachskomitee veranlasste bisher die Vergiftung von 25 Wasserläufen mit *Rotenon*. Diese natürliche Substanz aus tropischen Leguminosen[1] ist für Fische und viele andere Wassertiere hochgiftig. Sie wird schnell über Kiemen oder Tracheen[2]

breathing are inhibited in the mitochondria[3]. The poison does not just kill worm-infected salmon; it suffocates all fish. The majority of water insects, crustaceans, molluscs and worms fall victim too. Whilst birds and otters feeding off fish stocks are not directly affected, their chances of survival are bleak once all life in a river has been terminated.

Before the slaughter of river life begins, fish eggs and sperm are extracted from selected salmon for breeding purposes. The poison breaks down naturally in the water within a couple of weeks, but it takes years until rivers recover to an extent that young salmon bred in captivity can be re-introduced.

The variety of species in North American fish ponds has been controlled by rotenone since the thirties. It is mainly used to eliminate exotic species or to introduce species that fishermen love to catch and which would not have much of a chance of survival if other species were not wiped out beforehand. But that's North America. Why does Norway take such measures? Are they justified only to save the genetic variety of Norwegian salmon? Do the genes of other creatures wiped out by these measures not count? It is said that the aquatic fauna recovers within a year thanks to species immigration from neighbouring areas. But a case in Utah, USA, contradicts this: five years after all life in the Strawberry River had been poisoned with rotenone, 21 per cent of the aquatic fauna was still absent. Instead,

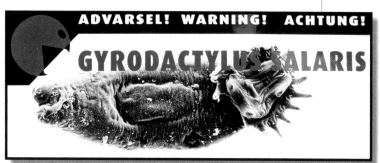

Wanted! Norway's most notorious inhabitant: the Gyrodactylus salaris.

other species have taken up home and the larva from stone flies, caddis flies and mayflies – which are lacking – do not have a lobby as powerful as the Norwegian Wild Salmon Committee.

And anyhow, the decline in the genetic variety of Norwegian salmon started long ago: every year between 500,000 and 2.6 million salmon bred in captivity escape from their farms. The proportion of farmed salmon in rivers has increased from 15 to 34 per cent and in some cases by up to 90 per cent. Salmon from farms do not have much in common with their wild counterparts: they are specifically bred to gain weight and size rapidly. Huge and aggressive, these food-guzzlers enter the rivers. Their genetic code mixes with that of the wild salmon and the different genetic varieties which have adapted to »their« specific river vanish: this endangers the survival of salmon populations in general.

In fact, wild salmon populations had started to decline long before Gyrodactylus was discovered in Norwegian

aufgenommen und hemmt die Atmungsenzyme in den Mitochondrien[3]. Nicht nur die infizierten Lachse fallen dem Giftanschlag zum Opfer, sondern auch alle anderen Fische des Flusses. Mit ihnen erstickt ein großer Teil der Wasserinsekten, Krebse, Weichtiere und Würmer. Fischfressende Tiere wie Vögel und Otter werden zwar nicht direkt durch das Gift beeinträchtigt, wohl aber wird ihnen die Nahrung entzogen.

Vor den Vergiftungsmaßnahmen entnimmt man Eier und Spermien einzelner Lachse und verwendet sie für die Nachzucht. Das Gift zersetzt sich innerhalb weniger Wochen im Wasser. Doch es dauert mehrere Jahre bis die Flüsse sich soweit regeneriert haben, dass sie mit den gezogenen Junglachsen besetzt werden können.

Seit den Dreißiger Jahren wird die Artenzusammensetzung in zahlreichen nordamerikanischen Fischteichen mit Rotenon kontrolliert. Meistens um exotische Spezies auszumerzen oder Bestände einzusetzen, die dem Anglerglück entgegenkommen. Doch warum greift Norwegen nun ebenfalls zu solchen Mitteln? Sind sie gerechtfertigt, um die genetische Vielfalt des norwegischen Lachses zu erhalten? Zählen die Gene anderer Lebewesen, die der Maßnahme zum Opfer fallen, weniger? Die aquatische Fauna regeneriere sich spätestens nach einem Jahr, indem sie aus benachbarten Gebieten neu einwandere, heißt es. Aus Utah ist anderes bekannt: Nach der Rotenonbehandlung des Strawberry-Rivers fehlte von 21 Prozent der aquatischen Fauna noch nach fünf Jahren jede Spur. Andere Arten haben sich stattdessen breitgemacht, und die vermissten Larven von Stein-, Köcher- und Eintagsfliegen haben keine Lobby, die dem Norwegischen Wildlachskomitee gleich käme.

Dabei hat unter den norwegischen Lachsen der Verlust an genetischer Vielfalt schon längst eingesetzt: Aus den Lachsfarmen entkommen jedes Jahr zwischen 500.000 und 2,6 Millionen Zuchtlachse. Der Anteil von Farmlachs stieg in den Flüssen auf 15 bis 34 Prozent, manchmal sind es sogar schon 90 Prozent. Der Lachs aus den Lachsfarmen hat nicht mehr viel mit seinem wilden Artgenossen gemein; er wurde auf Masse und schnelles Wachstum gezüchtet. Riesig und aggressiv wandern diese entflohenen Fressmaschinen in die Flüsse ein. Ihr Erbgut vermischt sich mit dem der Wildlachse, die spezifischen Eigenschaften der an ihren Fluss angepassten Lachsstämme verschwinden und beeinträchtigen die Überlebensfähigkeit der Populationen.

Tatsächlich gingen die Wildlachsbestände schon stark zurück, bevor Gyrodactylus in norwegischen Flüssen entdeckt wurde, sodass der von ihm verursachte Schaden nicht genau beziffert werden kann. Die Gründe für den Rückgang sind vielfältig und reichen von Überfischung über wasserbauliche Maßnahmen wie Wasserkraftwerke bis zu saurem Regen.

Zahlreiche Beispiele zeigen, dass Resistenzen gegenüber neuen Parasiten relativ schnell erworben werden können.

rivers which means that the damage caused by this worm cannot be determined exactly. Reasons for the decline range from over-fishing through to river regulation, hydroelectric power plants and acid rain.

Numerous examples show that resistance to new parasites can be built up relatively quickly. In the 1900s wild fish in England became infected on a large scale by *furunculosis* but are now immune. Another good example is the speed at which Australian rabbits adapted to *myxomatosis*. Why doesn't Norway let nature take its course and invest money in more sensible ecological projects? The decline in catches appears to cause a national identity crisis with Norwegian newspapers almost embarrassed to report bad figures. And dishonour is brought upon Norwegian fishermen when foreigners talk about a catastrophic fishing season. It appears almost impossible for Norway to sit back and watch the destructible power of *Gyrodactylus*.

Economic and political interests also have a key to the poison cabinet. The Norwegian salmon industry is the largest in the world, a major source of employment, and as far as exports are concerned, second only in importance to the country's oil industry. Diseases spread quickly in cramped fish cages and many fish farms have been forced to close due to *Gyrodactylus* or other parasites. Big business is naturally keen to see the parasite destroyed as quickly as possible. Tourism is almost as economically important as the salmon industry. Foreigners flock to enjoy perfect fishing expecting big shoals of jumping salmon and not feeble stocks struggling pathetically on the bumpy road to developing resistance to *Gyrodactylus*.

Norway is therefore continuing its policy of biological foolishness. Fifteen of the rivers »treated« by rotenone have since been declared healthy: eight of these have already been re-infected by the parasite. A further fourteen rivers are awaiting death by rotenone. The Driva, Norway's number one trout river, and two of its tributaries are amongst those on Death Row. In 2010 at the latest, poisoned fish will be drifting towards the sea and with them nearly every other form of life that once thrived in the Driva.

Antje Kahlheber,
Spektrum der Wissenschaft, Edition 1/2004

[1] leguminous: belonging to the family of pulses (seeds)
[2] trachea: respiratory passages of insects
[3] mitochondria: the power-plant of cells which serve cell breathing

Is Gyrodactylus harmful to humans?
Not really. The parasite is too specialised to do man any harm. If swallowed, it is simply digested.
Is rotenone poisonous to humans?
In the past, rotenone was used as a natural insecticide in ecological agriculture. Today, at least in Germany, it is forbidden. Animal tests with rats showed that there might be a link between rotenone and Parkinson's disease. The poison breaks down relatively quickly in water and should not represent a danger to paddlers.

Die Wildfische Großbritanniens erkrankten um 1900 massiv an *Furunkulose*, inzwischen sind die Populationen immun. Die noch schnellere Adaption australischer Kaninchen an das *Myxomatose-Virus* mag ein anderes Vorbild sein. Warum lässt man also in Norwegen der Natur nicht ihren Lauf und investiert das Geld in sinnvollere ökologische Maßnahmen? Auf der einen Seite scheint schon allein das Sinken der Fangzahlen eine norwegische Identitätskrise auszulösen. Fast verschämt berichten norwegische Zeitungen von schlechten Fangquoten und der norwegische Angler ist in seiner persönlichen Ehre getroffen, wenn Angeltouristen über eine katastrophale Fischsaison sprechen. Tatenlos dem verheerenden Werk des Parasiten zuzusehen, scheint da fast unmöglich.

Andererseits dürften auch kommerzielle und politische Interessen die Hand am Holzhammer steuern. Die norwegische Lachsindustrie ist die größte der Welt, nach der Ölindustrie der zweitwichtigste Export-Wirtschaftszweig des Landes und ein wichtiger Arbeitgeber. In den eng besetzten Farmkäfigen der Lachsfarmen breiten sich Krankheiten schnell aus. Viele Betriebe mussten wegen Gyrodactylus oder anderen Parasiten schließen. Sie haben ein Interesse daran, dass der Parasit verschwindet – und zwar möglichst schnell. Ein in wirtschaftlicher Hinsicht fast ebenso wertvolles Gut ist der Tourismus. Viele kommen, um ungetrübtes Angelvergnügen zu erleben, sie erwarten Massen von springenden Lachsen und keine Kümmerpopulationen auf dem steinigen Weg zur *Gyrodactylus*-Resistenz.

So wandert man in Norwegen weiter auf Pfaden biologischer Unvernunft. Fünfzehn der mit Rotenon behandelten Flüsse wurden bisher für gesund erklärt, acht weisen schon wieder eine Neuinfektion mit dem Parasiten auf. Weitere vierzehn Flüsse sollen in den kommenden Jahren vergiftet werden. Auch die Vorbereitungen für die Vergiftung von Norwegens forellenreichstem Fluss, der Driva, samt zweier Nebenflüsse laufen. Spätestens 2010 ist es dort so weit. Dann treiben wieder tote Fische ins Meer und mit ihnen fast alles, was in der Driva einst lebte.

Antje Kahlheber,
»Spektrum der Wissenschaft«, Ausgabe 1/2004

[1] Leguminosen: Hülsenfrüchte
[2] Tracheen: Atemwege der Insekten
[3] Mitochondrien: Kraftwerke der Zellen, die der Zellatmung dienen

Ist der Gyrodactylus salaris für den Menschen schädlich?
Eigentlich nicht. Der Parasit ist zu wirtspezifisch um dem Menschen zu schaden und wird bei einer oralen Aufnahme einfach verdaut.
Ist Rotenon für den Menschen giftig?
Rotenon wurde früher im ökologischen Anbau als natürliches Insektenbekämpfungsmittel eingesetzt und ist heute zumindest in Deutschland verboten. Es gab Tierversuche an Ratten, die einen Zusammenhang zwischen Rotenon und der Entstehung von Parkinson'scher Krankheit vermuten lassen. Das Gift zersetzt sich in der Umwelt aber relativ schnell und sollte so keine unmittelbare Gefahr für Paddler darstellen.

From the weather god

»Sunny for 50 metres and then cloudy for 100! The weather in Norway is as short-lived as today's rodeo boats.« Arnd Schäftlein

Judging by his degree of unpredictability and variety of moods, it would appear that the Norwegian weather god was born in April. Some sunshine, then again a short shower – the weather god cannot decide what to do. He is always game for a joke and one of his fads is three weeks of solid rain. But to be serious, there are reasons for the showery »April weather«: The northerly latitude, the wide flank to the ocean and the vertical differentiation due to the Skanden mountain range combine to ensure a varied climate.

The fact that Norway in its northerly latitude is not buried under snow and ice is due to the Gulf Stream which originates in Mexico as previously mentioned. The warm ocean currents heat up the air masses over the Atlantic which in turn are carried along by winds from the west which are particular to the northern hemisphere. When the warm air travels over the coastal mountains it is forced upwards and begins to cool. Warm air masses can absorb more moisture than cold ones and hence more precipitation occurs on the windward side of mountains. The town of Bergen on the west coast of Norway is one of the wettest in Europe.

By the time the Gulf Stream arrives at Norway it has cooled down even more. Its influence reduces and temperatures gradually cool down. Towards the east, i.e. inland, temperatures fall slightly due to the high altitude of the Skanden mountains. The ocean's effect on the climate declines.

Vom Wettergott

»50 Meter Sonne, 100 Meter Schatten! Das Wetter in Norwegen ist so schnelllebig wie die heutigen Rodeoboote.« Arnd Schäftlein

Der norwegische Wettergott scheint wohl im April geboren zu sein, seine Launen sind abwechslungsreich und unvorhersehbar. Etwas Sonne, dann wieder ein kurzer Regenschauer – er kann sich selten entscheiden. Er ist immer zu Späßen aufgelegt, und auch drei Wochen Dauerregen kann eine seiner Marotten sein. Aber mal im Ernst, das »Aprilwetter« hat auch seine Gründe: die nördliche Lage, die breite Meeresflanke und die vertikale Gliederung durch die Skanden variieren und bestimmen das Klima Norwegens.

Das Norwegen bei der nördlichen Lage nicht in Eis- und Schneemassen ertrinkt, bewirkt der Golfstrom aus Mexiko, soviel war schon erwähnt. Das warme Wasser der Meeresströmung erwärmt die Luftmassen über dem Atlantik, welche dann, getrieben von den bei uns vorherrschenden Westwinden, an den Küstengebirgen empor steigen und sich dabei abkühlen. Warme Luftmassen können mehr Feuchtigkeit als kalte speichern, so kommt es zu vermehrten Niederschlägen an der windzugewandten Seite, der Luvseite des Gebirges. Die Stadt Bergen an der Westküste Norwegens ist eine der regenreichsten Städte Europas.

Bis der Golfstrom Nordnorwegen erreicht, hat er sich weiter abgekühlt. Seine Auswirkungen lassen nach, die Temperaturen sinken allmählich ab. Auch Richtung Osten, also im Landesinneren, fallen aufgrund der höheren Lagen der Skanden die Temperaturen etwas ab, und der Einfluss des Seeklimas lässt nach.

If you're lucky enough to discover such a place to sleep, you won't need your tarp

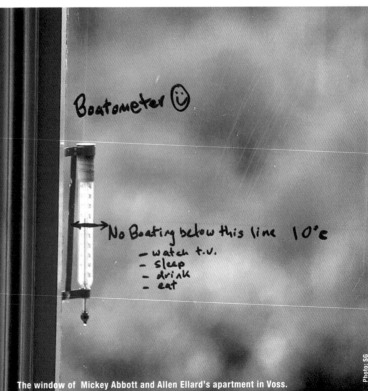

The window of Mickey Abbott and Allen Ellard's apartment in Voss.

The people, their art and culture

Norwegians radiate tranquillity: separated from hectic Europe by the North Sea and the Baltic Sea, they have retained their relaxed way of life. Whilst being the fifth largest member by size, Norway has Europe's second smallest population density but one of its highest living standards. Living to an average age of 77, Norwegians have one of the highest life expectancies in the world.

The Norwegians are described as being open, hospitable and full of humour. They are a free-and-easy, uncomplicated race but yet somewhat reserved. *Folkesjela* (the soul of the people) is what they call their typical patterns of thought and behaviour. We have come across an interesting piece of writing on this but unfortunately we do not know who the author is. Here is an excerpt:

A *Stavkirke* is a common traditional landmark in Norway: The »Bjølstad Kapell« in Heidal.

The Norwegian and the stranger

»The Norwegian is a down-to-earth person. He knows where he lives – on the outermost edges of Europe. And as a result, he is inclined to believe that people who live nearer the centre are more in-the-know than he is. This is particularly true as far as etiquette is concerned, for example the accurate choice of evening wear for the restaurant or the correct knife for a particular meal.

In short, when a Norwegian is surrounded by strangers, he feels like a small child in the forest, far away from mum and dad and the grandparents. He cannot help thinking that the stranger wants to take him for a ride, to steal his sandwich or short-change him.

But because the Norwegian is a proud son of the forest, he would never admit to himself having such childish thoughts – and certainly not to a stranger. So he tries to hide his thoughts as well as he can. If you catch a Norwegian in this very act, it is better to pretend you have not noticed and to talk about something completely different such as superb weather, the 1900 World Trade Fair in Paris or the rise and fall of the Roman Empire.«

Die Menschen, ihre Kunst und ihre Kultur

Norweger strahlen Ruhe aus: Durch Nord- und Ostsee vom hektischen Europa getrennt, ist ihnen eine entspannte Lebensart erhalten geblieben. Als flächenmäßig fünftgrößter Staat in Europa hat Norwegen zugleich die zweitniedrigste Bevölkerungsdichte – und einen der höchsten Lebensstandards in Europa. Die Norweger haben mit 77 Jahren sogar eine der höchsten Lebenserwartungen der Welt.

Norweger werden als offen und direkt beschrieben, als gastfreundlich und mit einem handfesten Humor ausgestattet. Sie gelten als ungezwungen und unkompliziert, allerdings auch als etwas zurückhaltend. *Folkesjela* (Volksseele) nennen sie selbst ihre typische Denk- und Verhaltensweise. Hierzu haben wir ein interessantes Schriftstück gefunden, dessen Autor uns leider nicht bekannt ist. Ein kurzer Auszug:

Der Norweger und der Fremde

»Der Norweger ist eine nüchterne Person. Er weiß wo er lebt – und zwar am äußersten Rande Europas. Und so ist er geneigt anzunehmen, dass Leute, die näher im Zentrum leben, besser Bescheid wüssten als er. Besonders in Angelegenheiten des Guten Benehmens, wie zum Beispiel bei der treffsicheren Wahl der Abendgarderobe für das Restaurant, oder des richtigen Messers für das jeweilige Gericht.

Kurz gesagt: Wenn der Norweger von Fremden umgeben ist, fühlt er sich manchmal wie ein Kleinkind im Wald, weit

weg von Mama und Papa und den Großeltern. Er wird das Gefühl nicht los, der Fremde will ihn übers Ohr hauen, seine Butterbrote klauen, oder zu wenig Wechselgeld rausgeben.

Aber, da der Norweger ein stolzer Sohn der Wildnis ist, würde er sich diese kindischen Gefühle selbst nie eingestehen – und erst recht keinem Fremden. Also versucht er sie zu überspielen so gut er kann. Wenn man einen Norweger genau dabei ertappt, ist das Beste so zu tun als sei nichts geschehen. Am besten spricht man sofort von etwas völlig anderem, wie zum Beispiel vom tollen Wetter, von der Weltmesse 1900 in Paris, oder vom Aufstieg und Fall des Römischen Imperiums.«

Their language: knotted and confusing

The language spoken for centuries was *Riksmål*, Danish with a Norwegian slant. Following the end of the union (1814) with Denmark, the language of *Landsmål*, a development of the rural dialects, began to compete for use. However, this new language could not take hold in the cities and a language battle became inevitable. To crown it all, as a result of a language reform in 1929 the languages were re-named: Landsmål became *Nynorsk* (New-Norwegian) and Riksmål became *Bokmål* (Book Norwegian). Today both languages are recognised, taught in schools and tested in university examinations. The long-serving language of Bokmål is however more commonly written whereas Nynorsk is the more spoken language.

In addition, these languages are accompanied by countless dialects and on every corner either the emphasis or spelling is different. The Norwegians take their dialects for a walk: every few kilometres they are different, just like the sky above a fjord. This fact has not particularly made the work involved preparing this book any easier because a webpage à la *www.correct-name-of-river.no* does not exist and different maps stylishly manage to slip a few different letters into a name.

Depending on the dialect, the Norwegian translation of »river« is *Elvi* or *Elva*. We will use the names of rivers which (we believe) are most common and deliberately forget about certain details in order not to cause any confusion. Uniquely the River Raundalselvi at Voss changes its name twice before it flows into Lake Vangsvatnet.

Their festivals: intensive and passionate

The Norwegians like to have celebrations and in this respect our Scandinavian neighbours do not differ from the rest of Europe. On 1st May they celebrate Labour Day, 17th May is a Norwegian Public Holiday and of course there are the Christian holidays at Easter, Whitsuntide and Christmas. There is a special celebration in the night from 23rd to 24th June called *Midsummer Night's Festival*. Large bonfires (*Bål*) are lit throughout the country in celebration of the summer solstice i.e. the longest day, and people dance, turn suddenly romantic and drink home-made alcoholic beverages – and surprisingly enough this coincides with the height of the canoeing season!

Ihre Sprache: Verknotet und verworren

Die Reichssprache war über Jahrhunderte die so genannte *Riksmål*: ein norwegisch eingefärbtes Dänisch. Nach dem Ende der Union mit Dänemark (1814) wurde aus den ländlichen Dialekten die norwegische Konkurrenzsprache *Landsmål* einwickelt. Diese konnte sich aber gerade in den Städten nicht durchsetzen und so war ein Sprachenstreit vorprogrammiert.

1929 wurden die Sprachen im Zuge einer Sprachreform zu allem Überfluss auch noch umbenannt: aus Landsmål wurde *Nynorsk* (Neunorwegisch) und aus Riksmål wurde *Bokmål* (Buchsprache). Heute sind beide Sprachen anerkannt, werden in den Schulen gelehrt und bei Uniprüfungen abgefragt. Das altgediente Bokmål wird jedoch häufiger geschrieben, Nynorsk hingegen vermehrt gesprochen.

Dazu gesellen sich unzählige Dialekte – an jeder Ecke wird ein wenig anders betont oder anders geschrieben. Die Norweger tragen ihre heimischen Mundarten spazieren, die alle paar Kilometer unterschiedlich sind, so wie der Fjordhimmel. Dies hat uns die Arbeit an unserem Buch nicht unbedingt einfacher gemacht, denn eine Internetseite à la *www.korrekte-flussnamen.no* gibt es nicht, und jede Landkarte versteht es mit Bravour ein paar andere Buchstaben ins Wort zu schummeln.

Je nach Dialekt wird im Norwegischen »Fluss« mit *Elvi* oder *Elva* übersetzt. Wir werden die (uns) geläufigsten Flussnamen verwenden und hin und wieder bewusst Einzelheiten unter den Tisch fallen lassen – um keine Verwirrung zu stiften. Allein die Raundalselvi bei Voss wechselt bis zur Mündung in den Vangsvatnet zwei Mal ihren Namen.

Ihre Feste: Intensiv und leidenschaftlich

Gefeiert wird in Norwegen gern, da unterscheiden sich unsere skandinavischen Nachbarn nicht vom Rest der Europäer: Am 1.Mai feiert man den Arbeitertag, am 17.Mai den Norwegischen Nationalfeiertag, und natürlichen die christlichen Feiertage wie Ostern, Pfingsten und Weihnachten. Ein besonderes Fest findet in der Nacht vom 23. zum 24. Juni statt: das *Mittsommernachtsfest*. Da werden in ganz Norwegen große Lagerfeuer (*Bål*) angezündet, um die Sommersonnenwende und den damit verbundenen längsten Tag des Jahres zu feiern. Ein Fest mit Romantik, Tanz und ein kleinwenig selbstgebranntem Alkohol – pünktlich zur Paddelhochsaison!

Norwegian cooking: simple and tasty

Traditional meals are a simple affair and were seldom offered to tourists in the past because the Norwegians were ashamed of their staple food. Whether the food is to your taste is for you to find out.

Rømmegrøt, the oldest warm dish in the country, is a sour cream pudding which is covered with melted butter and then sprinkled with either sugar and cinnamon or salt. *Labskaus* on the other hand is a substantial stew consisting of pieces of lamb and pork, carrots, onions and a brown sauce. All variations of fish are on offer; salmon, cod, mackerel or herring, whether raw, cooked, smoked or salted. There are even meatballs made of fishmeal, *Fiskeboller*, which most children detest, and *Fiskepudding* which is similar in taste and popularity. By contrast *Lefser*, a dessert consisting of a mixture of unleavened bread and biscuits, is much more popular and is served with sour cream and berry jam. The topping includes so-called *cloudberries* which are orange and have an unusual, slightly astringent, taste. Of all kinds of berries, cloudberries are one of the richest sources of vitamin C: they are not ready for picking in the mountains before August.

Tip: If you drink a cup of coffee in a Norwegian restaurant, the second cup known as the *Påtår* is usually cheaper or even free.

Ihre Küche: Einfach und schmackhaft

Die traditionelle Küche ist recht einfach und wurde den Urlaubern lange Zeit nur selten angeboten, da man sich für das Alltagsessen schämte. Ob es den Geschmacksnerv des Einzelnen trifft, muss wohl selbst herausgefunden werden.

Rømmegrøt, das älteste warme Gericht des Landes, ist eine Sauerrahmgrütze, die mit flüssiger Butter übergossen wird und mit Zucker und Zimt oder mit Salz bestreut wird. Im *Labskaus* hingegen tummeln sich Lamm und Schweinefleischstücken, die mit Kartoffeln, Zwiebeln und brauner Soße einen derben Eintopf ergeben. Fisch wird in allen Variationen angeboten, ob frisch oder gekocht, ob geräuchert oder gesalzen, ob Lachs, Dorsch, Makrele oder Hering. Es gibt sogar Fleischklößchen aus Fischmehl, *Fiskeboller*, die die meisten Kinder verabscheuen, und den ähnlich beliebten *Fiskepudding*. Wesentlich begehrter hingegen sind *Lefser*, ein Mischung aus Fladenbrot und Keks, die mit Sauerrahm und Beerenmarmelade als Nachspeise serviert werden. Die Krönung zu Lefser sind allerdings *Moltebeeren*, orangefarbene Beeren, die einen ganz eigenen, leicht herben Geschmack haben. Moltebeeren gehören zu den Vitamin-C-reichsten Beerensorten und sind in den Bergen nicht vor August reif.

Tipp: Trinkt man eine Tasse Kaffee in einem norwegischen Restaurant, ist der Nachschlag, der *Påtår*, meist billiger oder gar kostenlos.

If there's no party to go to, have your own!

Monuments in Oslo.

Famous Norwegians

Art which foreigners associate with Norway includes such items as wood carvings, animal ornaments from the Viking age, elaborately decorated wooden churches, traditional costumes and folk music. Scandinavia has long since been the birthplace to writers, painters and artists of all kinds, including Norwegians. Some became world famous due to their actions and works of art thereby succeeding in not only influencing Europe, but the whole world:

The author **Henryk Ibsen** (1828-1906) founded modern drama in Europe with his plays about society. He was the author of well-known *Peer Gynt*, one of Norway's most fantastic tales. Peer, the vagabond and show-off, loves his life of hunting in the countryside above all else, has skirmishes with a troll now and again and quite incidentally rescues an Alpine herdswoman from the monster. **Knut Hamson** (1859-1952), Norway's most important epic poet, received the Nobel Prize for literature in 1920 for his novel »Growth of the Soil«. Full of intuition, the story of the life of the Norwegian farmer Isak provides a deep insight into the simple farming life of the Norwegians and exposes the hypocrisy and lies of the middle class society. **Edvard Grieg** (1843-1907) made a name for himself by composing lyrical piano pieces but his music is often described as too simple – just typically Norwegian. He wrote the music to Ibsen's »Peer Gynt«, probably one of his most well-known works. **Edvard Munch** (1863-1944) on the other hand is Norway's most famous painter and founder of modern European expressionism. His style is unmistakable: Fear, love and death are the main themes of his paintings.

The polar scientist and zoologist, **Fridtjof Nansen** (1861-1930), and **Thor Heyerdahl** (1914-2002), expeditionist and someone who always knew how to make the best of things, proved that the Norwegians are the true successors of the Vikings. Nansen sailed through the Polar Sea in a wooden boat in 1893 hoping to arrive at the North Pole. Heyerdahl crossed oceans on simple wooden rafts and boats made of reeds to prove that man crossed the oceans much earlier than had been previously assumed.

Berühmte Norweger

Die norwegische Kunst verbindet man im Ausland häufig mit Holzschnitzereien und Tierornamenten der Wikingerzeit, mit kunstvoll ausgestalteten Stabkirchen, Trachten und Volksmusik. Skandinavien war schon immer eine Wiege für Schriftsteller, Maler und Künstler aller Art, so auch Norwegen. Einige von ihnen erlangten Weltruhm und konnten durch ihre Werke und ihr Handeln nicht nur Europa beeinflussen:

Der Schriftsteller **Henryk Ibsen** (1828-1906) begründete mit seinen Gesellschaftsstücken das moderne europäische Drama. Er ist der geistige Vater des berühmten *Peer Gynt*, eine der phantastischsten Erzählungen Norwegens. Der Herumtreiber und Prahlhans Peer liebt sein Jägerleben in der Natur über alles, prügelt sich hie und da mit einem Troll, und rettet mal ganz nebenbei eine Sennerin vor den Unholden. **Knut Hamson** (1859-1952), Norwegens bedeutendster Epiker, erhielt 1920 den Literaturnobelpreis für seinen Roman »Segen der Erde«. Die Erzählung über das Leben des norwegischen Bauers Isak gibt einen tiefen Einblick in das einfache bäuerliche Leben der Norweger und entlarvt voller Spürsinn die Heucheleien und Lügen der bürgerlichen Gesellschaft. Als Komponist lyrischer Klavierstücke machte sich **Edvard Grieg** (1843-1907) einen Namen, obwohl seine Musik oft als zu einfach, aber eben typisch norwegisch beschrieben wird. Er vertonte Ibsens »Peer Gynt«, welches wohl zu seinem bekanntesten Werk zählt. **Edvard Munch** (1863-1944) wiederum ist Norwegens berühmtester Maler und ein Begründer des modernen europäischen Expressionismus. Sein Stil ist unverkennbar: Angst, Liebe und Tod sind die wesentlichen Themen seiner Gemälde.

Polarforscher und Zoologe **Fridtjof Nansen** (1861-1930) und **Thor Heyerdahl** (1914-2002), Expeditionist und Lebenskünstler, beweisen, dass die wahren Nachfolger der Wikinger die Norweger sind. Nansen segelte schon 1893 mit einem Holzschiff durchs Polarmeer, in der Hoffnung zum Nordpool zu gelangen. Heyerdahl überquerte mit einfachen Holzflößen und Schilfbooten die großen Ozeane, um zu beweisen, dass man schon viel früher die Weltmeere überquerte als bisher angenommen.

From tribes of Vikings to a kingdom

The Vikings are probably the first we think about when we ponder Norwegian history. The sturdy men from the north influenced the image of Scandinavians in the world more than anyone else. Although the word Viking does not imply membership of a particular tribe, they are often assumed to be Norwegian. Early Norwegian legend is recorded in the »Heimskringla« of the poet *Snorre Sturlason* (1179-1241) and begins with King *Harald »Fairhair« Hårfagre* who, in 872, was able to put an end to the country's constant state of war which raged between many insignificant queens and tribal leaders and proclaim himself King of the whole of Norway. It is at this time that the country's name appears for the first time in English and French scripts where it is referred to as *Nortuagia*, *Norwegia* and *Nordweg*.

A glance further back in history reveals no information to specifically date man's first settlements in Norway but remains of early habitations are however thought to date back up to ten thousand years. At first, settlers lived mainly along the coastline fishing for a living and only moving inland at a later time hoping to find more favourable conditions for agriculture.

The society of farmers and fishermen began to change around 800 A.D. when yields from limited agricultural land proved insufficient and many settlers began to find their world too small. The first voyages were in the direction of Scotland where it was hoped that life would simply be easier. »Viking crusades« occurred regularly with ever larger dragon boats. They travelled to the Caspian Sea in the east and Ireland in the west, they crossed the Atlantic in the direction of Greenland and North America, and in the Mediterranean they got as far as Constantinople (Istanbul). The Vikings founded colonies on Iceland, the Faroes, The Shetland Islands and Normandy (France), and also played a key role in

Vom Wikingerhaufen zum Königreich

Die Wikinger sind wohl das erste was uns in den Sinn kommt, wenn wir an die norwegische Geschichte denken. Die derben Nordmänner haben das Bild der Skandinavier geprägt wie sonst niemand. Obwohl die Bezeichnung Wikinger keine Stammeszugehörigkeit beschreibt, werden sie oft mit den Norwegern gleichgesetzt. Die Sagen umwobene Vorzeit Norwegens ist in der »Heimskringla« des Dichters *Snorre Sturlason* (1179-1241) niedergeschrieben und beginnt mit König *Harald »Schönhaar« Hårfagre*. Dieser vermochte es im Jahre 872 den ewig wehrenden Krieg zwischen den vielen Kleinkönigen und Stammeshäuptlingen im Lande zu beenden und sich zum König von ganz Norwegen zu machen. Zu dieser Zeit wird auch der Name des Landes zum ersten Mal in englischen und französischen Schriften erwähnt: Dort heißt es *Nortuagia*, *Norwegia* und *Nordweg*.

Aber gehen wir noch etwas weiter zurück: Wann die ersten Menschen sich in Norwegen niederließen, ist nicht genau bekannt. Es wurden Wohnplätze gefunden, die bis zu zehntausend Jahre alt sein dürften. Anfangs lebten die Menschen als Fischer vorwiegend in Küstennähe, erst später drangen sie tiefer ins Landesinnere ein, da sie sich dort günstige Bedingungen für den Ackerbau erhofften.

Doch um 800 n. Chr. kam Bewegung in die Bauern- und Fischergesellschaft: Die Erträge der begrenzten Anbauflächen reichten nicht mehr aus, vielen Menschen wurden es zu eng in ihrer kleinen Welt. Erste Fahrten Richtung Schottland wurden unternommen, denn dort erhoffte man sich einfachere Lebensbedingungen. Es kam zu regelmäßigen »Wikingerfahrten« mit immer größeren Drachenbooten. Sie reisten bis zum Kaspischen Meer im Osten, segelten nach Irland im Westen, überquerten den Atlantik Richtung Grönland und Nordamerika und gelangten auf dem Mittelmeer bis nach Konstantinopel (Istanbul). Die Wikinger gründeten Kolonien auf Island, den Färöern, Shetland und in der Normandie (Frankreich) und wirkten Mitte des 9. Jahrhunderts maßgeblich an der Bildung des ersten russischen Großreiches, des sogenannten Kiewer Reiches mit. Der Volksname *Russen* ist von der finnischen Bezeichnung für die Wikinger, »Rus«, abgeleitet.

Die Wikingerfahrten brachten Reichtum ins Land – sei es durch Handel, oder Räuberei. Denn auch in schlechten Zeiten, als die Geschäfte nur spärlich liefen, wollte niemand mit leeren Händen zurückkehren. Und die schönsten »Souvenirs«, dass hatten die Normannen bald herausgefunden, waren in den Klöstern Englands und Irlands zu finden. Doch der steigende Drang nach Luxus zerstörte die Harmonie im eigenen Land: Es kam zu Missgunst und Streit, denn viele der Stammesoberhäupter wollten ihren Herrschaftsbereich erweitern – die Norweger waren ein riesiger, zerstrittener Haufen.

Erst der schon erwähnte Wikingerkönig *Harald Hårfagre* (*»Schönhaar«*) schaffte es wieder etwas Ordnung ins Land zu bringen. Nach den Überlieferungen des Snorre weigerte sich Haralds Auserwählte, sich ihrem Freier hinzugeben. Sie wollte keinen Stammeshäuptling, sie wollte einen Kö-

the formation of the first Russian Empire known as the Kiew Empire in the middle of the 9th century. The adjective *Russian* derives from the Finnish word for Vikings, »Rus«.

The Viking crusades brought wealth to the country – whether by trading or by plundering. In good times as well as bad, when trading was poor, nobody wanted to return empty-handed. And the Normans had soon discovered that the best »souvenirs« were to be found in the monasteries of England and Ireland. However, the constant quest for luxuries destroyed harmony at home. The results were envy, resentment and strife because many of the tribal leaders wanted to extend their powers: the Norwegians were simply an enormous quarrelling tribe.

It was the Viking King *Harald Hårfagre (»Fairhair«)*, mentioned above, who managed to bring some sort of order to the country. According to written records by Snorre, Harald's chosen one refused to bow down to her suitor. She did not want a tribal leader, she wanted a king, and not just any, but a proper one. *Hårfagre* accepted the challenge and brought further areas of the country together under his power. Incidentally, he gained the epithet of »Fairhair« because he did not have his hair cut until having completed the job at hand.

When he died in 931 the country fell apart again into individual parts and the Danish and Swedes had no trouble conquering it. Many years of guerrilla warfare followed during which a Norwegian man in particular made history. In 1015 *Olav Haraldsson* managed to win back the crown and introduce the country to Christianity. However, during a peasants' revolt, Haraldsson had to flee the country and the Danes once again had the country under their control. A short time later, in a renewed attempt to re-claim the throne, he was killed. But his death brought about a change of thinking amongst the people and in 1031 Olav Haraldsson became »Olav the holy one« and patron saint of the Norwegian people. The first wooden churches date back to the same period and are now the pride of every Norwegian village.

In the centuries that followed, Christianity became firmly established in Norway. As seats of bishoprics, the towns of *Nidaros* (Trondheim), *Christiania* (Oslo) and *Bjørgvin* (Bergen) increased in size considerably. Trade with Europe increased and enabled the German ports to gain a major influence on Norway's western ports. From 1387 Norway was ruled in union with Sweden and Denmark. The Reformation took hold in Norway in 1536 whereupon almost the entire population changed to the Lutheran faith.

The *peace settlement of Kiel* (1814) meant that the Danes, defeated allies of Napolean, had to concede Norway to Sweden. In the same year, Norway gave itself a constitution but was forced to recognise the Swedish king as its own. The personal union lasted until 1905 when Norway once again pronounced itself an independent kingdom under *Haakon VII*.

At the end of the 19th century industrialisation shook up Europe's conception of the world and brought about changes, also in Norway. The first factories shot up bringing employment and money to the towns. This opened the

nig, einen richtigen König. *Hårfagre* nahm die Herausforderung an und brachte weite Teile des Landes unter seine Kappe. Seinen Beinamen »Schönhaar« erhielt er übrigens, weil er sich seine Haare erst nach vollendeter Arbeit wieder schneiden ließ.

Nach seinem Tod 931 zerbrach das Land wieder in einzelne Teile, und so schafften es die Dänen und Schweden das Land zu erobern. Etliche Jahre Kleinkrieg folgten, in denen insbesondere ein Mann norwegische Geschichte schrieb. *Olav Haraldsson* schaffte es um 1015 den Thron zurückzuerobern und das Christentum im Land zu verbreiten. Doch bei einem Bauernaufstand musste Haraldsson fliehen, nun hatten die Dänen die Zügel wieder in der Hand. Bei dem Versuch den Thron erneut zu erkämpfen, kam er wenig später ums Leben. Doch sein Tod bewirkte einen Stimmungswandel im Volk: Olav Haraldsson wurde 1031 heilig gesprochen und als »Olav der Heilige« zum Schutzpatron der Norweger. In diese Zeit datiert man auch den Bau der ersten Stabkirchen, die heute als Stolz einer jeden norwegischen Ortschaft gelten.

In den folgenden Jahrhunderten festigte sich die Stellung des Christentums in Norwegen. Die Städte *Nidaros* (Trondheim), *Christiania* (Oslo) und *Bjørguen (Bergen)* vergrößerten sich als Bischofssitze erheblich. Der Handel mit Europa nahm zu und ermöglichte es den deutschen Hansestädten, großen Einfluss in den westlichen Hafenstädten Norwegens zu erlangen. Ab 1387 wurde Norwegen in Personalunion mit Dänemark und Schweden regiert. 1536 griff die Reformation in Norwegen, woraufhin fast die gesamte Bevölkerung zum lutherischen Glauben wechselte.

Im *Frieden von Kiel* (1814) mussten die Dänen als unterlegene Verbündete von Napoleon Norwegen an die Schweden abtreten. Im gleichen Jahr gab Norwegen sich eine eigene Verfassung, wurde aber gezwungen, den schwedischen König auch als den eigenen anzuerkennen. Diese Personalunion dauerte bis 1905, als sich Norwegen unter *Haakon VII.* wieder zum selbstständigen Königreich erhob.

Ende des 19. Jahrhunderts rüttelte die Industrialisierung am europäischem Weltbild und brachte Veränderungen mit sich, so auch in Norwegen: Erste Fabriken sprossen aus dem Boden und brachten Arbeit und Geld in die Stadt – eine Landflucht überrollte das Land. Die norwegische Schifffahrt erlebte eine Blütezeit, die erste Eisenbahnstrecke wurde gebaut (Oslo-Eidsvoll), auch in

floodgates and country dwellers flocked to the cities. Norwegian shipping flourished, the first railway lines were built (Oslo-Eidsvoll) and even output from agriculture was higher than Norway's own requirements. However, many people continued to live in remote and underdeveloped corners of the country, some in total poverty. These were the citizens who triggered an exodus of emigration to North America.

The Second World War

Having sided with Napoleon for the French Wars of 1813 only to lose, 125 years later Norway adopted a neutral stance in the run-up to World War II. However, this proved to be a futile tactic and Germany's lightning attack in April 1940 met unprepared resistance. Within a short space of time Norway's coastal cities in the west fell under occupation. It proved harder to conquer Oslo however, because a narrow area in the Oslofjord made access from the sea more difficult. The resulting delay gave the king and his government sufficient time to flee the country to England.

After a battle lasting two months which saw the retreat of the Allies, the Germans formally took over control of the country in June, but not its citizens. Not only did the great expanse of wilderness make total occupation difficult, but also the immense resistance shown by the Norwegians. Judges resigned, pastors adopted a confrontational approach to the newly appointed government and sportsmen boycotted international competitions. Even some teachers did not wish to teach new ideals and therefore ended up in concentration camps. At the same time, the British government kitted out Norwegian resistance fighters with equipment which included explosives to destroy the German-occupied Vemork chemical plant in Rjukan. This prevented the continued development of heavy water[1], which could have been useful to Germans for making atomic weapons. This single act of resistance, code-named »Operation Gunnerside« epitomised Norwegian resistance. One of several films made on the subject starred Kirk Douglas in »Heroes of Telemark«.

However, there were also collaborators: The newly appointed fascist Party of Norway under the leadership of *Vidkun Quisling* had got wind of the German attack long before it was able to take over power. Although Quisling was ousted a short time later, his name became a synonym for collaborators.

When the war ended, rebuilding the economy and job creation were the most important tasks. A considerable portion of the rural population migrated to the cities and large villages in hope of an easier life.

In 1965 the first drilling for oil commenced in Norwegian waters. With the discovery of the »Ekofisk« oil field, a major find, life changed irrevocably for Norwegians. Within the space of three decades, a country shaped by farmers and fishermen became one of the richest in the world.

[1] Water containing the isotope deuterium instead of hydrogen (relative molecular mass 20 as opposed to 18 for ordinary water).

der Landwirtschaft wurde nicht mehr nur für den eigenen Bedarf produziert. Trotzdem lebten noch viele Menschen in abgelegenen und unterentwickelten Ecken des Landes, teilweise in bitterer Armut. Sie waren es wohl, die die erste große Auswanderungswelle nach Nordamerika ins Rollen brachten.

Der Zweite Weltkrieg

Nachdem Norwegen in den französischen Kriegen 1813 auf der Seite von Napoleon den Krieg verloren hatte, suchten sie nun rund 125 Jahre später ihr Heil in der Neutralität – der Zweite Weltkrieg stand bevor. Doch ihre Bemühungen blieben erfolglos: Ein Blitzangriff der Deutschen im April 1940 traf die Norweger unvorbereitet, und so wurden die großen Küstenstädte im Westen kurzer Hand besetzt. Doch die Eroberung Oslos war problematischer, da eine Engstelle im Oslofjord den Zugang vom Meer erschwerte. Diese Verzögerung schaffte dem König und seiner Regierung genügend Luft für eine Flucht nach Großbritannien.

Nach zwei Monaten Kampf und dem Abzug der Alliierten übernahmen die Deutschen im Juni zwar formal die Macht über das Land, aber nicht die Kontrolle über die Einwohner. Nicht nur die Weitläufigkeit der Natur, auch die immense Widerstandskraft der Norweger erschwerte eine gänzliche Besetzung des Landes. Richter legten ihr Amt nieder, Pastoren stellten sich gegen die neu eingesetzte Regierung, Sportler boykottierten Wettkämpfe. Selbst einige Lehrer wollten das neue Ideal nicht unterrichten und landeten im Konzentrationslager. Die britische Regierung rüstete zeitgleich norwegische Widerstandskämpfer aus, unter anderem um in Rjukan das von Deutschen besetzte Vemork-Chemiewerk zu zerstören. Damit verhinderten sie die weitere Herstellung schweren Wassers[1], welches den Deutschen zum Bau der Atombombe hätte dienen sollen. Diese »Operation Gunnerside« steht als Symbol für den norwegischen Widerstand und wurde mehrmals verfilmt, unter anderem als »Kennwort: Schweres Wasser« (»Heroes of Telemark«) mit Kirk Douglas.

Doch natürlich gab es auch Kollaborateure: Die neu eingesetzte Regierung der faschistischen Partei Norwegens unter *Vidkun Quisling* hatte schon lange vor dem Angriff auf eine Machtübernahme gewittert. Auch wenn Quisling kurze Zeit später abgesetzt wurde, stand sein Name damals als Synonym für Verräter.

Nach dem Krieg stellte der Wiederaufbau von Wirtschaft und Erwerbsleben die wichtigste Aufgabe dar. Ein erheblicher Teil der Landbevölkerung wanderte in Städte und größere Ortschaften ab, da sie sich dort ein einfacheres Leben erhofften.

1965 begann man in den norwegischen Gewässern nach Erdöl zu bohren. Vier Jahre später hatte man Glück, das gewaltige Ekofisk-Ölfeld sollte das Leben der Norweger für immer verändern. Innerhalb von drei Jahrzehnten wurde aus einer von Bauern und Fischern geprägten Gemeinschaft eines der reichsten Länder der Erde.

[1] Im Gegensatz zu »normalem« Wasser sind hier die Wasserstoffatome durch Deuterium ersetzt.

Full sail ahead into the industrialised era

Let's get to the point: Norway today is one of the wealthiest countries in Europe. Reserves of oil and gas off the Norwegian coast heaved the country out of an economic crisis at the end of the 70s and created a healthy budget surplus. Despite the fact that costs of exploitation are approximately twenty times higher than those of the Arabic Gulf States, Norway is still able to hold its own in the competitive international oil market due to reduced transport costs to its European neighbours. A pipeline was laid especially to connect Germany up to Norwegian oil. Jobs on oil platforms are much sought-after and some of the best-paid in the country: two weeks of work non-stop followed by three weeks off.

The oil found paid off the country's debts, boosted industry, led to full employment and hiked social welfare benefits to exemplary levels. However, living costs rose too and prices are today approximately 50 percent higher than in Norway's European neighbours.

Oil exports brought more capital into the country than its small economy could cope with. The government

An interesting contrast: an industrial town in a beautiful setting.

now deposits enormous sums of money abroad in order to prevent further inflation. The industrial boom has died down considerably: Norwegian firms are too expensive in the international marketplace, their products too.

The sea has always played a key role in Norway, not just because of the oil fields which lie underneath. The search for food lured people out to sea and the urge to be mobile led them to build boats because where fjords squeeze between mountains, there is not much room left for roads. Norway is one of the world's greatest fishing nations and fish exports are the country's largest export after oil. It is no surprise that Norwegian shipbuilding is state-of-the-art; even in the middle ages shipbuilding was a lucrative business for many people.

Forestry is another of Norway's core industries: wood is needed to build boats and houses and is the raw material for paper-making. Wood-processing factories are mainly

Mit vollen Segeln ins Industriezeitalter

Gleich vorweg gesagt: Norwegen ist heute eines der wohlhabendsten Länder Europas. Erdgas- und Erdölfunde vor der Küste Norwegens haben das Land Ende der 70er Jahre aus der Wirtschaftskrise geholt und schwarze Zahlen schreiben lassen. Trotz der etwa zwanzigfach höheren Förderungskosten gegenüber den arabischen Golfstaaten kann Norwegen im Öl-Wettbewerb mithalten, und zwar durch die geringen Transportkosten zu den europäischen Nachbarn. Nach Deutschland wurde eigens eine Pipeline gelegt, die uns mit dem Öl aus dem Norden versorgt. Die Jobs auf den Bohrinseln zählen zu den begehrtesten und best-bezahlten im Lande: zwei Wochen nonstop arbeiten, danach drei Wochen frei.

Das gefundene Öl tilgte die Schulden des Landes, kurbelte die Industrie an, schaffte Voll-beschäftigung, und katapultierte die Sozialleistungen des Staates auf ein Vorzeigeniveau. Aber es stiegen auch die Lebenshal-tungskosten, das Preisniveau liegt heute etwa 50 Prozent über dem der europäischen Nach-barn.

Die Ölexporte brachten mehr Geld ins Land, als die kleine Volkswirtschaft verkraften konn-te. Die Regierung legt mittler-weile enorme Geldsummen im Ausland an, um einer weiteren Inflation vorzubeugen. Der Aufschwung der Industrie hat sich nämlich stark abge-schwächt: zu teuer sind norwegische Firmen im internatio-nalen Wettstreit, zu teuer ihre Produkte im Ausland.

Das Meer spielte in Norwegen schon immer eine wichtige Rolle, nicht nur wenn sich Ölfelder darunter befinden. Die Menschen zog es zur Nahrungs-suche auf das Wasser, auch der Drang zur Mobilität bewegte sie Boote zu bauen. Denn wo sich Fjorde zwischen Berge quetschen, lassen sie nur we-nig Platz für Straßen. Norwegen zählt zu den größten Fischfangnationen der Erde, nach dem Öl ist Fisch der größte Exportartikel. Die norwegische Schiffsbaukunst ist dem entsprechend ausgefeilt, schon im Mittelalter war der Bootsbau ein lukratives Geschäft für viele Menschen.

Ein weiteres Standbein der Norweger ist der Wald: Holz wird benötigt zum Schiffs- und Häuserbau, und als Roh-stoff für die Papierherstellung. Die holzverarbeitende Indus-

situated at the mouth of large rivers in the south east of the country because tree trunks from the forests can quickly be floated downriver to them.

The development of modern telephone connection technology is another key industry in Norway – the remoteness of the country makes telecommunications indispensable. Without a telephone, in many parts of the country a cosy chat face to face with the neighbour would mean hours of hiking. Nowhere else in Europe is the density of mobile phones higher than in Scandinavia, the public telephone network is fully digital and as far as high-speed data transmission is concerned, Norway leads the world.

A paradise for electricity

The Norwegians have been spoilt for power for years. Electricity is almost primarily generated by water power and as we all know, Norway is not short of rivers. For this reason electricity was cheap in the past which resulted in the Norwegians becoming the world's greatest power consumers per capita. It was not until the extremely dry summer of 2002 – when prices almost tripled – that people began to think about saving power.

»Water does not need man, but man needs water«

Norway and the world

Norway is situated on the periphery of Europe which appeals to the Norwegians, who voted against becoming a member of the European Union in 1972 and 1994. This does not mean that they want to isolate themselves – they could not afford the consequences because approx. 80 percent of exports go to EU countries. Norwegians probably only want to retain their peace and quiet as well as their independence – take whaling for example. When Norwegian paddlers say that they have never been canoeing in Europe, they usually mean that they have never canoed rivers in the Alps. They have everything they need to have a good time in Norway – what do they need Europe for?

Actually, Norwegian politics have had an international flair as long as anyone can remember. The first well-known pioneering champion of freedom and a mediator in international conflicts was the polar scientist and diplomat Fridtjof Nansen. As high commissioner of the League of Nations (the forerunner of the United Nations), he had a major impact on alleviating refugee problems and famine disasters following the First World War and the Russian Revolution. In 1922 Nansen was awarded the Nobel Peace Prize in recognition of his endeavours.

Even today Norway continues to play an active role in peace negotiations. In the Middle East, Norway has repeatedly worked to achieve agreements between Israel and the Palestinians, even if these did not prove successful very long due to the explosiveness and profundity of the conflict.

trie liegt hauptsächlich an den Mündungen großer Flüsse im Südosten, denn dorthin kann die Baumstämme aus den Wäldern am schnellsten herabgeflößt werden.

Die Entwicklung moderner Telekommunikationsverbindungen stellt einen weiteren Schwerpunkt der norwegischen Industrie dar – die Weitläufigkeit der Natur macht Kommunikation unerlässlich. Mal schnell den Nachbar auf einen Plausch zu besuchen, kann in vielen Teilen des Landes in stundenlangen Wanderungen enden. Die Mobiltelefondichte ist nirgendwo in Europa so hoch wie in Skandinavien, das Fernsprechnetz ist voll digitalisiert, und bei der Anzahl der ISDN-Anschlüsse liegt Norwegen sogar an der Weltspitze.

Das Strom-Paradies

Lange Zeit lebten die Norweger in einem Energie-Schlaraffenland: Strom wird beinah komplett aus Wasserkraft gewonnen, und wie wir wissen, hat Norwegen einiges an Flüssen zu bieten. Dadurch waren die Preise so niedrig, dass die Norweger an die Weltspitze der Pro-Kopf-Stromverbraucher vordrangen. Erst der extrem trockene Sommer 2002 ließ die Norweger über Stromsparen nachdenken – die Preise stiegen beinah um das Dreifache.

»Wasser braucht kein Mensch, aber Mensch braucht Wasser«

Norwegen und die Welt

Norwegen liegt etwas abseits in Europa, und das finden die Norweger auch gut: Zweimal, 1972 und 1994, stimmten sie gegen den Beitritt zur Europäischen Union. Das soll nicht heißen, dass sie sich abkapseln wollen, das können sie sich gar nicht erlauben (etwa 80 Prozent des norwegischen Exports gehen in die EU-Staaten). Die Norweger wollen wohl nur ihre Ruhe und Unabhängigkeit bewahren, denken wir beispielsweise an den Walfang. Reden norwegische Paddler davon, dass sie noch nie in Europa paddeln waren, meinen sie meist die Flüsse der Alpen. Sie haben in Norwegen alles was sie zum Leben brauchen – wozu brauchen sie Europa?

Doch eigentlich führen die Norweger seit eh und je eine international ausgerichtete Politik. Der erste bekannte Vorkämpfer für den Frieden und Vermittler bei internationalen Konflikten war der Polarforscher und Diplomat Fridtjof Nansen. Als Hochkommissar des Völkerbundes (dem Vorläufer der Vereinten Nationen) trug er zur Minderung der Flüchtlingsprobleme und Hungerkatastrophen nach dem Ersten Weltkrieg und der russischen Revolution bei. Hierfür wurde Nansen 1922 mit dem Friedensnobelpreis geehrt.

Die Norweger spielen auch heute noch eine aktive Rolle als Vermittler bei Friedensverhandlungen. Gerade im Nah-Ost-Konflikt konnten sie immer wieder zu Abkommen zwischen Israel und Palästina beitragen, auch wenn diese aufgrund der Brisanz und Tiefgründigkeit des Konflikts nie lange erfolgreich blieben.

Norway's five regions

Norway is split into five regions which are then organised in various districts. Each region has something special to offer, each region has its own merit:

Southern Norway (*Sørlandet*), which boasts the regions of *Aust-Agder* and *Vest-Agder*, is the number one holiday paradise for Norwegians and the south coast in summer seems to be the Norwegian Riviera. In this part of the country, the number of hours of sunshine are higher than anywhere else in Norway and many communities become centres of bustling activity with their populations increasing many times over. Skerry (rocky) gardens are southern Norway's trade mark and serve as protection against the harsh weather of the Skagerrak region.

Eastern Norway consists of the districts *Oslo*, *Akershus*, *Østfold*, *Vestfold*, *Buskerud*, *Telemark*, *Hedmark* and *Oppland*. It is the most populated area, at the heart of which is the country's capital, Oslo. As far as kayaking is concerned, the east – like the west – is one of the most accessible regions and over half of the rivers described in this book are in this area.

Western Norway consists of the districts of *Møre og Romsdal*, *Sogn og Fjordane*, *Hordaland* and *Rogaland*, and is renowned above all for its imposing mountains, waterfalls and fjords. It is therefore often referred to as »fjord Norway«. Each fjord has something special to offer: There are a number of impressive waterfalls at Geirangerfjord whereas Sognefjord is the longest fjord in the world, boasting lush farming villages on the banks of the fjord and narrow passages with cliffs which disappear into the water. Hardangerfjord also has a lot of variety to offer, the blossoming orchards being a particular highlight. At the Lysefjord you will find the Prekestolen cliffs which tower vertically approx. 600 metres above the water.

Central Norway is composed of *Nord-Trøndelag* and *Sør-Trøndelag* and is an important agricultural area in the country. It is also home to Norway's technology centre and capital of central Norway, the town of Trondheim, which is the country's third largest town. There is a lot of gossip about rivers worth canoeing here, but detailed information has to be paid for in pure gold.

Northern Norway consists of the regions of Nordland, Troms and Finnmark and is very much the Land of the Midnight Sun and the Northern Lights. In the middle of winter, dawn simply gives way to dusk without it becoming light. It is particularly at this time that you can see the Northern Lights (Aurora Borealis), a cascade of light in the sky for up to twenty hours. Thousands of birds on the sea and on islands have led to the entire stretch of coastline from the polar circle to Øst-Finnmark being referred to as »the bird cliff route«.

Die fünf Regionen Norwegens

Norwegen wird in fünf Regionen unterteilt, die wiederum in mehrere Bezirke gegliedert sind. Jede Region birgt Besonderheiten, jede hat ihr eigenes Flair:

Südnorwegen (*Sørlandet*) ist mit den Bezirken *Aust-Agder* und *Vest-Agder* das Ferienparadies der Norweger schlechthin, im Sommer wirkt die Südküste wie eine norwegische Riviera. Die Zahl der jährlichen Sonnenstunden ist in diesem Landesteil höher als im restlichen Norwegen, viele Gemeinden werden im Sommer von einem bunten Treiben erfasst und steigern ihre Bevölkerungszahlen um ein Vielfaches. Südnorwegens Markenzeichen ist der Schärengarten, der das Land gegen das raue Skagerrak schützt.

Zu **Ostnorwegen** gehören die Bezirke *Oslo*, *Akershus*, *Østfold*, *Vestfold*, *Buskerud*, *Telemark*, *Hedmark* und *Oppland*. Es ist das bevölkerungsreichste Gebiet, dessen Herz die Hauptstadt Oslo. Auch paddeltechnisch ist der Osten neben dem Westen eine der am weitesten erschlossenen Regionen – mehr als die Hälfte der beschriebenen Flüsse befindet sich hier.

Westnorwegen mit den Bezirken *Møre og Romsdal*, *Sogn og Fjordane*, *Hordaland* und *Rogaland* ist vor allem für seine imposanten Berge, Wasserfälle und Fjorde bekannt. Deshalb wird es auch oft als Fjordnorwegen bezeichnet. Jeder Fjord hat seine eigenen Attraktionen: Am Geirangerfjord gibt es eine Reihe imposanter Wasserfälle, der Sognefjord ist der längste Fjord der Welt, mit grünen Bauerndörfern am Ufer sowie engen Passagen mit ins Wasser ragenden Felsen. Der Hardangerfjord ist ebenso abwechslungsreich, sein besonderes Merkmal aber sind die blühenden Obstgärten. Am Lysefjord ragt der Prekestolen-Felsen etwa 600 Meter senkrecht über das Wasser.

Mittelnorwegen mit den Regionen *Nord-Trøndelag* und *Sør-Trøndelag* zählt zu den wichtigen Landwirtschaftsregionen des Landes. Hier liegt Trondheim, Norwegens Technologiehauptstadt, Hauptstadt Mittelnorwegens und drittgrößte Stadt des Landes. Paddeltechnisch munkelt man hier von jeder Menge lohnender Bäche, detaillierte Informationen erhält man jedoch nur im Tausch gegen pures Gold.

Nordnorwegen mit den Bezirken *Nordland*, *Troms* und *Finnmark* ist das Land der Mitternachtssonne und des Nordlichts. Mitten im Winter geht die Morgenröte in die Dämmerung über, ohne dass es Tag wird. Dann kann man das Nordlicht (Aurora Borealis) sehen, das bis zu zwanzig Stunden am Tag als Lichtkaskade über den Himmel flackert. Tausende von Vögeln auf dem Meer, auf Inseln sowie in der Luft haben dem gesamten Küstenstreifen vom Polarkreis bis in die Øst-Finnmark den Namen »Vogelfelsen-Route« eingebracht.

Finnmark
Troms
North Norway
Nordland
Nord-Trøndelag
Middle Norway
Sør-Trøndelag
Fjord Norway
Møre og Romsdal
East Norway
Sogn og Fjordane
Oppland
Hedmark
Buskerud
Horda-land
Oslo
Akershus
Roga-land
Tele-mark
Vest-fold
Øst-fold
Vest Agder
Aust Agder
South Norway

Norway: Facts and figures
Norwegen: Zahlen und Fakten

Kongeriket Norge • The Kingdom of Norway • Königreich Norwegen

Area **Fläche**	385,155 km², i.e. a little larger than Germany (Without the islands of Spitzbergen and Jan Mayen the area is 323,758 km²) 385.155 km², also etwas größer als Deutschland (ohne die Inseln Spitzbergen und Jan Mayen sind es 323.758 km²)
Inhabitants **Einwohner**	Approx. 4.5 million which represents a population density of 12 inhabitants per km² (Germany approx. 230/km², Great Britain approx. 240/km²) Etwa 4,5 Millionen; dies entspricht einer Einwohnerdichte von etwa 12 E/km² (Deutschland ca. 230 E/km², Großbritannien ca. 240 E/km²)
Capital / **Hauptstadt**	Oslo
Constitution / **Verfassung**	Hereditary constitutional monarchy Erblich konstitutionelle Monarchie
Official language **Amtssprache**	Norwegian (Bokmål and Nynorsk), Sámi Norwegisch (Bokmål u. Nynorsk), Samisch
Currency **Währung**	Norwegian crowns (NOK) Norwegische Krone (NOK) 1 NOK = 100 Øre = 0.13 € = 0.09 £ 1 € = 7.97 NOK, 1 £ = 11.6 NOK
Country code / **Landesvorwahl**	0047
Emergency numbers **Notruf**	Police 112, Accident Rescue 113 Polizei 112, Unfallrettung 113
Driving **Auto**	Lights on! Licht an!
Largest lake / **Größter See**	Mjøsa (362 km²)
Longest river / **Längster Fluss**	Glomma (600 km)
Highest waterfalls **Höchste Wasserfälle**	*not vertical:* Mardalsfossen (705 m), Mongefossen (700 m), Vedalsfossen (650 m) *highest vertical falls:* Skykkjedalsfossen (300 m), Vettisfossen (275 m), Søre Mardalsfossen (250 m)
Highest mountains **Höchste Berge**	Galdhøpiggen (2,469 m), Jotunheimen Glittertind (2,464 m), Jotunheimen
Largest glacier / **Größter Gletscher**	Jostedalsbreen (487 km²)
Longest fjord **Längster Fjord**	Sognefjorden (204 km)

TRAVELLING: OFF TO THE NORTH   AB IN DEN NORDEN

»Travelling is searching for wisdom«

On the road again.   Photo: DP

Before the journey: Where to go?

The Golden Route:

• for the grade III-IV paddler:
If you are looking for relaxing whitewater and are travelling with family, it's best to start in *Hedmark* in the east. Hedmark is the area with the easiest rivers. Having paddled the *Trysilelva, Setninga & Co.* you can look forward to paddling the *Sjoa* in *Oppland*. This region has everything to offer from easy open whitewater to pseudo-class V. Travelling north from Sjoa it is simple to get to *Jori* and *Lora*, to the south there is the *Frya* and to the west there is a wave to enjoy in *Skjåk* plus the *Bøvra* and *Ostri*. It is well worth making a detour to western Norway just to see the beautiful countryside even if there are fewer easy rivers to paddle than in the east.

• for the grade V paddler:
Let's assume you have enough time, you took along a creeker and want to paddle the finest whitewater in Europe. If this is the case, start your trip in southern Norway in mid-May and travel northwards to follow the meltwater. First canoe all the whitewater in *Telemark*, then go to *Hemsil* via *Numedalslågen*. You can begin a circular tour from Hemsil but first you need to set your objectives. Do you want to go west to *Voss* or to *Sjoa* in the north east? Both areas have rivers which are just as good to canoe with meltwater; alternatively go in late summer.

a) If you decide to begin in the west, you can take a short diversion through *Lærdal* and *Sogndal* or you can make straight for *Voss*. Voss is a good base for quite a while and the *Raundalselvi* alone can keep you busy for a few days. Once you've finished, travel north up the west coast via *Jølstra* and *Hellesylt* to *Valldall* and on to *Rauma*. From there you travel south to *Dombås*. If your holiday is nearly at an end, then it's time you head off to *Sjoa* for more fun. With time on your hands, it's worth first making a detour to *Trøndelag* for *Driva & Co.*

b) If you decide to head north east, it's a good idea to set up your next base camp near *Sjoa*. The Sjoa will keep you busy for a while, as will the other rivers in the surrounding area. When you've finished in this region you can either take the west route (above) in reverse i.e. via *Dumbås, Rauma* and *Hellesylt* to *Voss* or the quicker route to Voss via *Jotunheimen* and *Sogndal*.

Whichever route you choose, you will have a great time. Norway boasts a terrific number of rivers suitable for kayakers of which just a few are described in this guide. If you are looking for something new and feeling adventurous, Norway still has virgin territory just waiting to be discovered. The routes we have described are just tempting suggestions for your holiday; there are simply countless options which enable you to plan your own route.

Vor der Reise: Wo will ich hin?

Die Goldene Route:

• für den WW III-IV Paddler:
Ist man auf der Suche nach entspanntem Wildwasser und hat Kind und Kegel dabei, sollte man zuerst der *Hedmark* im Osten einen Besuch abstatten. Die Hedmark ist das Revier mit der höchsten Anzahl leichter Wildflüsse. Nach *Trysilelva, Setninga & Co* kann man sich auf die *Sjoa* in Oppland freuen. Diese Region bietet alles, von leichtem offenem Wildwasser bis hin zum Pseudo-Fünfer. Von Sjoa Richtung Norden sind *Jori* und *Lora* schnell erreicht, im Süden die *Frya* und gen Westen die Spielwelle in *Skjåk*, die *Bøvra* und der *Ostri*. Ein Abstecher nach Westnorwegen ist allein schon wegen der Landschaft lohnend, auch wenn das Angebot der leichten Flüsse nicht so reichhaltig ist wie im Osten.

• für den WW V Paddler:
Nehmen wir mal an, man hat genügend Zeit, ein Creek-boot dabei, und will das beste Wildwasser Europas paddeln: Man startet Mitte Mai in Südnorwegen und fährt der Schneeschmelze Richtung Norden nach. Erst alle Bäche in der *Telemark* abgrasen, dann über *Numedalslågen* zum *Hemsil*. Nun steht man am Anfang einer Rundreise und muss sich entscheiden, wohin man will: Richtung Westen nach *Voss*, oder Richtung Nord-Osten zur *Sjoa*. In beiden Gebieten gibt es Flüsse, die sowohl bei Schmelze als auch im Spätsommer am besten fahrbar sind.

a) Entscheidet man sich zuerst für den Westen, kann man einen kurzen Abstecher durchs *Lærdal* und *Sogndal* machen, oder direkt nach *Voss* aufbrechen. Voss ist ein gutes Basislager für einige Zeit, allein die *Raundalselvi* kann mehrere Tage beschäftigen. Danach geht es weiter gen Norden die Westküste entlang, über *Jølstra* und *Hellesylt* nach *Valldall*, und letztendlich zur *Rauma*. Von dort geht es südwärts nach *Dombås* weiter. Sieht man sich am Ende seines Urlaubes, wird es nun Zeit die *Sjoa* unsicher zu machen. Liegt der Rückreisetermin noch in ferner Zukunft, würde sich zuerst ein Abstecher nach *Trøndelag* zu *Driva & Co* lohnen.

b) Haben wir uns für den Nord-Osten entschieden, empfiehlt es sich das nächste Basislager bei *Sjoa* aufzuschlagen. Nicht nur die Sjoa, auch die Flüsse im Umland werden uns einige Zeit in Atem halten. Danach können wir entweder der zuerst beschriebenen West-Route entgegengesetzt folgen, also über *Dombås, Rauma* und *Hellesylt* nach *Voss*, oder man nimmt die schnellere Route nach Voss, übers *Jotunheimen* und *Sogndal*.

Egal wie man sich entscheidet, egal welchen Weg man wählt – man wird ein Abenteuer erleben. Norwegen bietet eine ungeheure Anzahl paddelbarer Flüsse, von denen in diesem Buch nur ein kleiner Teil beschrieben ist. Wer offen für Neues ist und etwas Abenteuergeist mitbringt, kann in Norwegen noch einiges an Neuland entdecken. Die beschrieben Routen sind lediglich Anreize für einen Urlaub, Möglichkeiten zur Kreation der »eigenen Runde« sind schier unbegrenzt vorhanden.

What do I need?

For a perfect tour of Norway you should have at least three weeks' holiday, enough money and a relaxed approach so that you can survive bad weather periods. Everyone needs good camping equipment, a reliable car and of course a shovel not just to bury your toilet paper! The most important item – your travel guide – you should keep to hand. The other items you need are listed as follows:

1. A good atlas and maps
2. A warm sleeping bag
3. Mosquito repellent
4. A lot of dry paddle clothes
5. Sun glasses (to help you fall asleep in June)
6. Spare paddle
7. A good book
8. Umbrella
9. Wellington boots

There are a few things you can have no qualms about leaving at home because there are plenty of alternative meal ideas in Norway: Canned fish, Syrup and Marmalade.

Tip: Very detailed maps (1:50000) are available from *Statens Kartverk Norge* (www.statkart.no). You can order them direct under the number +47/32118100. In Germany you can order the maps via the Homepage of Nordis Versand (www.nordis.versand.de) or by phoning +49/201/8482370. We highly recommend you purchase the map »Veiatlas Norge« in a scale of 1:300000 (ISBN 82-7945-028-9).

Was brauche ich?

Für die perfekte Norwegentour benötigt man mindestens drei Wochen Zeit, genügend Geld auf dem Konto und eine gelassene Mentalität, um auch mal Schlechtwetterperioden zu überstehen. Eine gute Campingausrüstung, ein verlässliches Auto und eine Schaufel, um das Klopapier zu vergraben, sollte jeder dabei haben. Das wichtigste, einen Flussführer, hältst du ja schon in der Hand. Was man noch mitbringen sollte, zeigt die folgende Liste:

1. Gute Land- und Straßenkarten
2. Einen warmen Schlafsack
3. Mückenspray
4. Jede Menge trockener Paddelsachen
5. Sonnenbrille (zum Einschlafen im Juni)
6. Ersatzpaddel
7. Ein gutes Buch
8. Regenschirm
9. Gummistiefel

Es gibt auch ein paar Sachen, die man getrost daheim lassen kann, denn davon gibt es in Norwegen gute Alternativen: Fischkonserven, Sirup und Marmelade.

Tipp: Sehr detaillierte Landkarten (1:50000) gibt das *Statens Kartverk Norge* (www.statkart.no) heraus. Sie können direkt unter der Nummer +47/3211 8100 bestellt werden. In Deutschland können diese Karten auf der Homepage des Nordis Versand (www.nordis.versand.de) oder unter der Tel. 0201/8482370 bestellt werden. Sehr zu empfehlen ist der »Veiatlas Norge« im Maßstab 1:300000 (ISBN 82-7945-028-9).

Erik Martinsen waiting for the ferry.

Arnd Schäftlein enjoys his »mothership«, Matze Brustmann his longboard.

How do I get to Norway?

• by plane:

Flying is surely the most relaxing way to travel and there are regular trains from Gardermoen airport (near Oslo) to Otta which take you to the kayaker's paradise in just a few hours.

A paddler without a car is in a bit of a fix and hiring one usually bursts the holiday budget. However, visitors arriving without one will find that they probably have to hire one anyway. Just a few quick mouse clicks on the homepage of the car rental company Hertz (*www.europcar.com*) will take you to Oslo airport.

Tip: You can hire used cars inexpensively under *www.rent-a-wreck.no* and roof racks are no problem to find because Norway is a nation of skiers.

• by car and ferry:

Probably the cheapest option for all Europeans is to go with your own car and to take the ferry. There are a lot of ferry crossings and, depending on the port of departure and destination, there are several routes to Norway to choose from. The long ferry crossings such as *Kiel - Oslo* or *Newcastle - Bergen* reduce the number of kilometres stuck behind the driving wheel but they do tend to make a hole in the wallet. The cheapest ferry companies (e.g. *»Vogelfluglinie«*) always take the shortest sea route but this does not leave much time to relax before the drive continues at the other side.

The ferry crossing you choose will of course depend on your chosen destination. If you want to go to *Telemark*, then Larvik is an obvious harbour to head for whereas if you are heading for *Voss*, take the *Fjordline* to Bergen. Oslo is the first choice if *Sjoa* is your destination.

The starting point is just as relevant. If you are travelling from England, then Newcastle is a good port to leave from. Alternatively, if your journey begins in Berlin, how about the direct crossing from *Saßnitz* to *Trelleborg* with a drive along the coast of Sweden to Oslo? If you travel up the western flank of Germany, it makes sense to take the ferry from Denmark.

If the metropolises of Amsterdam, Berlin or Copenhagen are en route, it pays to take a short break from driving and do a bit of sightseeing.

Tips galore:

Tip 1: Some ferry companies offer discounts if you book early.

Tip 2: Because you are likely to have boats on the car roof you need to be extra vigilant. Most vehicles over 2 metres in height are more expensive and tricks are usually unsuccessful (electronic height measurements).

Tip 3: Some companies e.g. *Kystlink* offer cheap crossings on freight ferries. These only take of few cars and there is no service whatsoever on board.

Wie komme ich nach Norwegen?

• mit dem Flugzeug:

Die entspannendste Art nach Norwegen zu reisen, ist sicherlich mit dem Flugzeug. Vom Gardermoen Flughafen bei Oslo gehen regelmäßig Züge nach Otta – in wenigen Stunden ist man am Ziel seiner Träume.

Als Paddler ohne Auto ist man allerdings aufgeschmissen, und ein Auto zu mieten sprengt bei vielen das Budget. Besucher aus Übersee werden oft nicht darum kommen ein Auto zu mieten. Auf der Homepage der Autovermietung Hertz (*www.hertz.de*) hat man sich schnell zum Flughafen Oslo durchgeklickt.

Tipp: Unter *www.rent-a-wreck.no* kann man alte gebrauchte Autos kostengünstig mieten. Dachträger erhält man recht unproblematisch, Norwegen ist eine Skifahrer-Nation.

• mit Auto und Fähre:

Die kostengünstigste Variante für alle Europäer ist die Anreise mit dem eigenen Auto und per Fähre. Die Auswahl der Fährverbindungen ist recht groß, je nach Ausgangspunkt und gewünschtem Zielhafen bieten sich mehrere Routen nach Norwegen an. Die langen Fährrouten (wie *Kiel - Oslo* oder *Newcastle - Bergen*) reduzieren zwar die Anzahl der lästigen Kilometer im Auto, strapazieren jedoch erheblich den Geldbeutel. Die günstigen Fährlinien (wie die *»Vogelfluglinie«* via Schweden) nehmen immer die kürzeste Route über das Wasser, lassen aber nur wenig Zeit zum Entspannen bevor die Autofahrt weitergeht.

Natürlich hängt die Wahl der Verbindung auch von der gewünschten Destination ab: Will man in die *Telemark*, bietet sich Larvik als Zielhafen an; will man nach *Voss*, nimmt man die *Fjordline* nach Bergen; und will man zur *Sjoa*, ist Oslo erste Wahl.

Ähnlich entscheidend ist der Ausgangspunkt: Startet man in England, bietet sich als Starthafen Newcastle an; kommt man über Berlin, wählt man die direkte Verbindung *Saßnitz - Trelleborg* und fährt dann die schwedische Küste entlang nach Oslo; reist man durch Deutschlands Westen an, nimmt man eine der Fährlinien von Dänemark.

Als kleine Verschnaufpause vom Autofahren bietet sich ein Zwischenstopp in Amsterdam, Berlin oder Kopenhagen an, wenn eine der Großstädte ohnehin auf dem Weg liegt.

Tippmarathon:

Tipp 1: Frühbucher bekommen bei einigen Fährgesellschaften Rabatt.

Tipp 2: Vorsicht mit Booten auf dem Dach: Bei den meisten Fährgesellschaften sind Autos über 2 Meter Höhe teurer. Tricksen meist erfolglos (elektronische Höhenmessung).

Tipp 3: Einige Fährgesellschaften, beispielsweise *Kystlink*, bieten billige Mitfahrgelegenheiten auf Frachtfähren an. Diese nehmen nur wenige Autos mit und bieten keinerlei Service an Bord.

What is important to know?

It is usually easy to enter Norway. An identity card is sufficient for EU nationals, Europeans without one (e.g. UK nationals) obviously need a passport. There are seldom customs checks but if you are winked out of the queue at the border, then you usually have to empty the car – of everything. All items intended for personal use may of course be imported without duties but this does not apply to drugs! There are limits on imported food, tobacco and alcohol and import taxes are exorbitant. If you do not overdo it with alcohol and tobacco and are friendly to the customs officials, they are usually happy to look the other way. Alcohol checks at the border are not uncommon because many holidaymakers cannot resist the tax-free alcohol on board only to drive off the ferry somewhat tipsy.

Worauf muss ich achten?

Generell ist die Einreise nach Norwegen problemlos. Der Personalausweis genügt, Kontrollen gibt es nur wenige. Sollten die Kollegen an der Grenze dich allerdings rauswinken, heißt es in der Regel ausräumen – und zwar komplett. Alle Gegenstände zum persönlichen Gebrauch dürfen natürlich abgabenfrei eingeführt werden (gilt nicht für Betäubungsmittel!). Bei Verpflegung, Tabakwaren und Alkohol gelten allerdings Grenzwerte, deren Überschreitung extreme Zollabgaben nach sich zieht. Übertreibt man es nicht mit Alkohol und Tabak und ist höflich zu den Beamten, drücken sie jedoch gern mal ein Auge zu. Auch Alkoholtests am Grenzhäuschen sind keine Seltenheit, da viele der Urlauber während der Überfahrt den zollfreien Alkoholpreisen nicht widerstehen können und leicht angeschwippst von der Fähre rollen.

There are several companies offering ferry crossings. Here are a few suggestions:
Die Fährrouten werden von verschiedenen Gesellschaften befahren, hier ein paar Vorschläge:

from Germany

Kiel - Oslo (Color Line)
Rostock - Trelleborg (TT-Line)
Sassnitz - Trelleborg (Skandlines)
»Vogelfluglinie«: Puttgarden - Rødby,
then Helsingør - Helsingborg (Skandlines)

from Denmark

Frederikshavn - Oslo (Stena Line)
Frederikshavn - Larvik (Color Line)
Hirtshals - Oslo (Color Line)
Hirtshals - Larvik (Color Line)
Hirtshals - Langesund (Kystlink)
Hirtshals - Stavanger - Bergen (Colorline)

from Great Britain

Newcastle - Bergen (Fjordline)
Newcastle - Stavanger (Fjordline)
(not shown on the map:)
Harwich - Hoek van Holland (Stena Line)
Harwich - Esbjerg (DFDS Seaways)

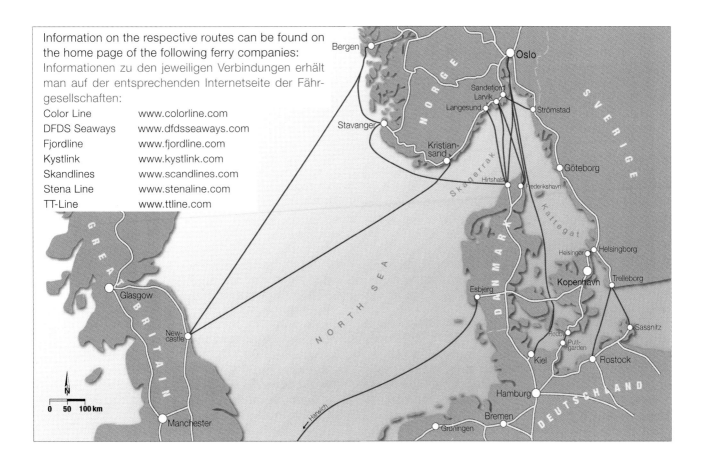

Information on the respective routes can be found on the home page of the following ferry companies:
Informationen zu den jeweiligen Verbindungen erhält man auf der entsprechenden Internetseite der Fährgesellschaften:

Color Line	www.colorline.com
DFDS Seaways	www.dfdsseaways.com
Fjordline	www.fjordline.com
Kystlink	www.kystlink.com
Skandlines	www.scandlines.com
Stena Line	www.stenaline.com
TT-Line	www.ttline.com

Near the Sumelvi - Jostedalsbreen Nasjonalpark.

On the roads

Driving in Norway is quite an agreeable experience, provided of course that you are suitably relaxed. Notorious speed merchants will despair because minor small roads tend to be somewhat narrow and full of bends and on the major roads nobody drives faster than 80 km/h. On top of this, the fuel prices make you think about every extra litre of petrol or diesel.

Although many rivers are quite close to one another, travelling can take up a lot of time because you can forget about covering vast distances at great speed which you can in Germany and other European countries. When you have found your next destination on the map and calculated a distance of one hundred kilometres, don't get any ideas about driving this distance in one hour. In addition to the eighty thousand kilometres of roads in Norway there are also ferries for twenty thousand kilometres which you have to take if you want to avoid the long journey around the fjords. Punctuated by stops to take the odd photo or two, you will be zigzagging up hills to the top only to be zigzagging back down the other side after a short stretch of level road in between.

Considering the conditions in Norway and the fact that the population density is so low, the road network is quite remarkable. Improvements are constantly being made and a great deal of money is being invested in tunnels in particular. Besides cutting out long winding roads and opening up remote regions, they make driving in winter much safer.

Auf den Straßen

Reisen in Norwegen ist angenehm, vorausgesetzt man bringt die nötige innere Ruhe mit. Notorische Raser werden in Norwegen verzweifeln: Die kleinen Straßen sind kurvenreich und nicht sehr breit, auf den großen Straßen fährt keiner schneller als 80 km/h – und auch die Spritpreise lassen über jeden zusätzlich verbrauchten Liter nachdenken.

Obwohl viele Flüsse eng beieinander liegen, kann bei der Anreise viel Zeit vergehen, denn eine Reisegeschwindigkeit wie in Deutschland oder in anderen europäischen Staaten kann man sich getrost abschminken. Hat man sein nächstes Ziel auf der Karte gefunden und eine Entfernung von hundert Kilometern ausgemacht, braucht man sich nicht einbilden, dass man diese hundert Kilometer dann in einer Stunde schafft. Zu den achtzigtausend Straßenkilometern gesellen sich mehr als zweitausend Kilometer, die mit Fähren zurückgelegt werden müssen, will man nicht den langen Weg um den Fjord wählen. Serpentine hoch, ein paar Kilometer über die Hochebene, Serpentine runter – und zwischendurch mal schnell anhalten zum Fotos machen.

Unter den norwegischen Bedingungen und einer derart geringen Bevölkerungsdichte ist das Straßennetz der Norweger eine bewundernswerte Leistung. Permanent wird an der Verbesserung gearbeitet, besonders in den Tunnelbau wird eine Menge Geld investiert. Dieser kürzt lange Serpentinenstrecken ab, erschließt entlegene Regionen und macht die Straßen wesentlich wintertauglicher.

Toll roads: the Bomveg

Many of the minor mountain roads are privately owned and financed according to the principle »if you use, you pay.« You pay at the start of each Bomveg section by putting the cash in an envelope which you deposit in the collection box. You then display the tear-off control slip in the front of your vehicle.

Always nice and slow!

Speeding is severely punished! Even though speeding checks are seldom carried out, given the size of the road network, fines are enormous. Unless signs indicate otherwise, when in inner city areas you should not drive faster than 50 km/h and on country roads not faster than 80 km/h. The speed limit is 90 km/h on the few motorways which exist. The blood alcohol limit is two parts per thousand and smoking when driving is not permitted in residential areas.

Tip: Norwegians do not appreciate your driving too close, so keep your distance!

Mautstraßen: der Bomveg

Viele der kleinen Bergstraßen werden von privater Hand betrieben und finanzieren sich nach dem Motto »Wer nutzt, soll zahlen.« Bezahlt wird am Anfang eines jeden Bomveg: Einfach das Geld in den Umschlag legen und in den Kasten einwerfen, den Kontrollabriss dann vorne im Auto platzieren.

Immer schön langsam!

Geschwindigkeitsüberschreitungen werden hart geahndet! Auch wenn auf Grund der Weitläufigkeit der Straßen Verkehrskontrollen verhältnismäßig selten stattfinden, sind die Geldstrafen enorm. So weit nicht anders ausgeschildert, sollte man innerorts nicht schneller als 50 km/h, und auf den Landstraßen nicht schneller als 80 km/h fahren. Auf den wenigen Autobahnen gilt 90 km/h. Die Promillegrenze liegt bei 0,2 Promille; rauchen am Steuer ist im Ortsbereich übrigens verboten.

Tipp: Norweger mögen es nicht, wenn man mit dem Auto zu dicht auffährt. Also Abstand halten, Platz ist genug!

STOP: Bomveg!

Driving in Norway:
A feast for the eyes.

»Where am I?«

The ferry is quite a common means of transport.

A great location for a delicious breakfast.

Camping

My tent is my castle

In accordance with Norway's »Countryside Usage Law« from 1947, every Norwegian has a basic right to camp. It is permitted to reside in the countryside and live off nature's fruits – whilst respecting other people, animals and plants of course. There are countless wild campsites which can be used with no problem if some basic rules are adhered to. To preserve this right, here are a few rules to follow:

Do not camp within sight of houses or holiday homes, avoid agricultural land, bury all human waste, keep to campsites if you are a big group, stick to rules and do not light fires in the period from 15 April to 15 September!

There is a proverb about this: »You can visit as often as you want provided nobody notices you have been here before!« It's best to leave everywhere clean and tidy just as you found it, because the canoeists with their coloured boats on the car roof attract the locals' attention more than anyone else.

Camping

Mein Zelt ist mein Schloss

In Norwegen gilt hinsichtlich Camping das Jedermannsrecht, welches im »Gesetz über das Leben im Freien« von 1947 festgeschrieben ist. Es erlaubt die Natur als Aufenthaltsort zu nutzen und sich der Früchte der Natur zu bedienen – natürlich mit der gebührenden Rücksicht auf Mensch, Tier und Pflanze. Es gibt zahlreiche wilde Campingplätze, die bei Einhaltung einiger Grundregeln problemlos genutzt werden können. Damit das so bleibt: Nicht in Sichtweite von Häusern oder Ferienhäusern campen, landwirtschaftliche Nutzflächen melden, Exkremente vergraben, Großgruppen nur auf Campingplätze, Verbote respektieren und vom 15. April bis 15. September keine offenes Feuer machen!

Das Sprichwort besagt: »Du darfst so oft wiederkommen wie du willst, solange man nicht sieht, dass du schon mal da warst!« Also am besten die Plätze sauberer verlassen, als man sie vorgefunden hat. Denn gerade Paddler, mit ihren bunten Booten auf dem Dach, bleiben den Einheimischen gern im Gedächtnis.

Tips galore:

Tip 1: Many campsites and hotels have saunas which the public can use. This is great when you need a break due to bad weather.

Tip 2: Out of season, small huts are quite inexpensive and make rainy days easier to cope with.

Tip 3: The camping guide issued by the Norwegian automobile club NAF contains good information about camping. *www.nafcamp.com*

Tip 4: You can find the weather forecast on the back page of the newspaper or on the internet under *www.weather.com*.

Tip 5: If you get the feeling the rain has come to stay, don't let it ruin the atmosphere in camp. If you pack up, check the weather forecast and drive for one or two hours, the situation can be completely different.

Der Tipp-Marathon:

Tipp 1: Viele Campingplätze und Hotels verfügen über Saunaanlagen, die öffentlich genutzt werden können. Optimal für eine Paddelpause bei schlechtem Wetter.

Tipp 2: Kleine Hütten sind in der Nebensaison recht preiswert und erleichtern es, kühle Regentage zu überstehen.

Tipp 3: Der Campingführer des Norwegischen Automobilverbandes NAF bietet viel Service rund ums Camping, *www.nafcamp.com*.

Tipp 4: Auf der letzten Seite der Tagesblätter findet man die aktuelle Wettervorhersage, oder im Internet *www.wetter.com* anklicken.

Tipp 5: Wenn es anfängt sich einzuregnen, darf man auf keinen Fall im Camp versauern. Sachen packen, Wettervorhersage checken, ein bis zwei Stunden Auto fahren und die Sache kann schon ganz anders aussehen.

Who said you would need a tent?

The journey to the supermarket

In the supermarkets you will find almost everything a hungry paddler could wish for. But there are limits to the fun to be had because the high prices make such a hole in your pocket, so you may have to refrain from extravagant feasts. If you stick to basic food and keep your finger off alcohol and tobacco, you can keep the costs of your holiday under control. Compared with the prices for meat, fish seems a good buy, so why not put it on the menu as a change from pasta with tomato sauce?

Here are a few culinary delights from the supermarket which you should not fail to try:
- Bamse Mums (chews covered in chocolate)
- Caviar creme in a tube (best mixed with mayonnaise)
- Ekte Geitost (goat's cheese with a caramel taste)
- Lomper (potato pancake) in which you wrap a sausage or something similar and eat like a Turkish pizza or Döner Kebab
- Scampis (type of crab)
- Jam made of cloudberries

Tip: »Tax Free for Tourists« means that you can get a refund of the value added tax/sales tax. In shops displaying this sign you can save between 11-18 per cent of the purchase price depending on the type of goods you buy (food 6-7 per cent) but you must export the product unopened. At borders, airports and international railway stations you can then get a refund of the value added tax/sales tax by cashing in your *Tax Free Shopping Cheque*.

Der Gang zum Supermarkt

In den Supermärkten findet man fast alles, was der hungrige Paddler begehrt. Doch macht das Einkaufen nur bedingt Spaß: Das hohe Preisniveau lässt das Herz schwerer, und den Geldbeutel leichter werden – auf ausgefallene Fressorgien sollte man verzichten können. Wer sich beim Einkaufen auf die Grundnahrungsmittel beschränkt und die Finger von Alkohol und Tabak lässt, kann die Kosten eines Trips im Rahmen halten. Meerestiere erscheinen in Hinsicht auf die Fleischpreise recht preiswert. Einfach mal in den Speiseplan integrieren – als Abwechslung zu Pasta mit roter Soße.

Hier einige kulinarische Leckerbissen aus dem Supermarkt, die man sich auf keinen Fall entgehen lassen sollte:
- Bamse Mums (Kaumasse mit Schokomantel)
- Kaviarcreme aus der Tube (am besten im Mayo-Mix)
- Ekte Geitost (Ziegenkäse mit Karamellgeschmack)
- Lomper (Kartoffelpfannkuchen), in die man Wurst oder ähnliches einwickelt und wie türkische Pizza oder türkischen Döner isst
- Scampis (Krebsart)
- Marmelade aus Moltebeeren

Tipp: »Tax Free for Tourists« ermöglicht es Ausländern beim Kauf in Norwegen die Mehrwertsteuer zurückerstattet zu bekommen. In Geschäften, die mit diesem Logo versehen sind, kann man je nach Ware 11-18 Prozent des Kaufpreises sparen (Lebensmittel 6-7 Prozent), muss das Produkt allerdings ungeöffnet ausführen. An Grenzstellen, Flughäfen und internationalen Bahnhöfen kann man dann bei der Ausreise seinen *Tax Free Shopping Cheque* einlösen und erhält die Mehrwertsteuer zurück.

Why does a Dutch oven take so damn long?

»I would sell my »Big Gun« for caviar paste... «

Photos: SG

And besides canoeing?

The number of options for a *culture day* are limited in Norway. Either you visit one of the wooden churches which you will find in nearly every village or you go to a museum. Oslo boasts a number of interesting museums which you can visit on your arrival and departure. You will find suggestions in the introduction to each particular area.

As far as sport is concerned, there are almost no limits to the options you have in Norway whether it be hiking or cycling or even »nerve-wracking« rafting. For the daredevil sorts there are a lot of BASE (Building, Antenna, Span or Earth) jumpers and parachutists

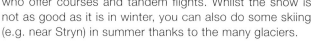
Stavkirke are boring!

Photo: SG

who offer courses and tandem flights. Whilst the snow is not as good as it is in winter, you can also do some skiing (e.g. near Stryn) in summer thanks to the many glaciers.

Tip for the camp cook: Pasta alla Marinara
Fry some scampi in oil with a little garlic, then shell them and eat with rémoulade and lemon. Put all the leftovers in a pan and cook with a little water for 15-20 minutes. Sieve the »stock« through a clean tea towel or a fine sieve, then thicken the liquid with butter and flour, bring to the boil and add seasoning to taste (garlic, lemon, white wine...). Add the cooked pasta and your seafood feast is ready to serve.

Did you know... ?

... that Norway's coastline is more than 25,000 kilometres long i.e. longer than half the circumference of the world? Measured straight without the fjord arms it would only be 2,650 kilometres.

... that it is 1,752 kilometres as the crow flies from the most southerly point of Norway to the North Pole? By road, the shortest distance would be approximately 2,500 kilometres.

... that at its narrowest point, Narvik, Norway is only just 6 kilometres wide? The widest point is 430 kilometres.

... that Scandinavia's smallest church is Undredal at Aurlandsfjord? It is not even 4 metres wide and has room for 40 people.

... that Europe's deepest lake at 514 metres is Hornindalsvatnet in western Norway? It also boasts the clearest water in the whole of Scandinavia.

... that nearly the same number of people live in the Greater Berlin area as in the whole of Norway?

Und außer paddeln?

Die Anzahl der Möglichkeiten zur Gestaltung eines *Kultur-Tages* sind in Norwegen begrenzt. Entweder man besucht eine der zahlreichen Stabkirchen, die es beinahe in jedem größeren Dorf gibt, oder man geht in ein Museum. Gerade Oslo bietet eine Reihe sehr interessanter Museen, denen man bei der An- oder Abreise einen Besuch abstatten kann.

Für sportliche Aktivitäten hingegen gibt es in Norwegen fast keine Grenzen: von wandern und radeln bis hin zum »Nerven aufreibenden« Rafting. Für Luftikusse gibt es gerade in Voss viele engagierter Basejumper und Fallschirmspringer, die Kurse und Tandemflüge anbieten. Auch Skifahren kann man im Sommer dank der vielen Gletscher (z.B. bei Stryn), allerdings unter schlechteren Schneebedingungen als im Winter.

Campingküche Rezept-Tipp: Pasta alla Marinara
Scampis mit Knoblauch in Öl etwas braten, dann schälen und mit etwas Remoulade und Zitrone genießen. Überreste in einen Topf, mit etwas Wasser 15-20 Minuten kochen. Den entstandenen Sud durch ein feines Sieb oder ein sauberes Geschirrtuch umgießen, mit etwas Butter und Mehl andicken, aufkochen und nach Belieben würzen (Knoblauch, Zitrone, Weißwein...). Die gekochte Pasta hinzugeben und fertig ist der Meeresschmaus.

Wussten Sie ... ?

... dass Norwegens Küstenlinie mehr als 25.000 Kilometer lang ist, also länger als der halbe Erdumfang? Geradlinig, ohne Fjordarme, wären es nur 2650 Kilometer.

... dass es vom südlichsten Punkt Norwegens bis zum Nordkap 1752 Kilometer Luftlinie sind? Auf der Straße wäre der kürzeste Weg etwa 2500 Kilometer lang.

... dass Norwegen an seiner schmalsten Stelle bei Narvik nur knapp 6 Kilometer breit ist? An der breitesten Stelle sind es 430 Kilometer.

... dass Skandinaviens kleinste Kirche in Undredal am Aurlandsfjord steht? Sie ist nicht mal 4 Meter breit und birgt 40 Plätze in sich.

... dass der Hornindalsvatnet in Westnorwegen mit 514 Metern der tiefste Binnensee Europas ist? Er ist zudem der See mit dem klarsten Wasser in ganz Skandinavien.

... dass allein der Großraum Berlin fast so viele Einwohner hat wie ganz Norwegen?

PADDLING: **WHITEWATER IN NORWAY WILDWASSER IN NORWEGEN**

Don Hölzl enters the first rapid of the Zambesi section, Numedalslågen.

Olaf Obsommer - Ulvåa, close to the confluence with the Rauma.

Whitewater in Norway

One day I asked a Norwegian why he had never been kayaking in the Alps. »Why should I?« was his astonished answer.

What is a typical Norwegian river? A great volume of water, a steep descent and open terrain is what many canoeists have in mind. This may well be true for the majority of rivers, but there is certainly no lack of variety in Norway, whether it be tight sections in gloomy canyons, playboating areas just next to the road, overcrowded but quite standard rivers or remote expedition rivers. If you keep your eyes open, you will find everything.

However, the focus of this book is mainly on rivers of typically alpine character with a route from A to B. There is just one difference to the Alps: everything is bigger, everything is higher and everything has more volume. You will need a couple of days to get used to the size of things but then there is nothing to stop you having fun.

Roughly speaking, Norwegian rivers are more spectacular but not necessarily more dangerous than those in the Alps. You may well ask what is meant by dangerous? Despite well-developed equipment and safety techniques, whitewater canoeing accidents occur again and again; this applies to Norway too. Although there are less undercuts and siphons lurking than in the western coastal area of New Zealand – and trees are often simply washed away due to the size of the riverbed – there are an increasing number of

Wildwasser in Norwegen

Irgendwann fragte ich einen Norweger, warum er noch nie in den Alpen paddeln war. »Warum sollte ich?« antwortete er verwundert.

Der typische norwegische Fluss? Viel Wasser, hohes Gefälle, offenes Gelände – dieses Bild hat so mancher vor Augen. Das mag zwar für einen großen Teil der Flüsse stimmen, aber an Vielfalt mangelt es in Norwegen nun wirklich nicht. Ob enge Rinnen in düsteren Schluchten oder die Spielstelle direkt neben der Straße, ob überlaufene Standardstrecke oder einsamer Expeditionsfluss. Wer seine Augen offen hält, findet alles.

Der Schwerpunkt liegt jedoch im alpinen Wildwasser im ursprünglichen Sinne, der Flussbefahrung von A nach B. Mit einem Unterschied zu den Alpen: alles ist größer, alles ist höher, alles ist wuchtiger! Man wird ein, zwei Tage brauchen um sich an die Dimensionen zu gewöhnen, doch dann steht dem Spaß nichts mehr im Wege.

Über den Daumen gepeilt sind die norwegischen Flüsse spektakulärer, aber nicht unbedingt gefährlicher als die der Alpen. Aber was heißt hier ungefährlich? Unfälle im Wildwasser passieren immer wieder, trotz ausgereifter Ausrüstung und Sicherheitstechniken – auch in Norwegen. Obwohl hier weniger Unterspülungen und Siphone lauern als an der Neuseeländischen Westküste, und Bäume aufgrund der Größe des Flussbettes oft einfach weggespült werden, hört man auch in Norwegen vermehrt von Unfällen. Doch

accidents in Norway. However, most incidents are usually the result of over-confidence. It is high waterfalls and rocky, messy landing areas which are often underestimated; the results are compression fractures and bruised organs.

Water temperatures range from ice cold to cold and only the larger rivers warm up slightly on their long journey to the coast. On high plateaux and in open countryside in particular, there can be an icy wind which will quickly chill you to the bone. Short-sleeved tops are seldom suitable and even in warm weather they should only be worn on short runs or for playboating. However, don't overreact; wearing gloves would be overdoing things.

Be careful on the river banks: Moss thrives on damp rocks and is pretty much like having a slippery banana skin under your feet. Moss also conceals crevices big enough to take your leg. Have you ever broken an ankle on a portage?

Difficulties with the difficulties
How do you classify whitewater?

»Like the River Loisach (southern Germany), just more water, more ledges, a steeper gradient i.e. generally considerably more difficult«, was a nice description of the Ardezer Schlucht on the River Inn (Austria) which the German Canoe Association (DKV) gave in their river guide. It is just as difficult for us to make comparisons and give examples. Basically, measured on the Norwegian scale, the Loisach is not a grade IV river and the Rissbach ravine (Rissbach-klamm) in southern Germany is not grade VI either.

handelt es sich dabei meistens um Verletzungen infolge von Übermut. Gerade hohe Wasserfälle und unsaubere Unterwasser werden oft unterschätzt und sind Grund für Kompressionsbrüche und Quetschungen von Organen.

Die Wassertemperaturen schwanken meist von eisigkalt bis kalt, lediglich die großen Flüsse haben sich auf ihrer weiten Reise etwas erwärmt. Gerade auf Hochebenen oder im offenen Gelände kann ein frischer Wind blasen, der schnell auskühlt. Die Kurzarmpaddeljacke wird selten benötigt und sollte auch bei warmem Wetter nur auf kurzen Etappen oder zum Spielen eingesetzt werden. Aber keine Panik, Handschuhe wären übertrieben.

Vorsicht am Ufer: Moos wächst gern auf feuchten Fels-platten, und wird zum Rutschkissen wenn sich Paddlers Füße darauf rumquälen. Ebenso verdecken sie mit Vorliebe kleine Felsspalten, in die ganze Beine reinpassen. Hast du dir schon mal beim Umtragen ein Fußgelenk gebrochen?

Schwierigkeiten mit den Schwierigkeiten
Wie bewertet man Schwierigkeiten im Wildwasser?

»Wie die Loisach, nur mehr Wasser, mehr Gefälle, mehr Stufen, also insgesamt erheblich schwieriger«, war ein schöner Vergleich der Ardezer Schlucht des Inns mit der Loisach im Flussführer des DKV. Ähnlich schwierig ist es auch für uns Vergleiche zu ziehen und Beispiele zu liefern, also sei eines kurz gesagt: Die Loisach ist am norwegischen Maßstab gemessen kein WW IV, genauso wenig wie die Rissbachklamm mit WW VI bewertet wird.

Sebastian Gründler running Spånemfossen on Austbygdåi. »If a lot of water flows in, then a lot also flows out!«

The ICF (International Canoe Federation) has brought the classification of running water down to a common denominator:

Die Skala der ICF (International Canoe Federation) hat die Bewertung der Schwierigkeiten von Fließgewässern auf einen Nenner gebracht:

	WW I easy unschwierig	WW II moderately difficult mäßig schwierig	WW III difficult schwierig	WW IV very difficult sehr schwierig	WW V extremely difficult äußerst schwierig	WW VI limit of navigability Grenze d. Befahrbarkeit
Line of sight **Sicht**		Open passages Freie Durchfahrten	Clearly visible passages Übersichtliche Durch-fahrten	Passages normally require scouting Durchfahrten nicht ohne weiteres erkenn-bar; Erkundung meist nötig	Scouting absolutely necessary Erkundung unerlässlich	Basically impossible Possible only at certain water levels Highly dangerous!
Water **Wasser**	Regular current, regular waves and small wave trains Regelmäßiger Strom-zug; regelmäßige Wel-len; kleine Schwälle	Irregular current; irregu-lar waves; mid-sized wave trains; small holes, whirlpools, boils and pillows Unregelmäßiger Stromzug; unregelmä-ßige Wellen; mittlere Schwälle; schwache Walzen, Wirbel und Presswasser	High, irregular waves; longer wave trains; holes, whirlpools, boils and pillows Hohe, unregelmäßi-ge Wellen; größere Schwälle, Walzen, Wir-bel und Presswasser	Higher, longer wave trains; strong holes, whirlpools, boils and pillows Hohe, andauernde Schwälle; kräftige Walzen, Wirbel und Presswasser	Extreme wave trains, holes, whirlpools, boils and pillows; undercuts and siphons possible Extreme Schwälle, Walzen, Wirbel und Presswasser; mgl. Unterspülungen und Siphone	Im allgemeinen unmöglich Bei optimalen Rahmen-bedingungen eventuell befahrbar Hohes Risiko!
Riverbed **Flussbett**	Simple obstacles Einfache Hindernisse	Few obstacles in the main current; small ledges and drops Einfache Hindernisse im Stromzug; kleinere Stufen	Isolated boulders, ledges and drops; other obstacles in the main current Einzelne Blöcke, Stu-fen; andere Hindernis-se im Stromzug	Offset boulders in the main current; higher ledges and drops with recirculating holes Blöcke versetzt im Stromzug; höhere Stufen mit Rücksog	Tightly offset boulders; high ledges and drops with difficult approach or exit Enge Verblockung; hohe Stufen mit schwierigen Ein- und Ausfahrten	

This classification was developed at the end of the seventies however and the alteration in maximum difficulties in the last ten years alone demonstrates the degree of inadequacy of the system; since the classification was published, no changes have been made to the top end of the scale. What was grade VI yesterday is today nothing more than V- to many people. To make statements on the levels of difficulty is always a subjective estimation based on several aspects which are difficult to compare i.e. water level, performance on the day and ability. When you read descriptions such as average water, difficult or steep, you should hopefully be aware of the vagueness of expression; we cannot do anything about this.

Diese Skala wurde allerdings schon Ende der siebziger Jahre entwickelt. Allein die Verschiebung der Höchst-schwierigkeiten in den letzten zehn Jahren zeigt die In-stabilität dieses Systems: eine offizielle Erweiterung nach oben hat es seit dem nicht mehr gegeben. Was noch gestern WW VI war, ist eine für viele heute nicht mehr als V-. Eine Angabe von Schwierigkeiten unterliegt immer einer subjektiven Einschätzung und hängt dadurch von mehreren schwer vergleichbaren Aspekten wie Wasser-stand, Tagesform und Können ab. Liest man Begriffe wie Mittelwasser, extrem oder steil, ist man sich hoffentlich deren Schwammigkeit bewusst, vor der auch wir uns nicht wehren können.

So what's the strategy?

The degree of difficulty must always be assessed on the spot. Only madmen rely on figures in a book. Changes in the river bed and authors' incorrect recollections due to high adrenaline levels on the paddle day must be taken into account. The difficulties of one section are a mixture of various criteria which are usually inextricably linked. Only when considered together can you begin to form an overall

Also was tun?

Schwierigkeiten sollten immer direkt vor Ort eingeschätzt werden. Auf Zahlen, die in einem Buch stehen, verlassen sich nur Wahnsinnige. Veränderungen des Flussbettes, sowie falsche Erinnerungen des Autors aufgrund des über-höhten Adrenalinspiegels müssen berücksichtigt werden. Die Schwierigkeiten eines Abschnitts setzen sich aus meh-reren Kriterien zusammen und hängen meist direkt vonein-

impression of the character of a river:

• **Gradient:** You can usually get an idea of the gradient of a river when driving to it and certainly when shuttling cars between put in and take out. You always need to differentiate between the average gradient and the gradient in the key sections of a stretch of river. Only then do you arrive at a decent assessment. Are you kayaking eddy to eddy alpine style or is the river a big green highway? Sometimes there are immense drops in height over short, steep passages and at other times you may race down the river with an even descent for kilometres i.e. the average drop of both rivers can be the same. You can portage around the steep descents quickly, but at motorway speeds in big water even stopping is hard work.

• **Force of water:** In order to draw conclusions about the force of water, you cannot just rely on the number of cubic metres of water. The volume of water is only a source of information when you look at the river bed and when you take the degree of slope and the character of the river into account. Twenty cubic metres of water gushing down a narrow steep gorge are a completely different kettle of fish to the same volume in a large open river. Even ten cubic metres of water forcing its way through a ravine represents a considerable force of water.

• **Obstacles:** What is the most technically demanding, what is more dangerous? Three perfect 5-metre waterfalls in quick succession or a few metres of bouldergarden rapids which descend a height of 15 metres, no ledge drop greater than one metre? Bouldergarden rapids do not just rob you of your vision, they also place different demands on your ability to control your boat.

• **Force of water vs. degree of obstacles:** Many sections of a river become technically more difficult – and the risk of being trapped rises – with low water and a decreasing force of water. Sometimes high water levels enable you to have a better run-up to a section but in return the holes are bigger. Low water therefore does not always mean that the river will become easier.

• **River accessibility:** This factor has a great influence on your psyche and is important for your safety: How well can you set up safety cover along the river banks for the difficult sections? Can you portage? Further questions you should ask yourself are: Can you finish the run at any point and how far away is the road?

• **Other important criteria:** How cold is the water? Is there a danger of someone suffering hypothermia if they end up swimming? How long is the stretch of river – how much energy do I need to keep in reserve? How strong is my group? Is the river running high water? Are vital eddies missing? What about driftwood, piles of strainers?

You need to answer all these questions in the back of your head before you put to water. It would be crazy to try to answer these with numbers. The classification of a natural river according to the whitewater grading system can only serve as a guide.

Don't count on numbers, listen to your inner voice!

ander ab. Nur zusammen ergeben sie das Gesamtbild, den Charakter eines Flusses:

• **Das Gefälle:** Häufig kann man sich schon bei der Anfahrt einen Überblick über das Gefälle eines Flusses verschaffen, spätestens beim Umsetzen des Autos. Man sollte allerdings immer zwischen dem Durchschnittsgefälle und dem Gefälle in den Kernstücken unterscheiden, nur diese Differenzierung gewährleistet eine reelle Einschätzung. Gumpenbach oder Autobahn? Manchmal werden immense Höhen in kurzen Steilabbrüchen abgebaut und manchmal rast man den Fluss über mehrere Kilometer stetig hinab – das Gesamtgefälle bleibt gleich. Die Steilabbrüche sind schnell umtragen, auf einer Autobahn hingegen fällt schon das Anhalten schwer.

• **Die Wasserwucht:** Um Rückschlüsse auf die Wasserwucht zu ziehen, reicht nicht allein die Kubikmeterzahl. Die Wassermenge kann nur beim Blick ins Flussbett und in Zusammenhang mit Gefälle und Flusscharakter Auskunft geben. Denn bilden zwanzig Kubikmeter Wasser auf einer engen, steilen Rinne ein ganz anderes Szenario als in einem offenen, großen Flussbett. Wasserwucht kann schon bei zehn Kubik entstehen, wenn sich der Fluss durch eine enge Klamm presst.

• **Die Verblockung:** Was ist technisch schwieriger, was ist gefährlicher? Drei saubere 5-Meter-Wasserfälle hintereinander oder ein Katarakt, der auf wenigen Metern 15 Höhenmeter abbaut, und dies ohne eine Stufen höher als einen Meter? Die Verblockung nimmt dir nicht nur die Sicht, sie stellt auch ganz andere Anforderungen an deine Bootskontrolle.

• **Wasserwucht vs. Verblockung:** Manche Flussabschnitte werden bei Niedrigwasser, also mit sinkender Wasserwucht, technisch schwieriger und klemmgefährlicher. Manchmal lassen höhere Wasserstände leichtere Anfahrten zu, dafür werden die Walzen größer. Niedrige Wasserstände müssen also nicht immer bedeuten, dass es leichter wird.

• **Die Zugänglichkeit des Flusses:** Diese hat großen Einfluss auf die Psyche, und ist ein wichtiges Indiz für deine Sicherheit: Wie gut kann man die schwierigen Stellen sichern? Und umtragen? Kann ich die Fahrt jeder Zeit beenden? Wie weit ist die Straße entfernt?

• **Weitere Kriterien:** Wie kalt ist das Wasser? Besteht die Gefahr der Unterkühlung bei einem möglichem Schwimmer? Wie lang ist das Stück – wie viele Kraftreserven brauche ich? Wie stark ist meine Gruppe? Führt der Fluss Hochwasser? Fehlen vielleicht wichtige Kehrwasser? Was ist mit Treibholz, mit Baumverhauen?

All diese Fragen sollten im Hinterköpfchen beantwortet werden, bevor man auf den Fluss geht. Sie in einer Zahl beantworten zu wollen, wäre aberwitzig. Die Einordnung eines Wildflusses in die Wildwasserskala kann nur als Anhaltspunkt dienen.

Equipment and safety

The correct boat

If the boats you bring are to suit the variety of rivers, then you will have a broad range of canoes on the roof rack of your car: creekers, cruisers, playboats. If this is not possible for logistical reasons, you should limit yourself to the boat which most suits your style of kayaking. For the Alpinist, a creeker is the option for fun in all situations on Norwegian rivers, whereas the connoisseur will prefer a funcruiser with some volume for safety. Whilst funcruisers have more playboating potential than pure creekers, it is better not to go to your limits with these but to change down a gear. Rodeo kids must definitely bring a quick boat to surf the best waves.

Safety begins in your head

Every single member of a group is responsible for safety and this includes having a complete and appropriate set of equipment; life jacket, adequate protection against the cold, helmet, paddle shoes, throwbag, dividable spare paddle, first-aid kit, pulleys and sun glasses.

Every whitewater paddler should know what equipment is needed and how to use it. Details of this would go beyond the scope of this book. However, one item is very important: we believe that safety begins in your head and is only maintained by regular safety training.

Tip: You can learn more about rescue and recovery techniques, dangers and their prevention in *Olli Grau*'s book »White Water Kayaking«. This gives you an overview of today's standard in whitewater kayaking and is in effect the Bible for every whitewater paddler!

Ausrüstung und Sicherheit

Das richtige Boot

Genauso vielfältig wie die Flussauswahl müsste dementsprechend auch die mitgebrachte Bootspalette auf dem Autodach aussehen: Creeker, Cruiser, Spielboot. Ist dies aus logistischen Gründen nicht umsetzbar, sollte man sich auf das Boot beschränken, welches dem eigenen Paddelstil am nächsten kommt. Für Alpinisten ist ein Creekboot die beste Waffe um sich in allen Situationen auf norwegischen Flüssen zu amüsieren, für Genießer ein schneller Funcruiser mit etwas Notreserven. Diese haben mehr Spielpotential als reinrassige Creeker, allerdings sollte man damit bei der Ausreizung seiner Grenzen einen Gang zurückschalten. Rodeokids müssen unbedingt eine schnelle Semmel mitbringen, um die Traumwellen zu reiten.

Sicherheit entsteht im Kopf

Jeder Einzelne ist für die Sicherheit seiner Gruppe verantwortlich, und dazu gehört eine intakte, angemessene Ausrüstung: Schwimmweste, ausreichender Kälteschutz, Helm, festes Schuhwerk, Wurfsack, teilbares Ersatzpaddel, Erste-Hilfe-Kit, Seilrolle, Sonnenbrille.

Jeder Wildwasserpaddler sollte wissen, welche Ausrüstung er benötigt und wie er damit umzugehen hat. Einzelheiten würden den Rahmen sprengen. Nur soviel sei gesagt: Sicherheit entsteht im Kopf und wird nur durch regelmäßiges Training gewährleistet. (Deutsche Gesellschaft für Wildwasserrettung: *www.dgwr.de*)

Tipp: Mehr über Rettungs- und Bergetechniken, Gefahren und deren Vorbeugung erfährt man in »Besser Wildwasserfahren«, der WW-Bibel von *Olli Grau*. Das Buch gibt einen Überblick über den heutigen Standard im Wildwasserfahren – die Bibel für jeden Wildwasserpaddler!

Make friends with your boat – you will need to be a team!

Safety first.

What have salmon got to do with paddlers?

The article »War in salmon's paradise« by Antje Kahlheber on page 19 gives details of the damage caused in Norway's rivers by the parasite *Gyrodactylus salaris*.

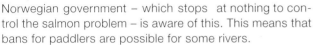

It is all the same to us whether there are fish in the rivers or not, isn't it? However, we need to take a broader view: This parasite can survive in warm and damp conditions for several days i.e. in our paddle equipment. This means that Gyro can hitch a ride with paddlers to the next river, and the Norwegian government – which stops at nothing to control the salmon problem – is aware of this. This means that bans for paddlers are possible for some rivers.

Paddlers should therefore adhere to the precautions stipulated! Information can be obtained from the regional tourist offices.

Help to stop the parasite spreading:

- It is forbidden to transport water or any life forms from one stretch of water to another!
- Kayaks and all accessories must be thoroughly dried or disinfected after use!
- Equipment which you are not able to dry completely prior to canoeing the next salmon river can be treated before use with chlorine or Virkon-S powder at specially designated areas (see information at put in and take out points). Dilute 1/2 litre of chlorine with 10 litres of water and either spray or thoroughly rinse the still damp equipment.

Was gehen uns Paddler Lachse an?

Im Beitrag »Mit dem Holzhammer« von Antje Kahlheber auf Seite 19 liest man vom Schaden, den der Parasit *Gyrodactylus salaris* in Norwegens Flüssen anrichtet. Ob Fische im Fluss schwimmen, kann uns Paddlern doch egal sein, oder? Eigentlich schon, aber wir müssen etwas weiter denken: Dieser Parasit kann mehrere Tage in feuchtwarmen Umgebungen überleben, zum Beispiel in unserer Paddelausrüstung. Somit bieten wir Paddler dem Gyro eine optimale Mitfahrgelegenheit zum nächsten Fluss – und dass weiß auch die norwegische Regierung. Um das Lachsproblem zu bekämpfen, sind alle Mittel Recht. Auch Sperrungen einzelner Flüsse für Paddler könnten die Folge sein.

Deshalb sollten alle Paddler die vorgeschriebenen Vorsichtsmaßnahmen befolgen! Informationen erhält man in den regionalen Touristeninformationen.

Helft den Parasiten zu stoppen:

- Es ist verboten Wasser oder Flusstiere von einem Gewässer zu einem Anderen zu transportieren!
- Kajaks und sämtliches Zubehör müssen nach Gebrauch sorgsam abgetrocknet oder desinfiziert werden! Feuchte Ausrüstung, die vor dem nächsten Lachsfluss nicht völlig zu trocknen scheint, kann an ausgeschriebenen Plätzen (siehe Informationen an Ein- u. Ausstiegen) oder eigenständig mit Chlor oder dem Pulver Virkon-S desinfiziert werden. Chlor im Verhältnis 1:10 mit Wasser verdünnen und das betroffene Material einsprühen oder gründlich abwaschen.

Salmon rivers in Norway / Lachsflüsse in Norwegen

Salmon are found in more or less all rivers which feed into a fjord unless high waterfalls or hydroelectric power stations block their path. The regions close to the coast are threatened by the Gyro parasite. The following list is a summary of the salmon rivers described in this book:

Lachse findet man in Norwegen mehr oder weniger in jedem Fluss der in ein Fjord mündet, es sei denn hohe Wasserfälle oder Wasserkraftwerke versperren den Tieren den Weg. So sind gerade die Meernahen Regionen vom Gyro bedroht. Die folgende Zusammenstellung gibt eine Übersicht über die im Buch beschriebenen Lachsflüsse:

Møre og Romsdal: Rauma, Toåa, Valldøla, Embla, Stordalselva
Sør-Trøndelag: Driva, Grøvu, Gaula
Sogn og Fjordane: Smeddalselvi/Lærdalselva, Jølstra, Sogndalselva
Telemark/Buskerud: Numedalslågen

»It is very important that you include this information in the book, because a fierce debate is raging which can end up with a ban on kayaking in Driva. Many people, including several politicians, want kayaking and riversports in Driva to be made illegal, especially for foreigners. Therefore: please disinfect all gear used in Driva and Rauma, be nice to fishermen (even if they are not nice to you), and don't throw garbage around! Please make a point of this in the book, Jensi!« **Tore Meirik, Oppdal - via email**

Further information can be obtained under / Weitere Informationen erhält man unter:
www.dyrehelsetilsynet.no
www.lakseelver.no/Elveoversikt/Elveoversikt.htm

If all salmon were in condoms, the Gyro wouldn't stand a chance.

Water levels in Norway

Water levels in the rivers depend on the weather; an accurate prediction is pretty much impossible. Not only rainfall influences the volume of water in a river, but also the amount of snow and the prevailing air temperature. And there is no regularity to these factors whatsoever. So on warm days in April the rivers can be flooding whereas cold dry weeks in July can cause water levels to be more typical of those in August. In autumn, heavy rainfall often helps to push up water levels that bit more. The exception proves the rule.

Water levels of course also depend on the size and height of the catchment area, possible dams and water take-offs. Some rivers take a few days of heavy rain before they begin to swell whereas others rise within a couple of hours. Glacier-fed rivers don't get in full swing until the height of summer when smaller rivers in lower levels have long since dried up. For some sections of rivers the maximum amount of water is best, whereas others can only be paddled at low water. On page 236 you will find an attempt to provide an overview of the sections of rivers described.

Tip: As early as the spring, start checking the snow levels in the ski areas via the Internet. The more snow there is, the longer the meltwater will last.   *www.nve.no/snokart*

Information on water levels

The following Internet pages may be useful:

- www.nve.no: This page boasts the most comprehensive list of river gauges but it is only in Norwegian, so here are some instructions: When on the home page, click on the box on the right named »Vannføring og vannstand« and then on the centre »Vis stasjonskart med vannstand«. After that select »Liste« followed by the river gauge you want.

- www.glb.no: click on »Vannstander«

- www.vosskajakkklubb.com: River gauges around Voss

- www.oppdalkajakklubb.com: River gauges around Oppdal

Wasserstände in Norwegen

Wasserstände von Flüssen sind abhängig vom Wettergeschehen, eine treffsichere Vorhersage kann eigentlich nicht gemacht werden. Nicht nur Regenfälle beeinflussen die Wasserführung eines Flusses, auch die vorhandenen Schneemengen und die gegenwärtigen Temperaturen – und diese unterliegen keinerlei Regelmäßigkeiten. So können im April die Flüsse an warmen Frühlingstagen Hochwasser führen, genauso können kalte und trockene Wochen im Juni »Augustwasserstände« verursachen. Im Herbst helfen oft starke Regenfälle um die Wasserstände noch einmal hochzujagen: Ausnahmen bestätigen die Regel.

Hinzu wirken auch die Größe und Höhe des Einzugsgebietes, mögliche Stauseen und Ableitungen auf die Wasserführung. Manche Flüsse brauchen auch bei heftigem Regen ein paar Tage um anzusteigen, andere schaffen es in ein paar Stunden. Gletscherbäche laufen erst im Hochsommer in vollen Touren, kleinere Flüsse in den unteren Lagen sind dann schon längst eingetrocknet. Für manche Flussabschnitte will man möglichst viel Wasser, andere gehen erst bei Niedrigwasser. Auf Seite 236 findet man den Versuch einer Übersicht über die beschriebenen Flussabschnitte.

Tipp: Schon im Frühjahr die Schneehöhen der Skigebiete im Internet studieren. Je mehr Schnee, je länger die Schmelze.   *www.nve.no/snokart*

Informationen zum Wasserstand

Folgende Internetadressen könnten nützlich sein:

- www.nve.no: Diese Seite liefert die umfangreichste Sammlung von Pegeln, sie existiert aber nur in norwegisch. Deshalb hier eine kurze Erklärung: Auf der Startseite rechts im Kasten auf »Vannføring og vannstand« klicken, dann in der Mitte auf »Vis stasjonskart med vannstand« gehen. Nun »Liste« und anschließend den betreffenden Pegel wählen.

- www.glb.no: auf »Vannstander« klicken

- www.vosskajakkklubb.com: Pegelstände um Voss

- www.oppdalkajakklubb.com: Pegelstände um Oppdal

River gauges you can phone (country code +47):
Telefonpegel (Vorwahl +47):

Otta	61231270
Sjoa, Faukstad	61234138
Lågen, Rosten	61233102
Bøvra, Akslen	61211992
Lågen, Eide/Vinstra	61290462
Otta, Lalm	61239016
Finna, Sælatunga	61237281

Olaf Obsommer with a good water level on the waterfall of the Jordalselvi.

TELEMARK

Arnd Schäftlein taking a ride down Popo falls - Gøyst.

Lake Sønstevatn

TELEMARK

Norway's southern most mountain range, the Telemark, reaches its highest point at Rjukan, with the Gaustatoppen (1883 metres). It then heads north and becomes the Hardangervidda. The name »Telemark« became world famous because of the skiing style which bears the same name, and one could claim, with some exaggeration, that the small village of Morgedal is the birthplace of modern skiing. Telemark is a region rich in tradition and folk art, and one of the oldest holiday destinations in Norway. Plentiful water masses formed the basis for numerous industrial branches, above all the timber industry.

Most of the rivers in the south of Telemark are diverted, but there is top class whitewater hidden in the north of the area, all around lake Tinnsjø. To the north of the lake are the Austbygdåi, Mår and Gøyst, in the west is the Skogsåa, and in the east the Skirva. All these rivers, with the exception of sections of the Mår and the Numedalslågen, require a good boat feel in WW V. We shall leave the »Project 2000« on the Husevollelvi out of the calculation for now, here things are just getting started at WW V.

Der südlichste der norwegischen Gebirgszüge, die Telemark, erreicht bei Rjukan mit dem Gaustatoppen eine Höhe von 1883 Metern und geht weiter nördlich in die Hardangervidda über. Die Bezeichnung »Telemark« wurde durch den gleichnamigen Ski-Stil weltbekannt, man kann etwas übertrieben behaupten hier, in dem kleinen Dorf Morgedal, liege die Wiege des modernen Skilaufens. Die Telemark ist eine an Traditionen und Volkskunst reiche Region und eines der ältesten Urlaubsgebiete Norwegens. Reichlich Wasserkraft bildete die Grundlage für verschiedene Industriezweige, vor allem der Holzindustrie.

Die Flüsse im Süden der Telemark sind zwar größtenteils abgeleitet, doch versteckt sich ein hochkarätiges Wildwasserrevier im Norden, rings um den Tinnsjø. Austbygdåi, Mår und Gøyst trumpfen im Norden des Sees auf, die Skogsåa im Westen und die Skirva im Osten. Alle Bäche, bis auf Abschnitte des Mår und des Numedalslågen, fordern ein gutes Bootsgefühl auf WW V. Das »Projekt 2000« auf der Husevollelvi lassen wir jetzt mal unter den Tisch fallen, hier geht es erst bei WW V los.

TELEMARK FACTS

Character: Mostly steep pushy creeks, flowing through forest canyons or open terrain. With the exception of the lower Mår and the lower Numedalslågen, almost all of the rivers come recommended more for the WW IV-V paddler.

Best time: End of April until mid June, depending on the snow melt. After winters with good snowfall the Austbygdåi can flow for longer. In summer even rainfall is rarely enough to fill the rivers to useful levels. A spring destination with a narrow window of opportunity.

Special remarks: A small time window for good water levels. Beware: Gyro is on the prowl! The lower Numedalslågen in the Vestfold region is a very popular salmon river.

Accommodation: Camping ground on the Tinnsjø at Austbygdi.

Charakter: Meist steile und wuchtige Flüsse, die in Waldschluchten oder offenem Gelände fließen. Bis auf den unteren Mår und den unteren Numedalslågen sind fast alle Etappen eher dem WW IV-V Paddler anzuraten.

Beste Zeit: Ende April bis Mitte Juni, je nach Einsetzen der Schneeschmelze. Untere Austbygdåi nach schneereichem Winter auch länger. Selbst Regenfälle reichen im Sommer kaum mehr aus, um der Telemark annehmbare Wasserstände zu verschaffen – ein Frühlingsrevier mit kleinem Fenster.

Besonderheit: Kleines Zeitfenster für gute Wasserstände. Achtung: Der Gyro geht um! Der untere Numedalslågen in der Region Vestfold ist ein sehr beliebter Lachsfluss.

Übernachtung: Campingplatz am Tinnsjø bei Austbygdi.

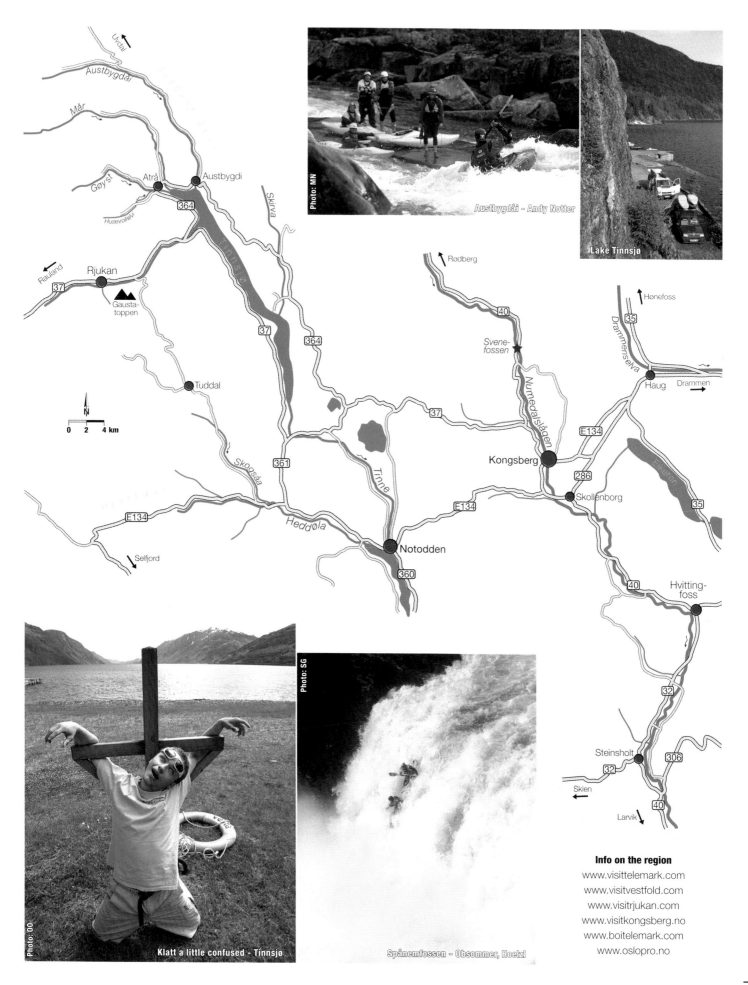

Austbygdåi – Andy Notter

Lake Tinnsjø

Klatt a little confused - Tinnsjø

Spånemfossen - Obsommer, Hoelzl

Info on the region

www.visittelemark.com
www.visitvestfold.com
www.visitrjukan.com
www.visitkongsberg.no
www.boitelemark.com
www.oslopro.no

NUMDEDALSÅGEN: LAKS RUN

BIG VOLUME FLATWATER WITH SOME SHORT RAPIDS

The lower Numedalslågen can be reached from Larvik in half an hour, and offers the first opportunity to catch a whiff of the big water atmosphere. Essentially it's all open whitewater (WW II) with a couple of boily rocky sections (up to WW IV) which can be portaged without any problem. There are dark rumours of excellent play spots here at high water.

The only catch: the Numedalslågen is one of the most popular salmon rivers in Norway. In 1999 around 20 tons of salmon was caught here, and the salmon stock is one of the few which has not yet been affected by diseases such as Gyro. Every year around 100,000 young fish are released into the Numedalslågen, and here you will also find the most popular spots to catch them again. Even the Norwegian King has fished here – no joke! What does this tell us? Exactly, that paddlers are not welcome here. But the rivers belong to us all! Not quite: the fishermen pay big money for their spots, and have no desire to have their catch quota ruined by a bunch of paddlers. In addition to this there is the problem of Gyro (see p. 53), which doesn't exactly leave us paddlers in the best light. So, if you get any sceptical looks from the fishermen at the put in, it is best to ask whether paddling is allowed at that time of year. The salmon don't come until the middle of June, before then paddling is no problem. But if the banks are crammed with fishermen, it is best to retreat. It's a question of the public profile of paddlers, and this is already not the brightest of shining lights!

But back to paddling: at the Kjærra Fossepark there is a powerful cataract, WW V-, immediately followed by another narrow passage. There are then

CLASS: III+ (IV)
LEVEL: 80 - 500 cumecs
LENGTH: 4 km
TIME: 1 - 2 h
SEASON: April - early June

another couple of difficult sections, but all can be well scouted. The long flat water section goes almost unnoticed due to the swift flow of the current.

However, in the interests of avoiding flatwater tedium and annoying the fishermen any more than necessary, it is best not to continue to the next bridge. After the difficult sections it is best to make your way to one of the hidden angler pathways, and head back up to the road. A good opportunity is after the river-wide drop, where you will find a camping ground on the left. Up the right bank, and then fight your way up to the road along the edge of the forest. (Not across the field!)

Tip: Watch the fishermen!
Tipp: Auf die Angler achten!

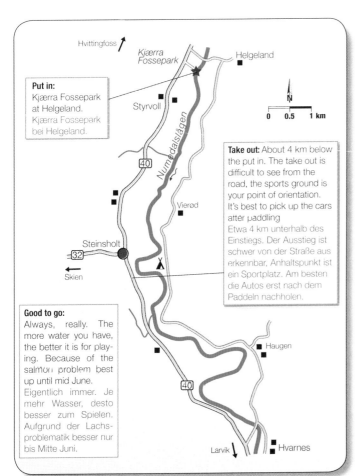

Hvittingfoss

Kjærra
Fossepark

Helgeland

Put in:
Kjærra Fossepark
at Helgeland.
Kjærra Fossepark
bei Helgeland.

Styrvoll

Numedalslågen

N

0   0.5   1 km

40

Take out: About 4 km below the put in. The take out is difficult to see from the road, the sports ground is your point of orientation. It's best to pick up the cars after paddling
Etwa 4 km unterhalb des Einstiegs. Der Ausstieg ist schwer von der Straße aus erkennbar, Anhaltspunkt ist ein Sportplatz. Am besten die Autos erst nach dem Paddeln nachholen.

Vierød

Steinsholt

32

Skien

Good to go:
Always, really. The more water you have, the better it is for playing. Because of the salmon problem best up until mid June.
Eigentlich immer. Je mehr Wasser, desto besser zum Spielen. Aufgrund der Lachsproblematik besser nur bis Mitte Juni.

Haugen

40

Larvik   Hvarnes

Der untere Numedalslågen ist von Larvik in einer halben Stunde erreicht, und bietet die erste Gelegenheit Wuchtwasseratmosphäre zu schnuppern. Im Grunde handelt es sich um offenes Wildwasser (II) mit ein paar wirbeligen Felsgassen (bis WW IV), die ohne Probleme umtragen werden können. Bei viel Wasser munkelt man hier von richtig guten Spielstellen.

Der einzige Haken: der Numedalslågen ist einer der beliebtesten Lachsflüsse Norwegens. 1999 wurden hier etwa 20 Tonnen Lachs gefangen, außerdem ist der Lachsbestand dort einer der wenigen der noch nicht von Krankheiten wie dem Gyro befallen ist. Jedes Jahr werden im Numedalslågen etwa 100.000 Jungfische ausgesetzt, und genau hier befinden sich die beliebtesten Fangplätze. Selbst der norwegische König, das ist kein Witz, war hier schon zum Angeln. Was sagt uns das? Genau, Paddler sind hier nicht gern gesehen. Aber die Flüsse gehören doch uns allen! Nicht ganz: die Angler bezahlen teures Geld für ihre Standorte und haben keine Lust, sich ihre Fangquoten von Paddlern ruinieren zu lassen. Hinzu kommt die Gyro-Problematik (siehe S. 53), die uns Paddler nicht unbedingt im besten Licht stehen lässt. Also, wird man schon am Einstieg von den Anglern skeptisch begutachtet, am besten mal nachfragen ob paddeln zurzeit erlaubt ist. Die Lachse kommen erst Mitte Juni, vorher ist paddeln kein Problem. Sind die Ufer jedoch überfüllt von Anglern, sollte man besser den Rückzug antreten. Es geht hier um das Bild der Paddler in der Öffentlichkeit, und das strahlt ohnehin nicht im hellsten Licht.

Aber zurück zum Paddeln: Am Kjærra Fossepark bricht ein mächtiger Katarakt zu Tale, WW V-, direkt danach eine weitere Engstelle. Es folgen noch ein paar schwierige Passagen, die aber alle gut zu besichtigen sind. Der große Flachwasseranteil fällt aufgrund der hohen Fliessgeschwindigkeit gar nicht auf.

Um jedoch längere Flachwasserquälereien zu vermeiden und den Anglern nicht noch länger auf die Nerven zu gehen, sollte man nicht bis zur nächsten Brücke weiterfahren. Besser ist es, nach Abklang der Schwierigkeiten auf einem der verstockten Fischerpfade den Weg zur Straße anzutreten. Eine gute Gelegenheit dazu bietet sich nach einer flussüberquerenden Stufe, nach der links ein Zeltplatz auftaucht. Hier rechtsufrig die Böschung hoch und dann am Waldrand zur Straße kämpfen (nicht quer über den Acker!).

SKOGSÅA: UPPER RUN

ONE OF THE BEST RUNS IN THE COUNTRY

Whitewater doesn't get any more varied than this! Open rapids and cataracts, low gorges and ravines with bed rock passages, slides and waterfalls. For many Norwegians the Skogsåa counts as one of the most beautiful rivers in the country. When the upper Skogsåa has good water, there are always plenty of tales to tell around the campfire at night!

Just 300 metres after the put in is the first spectacular section which is best scouted and, if necessary, portaged on the right. The water gets pressed through a 2 metre wide slot, with about 5 metres of drop. The catch: half way down lies a diagonal hole which loves to tip paddlers over and scrape them down the rocks – elbow pain guaranteed here!

The next two kilometres runs quietly over a number of small slides and drops, which can become powerful holes at higher water levels. When you get to the 7 metre waterfall, you have reached the entrance to the gorge. The waterfall should be portaged on the right, there are hidden dangers below the surface. A run may be possible at higher flows. From here you can scout the following gorge from the right bank, because after the next left bend waits a cataract with no clear line of sight. This is however not absolutely necessary, as it is generally no more difficult than WW IV, and everything can be run in the main current. It is sometimes possible to put out on the right bank of the gorge. After about 400 metres the gorge opens out once more.

After another kilometre caution becomes the order of the day: after a left bend there is a powerful slide which likes to eat red boats! Exit on the right and scout. Swimming here could have fatal consequences because shortly after the hole there is a massive 14 metre slide/waterfall. After that you have to carry up to the road on the right to reach the parking bay.

CLASS:	V - VI
LEVEL:	15 - 30 cumecs
LENGTH:	5 km
TIME:	3 - 4 h
SEASON:	April - early June

Obsommer

Abwechslungsreicher kann Wildwasser nicht sein: offene Schwälle und Katarakte, Niederklammen und Schluchten mit Grundgesteinspassagen, Rutschen und Wasserfälle. Die Skogsåa im Tuddalsdalen zählt für einige Norweger zu den schönsten Bächen des Landes. Die obere Skogsåa mit satt Wasser sorgt am Abend für jede Menge Gesprächsstoff.

Schon etwa 300 Meter nach dem Einstieg wartet die erste spektakuläre Stelle, die man am besten rechts anschaut und gegebenenfalls umträgt. Das Wasser wird durch einen 2 Meter engen Schlitz gepresst und macht dabei etwa 5 Meter Gefälle. Die Gemeinheit dabei: auf halber Höhe lauert eine Querwalze, die Paddler gerne umhaut und somit über die Steine schleift – Ellenbogenschmerzen vorprogrammiert.

Die nächsten 2 Kilometer geht es über einige kleine Rutschen und Stufen dahin, die bei höheren Wasserständen zum Teil kräftige Walzen bilden können. Erreicht man einen 7 Meter hohen Wasserfall, steht man am Eingang zur Klamm. Den Wasserfall sollte man rechts umtragen, da das Unterwasser unsauber ist. Bei höheren Wasserständen eventuell fahrbar. Man kann die folgende Schlucht gleich vom rechten Ufer besichtigen, da nach der nächsten Linkskurve ein etwas unübersichtlicher Katarakt wartet. Dies ist aber nicht dringend notwendig, da die Schwierigkeiten nicht wesentlich über WW IV steigen und eigentlich alles im Hauptwasser fahrbar ist. Anlanden ist in der Schlucht zum Teil am rechten Ufer möglich. Nach etwa 400 Metern macht die Schlucht wieder auf.

Nach einem weiteren Kilometer ist Vorsicht geboten: Nach einer Linkskurve folgt eine mächtige Rutsche, deren Ausgangswalze gern rote Boote frisst. Rechts anlanden und besichtigen. Hier zu schwimmen kann fatale Konsequenzen haben, da kurz nach der Walze eine riesige wasserfallartige Rutsche von etwa 14 Metern Höhe wartet. Dahinter muss man rechts zur Straße hoch tragen, um zur Parkbucht zu gelangen.

Photo: SG

The first drop - Klatt

SKOGSÅA: LOWER

NICE RAPIDS IN A WOODED GORGE

On the lower section of the Skogsåa things are a little quieter. But you are still guaranteed fun here, as long as there's a decent roar coming from the river bed. The Skogsåa offers mostly open whitewater, sometimes flowing through a wooded gorge.

CLASS: IV - V-
LEVEL: 15 - 40 cumecs
LENGTH: 6 km
TIME: 3 h
SEASON: April - early June

Take care on the two man-made concrete ledges shortly after the put in; part of the water flows under the concrete ledge. After a couple of kilometres of quiet water there are a number of nice sections up to WW V-, until the river flows into a wooded gorge. In the gorge you'll find lively whitewater up to WW IV.

Auf dem unteren Abschnitt der Skogsåa geht es etwas ruhiger zu. Aber auch hier ist der Spaß garantiert, vorausgesetzt es rauscht ordentlich im Flussbett. Die Skogsåa bietet hier meist offenes Wildwasser, zum Teil in einer Waldschlucht.

Vorsicht an zwei künstlich betonierten Furten bald nach dem Einstieg, ein Teil des Wassers zieht unter dem Beton der Furt durch. Nach ein paar Kilometern ruhigen Wassers folgen noch einige schöne Stellen bis WW V-, bis es in eine Wald-schlucht geht. In der Schlucht spritziges Wildwasser bis WW IV.

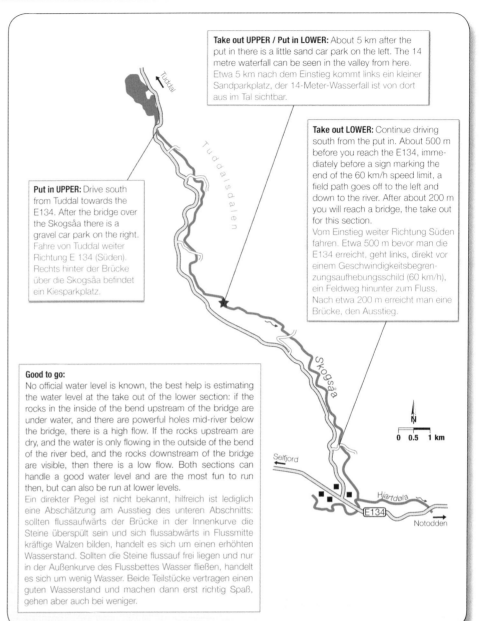

Take out UPPER / Put in LOWER: About 5 km after the put in there is a little sand car park on the left. The 14 metre waterfall can be seen in the valley from here.
Etwa 5 km nach dem Einstieg kommt links ein kleiner Sandparkplatz, der 14-Meter-Wasserfall ist von dort aus im Tal sichtbar.

Put in UPPER: Drive south from Tuddal towards the E134. After the bridge over the Skogsåa there is a gravel car park on the right.
Fahre von Tuddal weiter Richtung E 134 (Süden). Rechts hinter der Brücke über die Skogsåa befindet ein Kiesparkplatz.

Take out LOWER: Continue driving south from the put in. About 500 m before you reach the E134, immediately before a sign marking the end of the 60 km/h speed limit, a field path goes off to the left and down to the river. After about 200 m you will reach a bridge, the take out for this section.
Vom Einstieg weiter Richtung Süden fahren. Etwa 500 m bevor man die E134 erreicht, geht links, direkt vor einem Geschwindigkeitsbegren-zungsaufhebungsschild (60 km/h), ein Feldweg hinunter zum Fluss. Nach etwa 200 m erreicht man eine Brücke, den Ausstieg.

0 0.5 1 km

Good to go:
No official water level is known, the best help is estimating the water level at the take out of the lower section: if the rocks in the inside of the bend upstream of the bridge are under water, and there are powerful holes mid-river below the bridge, there is a high flow. If the rocks upstream are dry, and the water is only flowing in the outside of the bend of the river bed, and the rocks downstream of the bridge are visible, then there is a low flow. Both sections can handle a good water level and are the most fun to run then, but can also be run at lower levels.
Ein direkter Pegel ist nicht bekannt, hilfreich ist lediglich eine Abschätzung am Ausstieg des unteren Abschnitts: sollten flussaufwärts der Brücke in der Innenkurve die Steine überspült sein und sich flussabwärts in Flussmitte kräftige Walzen bilden, handelt es sich um einen erhöhten Wasserstand. Sollten die Steine flussauf frei liegen und nur in der Außenkurve des Flussbettes Wasser fließen, handelt es sich um wenig Wasser. Beide Teilstücke vertragen einen guten Wasserstand und machen dann erst richtig Spaß, gehen aber auch bei weniger.

The gorge of the upper section - Klatt, Obsommer

Photos: SG

»Did you say G-R-A-B?« - Obsommer, Wimsett

AUSTBYGDÅI (TESSUNGSELVA): UPPER SECTION   A BEAUTIFUL RUN WITH SEVERAL REAL HIGHLIGHTS

The Austbygdåi is the Queen of the Telemark, her trademark the icing on the cake. She is the salt in the soup, the cherries on top, the First Lady of Whitewater. Without her the Telemark would not be complete, a part of river history would be missing. The upper part of the Tessungselva is really just there to warm you up and get your appetite going for the California Section, but it also offers a few highlights which make a day on »the upper« unforgettable.

Most of the sections can easily be scouted and portaged, and are mostly between WW IV-V. The first bomb hits once you've flown over the kicker on the monster slide – full adrenalin hit! This is directly beside the road but is easy to miss. However, beware: 50 metres after the slide waits a rather unnice waterfall. This can either be portaged on the left, or you can gain a full appreciation of its height with a super-duper 7 metre cliff start on the right.

The Austbygdåi takes a leisurely course through the countryside, WW III, until it reaches the Spånemfossen, its absolute highlight. The Spånemfossen is an 8 metre high waterfall which is as soft as butter, provided there's enough juice in the creek. If this is not the case take care: because the drop is so wide, the water scatters quickly and can not break through the surface water in the pool – makes for a hard landing! What's more, half way down on the left is a rock jutting out, a rock which has already cost one paddler a compression fracture.

Then follows 2 km of WW II-III to the take out. Important at the take out: the river splits into two channels. The bridge is only in the left channel, in the right channel it is easy to miss the take out.

CLASS:	III - IV (V, X)
LEVEL:	10 - 25 cumecs
LENGTH:	10 km
TIME:	3 - 6 h
SEASON:	late April - June

Die Austbygdåi ist die Königin der Telemark, ihr Wahrzeichen, das Tüpfelchen auf dem »i«. Sie ist das Salz in der Suppe, die Sahne auf dem Stück Kuchen, die First Lady des Wildwassers. Ohne sie wäre die Telemark nicht vollständig, ein Stück Flussgeschichte würde fehlen. Der obere Teil der Austbygdåi ist zum Aufwärmen und Appetit holen für die untere California Section, bietet aber doch ein paar Höhepunkte, die den Tag auf der »Oberen« unvergesslich machen.

Alle Stellen können einfach besichtigt und umtragen werden und liegen meist zwischen WW IV-V. Die erste Bombe schlägt ein, wenn man über den Kicker der monstermäßigen Rutsche geflogen ist – Adrenalin in vollem Maße. Diese liegt direkt an der Straße, ist jedoch leicht zu übersehen. Doch Obacht: 50 Meter nach der Rutsche wartet ein unschöner Wasserfall, der entweder flusslinks umtragen wird, oder dessen Höhe rechts mit einem supi-dupi 7-Meter-Klippenstart nachempfunden werden kann.

Bis zum unbestrittenen Höhepunkt der Austbygdåi, dem Spånemfossen, plätschert sie gemächlich durchs Land, WW III, Zeit um tief Luft zu holen. Der Spånemfossen ist ein 8 Meter hoher Wasserfall, der butterweich ist, vorausgesetzt es ist ordentlich Brühe im Bach. Ist dem nicht so, sei Vorsicht geboten: Durch die Breite der Abrisskante verläuft sich das Wasser schnell und kann das Unterwasser nicht durchsetzen, der Aufprall wird hart. Außerdem schaut dann links von der Mitte auf halber Höhe eine Felsnase heraus, die schon einen Kompressionsbruch eines Paddlers zufolge hatte.

Dann bis zum Ausstieg 2 Kilometer WW II-III. Wichtig beim Ausstieg: Der Fluss teilt sich in zwei Kanäle. Die Brücke befindet sich nur im linken Kanal, im rechten kann der Ausstieg leicht verpasst werden.

»Yeah, G-R-A-B!«

Photos: SG

Spånemfossen - Klatt

AUSTBYGDÅI: CALIFORNIA SECTION

A POOL + DROP ADVENTURE WITH AWESOME SLIDES AND DROPS

The lower Austbygdåi has as many bedrock slides as all of the Austrian rivers put together. Well ok, that's perhaps a small exaggeration, but we hope you'll forgive that. When we named the section, California was the first thing to come to mind.

About 600 metres after the first fiery slide you'll hear the roar of a recirculating double drop, immediately followed by a slot – not really paddleable. Portage on the left or right. The drop which follows looks worse than it actually is, simply boof out to the left.

Under a dilapidated wooden suspension footbridge is a slide which feeds into a slot. If you're not sure of hitting your line, best to portage.

At some stage you will reach an

CLASS: V - VI (X)
LEVEL: 15 - 20 cumecs
LENGTH: 8 km
TIME: 4 - 6 h
SEASON: April - early July

impressive double drop directly beside the road – a dream combination!

In the last kilometre before Austbygdi the Austbygdåi makes another bold downhill charge – magnificent combinations await us! However, as soon as you reach the houses on your right, it's time to exercise caution once more: the entrance to the last short low canyon comes rather unexpectedly, after a small drop. This mighty final canyon demands both skill and guts. To date the entrance has never been paddled. So be careful and take out on the right in good time, then carry the 200 metres up to the carpark by the road.

Tip: The road follows the river for the most part, so it's possible to get off the river at any stage.

Photo: MN

The last drop of Austbygdäi in 1997 - Obsommer...

Die untere Austbygdåi hat so viele Grundgesteinsrutschen wie ganz Österreich zusammen. Nun gut, das ist etwas übertrieben, aber das wird man ja auch mal dürfen. Als Bezeichnung für diesen Abschnitt kam uns spontan Kalifornien in den Sinn.

Nach den ersten pfeffrigen Rutschen schreit etwa 600 Meter nach dem Start eine rückläufige Doppelstufe laut auf, direkt danach folgt ein Schlitz, eher unfahrbar. Rechts oder links umtragen. Die Stufe im Anschluss sieht nur so wild aus, einfach nach links rausboofen.

Unter einer zerfallenen Hängebrücke wartet eine Rutsche, deren Ausgang rechts in einen Schlitz fällt. Wer sich nicht sicher ist, sollte besser umtragen. Irgendwann erreicht man eine imposante Doppelstufe direkt an der Straße – eine Traumkombination!

Im letzten Kilometer vor Austbygdi bricht die Austbygdåi noch mal richtig zu Tale, wunderschöne Kombinationen warten auf uns. Sobald man rechts die Häuser in greifbarer Nähe hat, ist Vorsicht geboten: Der Eingang zum letzten Durchbruch kommt unverhofft nach einer kleinen Stufe.

Dieser mächtige Abschlusscanyon fordert Mut und Können zu gleich. Der Eingang ist bis dato noch nicht gepaddelt worden. Also aufpassen und rechtzeitig rechts anlanden, und die 200 Meter zum Parkplatz auf der Straße laufen.

Tipp: Die Straße verläuft meist in Flussnähe, somit ist ein Abbruch jederzeit möglich.

... and in 2004 - Brustmann

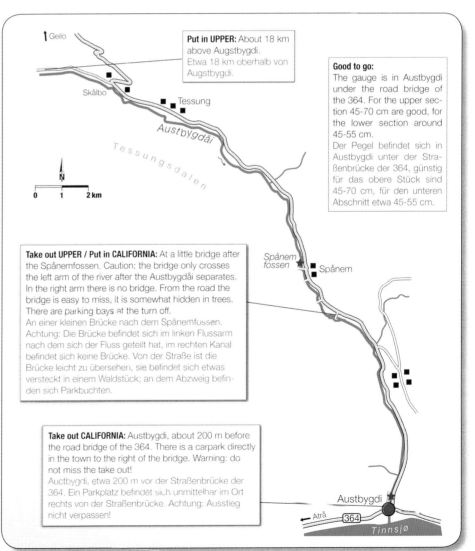

↑ Geilo

Skålbo

Tessung

Put in UPPER: About 18 km above Augstbygdi.
Etwa 18 km oberhalb von Augstbygdi.

Good to go:
The gauge is in Austbygdi under the road bridge of the 364. For the upper section 45-70 cm are good, for the lower section around 45-55 cm.
Der Pegel befindet sich in Austbygdi unter der Straßenbrücke der 364, günstig für das obere Stück sind 45-70 cm, für den unteren Abschnitt etwa 45-55 cm.

Austbygdåi

Tessungsdalen

N

0   1   2 km

Take out UPPER / Put in CALIFORNIA: At a little bridge after the Spånemfossen. Caution: the bridge only crosses the left arm of the river after the Austbygdåi separates. In the right arm there is no bridge. From the road the bridge is easy to miss, it is somewhat hidden in trees. There are parking bays at the turn off.
An einer kleinen Brücke nach dem Spånemfossen. Achtung: Die Brücke befindet sich im linken Flussarm nach dem sich der Fluss geteilt hat, im rechten Kanal befindet sich keine Brücke. Von der Straße ist die Brücke leicht zu übersehen, sie befindet sich etwas versteckt in einem Waldstück; an dem Abzweig befinden sich Parkbuchten.

Spånem fossen ★   Spånem

Take out CALIFORNIA: Austbygdi, about 200 m before the road bridge of the 364. There is a carpark directly in the town to the right of the bridge. Warning: do not miss the take out!
Austbygdi, etwa 200 m vor der Straßenbrücke der 364. Ein Parkplatz befindet sich unmittelbar im Ort rechts von der Straßenbrücke. Achtung: Ausstieg nicht verpassen!

Austbygdi

← Atrå   364

Tinnsjø

Disputed name:

The Austbygdåi flows through the Tessungsdalen and into lake Tinnsjø at Austbygdi. The Norwegian cartographers are divided in their naming of this river: Tessungselva or Austbygdåi? We asked locals in Austbygdi and promptly received a plausible answer: until around 150 years ago, the upper part of the river was called the Tesse, the section to Tinnsjø called Austbygdåi. Tessungselva is indeed a name that we Germans have thought up for ourselves! So we would like to adhere to the Norwegian protocol: Austbygdåi!

Namensstreit:

Die Tessungselva, ähh Austbygdåi, fließt durch das Tessungsdalen und mündet bei Austbygdi in den Tinnsjø. Die norwegische Landkartenkultur ist gespalten in der Bezeichnung des Flusses: Tessungselva oder Austbygdåi? Wir fragten Einheimische in Austbygdi und bekamen prompt eine plausible Antwort: Der oberste Teil des Flusses wurde bis vor rund 150 Jahren Tesse genannt, der Teil bis zum Tinnsjø Austbygdåi. Tessungselva ist wohl ein Name, den wir Deutsche uns ausgedacht haben. Also, wir wollen uns an die norwegische Sprachgewohnheiten halten: Austbygdåi!

Photo: MN

California section - Austbygdåi

MÅR: UPPER

The Mår in the Gausetdalen actually has a huge catchment area in the Hardangervidda, and a-c-t-u-a-l-l-y should run well into the summer. Actually! If only it was not for the giant dams which feed the hydroelectric station at Rjukan! Thus for us paddlers there is not much left over, aside from the peak melt times and after heavy rainfall, when the Mår is transformed into a paradise.

300 metres after the start we are greeted by the first mean section: the water is pressed through a slot into a low gorge with rounded, potholed walls, creating an interesting cocktail mix of towback and recirculating eddy. If you don't want to run it you will need

CLASS:	IV - V (VI, X)
LEVEL:	15 - 30 cumecs
LENGTH:	9 km (6 km)
TIME:	3 - 5 h
SEASON:	late April - June

to make a big portage on the right, or climb your way around the left wall on slippery rocks. In the next 500 metres there are several small slides and drops which can all be paddled with a reasonable feel for the right line and a long enough neck. The next 1.5 kilometres allow you time to appreciate the scenery, before the first gnarly slides and drops come up.

When you see a wooden footbridge over the river (Take out 1) things start to get more gorge-like and challenging. The 2 metre drop just before the bridge is worthy of safetying, especially at high levels. The waterfall after the bridge is paddleable, but extremely dangerous. Take out and scout on the right directly after the bridge. You should

portage over the bridge and then along the road on the left bank. Seasoned paddlers can also drop in river right from the table top of the waterfall.

The Mår now leaves the road and digs its way into a gorge. After about a kilometre the difficulties get up to WW IV again. Be careful at the end of the gorge: the Mår thunders down a monster Foss, make absolutely sure you get out on the left in good time! You should check out the take out eddy before putting on the river, because it really is the last eddy, and at high levels doesn't really fulfil the function of an eddy!

Tip: Those who are still full of beans paddle the Homerun too.

Der Mår im Gauset-dalen hat eigentlich ein riesiges Ein-zugsgebiet aus der Hardangervidda, und müsste e-i-g-e-n-t-l-i-c-h bis in den Sommer hinein laufen. Eigentlich! Wären da nicht die riesigen Stauseen, die das Kraftwerk von Rjukan mit Wasser versorgen. So bleiben für uns Paddler die kläglichen Überreste, die nur in der Hochschmelze und nach kräftigem Regen den Mår in ein Paradies verwandeln.

Gleich 300 Meter nach dem Start grüßt die erste gemeine Stelle: Das Wasser wird durch einen Schlitz in eine Niederklamm gepresst und bildet eine Mischung aus Rücklauf und rotierendem Kehrwasser, natürlich mit Kolk. Wer nicht fährt,

umträgt rechts weiträumig oder umhebt links an der Wand auf glitschigem Fels. Auf den nächsten 500 Metern folgen mehrere kleine Rutschen und Stufen, die alle mit langem Hals und etwas Gefühl für die richtige Route befahren werden können. Die folgenden 1,5 Kilometer geben Zeit die Natur zu genießen, bevor die ersten knackigen Rutschen und Stufen warten.

Es wird wieder schluchtiger und anspruchsvoller, spätestens wenn man eine hölzerne Fußgängerbrücke über dem Fluss sichtet (Take out 1). Die 2 Meter hohe Stufe kurz vor der Brücke lädt gerade bei viel Wasser zum Sichern ein. Der Wasserfall nach der Brücke ist fahrbar, aber extrem gefährlich. Direkt hinter der Brücke rechts aussteigen und besichtigen. Umtragen sollte man über die

Brücke und dann linksufrig auf der Straße. Sehr sichere Paddler können auch flussrechts auf dem Schanzentisch des Wasserfalls reinrutschen.

Nun trennt sich der Mår wieder von der Straße und gräbt sich langsam in eine Schlucht. Nach etwa 1 Kilometer wachsen die Schwierigkeiten wieder auf WW IV an. Vorsicht am Ausgang der Schlucht: der Mår bricht über einen Monsterfossen hinab, unbedingt rechtzeitig links aussteigen! Vor einer Befahrung sollte das letzte Kehrwasser links erkundet werden, da es wirklich das Letzte ist und bei viel Wasser der Funktion eines Kehrwassers nicht mehr richtig nachkommt.

Tipp: Wer noch fit ist, paddelt den Homerun gleich mit.

Motoko Ishida from Japan - Homerun

Obsommer filming Kagel

MÅR: HOMERUN

5 WATERFALLS, WHICH JUST BEG TO BE PADDLED OVER AND OVER AGAIN

The Homerun is a beautiful waterfall combination – paddling it can take you to heights you've never been before! Scout from the left bank, beginning at the take out and moving up. At this spot there is a path which follows the river, until you reach a large pool where the waterfalls appear.

It is possible to paddle around the clock here, especially in June. Our most unusual paddling time was three o'clock in the morning – without a headlamp of course! Have fun!

CLASS:	IV - V
LEVEL:	10 - 15 cumecs
LENGTH:	1 km
TIME:	10 min
SEASON:	April - June

Der Homerun ist eine wunderschöne Wasserfallkombination, deren Befahrung zu Höhenflügen verleitet. Besichtigung vom flusslinken Ufer, am besten vom Ausstieg beginnend. Dort führt ein Feldweg den Fluss entlang, bis nach einem großen Pool die Wasserfälle auftauchen. Gerade im Juni kann man hier rund um die Uhr paddeln. Unsere ausgefallenste Uhrzeit liegt bei 3 Uhr in der Nacht – natürlich ohne Stirnlampe. Viel Spaß!

Tip: The Homerun is the most amazing waterfall combo in Telemark. Don't miss it!

Tipp: Der Homerun ist die schönste Wasserfallstrecke der Telemark. Nicht verpassen!

The last drop of the Homerun - Klatt

Photo: SG

MÅR: LOWER

AN OPEN RUN, GOOD WITH A LOT OF WATER

The lower Mår is the easiest section around lake Tinnsjø, and so it is perfect to warm up on, or as a quick afternoon run on the side. It seldom gets more difficult than WW IV, and this is only when the river is really full. The first difficult section can be seen from the gravel road, about 500 metres below the put in.

After the road bridge of the 364 there is a nice slide, which develops a big hole at high flows. After that life gets easier again.

Der untere Mår ist der leichteste Abschnitt am Tinnsjø und somit perfekt geeignet zum Einfahren oder als schneller Nachmittagsabstecher. Die Schwierigkeiten steigen selten über WW IV, und dies auch nur, wenn viel Wasser im Flussbett rauscht. Die erste schwierige Stelle kann von der Schotterstraße aus besichtigt werden, sie befindet sich etwa 500 Meter unterhalb des Einstieges.

Nach der Straßenbrücke der 364 folgt eine schöne Rutsche, die bei hohen Wasserständen eine kräftige Walze bildet. Danach lassen die Schwierigkeiten nach.

CLASS: III - IV (V-)
LEVEL: 10 - 40 cumecs
LENGTH: 2 km
TIME: 1 - 2 h
SEASON: April - June

Manuel Arnu in 1997 - Homerun

Photo: MN

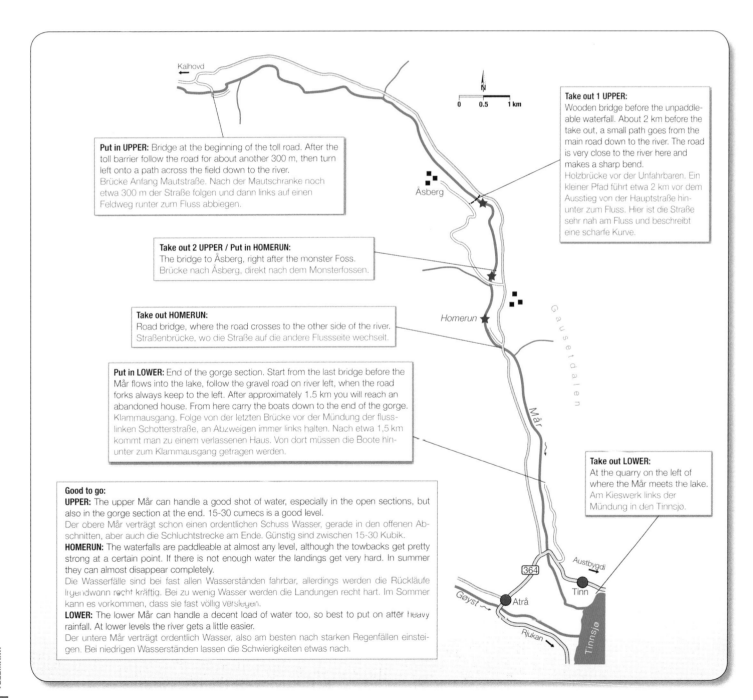

Take out 1 UPPER: Wooden bridge before the unpaddleable waterfall. About 2 km before the take out, a small path goes from the main road down to the river. The road is very close to the river here and makes a sharp bend.
Holzbrücke vor der Unfahrbaren. Ein kleiner Pfad führt etwa 2 km vor dem Ausstieg von der Hauptstraße hinunter zum Fluss. Hier ist die Straße sehr nah am Fluss und beschreibt eine scharfe Kurve.

Put in UPPER: Bridge at the beginning of the toll road. After the toll barrier follow the road for about another 300 m, then turn left onto a path across the field down to the river.
Brücke Anfang Mautstraße. Nach der Mautschranke noch etwa 300 m der Straße folgen und dann links auf einen Feldweg runter zum Fluss abbiegen.

Take out 2 UPPER / Put in HOMERUN: The bridge to Åsberg, right after the monster Foss.
Brücke nach Åsberg, direkt nach dem Monsterfossen.

Take out HOMERUN: Road bridge, where the road crosses to the other side of the river.
Straßenbrücke, wo die Straße auf die andere Flussseite wechselt.

Put in LOWER: End of the gorge section. Start from the last bridge before the Mår flows into the lake, follow the gravel road on river left, when the road forks always keep to the left. After approximately 1.5 km you will reach an abandoned house. From here carry the boats down to the end of the gorge.
Klammausgang. Folge von der letzten Brücke vor der Mündung der flusslinken Schotterstraße, an Abzweigen immer links halten. Nach etwa 1,5 km kommt man zu einem verlassenen Haus. Von dort müssen die Boote hinunter zum Klammausgang getragen werden.

Take out LOWER: At the quarry on the left of where the Mår meets the lake.
Am Kieswerk links der Mündung in den Tinnsjø.

Good to go:
UPPER: The upper Mår can handle a good shot of water, especially in the open sections, but also in the gorge section at the end. 15-30 cumecs is a good level.
Der obere Mår verträgt schon einen ordentlichen Schuss Wasser, gerade in den offenen Abschnitten, aber auch die Schluchtstrecke am Ende. Günstig sind zwischen 15-30 Kubik.
HOMERUN: The waterfalls are paddleable at almost any level, although the towbacks get pretty strong at a certain point. If there is not enough water the landings get very hard. In summer they can almost disappear completely.
Die Wasserfälle sind bei fast allen Wasserständen fahrbar, allerdings werden die Rückläufe irgendwann recht kräftig. Bei zu wenig Wasser werden die Landungen recht hart. Im Sommer kann es vorkommen, dass sie fast völlig versiegen.
LOWER: The lower Mår can handle a decent load of water too, so best to put on after heavy rainfall. At lower levels the river gets a little easier.
Der untere Mår verträgt ordentlich Wasser, also am besten nach starken Regenfällen einsteigen. Bei niedrigen Wasserständen lassen die Schwierigkeiten etwas nach.

The International WhiteWater Magazine

KAYAK
session

©D.HARDY

GØYST

The Gøyst flows through the Gøystdalen, and is the third in the group of northern headwaters feeding lake Tinnsjø. About 2 kilometres after the put in it flows through a gorge, WW III with two WW V-sections. Under the first bridge after the gorge there is a slot waterfall, and 150 metres after that the highest waterfall, the Gøyst. The Gøyst is 5 metres high and has hidden dangers under the surface in the pool, so your line must be perfect here. The following V+ section can be portaged on the left.

CLASS:	IV - V (V+)
LEVEL:	10 - 15 cumecs
LENGTH:	10 km
TIME:	3 - 6 h
SEASON:	April - June

Countless bedrock slides then follow, interrupted by a small weir, which springs up somewhat unexpected (no real eddy in front of it). The pool isn't too safe to drop into, so it's better to boat out on the island in the middle, and carry around the weir.

Photo: SG

Wimsett, Klatt - enjoying the slides

The Bum's Rush Falls slide combination comes about 2 kilometres before the Gøyst flows into the lake. It is easy to reach from the road, directly behind a large gravel car park with toilets. Why Bum's Rush Falls? If you swim in the hole at the start, you do the rest of the slide on your rosy little cheeks.

Tip: When the sun is shining, you can sometimes sight the odd frolicking mermaid at the Bum's Rush Falls (a.k.a. Popo-Falls).

Der Gøyst fließt durch das Gøystdalen und ist der Dritte im Bunde der nördlichen Tinnsjøzuflüsse. Etwa 2 Kilometer nach dem Einstieg strömt er durch eine Schlucht, WW III mit zwei Stellen WW V-. Unter der ersten Brücke nach der Schlucht wartet ein Schlitzwasserfall, gleich 150 Meter dahinter der höchste Fall des Gøyst, der mit seinen 5 Metern und unsauberem Unterwasser genau befahren werden will. Die folgende WW V+ Stelle kann linksufrig umtragen werden.

Es folgen zahlreiche Grundgesteinsrutschen, unterbrochen von einem kleinen Wehr, welches recht unverhofft auftaucht (wenig Kehrwasser davor). Das Unterwasser ist unsauber und somit ist es besser, das Wehr auf der Insel in der Mitte zu umheben.

Die Rutschenkombination Popo-Falls liegt etwa 2 Kilometer vor der Mündung in den See. Sie ist ganz einfach von der Straße aus erreichbar, direkt hinter einem großen Schotterparkplatz mit Toilettenhäuschen. Warum Popo-Falls? Schwimmt man in der Eingangswalze, legt man den Rest der Rutsche auf dem Allerwertesten zurück.

Tipp: Wenn die Sonne brennt, tummelt sich die eine oder andere Badenixe an den Popo-Falls.

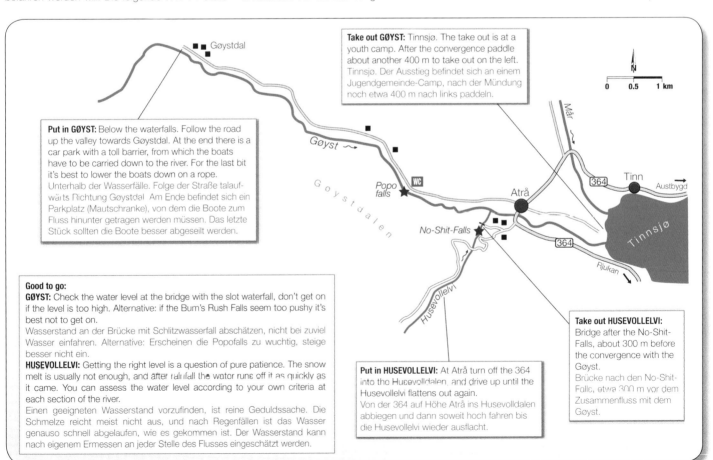

Take out GØYST: Tinnsjø. The take out is at a youth camp. After the convergence paddle about another 400 m to take out on the left. Tinnsjø. Der Ausstieg befindet sich an einem Jugendgemeinde-Camp, nach der Mündung noch etwa 400 m nach links paddeln.

Put in GØYST: Below the waterfalls. Follow the road up the valley towards Gøystdal. At the end there is a car park with a toll barrier, from which the boats have to be carried down to the river. For the last bit it's best to lower the boats down on a rope. Unterhalb der Wasserfälle. Folge der Straße talaufwärts Richtung Gøystdal. Am Ende befindet sich ein Parkplatz (Mautschranke), von dem die Boote zum Fluss hinunter getragen werden müssen. Das letzte Stück sollten die Boote besser abgeseilt werden.

Good to go:
GØYST: Check the water level at the bridge with the slot waterfall, don't get on if the level is too high. Alternative: if the Bum's Rush Falls seem too pushy it's best not to get on.
Wasserstand an der Brücke mit Schlitzwasserfall abschätzen, nicht bei zuviel Wasser einfahren. Alternative: Erscheinen die Popofalls zu wuchtig, steige besser nicht ein.
HUSEVOLLELVI: Getting the right level is a question of pure patience. The snow melt is usually not enough, and after rainfall the water runs off it as quickly as it came. You can assess the water level according to your own criteria at each section of the river.
Einen geeigneten Wasserstand vorzufinden, ist reine Geduldssache. Die Schmelze reicht meist nicht aus, und nach Regenfällen ist das Wasser genauso schnell abgelaufen, wie es gekommen ist. Der Wasserstand kann nach eigenem Ermessen an jeder Stelle des Flusses eingeschätzt werden.

Put in HUSEVOLLELVI: At Atrå turn off the 364 into the Husevolldalen, and drive up until the Husevollelvi flattens out again. Von der 364 auf Höhe Atrå ins Husevolldalen abbiegen und dann soweit hoch fahren bis die Husevollelvi wieder ausflacht.

Take out HUSEVOLLELVI: Bridge after the No-Shit-Falls, about 300 m before the convergence with the Gøyst. Brücke nach den No-Shit-Falls, etwa 300 m vor dem Zusammenfluss mit dem Gøyst.

HUSEVOLLELVI: PROJECT 2000

SOUNDS LIKE »HOSE VOLL« TO ME (FILL YOUR PANTS)

One thing is for sure, this river is a Mecca for adrenalin and drop junkies. It is simply a continuous series of waterfalls and slides, which could theoretically all be run at the optimal water level. We will not bother with a description here, as scouting is an absolute must.

The Husevollelvi is a source of inspiration for artists of all persuasion. This spectacle of nature doesn't go unnoticed by the tourists either, particularly the highest waterfall of the Husevollelvi, the Bear Falls, which has served as the subject of many painters. It was given its name because of the bear cave which hides behind it, and can only be seen at low water. But for us it will always be the »No-Shit-Falls«.

CLASS:	**V - VII (X)**
LEVEL:	**1 km**
LENGTH:	**5 - 8 cumecs**
GRADIENT:	**200 m/km**
TIME:	**8 h**
SEASON:	**April - early June**

Why the No-Shit-Falls? Mmm, shouldn't really talk about it actually. But since you ask… one of the first paddlers to run the falls, whose name doesn't necessarily need to be mentioned here, hit the kicker just under the edge of the drop and landed too far right in the pool – flat as a pancake. Bang! The impact was so huge it even spun the heads of the people on land. The result: no bowel movements for six days and unbearable stomach pain. On the seventh day grace was granted, in the form of a toilet seat.

Why Project 2000? It was some time in the middle of the nineties that Olaf first noticed the Husevollelvi. From the road into the Gøystdal he caught sight of a white streak running down the opposite valley wall. After close examination a theoretical possible for line was hatched for almost every section – at the right water level. But the years to follow failed to provide the right conditions. Or was it fear which caused the first paddlers to falter? The name was coined on one of the many reconnaissance missions, when it was decided that the river was to be run in the year 2000 – at the very latest! 2000 grew somehow into 2001, but who's counting?

From Olaf's memories: »As we reached the combination, we were greeted by a rainbow. I could therefore paddle, in the truest sense of the word, where the rainbow stood at its highest. So, put on the spraydeck, boofed the first drop, focussed on the edge of the second drop. The thrill of anticipation is rushing through my mind. But there's going to be none of that today: just before the second drop the water pushes me into the left wall. I push off against it with both hands to prevent my boat and its contents from disappearing under it. I throw a panicked look to Jens, standing on the bank. He signals to me: »keep cool, you can kook down hard left too. You'll just hit the wall a bit.« Okay, after such fitting advice I shove myself out into the current as hard as I can, and try to get as far into the middle as possible. But I just clip a rock, and bomb off the edge old school style. Where was the rainbow again?«

Dieser Bach ist ein Mekka für adrenalinsüchtige Stürzer, soviel steht fest. Es handelt sich um eine Aneinanderreihung von Wasserfällen und Rutschen, die theoretisch fast alle bei optimalem Wasserstand befahren werden können. Auf eine Beschreibung verzichten wir, da eine Erkundung unerlässlich ist.

Die Husevollelvi ist eine Inspirationsquelle für Künstler jeglicher Art, auch Touristen schätzen dieses Naturschauspiel. Vor allem der höchste Abfall der Husevollelvi, die Bear Falls, dienen Malern gern als Motiv. Der Namen stammt von der dahinter liegenden Bärenhöhle, die bei wenig Wasser zum Vorschein tritt. Für uns bleiben es jedoch die »No-Shit-Falls«.

Warum No-Shit-Falls? Mmm, darüber sollte man eigentlich gar nicht sprechen. Aber, weil ihr es seid: Einer der Erstbefahrer, der hier nicht unbedingt namentlich erwähnt werden muss, erwischte einen Kicker kurz unter der Kante und landete etwas zu weit rechts im Pool – brettflach im fast grünen Wasser. Bang! Der Aufschlag war so laut, dass selbst den Leuten an Land schwindelig wurde. Das Resultat: Sechs Tage kein Stuhlgang und unerträgliche Bauchschmerzen – am siebenten Tag die Erlösung in Form einer Darmentleerung.

Warum eigentlich Projekt 2000? Es war irgendwann Mitte der Neunziger als Olaf das erste Mal auf die Husevollelvi aufmerksam wurde. Von der Straße ins Gøystdal erblickte er eine weiße Rinne auf der anderen Talseite. Die genaue Erkundung ergab eine theoretische Befahrungslinie für fast jede Stelle – beim richtigen Wasserstand. Doch auch die folgenden Jahre brachten keine günstigeren Bedingungen. Oder war es die Angst, die die Erstbefahrer hemmte? Die Namensgebung fand bei einer der etlichen Erkundungstouren statt,

Obsommer

bei der man beschloss spätestens im Jahr 2000 diesen Fluss zu befahren. Aus dem Jahr 2000 wurde zwar 2001, aber das spielt ja keine Rolle. Oder?

Aus Olafs Erinnerungen: »Als wir die eine Kombination erreichten, empfing uns ein Regenbogen. Also konnte ich im wahrsten Sinne des Wortes dort paddeln, wo der Regenbogen am höchsten stand. Also Spritzdecke zu, erste Stufe gebooft, zweite Fallkante fokussiert. Vorfreude über die schöne Linie durchströmte mein Gehirn. Doch nix da: kurz vor der zweiten Kante drückt mich das Wasser an die linke Felswand. Mit beiden Händen stemme ich mich dagegen, um zu verhindern, dass mein Boot samt Inhalt darunter verschwindet. Ich werfe panische Blicke zu Jens ans Ufer, der mir signalisiert: »Locker bleiben, kannst auch ganz links runterplumpsen! Fällst aber ein wenig in die Wand.« Okay, nach so einem adäquaten Rat drücke ich mich energisch in die Strömung und versuche möglichst weit in die Mitte zu kommen, touchiere jedoch noch leicht den Fels, um anschließend oldschoolmäßig einzubomben. Wo war noch der Regenbogen?«

Nils Kagel

Obsommer looking for the rainbow

Obsommer

Sebastian Gründler running the last drop into lake Tinnsjö

SKIRVA

CONTINUOUS CLASS III-IV WITH AT LEAST 2 PORTAGES

This section of the Skirva is actually also well suited for WW III-IV paddlers, as long as they have a bit of alpine experience, in particular when it comes to portaging. In addition, exiting before the difficult sections is not always easy, so bomb-proof eddy technique is a must.

Directly after the put in there is a WW V- slide, after which the Skirva digs itself down into a deep gorge. After the bridge there is a further WW V- combination, then the first unrunnable section, portage on the right. The second »portage« has already been kagelled, WW VI. At more than 10 cumecs it is no longer possible to put straight onto the river, and the portage is difficult. It is necessary to abseil down about 20 metres on the right.

CLASS: III - IV (V, VI, X)
LEVEL: 9 km (11 km)
LENGTH: 10 - 20 cumecs
TIME: 3 - 6 h
SEASON: April - June

You can get off the river on the right, before the next road bridge. If you still haven't had enough, you can try the mini gorge which follows, or just the 15 metre high slide which marks the end of the gorge. The last kilometre to the Skirva's final destination in the lake holds a couple of difficult sections, but the double waterfall into the lake is a thing of pure joy!

Dieser Abschnitt der Skirva ist eigentlich auch für WW III-IV Paddler geeignet, vorausgesetzt man bringt etwas alpine Erfahrung mit, insbesondere zum Umtragen. Zudem ist das rechtzeitige Anlanden vor den schweren Passagen nicht immer einfach, so ist eine sichere Kehrwassertechnik Pflicht.

Direkt nach dem Einstieg folgt eine WW V- Rutsche, anschließend gräbt sich die Skirva schnell in eine tiefe Schlucht. Nach der Brücke folgt eine weitere WW V- Kombination, dann die erste unfahrbare Stelle, flussrechts umtragen. Die zweite »Umtragestelle« ist schon bekagelt worden, WW VI. Bei über 10 Kubik kann hier nicht mehr direkt am Fluss eingebootet werden, das Umtragen gestaltet sich schwierig. Es muss rechts etwa 20 Meter abgeseilt werden.

Vor der nächsten Straßenbrücke kann rechts ausgebootet werden. Wer noch nicht genug hat, kann sich an der folgenden Miniklamm versuchen, oder lediglich an der abschließenden 15 Meter hohen Rutsche. Der letzte Kilometer bis zur Mündung in den See birgt noch ein paar schwierige Stellen in sich, wobei der Doppelwasserfall in den See ein Hochgenuss ist.

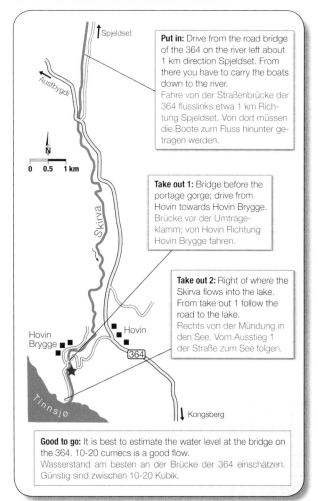

Put in: Drive from the road bridge of the 364 on the river left about 1 km direction Spjeldset. From there you have to carry the boats down to the river.
Fahre von der Straßenbrücke der 364 flusslinks etwa 1 km Richtung Spjeldset. Von dort müssen die Boote zum Fluss hinunter getragen werden.

Take out 1: Bridge before the portage gorge; drive from Hovin towards Hovin Brygge.
Brücke vor der Umtrageklamm; von Hovin Richtung Hovin Brygge fahren.

Take out 2: Right of where the Skirva flows into the lake. From take out 1 follow the road to the lake.
Rechts von der Mündung in den See. Vom Ausstieg 1 der Straße zum See folgen.

Good to go: It is best to estimate the water level at the bridge on the 364. 10-20 cumecs is a good flow.
Wasserstand am besten an der Brücke der 364 einschätzen. Günstig sind zwischen 10-20 Kubik.

STORY: AUSTBYGDÅI NICK WIMSETT

PEPSI CHALLENGE AND MELTDOWN MADNESS

Jens and Olaf had called the California section on the Austbygdåi the most beautiful whitewater Norway has to offer. They were right: We spent a gorgeous day on the river. Perfect water levels, sunshine and clean lines made us forget everything else around us. We felt like five-year-olds playing with their Lego.

It was almost at the end of the trip that we reached a small ledge. »Last year, we simply bombed down the middle and did huge meltdowns,« remembered Jensi. »But I think we have a little more water today«. I could see the twinkling in his eyes. Ever since I had explained to him what Kiwis call a Pepsi Challenge, he was constantly looking for one. Jensi had never heard this expression before and maybe you haven't either. So what exactly is a Pepsi Challenge? It's a competition among friends which is done just for fun. Anyone can call out a Pepsi Challenge, no matter where and when. The winner gets to triumph over his opponents and on top of that, a can of Pepsi.

We were still standing by the drop wondering who should run it first. We decided to deal with the issue like real men and played paper, scissor, and rock. The scissors won – and of course I was the one with the paper.

So I jumped into my boat and prepared myself mentally for a long meltdown. I took up a lot of speed. Boom! It wasn't actually a meltdown, but a backloop into the bottom hole. I tried desperately to work my way toward the flushing water but without success. I felt trapped in the recirc like a cork. The boys were throwing one rope after the other, but I couldn't catch any of them. Soon, I ran out of air and decided to pop my skirt. And then, everything around me became quiet. It felt as if I was being sucked down towards the centre of the earth. Back to the surface, the sun shone cheerfully on my face. The boys applauded and thanked me for the great entertainment.

»Next please,« I gasped to Jensi. The comment was of course meant as a joke, but he felt bad because of my swim and remembered that it had been his idea to begin with. The boys cheered as if Jensi was about to be crowned as king and the pressure was on. I took my throwbag, sat down on a rock beneath the ledge, and looked upstream with anticipation.

A few minutes later, Jensi came swimming in my direction. When he crawled on shore, I congratulated him on his success, and we shook hands. We both burst out laughing. »Next year, you'll go first,« I said, and his face went blank. It looked like Jensi had been cured of the Pepsi Challenge bug for quite some time.

PEPSI CHALLENGE UND MELTDOWN MADNESS

Jens und Olaf hatten die California Section auf der Austbygdåi als einen von Norwegens besten Abschnitten angekündigt, und sie hatten recht: Wir hatten einen großartigen Tag auf dem Fluss. Ein perfekter Wasserstand, sonniges Wetter, saubere Linien – alles andere war vergessen. Wir fühlten uns wie fünf Jahre alte Jungen, die mit ihrem Playmobil spielen.

Wir waren schon fast am Ende des Trips, als wir eine kleine, unscheinbare Stufe erreichten. »Letztes Jahr sind wir einfach in der Mitte runter gebombt und haben dicke Meltdowns gemacht«, erinnerte sich Jensi. »Aber ich glaube es ist heute etwas mehr Wasser« Ich konnte schon wieder das Glänzen in seinen Augen sehen. Seitdem ich ihm erklärt hatte, was wir Neuseeländer unter einer *Pepsi Challenge* verstehen, war er andauernd auf der Suche nach einer. Er hatte noch nie von dieser Bezeichnung gehört, und du ja vielleicht auch noch nicht. Also was ist eigentlich eine Pepsi Challenge? Ein Wettkampf zwischen Freunden, eine Herausforderung bei der es einzig um den Spaß geht. Jeder kann eine Pepsi Challenge ausrufen, egal wann und wo. Der Gewinner darf sich glücklich schätzen den Gegner besiegt zu haben, und bekommt allenfalls eine Dose Pepsi Cola.

Immer noch grübelnd vor dem Drop stehend, konnten wir uns nicht recht entscheiden, wer es denn nun zuerst probieren solle. Also trugen wir es aus wie echte Männer: Wir spielten Stein, Schere, Papier! Schere gewann – und natürlich war ich derjenige mit dem Papier.

Also hüpfte ich in mein Boot, bereitete mich seelisch und moralisch auf einen langen Meltdown vor und gab ordentlich Gas. Boom! Doch das war kein Melt, das war ein Überschlag zurück ins Loch! Ich versuchte mich krampfhaft ins ablaufende Wasser zu arbeiten – erfolglos, der Rücklauf hatte mich einbetoniert. Die Jungs warfen mir ein Seil nach dem anderen zu, doch ich bekam keines zu fassen; die meisten konnte ich nicht mal richtig sehen, ich war ja noch mit dem Rücklauf beschäftigt. Schnell ging mir die Puste aus und ich entschied auszusteigen. Alles um mich wurde ruhig – es fühlte sich an, als ob ich zum Mittelpunkt der Erde gesaugt werde. Zurück an der Oberfläche lachte mir das Tageslicht in die Augen. Die Jungs applaudierten und dankten mir für die tolle Unterhaltung.

»Der Nächste bitte«, hechelte ich zu Jensi, natürlich nur aus Spaß. Aber er fühlte sich schuldig an meinem Schwimmer und erinnerte sich an die Herausforderung aus seinem Munde. Die Jungs feuerten ihn an als ob er zum König gekürt werden solle: die Stimmung war kurz vorm Überkochen. Ich setzte mich mit meinem Wurfsack auf einen Stein unterhalb und blickte gespannt flussauf.

Kurze Zeit später kam auch Jensi angeschwommen, genau in meine Richtung. Als er ans Ufer kroch, gratulierte ich ihm per Handschlag zu seinem riesen Erfolg, wir beide mussten lachen. »Nächstes Jahr fährst du vor« sagte ich – sein Lachen verstummte. Mir schien, als wäre er vorerst geheilt von der Pepsi Challenge.

NICK WIMSETT 1980

A kiwi with style on the water as well as on shore. His favourite hobbies are collecting hats, smoking fat Marleys and sitting in a boat – for freestyle and creeking. After the rodeo worlds in Graz 2003, he came to visit Norway and was simply stoked about the paddling.

Ein Kiwi mit Stil, ob auf dem Wasser oder an Land. Am liebsten sammelt er Kopfbedeckungen, raucht dicke Marleys oder sitzt in seinem Boot – egal ob Rodeo oder Creeker. Nach der Rodeo-WM in Graz 2003 konnte er Norwegen einen Besuch abstatten, und war grenzenlos begeistert.

BUSKERUD

Daniel Herzig - Hallingdalselvi

Road to Dagali - Numedalslågen

BUSKERUD

The Buskerud region stretches northwest of the Hardangervidda. There are not so many worthwhile rivers here, but those that are here are a force to be reckoned with. The upper Numedalslågen before Dagali, at high flow, is one of the best big water runs in the country. The Hemsil, if it has water, is one of the most awesome steep creeks you'll find anywhere.

The Hardangervidda is Europe's largest highland plateau, and is home to the largest population of wild reindeer. The Hardangerjøkulen in the north is the region's largest glacier, and right next to it is the Hallingskarvet mountain ridge. The part of Buskerud of interest to paddlers is a very quiet area. Despite its proximity to Oslo, the tourism there is still under control. The main city in the Hallingdal, Gol, has just on 4,000 inhabitants, and is at the mouth of the Hemsedal. Here you will also find a typical Norwegian church (Stavkirke) which is well worth a visit.

Die Region Buskerud erstreckt sich nordöstlich der Hardangervidda. Hier gibt es nicht viele lohnende Flüsse, aber die wenigen haben es in sich: Der obere Numedalslågen vor Dagali ist bei Hochwasser eines der besten Wuchtwasser des Landes, der Hemsil, wenn er mal läuft, einer der geilsten Sturzbäche überhaupt.

Die Hardangervidda ist Europas größte Gebirgshochfläche, die obendrein den größten Bestand wilder Rentiere beheimatet. Im Norden liegt der Hardangerjøkulen, der größte Gletscher der Region, gleich daneben der Gebirgsrücken Hallingskarvet. Der für Paddler interessante Teil der Region Buskerud ist trotz der Nähe zu Oslo ein recht ruhiges Pflaster, der Tourismus hält sich in Grenzen. Der Hauptort im Hallingdal, Gol, mit knapp 4.000 Einwohnern, liegt am Eingang zum Hemsedal. Hier steht übrigens eine sehenswerte Stabkirche.

BUSKERUD FACTS

Character: Mostly open and pushy whitewater between WW III-V. Only the Usteåni flows through a canyon with WW V must-run sections, on the other rivers (almost) everything can be portaged without difficulty.
Best time: End of April until start of June. The Numedalslågen also runs into the high summer.
Special remarks: Whether the Hemsil can be run depends on the flow being released from the Eikredammen dam.
Accommodation: Free camping area at the Eikredammen on the 52, north of Hemsedal.

Charakter: Meist offen und wuchtiges Wildwasser zwischen III-V. Lediglich auf der Usteåni geht es durch eine Schlucht mit WW V Zwangspassagen, auf den anderen Bächen kann (fast) alles problemlos umtragen werden.
Beste Zeit: Ende April bis Anfang Juni, Numedalslågen auch bis in den Hochsommer.
Besonderheit: Die Befahrbarkeit des Hemsils ist abhängig vom Stausseeablass am Eikredammen.
Übernachtung: Wildcampingplatz am Eikredammen an der 52 nördlich von Hemsedal.

Info on the region

www.golinfo.no
www.geilo.no
www.hemsedal.net
www.hardangervidda.org

Eikredammen

STRØMHVIRVEL, DYKKET INNTAK

WATER SWIRL, SUBMERGED OUTLET

WASSER SPIRALE, ABWASSER UNDERGETAUCHT

Tyinkrysset

Smedalselvi

Lærdal

Mørkedøla

Grøndøla

Mørkedøla

Hemsedal

Tyinkrysset ← E16 Fagernes ↑ Randsverk

Etna

251 Bruflat

Dokka →

E16 33

52 51

Begna

Hemsil

Aurland

Urunda

N

0 2 4 km

Gol

Noresund
Nesbyen ↓

Hønefoss

Hallingdalselvi

7

50

Geilo

Usteani

7

Usevatnet

Eidfjord

Tunhovd

Dagali

Numedalslågen

40 ↓ Uvdal

Rødberg ↓

Where are the fish?

Hemsedal

Numedalslågen - Schorschi Schauf

The first rapid - Obsommer

NUMEDALSLÅGEN: ZAMBEZI SECTION

BIG VOLUME RUN IN AN OPEN RIVERBED

The Numedalslågen is the third longest river in Norway, and flows from Hardangervidda to the Baltic Sea. It is often referred to as the Zambezi of Norway, and at least in spring it certainly lives up to its name: at this time of year 500 cumecs ensure you have sufficient water under your butt! Massive wave trains, giant waves, and now and again a monster hole. From your boat the waves seem so enormous that you expect a killer hole behind each one. The butterflies in your stomach never stop until you're at the take out, they merely recede slightly on the quieter intervals. It's not a good idea to turn up in too short a boat, even if you do hear the waves calling. A fast boat which surfs well is perfect here, as some waves are truly world class – actually good enough to allow blunts in a creek boat! At medium to low water the Numedalslågen quickly loses its power, but is still fun to paddle.

The put in is the beautiful Ossjøen Lake. The Numedalslågen only offers you a few minutes to warm up before it bucks and roars, crashing into the next lake. This cataract can be sighted from the road.

After the 1 kilometre paddle over the lake, which flies by thanks to its gentle current, the level of difficulty slowly begins to increase. After the next 90° bend to the right the Numedalslågen splits into two arms, and after these converge once more, a river-wide hole awaits us. Keep hard left here. The following straight section, with a rock wall on the left, should be scouted from the right at high water levels. Here the current pulls to the left into a mighty »room of doom« – a huge circulating eddy. But if you break out through the diagonal to the right beforehand, all is well. What follows are beautiful cataracts, several of which should be scouted. The old wooden tower on the left signals the last cataract, before the bridge at the take out spoils all the fun.

CLASS:	III - V
LEVEL:	30 - 300 cumecs
LENGTH:	10 km
TIME:	3 h
SEASON:	May - August

Der Numedalslågen ist der dritt-längste Flusslauf Norwegens, er bahnt sich seinen Weg von der Hardangervidda bis in die Ostsee. Hier oben wird er gern als Sambesi Norwegens bezeichnet, und zumindest im Frühjahr wird er seinem Ruf auch gerecht: dann sorgen bis 500 Kubik für ordentlich Wasser unterm Popo. Massive Wellenzüge, Riesenwellen – und ab und zu die ein oder andere große Walze. Die Wellen erscheinen aus dem Boot so riesig, dass man hinter jeder Einzelnen eine Killerwalze erwartet. Das Kribbeln im Bauch hört bis zum Ausstieg nicht auf, es lässt lediglich auf den ruhigeren Zwischenstücken nach. Hier sollte man nicht im zu kurzen Schiff antreten, auch wenn man die Wellen schon rufen hört. Perfekt ist ein schnelles Boot mit hohem Surfpotential, denn einige Wellen sind echte Weltklasse. Eigentlich gut genug um auch im Creekboot zu blunten. Bei Mittel- und Niedrigwasser im Sommer verliert der Numedalslågen schnell an Kraft, macht jedoch immer noch Spaß.

Gestartet wird an einem wunderschönen See, dem Ossjøen. Nur wenige hundert Meter lässt einem der Numedalslågen um sich warm zu paddeln, schon tost er mit Gebrüll in den nächsten See. Dieser Katarakt ist von der Straße aus sichtbar.

Nach dem folgenden Kilometer über den See, der Dank der leichten Strömung wie im Flug vergeht, steigern sich die Schwierigkeiten langsam. Hinter der nächsten 90-Grad-Rechtskurve teilt sich der Numedalslågen kurz in zwei Arme, nach dem Zusammenfluss wartet eine flussbreite Walze, hier ganz links halten. Die folgende Gerade mit linker Hand ansteigender Felswand sollte bei viel Wasser kurz von rechts besichtigt werden. Hier zieht die Strömung nach links in ein mächtiges rotierendes Kehrwasser. Aber wenn man die Diagonale vorher bricht und nach rechts kommt, wird alles gut. Es warten noch schöne Katarakte, von denen einige besichtigt werden sollten. Der alte Holzturm auf der linken Seite läutet den letzten Katarakt ein, bevor die Ausstiegsbrücke einem den Spaß verdirbt.

Good to go:
All year round, at best in spring at high flow. At low flow the difficulty drops significantly.
Ganzjährig, am besten im Frühjahr bei hohem Durchfluss. Bei niedrigen Wasserständen nehmen die Schwierigkeiten deutlich ab.

N
0   0.5   1 km

Gello
Dagali
WC
40
Numedalslågen
Sæterdalen
Uvdal
Ossjøen

Put in: Ossjøen. From the take out follow the toll road on river left for about 10 km. The put in is at the outlet of the second lake.
Ossjøen. Folge vom Ausstieg der Mautstraße auf der flusslinken Seite für etwa 10 km. Am Auslauf des zweiten Sees befindet sich der Einstieg.

Take out:
Road bridge on the 40 at Dagali.
Straßenbrücke der 40 bei Dagali.

Tip: Dress warmly in spring, even in sunny weather; the cold water is accompanied by cold winds.
Luxury tip: If you follow the 40 a further 200 m towards Dagali you'll find a rest area with toilets and showers.

Tipp: Im Frühjahr auch bei Sonne warm anziehen: zum kalten Wasser gesellt sich ein kalter Wind.
Luxus-Tipp: Folgt man der 40 weitere 200 m Richtung Dagali, erreicht man einen Rastplatz mit Toilettenhaus und Duschraum.

Photo: SG

Yeah! - Schauf

Schauf, Vujkow, Preuss

Obsommer, Wimsett

Portage!

USTEÅNI: GORGE RUN

A NICE GORGE RUN WITH 2 MUST-RUNS

The Usteåni flows through a beautiful gorge in the Ustedalen, which already gives a mysterious impression when seen from the road. And there is a catch; two must-runs await the intrepid paddler. The first is a 2-3 metre wide slot with a powerful towback which should be run to the left. With a great deal of fantasy, willpower and the right equipment, this section can be portaged on the right. In the second must-run rapid you start from the right, catch the eddy behind the rock for a quick breather, and then fight on down the right.

The must-run sections can be scouted from the left bank, steps and ropes should be there to make this easier. If the steps are damaged scouting becomes extremely difficult. To get an idea of the level of difficulty before putting in, it is possible to fight your way through the forest down to the river, 1.5 km after the put in.

Shortly after the second must-run section there is a siphon, portage on the left. It is advisable to put out at the suspension bridge approximately 200 metres before the 15 metre waterfall. From here it is necessary to carry the boats about 500 metres to the road, following the path on river left. For those who wish to run the waterfall, or attempt the complicated abseil, it is then possible to continue until the next bridge over the Hallingdalselvi (further in the direction of Gol). There follows a number of cataracts, WW III-IV.

If you wanna scout it first, go that way!

Tip: Check out the must-run sections beforehand, it'll ease your mind.

CLASS:	V (VI, X)
LEVEL:	10 - 15 cumecs
LENGTH:	5 km
TIME:	2 - 4 h
SEASON:	May - June

Die Usteåni durchfließt eine sehr schöne Schlucht im Ustedalen, die schon von der Straße einen mysteriösen Eindruck macht. Und die Sache hat einen Haken, hier warten zwei Zwangspassagen: Bei der Ersten handelt es sich um einen 2-3 Meter breiten Schlitz mit starkem Rücklauf, der nach links rausgeschnitten werden sollte. Mit viel Fantasie, Willensstärke und der richtigen Ausrüstung ist diese Stelle auch rechts umtragbar. Beim zweiten Zwangskatarakt startet man von rechts, atmet mittig im Kehrwasser hinter dem Stein kurz durch und kämpft sich dann rechts weiter durch.

Die Zwangspassagen können vom linken Ufer besichtigt werden, Tritte und Seile sollten vorhanden sein. Sind die Tritte beschädigt, ist ein Besichtigen nur schwer möglich. Um sich schon vor dem Paddeln ein Bild von den Schwierigkeiten zu machen, kann man sich seinen Weg von der Straße aus bahnen, indem man etwa 1,5 Kilometer nach dem Einstieg den Wald hinunter zum Fluss läuft.

Schnell nach der zweiten Zwangspassage erreicht man einen Siphon, links umtragen. Es sollte an einer Hängebrücke etwa 200 Meter vor dem 15-Meter-Wasserfall ausgestiegen werden. Von dort muss man die Boote etwa 500 Meter zur Straße tragen, immer dem Pfad flusslinks folgen. Wer den Wasserfall fahren oder aufwendig umseilen möchte, kann danach noch bis zur nächsten Brücke über die Hallingdalselvi paddeln (weiter Richtung Gol). Es folgen noch einige Katarakte, WW III-V.

Tipp: Schau dir die Zwangspassagen vorher an, und die Aufregung lässt nach.

Good to go:
There should be no water running through the fields at the put in, 10-15 cumecs is a good level.
Am Einstieg sollte kein Wasser durch die Wiesen laufen, günstig sind 10-15 Kubik.

Put in: From Geilo follow the 7 towards Gol and take the first road on the right.
Von Geilo der 7 Richtung Gol folgen und die erste Möglichkeit rechts abbiegen.

Hagafoss ■ □ 50 ■ ← Aurland

Hallingdalen

7

Gol →

Ustedalen

Usteåni

Take out: Suspension bridge before the 15 m waterfall. From the put in drive further along the 7 and turn right between the houses as soon as the road changes from two lanes to one. When you reach the bridge over the Usteåni, walk up river left to the waterfall.
Hängebrücke vor dem 15-Meter-Fall. Vom Einstieg weiter auf der 7 fahren und rechts zwischen Häusern abbiegen, sobald die Fahrbahn sich von zwei auf eine Spur verjüngt. Sobald man die Brücke über die Usteåni erreicht, flusslinks zum Wasserfall hoch laufen.

Eidfjord ← Geilo

↑ N

0   0.5   1 km

40 ↓ Dagali

HEMSIL

ONE OF THE BEST RUNS IN THE COUNTRY, WHEN IT HAS WATER

The Hemsedal is world renowned for skiing, so why not the Hemsil for paddling? Good question. One reason for this could be the Eikreddammen, which drown the waters of the river in a lake. Only at sufficient flow releases does the Hemsil become a true gem, at which point it earns itself an immediate entry in the Norwegian Top Ten list. The whitewater hero can look forward to a spectacular giant slide, a must-run section starting at 15 cumecs, a no-run section (which has already been kagelled), and then the show-down to finish with: waterfalls. The Hemsil offers fantastic whitewater under the motto »Tough but Fair«, to tempt the heart of every drop junkie!

Back to the facts: shortly after the put in you reach a narrow drop, after which is a mini gorge. This should best be scouted. After the gorge come several difficult sections, which can all be easily portaged. Under the wooden bridge is a supposedly unrunnable section, which has in fact been paddled by Nils Kagel, but this does not come recommended.

CLASS: IV - VI (X)
LEVEL: 9 km (6 km)
LENGTH: 10 - 25 cumecs
TIME: 3 - 6 h
SEASON: May - early July

After the portage comes the most difficult section of the Hemsil. If you have not felt comfortable up to this point, it is time to get off the river. The giant slide here is in fact not difficult, but there is no room for error: all the water on river right disappears into a cave, and safetying is almost impossible.

After this adrenaline hit the trip continues through the second gorge, where the must-run section shortly before Gol is worthy of mention. None of the lines through this cataract is nice, none is impossible. Up to 15 cumecs you can portage on the right hand side, but the Hemsil is really only worth running at 15 cumecs and up. Then scout from the left bank and best run it down the middle. He who goes left with the main current can expect to meet the wall!

The waterfalls in Gol are the crowning glory of the Hemsil. They are not particularly easy, and develop strong towbacks at decent flows. The waterfall under the bridge is several metres undercut and very dangerous.

Tip: If the Hemsil has too much water, there is an awesome play wave after the bridge in Gol. It can be seen from the bridge.

Photo: 00

Michi Neumann

Das Hemsedal ist bei Skifahrern in aller Welt bekannt, warum dann nicht der Hemsil für uns Paddler? Gute Frage. Grund dafür dürfte der Eikreddammen sein, der das Wasser des Flusses in einem See ertrinken lässt. Nur bei ausreichendem Durchlass wird der Hemsil zu einem wirklichen

Schmankerl, dann verdient er sich im Nu einen Eintrag in die norwegische Top-10-Liste. Es wartet eine spektakuläre Riesenrutsche auf ihre Helden, eine Zwangspassage ab 15 Kubik, eine Unfahrbare (die schon bekagelt wurde) und dann noch der Showdown zum Schluss: Wasserfälle. Der Hemsil

bietet traumhaftes Wildwasser getreu dem Motto »Schwer aber fair«. Da juchzt das Stürzerherz!

Zurück zu den Tatsachen: Kurz nach dem Einstieg erreicht man eine schlitzige Stufe, danach geht es in eine Miniklamm, diese am besten schon vorher besichtigen. Nach der Klamm folgen

etliche schwere Stellen, die aber auch alle gut zu umtragen sind. Unter einer Holzbrücke wartet eine vermeintlich unfahrbare Stelle, die zwar schon von Nils Kagel befahren wurde, jedoch nicht zu empfehlen ist.

Nach der Umtrage folgt der schwerste Teil des Hemsil. Wer sich bis hierhin nicht sicher fühlte, sollte die Fahrt beenden. Die folgende große Rutsche ist eigentlich nicht schwer, jedoch sind Fahrfehler verboten: Das gesamte Wasser der rechten Flussseite verschwindet in einer Höhle, sichern ist fast unmöglich.

Nach diesem Adrenalinschub geht es weiter durch die letzte Schlucht, erwähnenswert ist die Zwangsstelle kurz vor Gol: keine der Routen durch diesen Katarakt ist schön, keine ist unmöglich. Bis etwa 15 Kubik kann man sie rechts umtragen, jedoch wird der Hemsil erst ab 15 Kubik richtig lohnend. Dann von links anschauen und am besten in der Mitte fahren. Wer links im Hauptwasser paddelt, muss damit rechnen die Wand zu treffen.

Die Wasserfälle in Gol setzen dem Hemsil die Krone auf. Sie sind nicht recht einfach, bei einem ordentlichen Wasserstand entstehen starke Rückläufe. Der dritte Fall muss sauber und weit gebooft werden, da sich hinter dem Fall eine Höhle befindet. Der Fall unter der Brücke ist rechts mehrere Meter unterspült und somit sehr gefährlich.

Tipp: Führt der Hemsil zuviel Wasser, entsteht nach der Brücke in Gol eine herrliche Spielwelle. Man sieht sie von der Brücke aus.

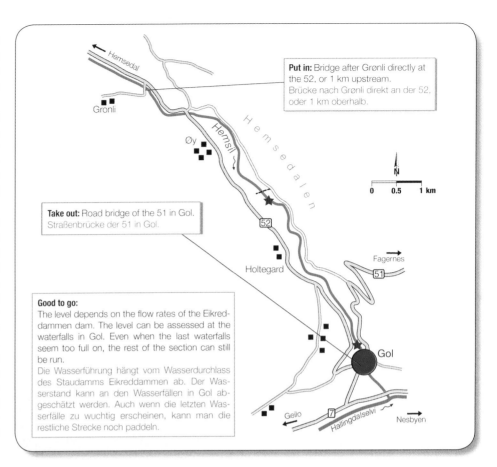

Put in: Bridge after Grønli directly at the 52, or 1 km upstream.
Brücke nach Grønli direkt an der 52, oder 1 km oberhalb.

Take out: Road bridge of the 51 in Gol.
Straßenbrücke der 51 in Gol.

Good to go:
The level depends on the flow rates of the Eikreddammen dam. The level can be assessed at the waterfalls in Gol. Even when the last waterfalls seem too full on, the rest of the section can still be run.
Die Wasserführung hängt vom Wasserdurchlass des Staudamms Eikreddammen ab. Der Wasserstand kann an den Wasserfällen in Gol abgeschätzt werden. Auch wenn die letzten Wasserfälle zu wuchtig erscheinen, kann man die restliche Strecke noch paddeln.

Photos: MN

Obsommer in the first short canyon - 1995

ETNA: BRUFLAT SECTION
MOSTLY OPEN GRADE IV WHITEWATER WITH SOME HIGHLIGHTS

Obsommer in 1997

Photo: MN

The Etna feeds into the Dokka at Dokka (nice, huh?) and can be run in several sections. We shall confine ourselves here to the lower section at Bruflat, it is ideal for testing your limits a bit. Between the difficult sections there are always easy, open sections.

The entrance to the short canyon at Bruflat might have to be portaged, as it is followed by a difficult waterfall combination which can be well scouted from river left. There are two possible lines here: either boof the first waterfall (4 metres) to the right, or take the action line straight down the middle. We tried both lines, but no-one really made a clean run of the second waterfall (3 metres). After that the Etan gets quieter and more open. But you are regularly entertained with nice bedrock slides. Especially just before the take out, two impressive slides await you.

CLASS:	**IV - V**
LEVEL:	**10 - 20 cumecs**
LENGTH:	**4 km**
TIME:	**2 - 5 h**
SEASON:	**April - June**

Tip: In the upper section, from the outflow of the Etnsenn, the Etna offers almost constantly nice WW II-IV.

Die Etna mündet bei Dokka in die Dokka (toll, oder?) und kann auf mehreren Abschnitten befahren werden. Wir werden uns auf das untere Teilstück bei Bruflat beschränken, es ist ideal um ein bisschen die eigenen Grenzen auszuloten. Zwischen den schweren Stellen folgen immer wieder leichte und offene Abschnitte.

Der Eingang zur kurzen Klamm von Bruflat muss eventuell umhoben werden, danach folgt eine schwere Wasserfallkombination, die linksufrig gut zu besichtigen ist. Es gibt zwei Linien: entweder den ersten Fall (4 Meter) nach rechts rausboofen oder die Action-Line direkt über die Mitte. Wir haben beide Linien versucht, doch niemand ist vernünftig über den zweiten Fall (3 Meter) gekommen. Danach wird die Etna offener und ruhiger, es folgen aber immer wieder nette Grundgesteinsrutschen. Gerade kurz vor dem Ausstieg warten noch zwei imposante Rutschen.

Tipp: Im oberen Verlauf, vom Ausfluss des Etnsenn, bietet die Etna fast durchweg schönes WW II-IV.

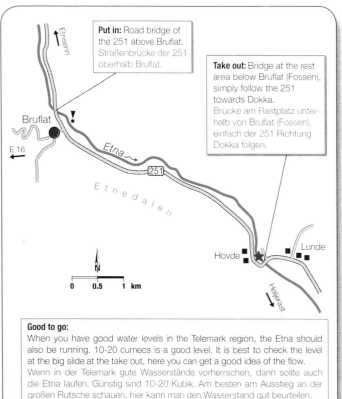

Put in: Road bridge of the 251 above Bruflat. Straßenbrücke der 251 oberhalb Bruflat.

Take out: Bridge at the rest area below Bruflat (Fossen), simply follow the 251 towards Dokka. Brücke am Rastplatz unterhalb von Bruflat (Fossen), einfach der 251 Richtung Dokka folgen.

Etnsenn
Bruflat
E 16
Etna
251
E t n e d a l e n
Hovde
Lunde
Høllerast

N
0   0.5   1 km

Good to go:
When you have good water levels in the Telemark region, the Etna should also be running. 10-20 cumecs is a good level. It is best to check the level at the big slide at the take out, here you can get a good idea of the flow.
Wenn in der Telemark gute Wasserstände vorherrschen, dann sollte auch die Etna laufen. Günstig sind 10-20 Kubik. Am besten am Ausstieg an der großen Rutsche schauen, hier kann man den Wasserstand gut beurteilen.

MØRKEDØLA

A NICE RUN WITH SOME TECHNICAL DROPS

Together with the Grøndøla, this Mørkedøla is one of the sources feeding the Hemsil. To add confusion, however, the northern run-off of this fjell, feeding the Lærdalselvi, is also called the Mørkedøla. So be aware that we are here referring to the Mørkedøla, headwaters of the Hemsil.

For the first kilometre the Mørkedøla flows swiftly, WW III-IV, and everything can be run on sight. After that it becomes quieter once more, allowing time to take in the landscape of the valley, before the next slides and drops demand your attention.

At the halfway point of the trip you reach a triple combination under a wooden bridge, WW IV+. After another 2 kilometres a suspension foot bridge stretches across the river: the signal to sit up and pay attention. Immediately after the next drop, directly before the large road bridge of the 52, you must put out of the Mørkedøla on the left, and portage over the bridge. Beneath the bridge a crevice waterfall lies in wait, nestled in a low gorge with no foot access.

Once back on the water, things quickly get interesting again: there follows a low gorge with several drops, scout from the right. Depending on water level, up to WW V. At the very latest you should portage the last potholed drop, if not those previous, as it has a strong towback, even at normal levels. Portage on the left or on the right beneath the wall.

When the road is once more on the river left, you don't have much further to go to the take out. After approximately another 700 metres you'll find the tourist attraction of the Rjukandefossen plunging into the valley, it is advisable to exit left beforehand.

CLASS: III - IV+ (V, X)
LEVEL: 10 - 20 cumecs
LENGTH: 9 km
TIME: 3 - 4 h
SEASON: May - early July

Diese Mørkedøla ist neben der Grøndøla einer der Quellbäche des Hemsil. Gleichzeitig wird aber auch der nördliche Abfluss dieses Fjells, also der Zufluss zur Lærdalselvi, Mørkedøla genannt. Also nicht verwechseln, wir reden von dem Oberlauf des Hemsils.

Auf dem ersten Kilometer fließt die Mørkedøla zügig dahin, WW III-IV, es kann eigentlich alles auf Sicht gefahren werden. Danach wird es ruhiger, Zeit für einen Blick durchs Tal, bevor die nächsten Rutschen und Stufen die Aufmerksamkeit fordern.

Auf der Hälfte der Strecke erreicht man eine Dreier-Kombination unter einer Holzbrücke, WW IV+. Nach weiteren 2 Kilometern zieht sich eine Fußgänger-Hängebrücke über den Fluss: Zeichen Obacht zu geben. Gleich nach der nächsten Stufe, direkt vor der großen Straßenbrücke der 52, muss man links die Mørkedøla verlassen und über die Brücke umtragen. Unter der Brücke treibt ein Schlitzwasserfall sein Unwesen, eingebettet in eine unbegehbare Niederklamm.

Nachdem man wieder auf dem Wasser ist, wird es schnell wieder spannend: Es folgt eine Niederklamm mit mehreren Stufe, von rechts be-sichtigen. Je nach Wasserstand bis WW V. Spätestens am Ende sollte man umtragen, die letzte Stufe mit Kolk ist schon bei Normalwasserstand extrem rückläufig. Rechts unter der Wand oder links umtragen.

Wenn die Straße wieder auf die linke Flussseite wechselt, ist es nicht mehr weit zum Ausstieg. Etwa 700 Meter entfernt bricht der Rjukandefossen als Touristenattraktion zu Tale, ein Ausstieg vorher links ist ratsam.

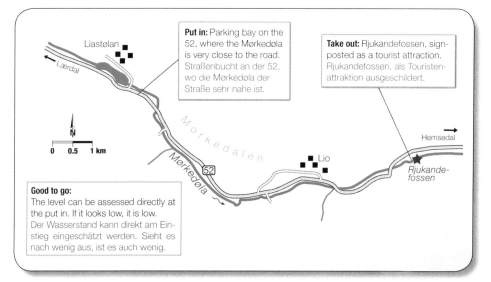

Put in: Parking bay on the 52, where the Mørkedøla is very close to the road. Straßenbucht an der 52, wo die Mørkedøla der Straße sehr nahe ist.

Take out: Rjukandefossen, signposted as a tourist attraction. Rjukandefossen, als Touristen-attraktion ausgeschildert.

Good to go:
The level can be assessed directly at the put in. If it looks low, it is low.
Der Wasserstand kann direkt am Einstieg eingeschätzt werden. Sieht es nach wenig aus, ist es auch wenig.

Obsommer at Rjukandefossen

(Matze)

(Olli)

Europas
größte
Zeitschrift
für Paddler

(www.kanumagazin.de)

(Jutta)

STORY: NORWEGIAN FAIRYTALES MARIANN SÆTHER

PREFACE: Does anyone here believe in fairytales? **Jens Klatt**

For a long time, I associated trolls with the wooden figures which you can find in front of any shop or gas station in Norway, even in the most remote province. Is the image of the troll spoilt through its use as gas station decoration? To us foreigners this may be so, but not to the Norwegians: for generations and generations, grandmothers have been telling their grandchildren about trolls, elves and forest spirits on long winter evenings. Horrible looking creatures with big noses, several heads, long tails, and a terrifying laugh haunt the Norwegian fairy world. Together with heroic sagas and legends, they make up the content of the original Norwegian folktales. In these tales, humans remain suspicious and fearful of nature and thus change their fears into myths. These tales are of course a bit silly and no one would believe in these mythical creatures today.

Still, an image of these gas station decorations should not be missing in this book. I had collected a few nice pictures of trolls over the past few years and the choice was tough. I compared all the pictures carefully under a magnifying glass. And suddenly, I had doubts whether the Norwegian myths were in fact only a product of fantasy: the troll in my picture had winked. Just once, and very quickly – but I swear I saw it! And then, I began to remember all the strange things that had happened on our trip: my skirt that popped on the Teigendalen waterfall, my defective camera during the »Project 2000«, the wheel suspension that broke right before the ferry, the tree on the Mår, and Olaf's crazy video camera. Did trolls maybe have their fingers in there? Could a small wooden troll possess such magical powers?

These thoughts kept spinning in my head for a while and all of a sudden, I read Marianne's story with different eyes. I thought I knew now why trolls have it in for tourists; they are trying to keep people from intruding into their sacred territory and disturbing them. Now that you know, be nice to them, and they may be nice to you!

Mariann Seather is a Norwegian kayaker who knows these myths and legends much better than any foreigner, since she has learned them from her grandmother and she will probably teach them to her grandchildren one day. Mariann has summarized the Norwegian fairy world for us, so that we'll be prepared for our next visit to Norway.

OF ELVES, TROLLS AND WATER SPIRITS

Did you ever wonder where that duck-tape went that you held in your hand just a few minutes ago? Or that chocolate bar you had saved, for when you finally reached the take out after hours of paddling? And what about the fact that you always trip and fall when you carry your kayak around a gnarly drop on the river? Well, if these things keep happening to you when you're on a paddling mission in Norway, there might be a plausible explanation.

Most kayakers camp while travelling around Norway, due to the outrageous prices for accommodation. However, there are a few things you should be aware of when sleeping outside on starlit summer nights. Norway is not only the country of waterfalls, it is also the home of numerous trolls, the water spirit »Nøkken«, »Hulder«, elves, and last but not least the »Little People«.

Let's start with the trolls: these ugly and evil creatures love human flesh. Most of them are huge and dwell in the mountains, but they can also be small and live under bridges. They are generally dressed in filthy clothes and sometimes they have a tree growing on their nose. They are

---

VORWORT: Glaubt hier jemand an Geister? **Jens Klatt**

Lange Zeit erschienen mir Trolle als nichts anderes als Figuren aus Holz, zu finden vor Geschäften und Tankstellen selbst in der hintersten Provinz. Ist der Troll geprägt durch die Schmach als Tankstellendekoration? Für uns Ausländer schon, für die Norweger nicht: von Trollen, Dämonen und Waldgeistern erzählen Großmütter an langen Winterabenden ihren Enkeln seit eh und je. Grässlich anzusehende Wesen mit großen Nasen, mehreren Köpfen, langen Schwänzen und einem erschütternden Lachen spuken durch die norwegische Fabelwelt. Verknüpft mit Heldensagen und Legenden bilden sie den Inhalt für die ursprünglichen norwegischen Volksmärchen. Wo die Natur den Menschen unheimlich bleibt, verwandeln sie ihre Ängste in Mythen. Natürlich sind diese Märchen feinster Tobak – kein Mensch glaubt heute noch an Fabelwesen.

Trotzdem sollte auch ein Bild von einer dieser Tankstellendekos in unserem Buch zu sehen sein. Mehrere nette Bilder von Trollen hatte ich in den letzten Jahren gesammelt, die Auswahl fiel schwer. Sorgsam verglich ich alle Bilder unter der Lupe. Doch plötzlich kamen mir Zweifel, ob es sich bei diesen norwegischen Mythen wirklich nur um Ausgeburten der Fantasie handelt: Der Troll auf meinem Dia zwinkerte mir zu! Nur kurz, nur einmal – aber ich hab's gesehen! All die merkwürdigen Ereignisse unserer letzten Touren kamen mir wieder in den Sinn. Die offene Spritzdecke am Teigdalen-Wasserfall, mein defekter Fotoapparat am »Projekt 2000«, die kaputte Radaufhängung kurz vor der Fähre, der Baum auf dem Mår, Olafs verrückte Videokamera – hatten da Trolle die Finger im Spiel? Hat ein kleiner Holztroll eine solche Macht, lauern da magische Kräfte in ihm?

Diese Gedanken spukten noch lange Zeit in meinem Kopf herum, auch Marianns Geschichte über die norwegische Fabelwelt las ich plötzlich mit anderen Augen. Und ich glaube jetzt auch zu wissen, warum Trolle uns Touristen auf dem Kieker haben: Sie wollen uns fernhalten von ihrem gelobten Land und verhindern, dass noch mehr Menschen nach Norwegen kommen, in ihre Wälder eindringen und ihre Ruhe stören. Also, seid lieb zu ihnen, dann sind sie auch lieb zu euch!

Wesentlich besser kennt sich die Norwegerin Mariann Sæther mit diesen Mythen und Geschichten aus. Sie hat sie einst von ihrer Großmutter erzählt bekommen, und wird sie wohl irgendwann an ihre eigenen Enkel weitergeben. Für uns hat sie die norwegische Sagenwelt kurz zusammen gefasst, damit wir für unseren nächsten Norwegenurlaub gegen alles gewappnet sind.

VON ELFEN, TROLLEN UND WALDGEISTERN

Hast du dich schon mal gefragt, wo das Klebeband hin ist, welches du gerade noch in der Hand hattest? Oder der Schokoriegel, den du dir eigentlich bis zum Ausstieg aufbewahren wolltest? Und hast du dir schon mal Gedanken gemacht, warum du immer stolperst, wenn du einen Katarakt umträgst? Tja, wenn dir diese Sachen ständig passieren, muss es dafür doch eine einleuchtende Erklärung geben.

Die meisten Paddler schlafen im Zelt oder im Auto, wenn sie in Norwegen unterwegs sind. Aber nur die wenigsten wissen, dass es da ein paar Dinge gibt, vor denen sie sich nachts unterm Sternenhimmel hüten sollten. Norwegen ist nicht nur das Land der Wasserfälle, es ist auch die Heimat zahlreicher Trolle, des Wassergeistes »Nøkken«, der »Hulder«, Elfen und nicht zu vergessen der »Kleinen Leute«.

Aber fangen wir mit den Trollen an: Diese ekelhaften und gemeinen Kreaturen lieben menschliches Fleisch. Die meisten von ihnen sind riesig und stapfen nachts durch die Berge, aber es gibt auch kleinere, die gern unter der einen oder anderen Brücke hausen. Sie tragen schäbige Kleidung und manchmal wächst ihnen sogar ein Bäumchen auf der

especially fond of princesses, but since we only have one left in Norway, it's not really a big issue anymore. If chased by a troll, the trick is to lure it out of the protecting darkness of its cave. When the first ray of the morning light falls on the troll, it will turn to stone. I am sure you have seen all the huge, strangely-shaped stones all over Norway, placed in the oddest locations? Well, there you go, now you know where they've come from.

You can find some very beautiful women in Norway, but there are some you better leave alone: if you run into a beautiful woman with long, blond hair, wearing a traditional dress, and if she tries to lure you deep into the woods – watch out! If you follow her, you may never come back. »Hulder« are beings from the old days, and even these days many people claim to have met them. Sometimes you can hear their beautiful song when they are calling for their cattle high up in the mountains.

The only way you can recognize a Hulder before it's too late is by checking her back: a Hulder has a cow's tail. Of course she will try to hide it from you. But if you do see a cow's tail, turn and run away as fast as you can – or throw a knife over her head. It is said that if you throw steel over a Hulder, she can not harm you anymore. Whatever »harm« means.

Then we come to the »Nøkken«: he is the spirit of all waterfalls and small hidden ponds in the forest. He is a merry little fellow, and plays the fiddle like a god. Sometimes, especially during quiet nights, you can hear him as he tries to enchant virgins with his play. He loves to sit close by a waterfall and play, because there he is accompanied by the sound of falling water.

Elves are beautiful, humanlike creatures that have been living on earth since long before us. Some of them are good, such as the »light elves«, and some of them are evil, such as the »dark elves«. Elves live inside the mountains and are known to be amazing blacksmiths. Their king is famous for fooling young virgins into coming and living with him inside the mountain. Sometimes the trapped people will be treated like royals; sometimes they will be treated like slaves. There are stories about girls who have been away for years, and when they reappear in the light, all they want is to return to the elves. If you ever want to free someone from the elves' grasp, ring a church bell at great length. The elves might get scared and open their doors to the mountain to set their prisoner free.

The »Little People« live in the forest, and they love to play tricks on you. They like to hide your things while you are kayaking. And if they see you carrying your kayak around a rapid, they will try and make you trip, and giggle and snigger when successful. Since they hardly reach up to our knees, it is no problem for them to hide from frustrated kayakers. Here is a good old Norwegian rule: when you pour your hot dishwashing water onto the ground, make sure you give them a warning first, otherwise they will make your day a lot harder!

By the way: one of the most famous Norwegian fairytales takes place in Heidal, the valley where the mighty Sjoa flows. It is called »The Troll of the Heidal forest«. So the next time you are in Norway, look around while walking in the forest, you might see things you have never noticed before. Listen for Nøkken playing his fiddle under a waterfall, and for the Hulder's song as she tries to find her cattle. So remember, when your Swiss army knife goes missing next time, don't blame your friends straight away. Instead listen for the giggling sound coming from the woods!

Have fun!
Mariann Sæther

Nase. Eigentlich sind sie immer auf der Suche nach einer Prinzessin, aber seitdem es in Norwegen nur noch eine gibt, geht es ihnen gar nicht mehr nur darum. Wirst du von einem Troll gejagt, musst du ihn ins Licht locken! Denn sobald ihn die ersten Sonnenstrahlen erwischen, verwandelt er sich zu Stein. Ich bin mir sicher, dass du schon mal einen dieser seltsamen Felsbrocken gesehen hast, die an den unmöglichsten Orten herumliegen. Jetzt weißt du auch, wo sie herkommen.

In Norwegen gibt es einige hübsche Frauen, aber es gibt auch einige, von denen man besser die Finger lassen sollte: Triffst du eine schöne Frau mit langem, blondem Haar in traditionellem Gewand, die dich versucht tiefer in die Wälder zu locken, ist Vorsicht geboten – es kann sein das du nie zurückkehrst. Die »Hulder« sind Wesen aus vergangenen Zeiten, doch viele Menschen begegnen ihnen auch heutzutage noch. Manchmal kann man sogar ihren Gesang aus den Bergen hören, wenn sie ihr Vieh zusammen treiben.

Dir bleibt nur eine Möglichkeit rechtzeitig zu erkennen, ob sie eine Hulder ist oder nicht: Hulder haben einen Kuhschwanz. Allerdings wird dir eine Hulder nie freiwillig den Rücken zukehren. Entdeckst du jedoch einen Schwanz, renne so schnell du kannst! Oder wirf ihr ein Messer über den Kopf, denn die Sage besagt, dass sie dir keinen Schaden mehr zufügen kann, sobald man ein Stück Eisen über sie geworfen hat. Was immer das bedeuten mag.

Kommen wir zu Nøkken: Er ist der Geist aller Wasserfälle und der kleinen Tümpel im Wald. Er ist ein kleiner fröhlicher Kerl und spielt Geige wie ein Gott. Manchmal, in besonders ruhigen Nächten, kann man ihn hören, wenn er versucht mit seinem Geigenspiel Jungfrauen zu verzaubern. Am liebsten spielt er an einem Wasserfall, denn dort wird er vom Klang des Wassers begleitet.

Elfen sind wunderschöne, menschenähnliche Wesen, die schon lange vor uns auf der Erde lebten. Es gibt freundliche Elfen, wie die »Lichtelfen«, und es gibt böse Elfen, die »Dunklen Elfen«. Sie leben unter der Erde in Hügeln und sind begnadete Schmiede. Der Elfenkönig lockt immer wieder Jungfrauen zu sich, um mit ihnen unter der Erde zu wohnen. Die meisten Gefangenen werden wie Sklaven behandelt, andere wie Adlige. Es werden Geschichten von Mädchen erzählt, die jahrelang verschollen waren, und als sie endlich wieder ans Tageslicht kamen, wollten sie nichts anderes als zurück zu den Elfen. Um einen verschollenen Menschen zurückzuholen, muss man vor dem vermeintlichen Hügel die Kirchenglocken läuten – und zwar äußerst lang. Denn dann bekommen die Elfen Angst und lassen ihre Gefangenen möglicherweise frei.

Die »Kleinen Leute« leben im Wald und lieben es dir Streiche zu spielen. Sie verstecken deine Sachen während du auf dem Wasser bist, lassen dich stolpern, wenn du einen Katarakt umträgst – und lachen sich kaputt, wenn du dich dann darüber ärgerst. Da sie uns gerade mal bis zu den Knien reichen, ist es kein Problem für sie sich vor uns frustrierten Paddlern zu verstecken. Anbei noch eine alte norwegische Regel: Wenn du heißes Wasser auf den Boden schüttest, sei es von Kartoffeln oder vom Abwasch, warne die Kleinen Leute vorher – oder sie machen deinen Tag zur Hölle.

Und ganz nebenbei: Eine der bekanntesten norwegischen Sagen, »Der Troll aus dem Wald von Heidal«, spielt im Tal der beliebten Sjoa. Also, wenn du mal wieder in Norwegen bist, halte deine Augen offen und du wirst Dinge sehen, die dir vorher nie aufgefallen sind. Lausche Nøkken, wenn er seine Geige spielt, und den Huldern, wenn sie ihr Vieh zusammentreiben. Und wenn dein Schweizer Taschenmesser mal wieder verschwunden ist, beschuldige nicht gleich deine Freunde – lausche lieber in den Wald, vielleicht hörst du ja ein leises Kichern.

Have fun!
Mariann Sæther

HEDMARK

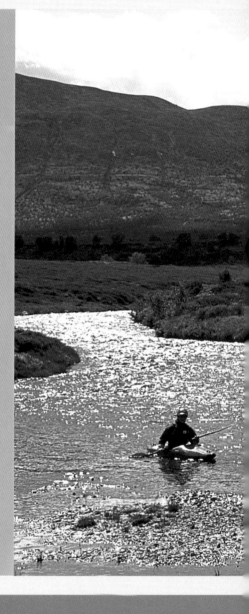

Nina Wittig enjoying her cruise down the Grimsa.

Rondane Nasjonalpark

HEDMARK

It is rumoured that only hard core paddlers get their money's worth in Norway, but kayak teacher Manfred Eckert knows better, and he presents here a region which combines all the Norwegian highlights, with finest middle-class whitewater: the Hedmark. This area is the Tuscany of Norway, blessed with rolling hills and a pleasant climate.

Hedmark is the eastern-most region described in this guide, and lies on the border to Sweden. Here you will find 12 tours perfect for the WW II-IV paddler, the WW V paddler will really only get his thrills on the upper Atna.

In the north of Hedmark lies Lake Femund, Norway's third largest inland body of water, and east

of there the Femundsmarka Nasjonalpark. In the northwest of Hedmark is the Rondane Nasjonalpark. Both areas offer beautiful Fjell landscape and are perfectly suited for hiking. The culture vultures may have to look a little harder to find what they want, but the Forestry Museum and the Glomsdalsmuseum in Elverum are well worth a visit.

HEDMARK FACTS

Character: Mostly rivers of medium difficulty in mid alpine landscape. They flow through rock or forest canyons, but these are seldom very deep. One exception: the upper Atna.

Water: Most of the rivers flow out of moors, and so have clear brown water. You will often see collections of foam on the surface of the water. These are the result of a natural biological process, and do not indicate unclean water.

Best time: June and July. In August it is only worth coming here after rainfall. Several of the rivers have enough water for a run from May to September, but are more fun to paddle when their levels are higher. Be careful at high flows: the difficulties in the canyons are then considerably higher than those given here!

Special remarks: From the many forking paths it is often difficult to choose which is the right one to take you down to the river. As the anglers also suffer a similar lack of orientation, they have marked most of the correct paths with small wooden fish.

Accommodation: At the put in of the Åsta and at the Atna bridge at Mogrenda. The paddlers' camp ground on the Setninga no longer exists. The camp ground of Sølenstua on the Trysilelva can be recommended.

Charakter: Meist mittelschwere Flüsse in einer Mittelgebirgslandschaft. Sie fließen in Fels- und Waldschluchten, die aber nur selten tief eingeschnitten sind. Ausnahme: die obere Atna.

Wasser: Die meisten Flüsse entspringen in Mooren und sind deshalb braun gefärbt, aber klar. Häufig sieht man leichte Schaumkronen, die von einem natürlichen Verseifungsprozess zeugen und keine Verschmutzungen darstellen.

Beste Zeit: Juni und Juli, im August lohnt das Gebiet nur noch nach Regen. Einige Flüsse führen von Mai bis September genügend Wasser für eine Befahrung, machen jedoch mehr Spaß, wenn der Wasserstand höher liegt. Achtung bei Hochwasser: die Schwierigkeiten liegen in den Schluchten dann wesentlich höher als angegeben.

Besonderheit: Oft ist es schwer aus den vielen abzweigenden Fahrwegen denjenigen herauszufinden, der zum Fluss führt. Da Fischer wohl ähnlich orientierungslos sind, haben sie die richtigen Abzweigungen meist mit Holzfischen markiert.

Übernachtung: Am Einstieg der Åsta und an der Atna-Brücke bei Mogrenda. Der Paddlercampingplatz an der Setninga existiert nicht mehr. An der Trysilelva empfiehlt sich der Campingplatz von Sølenstua.

Ein Gerücht besagt, dass in Norwegen nur Hardcore-Paddler auf ihre Kosten kommen. Kanulehrer Manfred Eckert weiß es besser und stellt für uns einen Landstrich vor, der alle Vorzüge Norwegens mit feinstem Mittelklasse-Wildwasser kombiniert: die Hedmark. Sie ist die Toskana Norwegens, hier begeistern liebliche Hügel und ein ausgeglichenes Klima. Die Hedmark ist die östlichste beschriebene Region an der Grenze zu Schweden. Vornehmlich für den WW II-IV Paddler bieten sich hier 12 beschriebene Touren, der WW V Paddler wird lediglich auf der oberen Atna glücklich.

Im Norden der Hedmark liegt der Femundsee, Norwegens drittgrößtes Binnengewässer, östlich davon der Femundsmarka Nasjonalpark. Im Nordwesten der Hedmark liegt der Rondane Nasjonalpark. Beide Gebiete bieten eine wunderschöne Fjelllandschaft und eignen sich zudem vorzüglich zum Wandern. Das Kulturangebot in der Hedmark ist etwas dürftig, lohnend sind das Forst- und das Glomsdalsmuseum in Elverum.

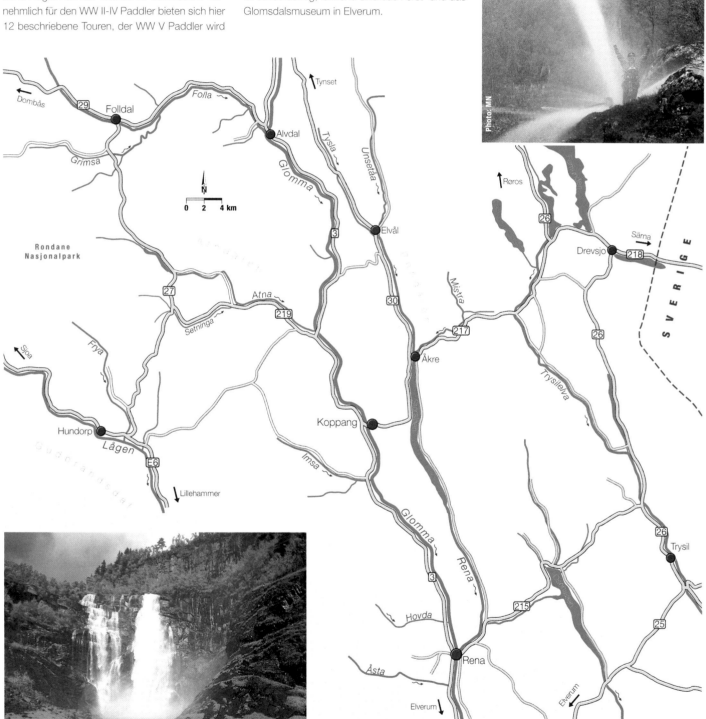

Photo: MN

Photo: MN

Info on the region
www.trysil.com
www.hedmark.com
www.femund.no

Mannis Wildwasserkurse und Kanutouren
Tel: +49/7681/1844, Fax: 490722
Email: kajakkurs4u@gmx.de

ÅSTA

BEAUTIFUL WHITEWATER WITH SHORT GORGES

The Åsta is the southern most river in the area. Newcomers have their first chance to check out the water situation at the road bridge of the E 3. If the Åsta is good to go, then you can reckon with good water for the whole Hedmark region.

The clear, red-brown moor water of the Åsta first offers several kilometres of open

CLASS: III+ (IV)
LEVEL: 20 - 40 cumecs
LENGTH: 11 km
TIME: 2 - 4 h
SEASON: May - July

rapids over gravel banks and through boulder gardens. Shortly after the river runs into a low gorge you reach the key rapid: a pushy rock slide which absolutely must be scouted beforehand. After another 2 kilometres the Åsta splits at the entrance of another gorge. On the left is a dangerous 2 metre drop with major pin potential, to the right is a simple rapid. After that it's WW II in a beautiful low gorge to the take out bridge.

Die Åsta ist der südlichste Bach des Reviers. Jeder Neuankömmling hat an der Straßenbrücke der E 3 zum ersten Mal die Chance, die Wassersituation zu beurteilen: Ist die Åsta gut fahrbar, kann man in der ganzen Hedmark mit Wasser rechnen.

Die Åsta fließt mit klarem, rotbraunem und warmem Moorwasser zuerst einige Kilometer über offene Geröllbankschwälle mit leichter Verblockung. Kurz nachdem der Fluss das erste Mal in eine Niederschlucht fließt, folgt die Schlüsselstelle: eine wuchtige Felsrutsche, die man sich unbedingt vorher ansehen sollte. Etwa 2 Kilometer später teilt sich die Åsta am Eingang einer weiteren Schlucht. Links lauert eine steckgefährliche 2-Meter-Stufe, rechts nur ein einfacher Schwall. Danach WW II+ in einer schönen Niederschlucht bis zur Ausbootbrücke.

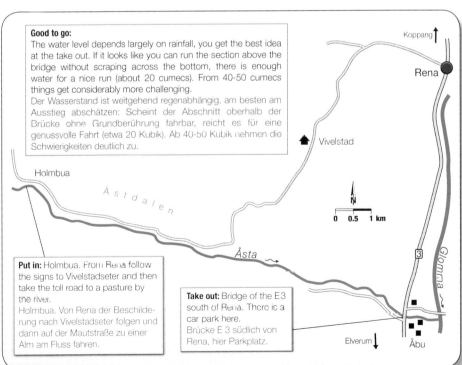

Good to go:
The water level depends largely on rainfall, you get the best idea at the take out. If it looks like you can run the section above the bridge without scraping across the bottom, there is enough water for a nice run (about 20 cumecs). From 40-50 cumecs things get considerably more challenging.
Der Wasserstand ist weitgehend regenabhängig, am besten am Ausstieg abschätzen: Scheint der Abschnitt oberhalb der Brücke ohne Grundberührung fahrbar, reicht es für eine genussvolle Fahrt (etwa 20 Kubik). Ab 40-50 Kubik nehmen die Schwierigkeiten deutlich zu.

Koppang

Rena

Vivelstad

Holmbua

Åstdalen

N

0   0.5   1 km

Åsta

Put in: Holmbua. From Rena follow the signs to Vivelstadseter and then take the toll road to a pasture by the river.
Holmbua. Von Rena der Beschilderung nach Vivelstadseter folgen und dann auf der Mautstraße zu einer Alm am Fluss fahren.

Take out: Bridge of the E3 south of Rena. There is a car park here.
Brücke E 3 südlich von Rena, hier Parkplatz.

Glomma

3

Elverum

Åbu

IMSA: UPPER

FROM THE LAKE TO THE WATERFALL

The Imsa flows through the gentle Imsdalen before it converges with the Glomma at Imsroa. The upper Imsa is much more *Norwegian* than the lower section, the individual sections here are much more distinctive. After the lake there follows an open highland valley, with whitewater of medium difficulty. Just as typically Norwegian is the take out: directly before unpaddleable waterfalls. The take out should be clearly determined before putting on, as the waterfalls begin somewhat unexpectedly. It is best to take out 200 metres upriver, where the road is nearby.

Tip: The Kvitkallen waterfalls may be paddleable at low water, WW V-VI, but then the section above definitely has too little water.

CLASS: III - IV
LEVEL: 10 cumecs
LENGTH: 5 km
TIME: 1 - 2 h
SEASON: May - June

Die Imsa durchfließt das ruhige Imsdalen bevor sie bei Imsroa in die Glomma mündet. Die obere Imsa ist viel *norwegischer* als die Untere, die Einzelstellen sind hier wesentlich ausgeprägter. Nach dem See folgt mittelschweres Wildwasser in einem offenen Hochtal. Genauso typisch norwegisch ist der Ausbootpunkt: direkt oberhalb von unfahrbaren Wasserfällen. Der Ausstieg sollte schon vorher festgelegt werden, da die Wasserfälle recht unvermutet beginnen. Am besten 200 Meter oberhalb aussteigen, wo die Straße in Flussnähe liegt.

Tipp: Die Kvitkallen-Wasserfälle sind bei Niedrigwasser eventuell fahrbar, WW V-VI, aber dann hat die Strecke oberhalb definitiv zu wenig Wasser.

IMSA: LOWER

A CONTINUOUS RUN THROUGH A WOODED GORGE

Of all the Hedmark rivers, the lower Imsa's character is most like that of a Central European river in the lower mountain ranges: fast and short of eddies, it races down a remote wooded gorge, whose trees have also been known to block the relatively narrow Imsa with nasty tree jams.

CLASS: III - IV
LEVEL: 10 - 30 cumecs
LENGTH: 9 km
TIME: 1 - 2 h
SEASON: May - early July

After the bridge at the put in the riverbed is initially fairly open, WW II-III. In the beautiful wooded gorge to follow things pick up pace considerably, running over steep boulder rapids, up to WW IV. Good eddies are very hard to come by here, a good reason to be particularly careful of tree jams.

About 500 metres before the Imsa meets the E 3 there is a dangerous weir in the township of Imsroa. It is not the towback, but the reinforcing iron which poses the danger here. It is best to end the trip before the weir.

Tip: Don't miss the take out!

Von allen Hedmarkflüssen hat die untere Imsa am ehesten den Charakter eines mitteleuropäischen Mittelgebirgsbaches: schnell und kehrwasserarm rauscht sie durch eine abgelegene Waldschlucht, deren Bäume auch einmal querliegend die relativ schmale Imsa blockieren können.

Ab der Einbootbrücke ist das Flussbett zunächst relativ offen, WW II-III. In der folgenden, sehr schönen Waldschlucht geht es dann wesentlich zügiger über steile Geröllschwälle bergab, bis WW IV. Gute Kehrwasser sind hier recht selten, gerade deshalb sollte auf Baumhindernisse geachtet werden.

Etwa 500 Meter bevor die Imsa auf die E 3 trifft, befindet sich noch im Ortsbereich von Imsroa ein gefährliches Wehr. Nicht der Rücklauf, sondern die herausragenden Armiereisen bilden hier die Gefahr. Die Fahrt sollte am besten vorher beendet werden.

Tipp: Nicht den Ausstieg verpassen!

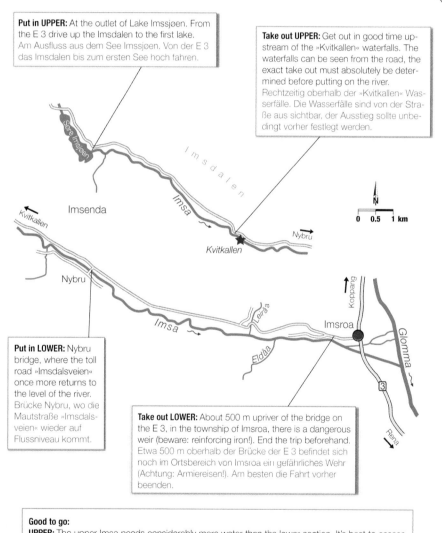

Put in UPPER: At the outlet of Lake Imssjøen. From the E 3 drive up the Imsdalen to the first lake.
Am Ausfluss aus dem See Imssjøen. Von der E 3 das Imsdalen bis zum ersten See hoch fahren.

Take out UPPER: Get out in good time upstream of the »Kvitkallen« waterfalls. The waterfalls can be seen from the road, the exact take out must absolutely be determined before putting on the river.
Rechtzeitig oberhalb der »Kvitkallen« Wasserfälle. Die Wasserfälle sind von der Straße aus sichtbar, der Ausstieg sollte unbedingt vorher festlegt werden.

Put in LOWER: Nybru bridge, where the toll road »Imsdalsveien« once more returns to the level of the river.
Brücke Nybru, wo die Mautstraße »Imsdalsveien« wieder auf Flussniveau kommt.

Take out LOWER: About 500 m upriver of the bridge on the E 3, in the township of Imsroa, there is a dangerous weir (beware: reinforcing iron!). End the trip beforehand.
Etwa 500 m oberhalb der Brücke der E 3 befindet sich noch im Ortsbereich von Imsroa ein gefährliches Wehr (Achtung: Armiereisen!). Am besten die Fahrt vorher beenden.

Good to go:
UPPER: The upper Imsa needs considerably more water than the lower section. It's best to assess the water level yourself from the toll road which follows the river. Further down at the E 3 there should be at least 20 cumecs coming down.
Die obere Imsa benötigt deutlich mehr Wasser als der untere Abschnitt, am besten schätzt man den Wasserstand von der begleitenden Mautstraße selbst ein. Unten an der E 3 sollten mindestens 20 Kubik ankommen.
LOWER: The Imsa runs somewhat more often than the Åsta. When the water level is sufficient for the flattened section at the bridge on the E 3, it is also sufficient for the rest of the section.
Die Imsa läuft etwas häufiger als die Åsta. Wenn der Wasserstand auf dem begradigten Abschnitt an der Brücke der E 3 gut ausreicht, reicht er auch für den Rest der Strecke.

ATNA: UPPER CANYON

A NARROW CANYON SECTION WITH MUST-RUN RAPIDS

The upper Atna gorge is the hidden WW V- highlight of Hedmark! The gorge is quite atypical of Norway, it reminds you more of a river in Ticino or Piemont. This section is described by intrepid paddlers as »a real treat«, you just mustn't be too alarmed by the must-run sections.

CLASS:	V (VI, X)
LEVEL:	8 km
LENGTH:	3 - 7 cumecs
TIME:	4 - 6 h
SEASON:	July - September

Straight after the put in is a short low gorge with beautiful WW IV over bedrock. After about 2 kilometres there is striking 90° bend to the left – it is vital to get off on the right here! Behind the next bend a siphon lies in wait. Carry up about 30 metres to the top of the gorge, then follow it along for another 250 metres.

A bit later you reach a difficult rapid. Scout and, if necessary, portage on the right, then follows the first real must-run rapid. A 15 metre long rock channel, with about 4 metres vertical drop. From the last eddy you have to guess the line, but it's very clear anyway.

About 1.5 kilometres before the end of the gorge waits another twisting double drop, WW V. Scout and, if necessary, portage on the right. After the end of the gorge you splash your way over the pebble beds for another 2-3 kilometres before you reach the take out on the right.

Tip: From the take out tramp to the exit of the gorge.

Die obere Atnaklamm ist der versteckte WW-V-Höhepunkt der Hedmark! Die Klamm ist recht untypisch für Norwegen, sie erinnert vielmehr an einen Fluss im Tessin oder Piemont. Dieser Abschnitt wird von nervenstarken Paddlern als Schmankerl beschrieben, man darf sich bloß nicht von den Zwangspassagen schocken lassen.

Gleich nach dem Einstieg folgt eine kurze Niederklamm, sie bietet sehr schönes WW IV über Grundgestein. Nach etwa 2 Kilometern folgt eine markante 90-Grad-Linkskurve, hier unbedingt rechts aussteigen. Hinter der nächsten Kurve lauert ein Siphon. Etwa 30 Meter zum Schluchtrand hoch tragen, dann 250 Meter entlang laufen.

Etwas später erreicht man einen schweren Katarakt, rechts besichtigen und gegebenenfalls umtragen, dann folgt die erste wirkliche Zwangspassage: eine 15 Meter lange Felsrinne mit etwa 4 Metern Höhenunterschied. Aus dem letzten Kehrwasser muss man die Route erahnen, aber die ist ohnehin recht eindeutig.

Etwa 1,5 Kilometer vor dem Ausgang der Klamm wartet noch eine verwinkelte Doppelstufe, WW V. Rechts besichtigen und gegebenenfalls umtragen. Nach dem Klammausgang kann man noch 2-3 Kilometer übers Kiesbett plätschern, bevor rechts der Ausstieg erreicht ist.

Tipp: Vom Ausstieg zum Klammausgang wandern.

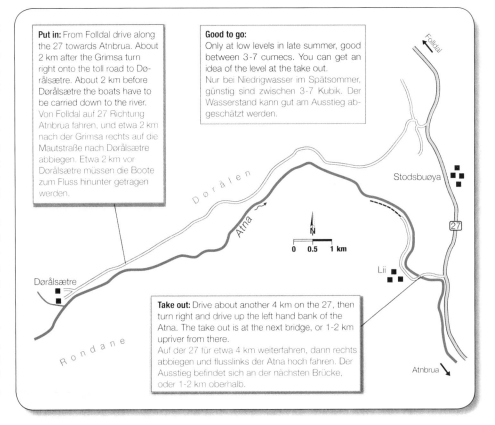

Put in: From Folldal drive along the 27 towards Atnbrua. About 2 km after the Grimsa turn right onto the toll road to Dørålsætre. About 2 km before Dørålsætre the boats have to be carried down to the river. Von Folldal auf 27 Richtung Atnbrua fahren, und etwa 2 km nach der Grimsa rechts auf die Mautstraße nach Dørålsætre abbiegen. Etwa 2 km vor Dørålsætre müssen die Boote zum Fluss hinunter getragen werden.

Good to go: Only at low levels in late summer, good between 3-7 cumecs. You can get an idea of the level at the take out. Nur bei Niedrigwasser im Spätsommer, günstig sind zwischen 3-7 Kubik. Der Wasserstand kann gut am Ausstieg abgeschätzt werden.

Take out: Drive about another 4 km on the 27, then turn right and drive up the left hand bank of the Atna. The take out is at the next bridge, or 1-2 km upriver from there. Auf der 27 für etwa 4 km weiterfahren, dann rechts abbiegen und flusslinks der Atna hoch fahren. Der Ausstieg befindet sich an der nächsten Brücke, oder 1-2 km oberhalb.

ATNA: MIDDLE

A LONG RUN WITH TWO VERY DIFFERENT PARTS

The middle Atna is divided into two completely different parts. For the first 7 kilometres it flows through a wide highland valley, varying between gentle swift water sections with easy rapids, bed rock slides and angled holes. Mostly WW II. About 3 kilometres after putting on you reach quite a high drop which you should look at before running. Depending on water level, up to WW IV. If necessary, there is an easy portage over the flat rocks on the right.

Half way down the section, after a road bridge, the forestry road following the river is closed. This is an alternative put in. The Atna now breaks through a moraine, and offers pushy boulder rapids up to WW IV. These gradually get easier, and are good to paddle on site. Shortly after the convergence of the Setninga you reach the take out.

Tip: For Foss collectors: the Atnafoss directly above the put in has already been paddled at low water.

Die mittlere Atna teilt sich in zwei völlig unterschiedliche Abschnitte. Auf den ersten 7 Kilometern fließt sie durch ein breites Hochtal, hier wechseln ruhige Fließstrecken mit leichten Schwällen und Grundgesteinsrutschen mit Schrägwalzen ab, meist WW II. Etwa 3 Kilometer nach dem Start folgt ein höherer Abfall, den man sich vor einer Befahrung ansehen sollte, je nach Wasserstand bis WW IV. Ein eventuelles Umtragen ist rechts über die Felsplatten ganz einfach.

Ab einer Straßenbrücke auf Hälfte der Strecke ist die begleitende Forststraße gesperrt, hier kann auch alternativ eingebootet werden. Die Atna durchbricht nun einen Moränenriegel und bietet wuchtige Geröllkatarakte bis WW IV, die allmählich leichter werden. Sie sind alle gut auf Sicht fahrbar.

Kurz nach der Mündung der Setninga erreicht man den Ausstieg.

Tipp: Für Fossensammler: der Atnafoss direkt oberhalb des Einstiegs wurde bei Niedrigwasser schon befahren.

CLASS: II - IV
LEVEL: 20 - 100 cumecs
LENGTH: 23 km
TIME: 4 - 6 h
SEASON: May - August

ATNA: LOWER

A CALM FAMILY SECTION WITH ONE EXCITING RAPID

This section is not exactly a classic, but for warming up, as a high water alternative, or simply to rest and recover between two difficult rivers – it's perfect. Moreover, there is the play spot at Fossum, where the Atna has carved an S-bend into a slab of bed rock (WW III). The holes here have surely robbed many a touring paddler of his equipment. This section is easy to reach from the road, and can be seen from the 27.

CLASS: I - II (III)
LEVEL: 20 - 100 cumecs
LENGTH: 26 km
TIME: 2 - 4 h
SEASON: May - early July

Tip: For those who enjoy floating down gentle rapids through the wide open landscape of Hedmark, it is possible to continue the trip for another 25 km down the Glomma to Koppang. Especially in early summer you can get a real sniff of the Canada feeling, you hardly notice the road following the river.

Diese Strecke ist nicht gerade ein Klassiker, aber zum Einpaddeln, als Ausweichziel bei Hochwasser oder zum Erholen zwischen zwei schweren Bächen eignet sie sich sehr gut. Außerdem gibt es ja noch die Spielstelle von Fossum, wo sich die Atna S-förmig durch einen Riegel aus Grundgestein gefressen hat (WW III). Deren Walzen haben sicher schon so manchen Wanderpaddler von seiner Ausrüstung getrennt. Diese Stelle ist von der Straße einfach erreichbar, sie ist von der 27 aus zu sehen.

Tipp: Wer Gefallen daran findet sich auf leichten Schwällen durch die Landschaft treiben zu lassen, kann die Fahrt noch 25 km auf der Glomma bis Koppang fortsetzen. Besonders im Frühsommer kann man echtes Kanadafeeling spüren, die begleitende Straße nimmt man kaum wahr.

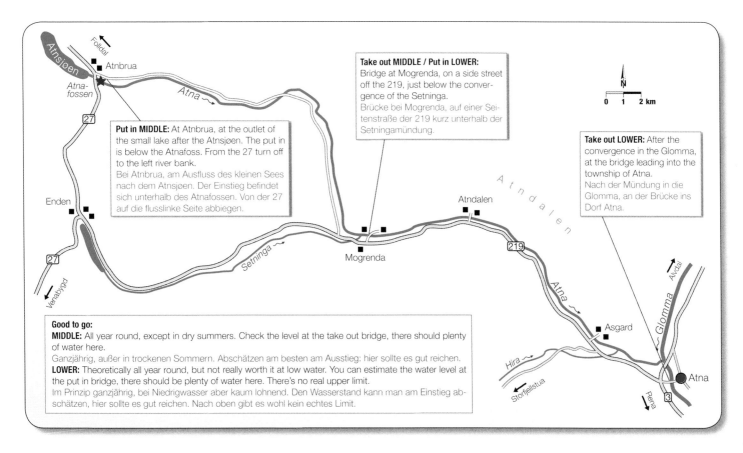

Take out MIDDLE / Put in LOWER:
Bridge at Mogrenda, on a side street off the 219, just below the convergence of the Setninga.
Brücke bei Mogrenda, auf einer Seitenstraße der 219 kurz unterhalb der Setningamündung.

Put in MIDDLE: At Atnbrua, at the outlet of the small lake after the Atnsjøen. The put in is below the Atnafoss. From the 27 turn off to the left river bank.
Bei Atnbrua, am Ausfluss des kleinen Sees nach dem Atnsjøen. Der Einstieg befindet sich unterhalb des Atnafossen. Von der 27 auf die flusslinke Seite abbiegen.

Take out LOWER: After the convergence in the Glomma, at the bridge leading into the township of Atna.
Nach der Mündung in die Glomma, an der Brücke ins Dorf Atna.

0 1 2 km

Good to go:
MIDDLE: All year round, except in dry summers. Check the level at the take out bridge, there should plenty of water here.
Ganzjährig, außer in trockenen Sommern. Abschätzen am besten am Ausstieg: hier sollte es gut reichen.
LOWER: Theoretically all year round, but not really worth it at low water. You can estimate the water level at the put in bridge, there should be plenty of water here. There's no real upper limit.
Im Prinzip ganzjährig, bei Niedrigwasser aber kaum lohnend. Den Wasserstand kann man am Einstieg abschätzen, hier sollte es gut reichen. Nach oben gibt es wohl kein echtes Limit.

SETNINGA

A WHITEWATER PEARL IN A DEEP AND REMOTE GORGE

The Setninga is undoubtedly one of the most beautiful Norwegian class fours you will find. Way below the road, it carries paddlers on crystal clear water over slides and drops through short low gorges.

Shortly after the release from the lake, the difficulties get up to WW III, hopefully you should be warmed up by the time you reach the first low gorges. The following gorge is the key section of the Setninga where many of the rapids and drops get up to WW IV. The line can usually be spotted from your boat, but you should take care, there can be tree jams hidden in the blind sections. Because of this, a trip at high water can be very dangerous. Scouting and portaging is possible everywhere, but is often very hard work, as is carrying out if you have to.

The last kilometres are then easier, before the Setninga kicks into gear again just before the bridge of the 27 (WW III-IV). Shortly after this, when you reach the Åtna, you're almost at the take out.

Tip: It may be worth checking out the upper section of the Setninga, above the lakes by the 27.

CLASS:	III - IV
LEVEL:	10 cumecs
LENGTH:	18 km
TIME:	4 - 6 h
SEASON:	May - July

Die Setninga ist sicherlich einer der schönsten Norwegen-Vierer überhaupt.

Weit unterhalb der Straße führt sie den Paddler auf glasklarem Wasser über kleine Rutschen und Stufen durch kurze Niederklammen.

Schon bald nach dem Ausfluss aus dem See steigert sich das Gefälle bis WW III. Bis die ersten Niederklammen zu sehen sind, hat man sich hoffentlich eingepaddelt. Denn in der folgenden

Schlucht, der Kernstelle der Setninga, erreichen viele Passagen den vierten Grad. Im Prinzip ist die Linle immer vom Boot aus zu erkennen, allerdings ist Vorsicht geboten, da Baumhindernisse an unübersichtlichen Stellen nicht auszuschließen sind. Dadurch kann eine Befahrung bei Hochwasser recht gefährlich werden. Besichtigen und Umtragen ist zwar überall möglich, aber zum Teil sehr mühsam, ebenso ein Fahrtabbruch.

Die letzten Kilometer sind dann wieder einfacher, bevor die Setninga kurz vor der Brücke der 27 noch einmal loslegt, hier WW III-IV. Erreicht man kurz danach die Atna, hat man auch bald den Ausstieg erreicht.

Tipp: Eventuell lohnt es sich, den Oberlauf der Setninga oberhalb der Seen an der 27 zu erkunden.

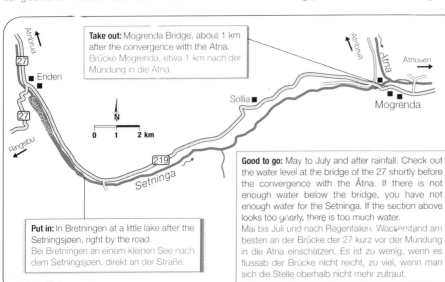

Take out: Mogrenda Bridge, about 1 km after the convergence with the Atna.
Brücke Mogrenda, etwa 1 km nach der Mündung in die Atna.

Good to go: May to July and after rainfall. Check out the water level at the bridge of the 27 shortly before the convergence with the Åtna. If there is not enough water below the bridge, you have not enough water for the Setninga. If the section above looks too gnarly, there is too much water.
Mai bis Juli und nach Regenfällen. Wasserstand am besten an der Brücke der 27 kurz vor der Mündung in die Atna einschätzen. Es ist zu wenig, wenn es flussab der Brücke nicht reicht, zu viel, wenn man sich die Stelle oberhalb nicht mehr zutraut.

Put in: In Bretningen at a little lake after the Setningsjøen, right by the road.
Bei Bretningen an einem kleinen See nach dem Setningsjøen, direkt an der Straße.

GRIMSA

Nina Wittig

Photos: SG

The Grimsa is a tributary to the Folla, and for us the lower section is the most interesting. It flows with easy whitewater and flatwater sections through a beautiful highland valley. The vegetation consists of moors and low bush, and occasionally reveals a glimpse of the mountains in the Rondane National Park.

The only cause for excitement is the double drop, which most paddlers portage. This you will find under the second bridge, about 5 kilometres from the start. After that the difficulties diminish, and you'll find countless little gravel bank sections.

CLASS:	**II (V)**
LEVEL:	**20 cumecs**
LENGTH:	**18 km**
TIME:	**2 - 4 h**
SEASON:	**May - September**

The actual take out is at the Folla bridge at Brimsbu, about 1.5 kilometres below the convergence with the Folla. Because the last kilometres are very flat, the wooden bridge at the end of the wooded valley offers a good alternative. Here, about 5 kilometres before the convergence, the Grimsa meets the Folla Valley.

Die Grimsa ist ein Nebenbach der Folla, für uns ist der untere Abschnitt interessant. Sie fließt mit leichtem Wildwasser und Zahmwasserabschnitten durch ein schönes Hochtal. Die Vegetation besteht aus Mooren und Niederwald und gibt gelegentlich den Blick auf die Berge des Rondane National-parks frei.

Der einzige Aufreger ist eine Doppelstufe, die jedoch meist umtragen wird. Sie befindet sich un-terhalb der zweiten Brücke, etwa 5 Kilometer nach dem Start. Danach lassen die Schwierigkeiten nach, es folgen unzählige Kiesbankschwälle.

Der eigentliche Ausstieg befindet sich an der Follabrücke bei Grimsbu, ungefähr 1,5 Kilometer unterhalb des Zusammenflusses mit der Folla. Da die letzten Kilometer sehr flach sind, bietet die Holzbrücke am Ende des Waldtales eine Alterna-tive. Hier, etwa 5 Kilometer vor der Mündung, trifft die Grimsa auf das Follatal.

Map labels:

N
0 0.5 1 km

Alvdal

Grimsbu

Take out: Folla bridge at Grimsbu, east of Folldal on the 29, about 1.5 km below the convergence.
Follabrücke bei Grimsbu an der 29 östlich von Folldal, ungefähr 1,5 km unterhalb der Mündung.

Geitberget

Folldal

Folldalen

29

Folla

Grimsmoen

Streitlii

27

Put in: Bridge on the 27, approximately 10 km south of Folldal.
Brücke der 27, etwa 10 km südlich von Folldal.

Grimsa

Good to go:
All year round, except in very dry summers. 20 cumecs at the put in is a good level.
Ganzjährig, außer in sehr trocke-nen Sommern. Günstig sind ge-schätzte 20 Kubik am Einstieg.

Atnbrua

FOLLA: WOODED GORGE

A BIG RIVER WITH SOME POWERFUL STOPPERS (AT HIGH WATER)

Over the length of its 80 kilometre course in the Glomma, the Folla offers mostly calm water. Only in the upper reaches in the lower section does it become more interesting for whitewater paddlers. In the lower section the Folla flows through a wooded gorge, the first third of which has several challenging rapids.

Especially at high flows, you should make good use of the first 1.5 kilometres to warm up. As soon as the road and a farmstead come into sight on the left, up on the hillside, take the first eddy you can on the right. Otherwise you can easily miss the line between the big stoppers bunched in the next 300 metres. This is the most difficult section of the Folla, at high flows WW IV. After that things get progressively easier, giving you time to enjoy the landscape.

CLASS: II - IV
LEVEL: 20 - 50 cumecs
LENGTH: 10 km
TIME: 3 - 4 h
SEASON: May - August

Die Folla bietet auf ihrer 80 Kilometer langen Reise zur Glomma zumeist Zahmwasser, lediglich im Oberlauf und im unteren Durchbruch ist sie für Wildwasserpaddler interessant. Auf dem beschriebenem unteren Abschnitt durchfließt die Folla eine Waldschlucht, die im ersten Drittel einige sportliche Katarakte bietet.

Gerade bei hohen Wasserständen sollte man die ersten 1,5 Kilometer ausgiebig zum Warmfahren nutzen und sofort rechts ein Kehrwasser nehmen, sobald links oben am Hang die Straße und ein Gehöft zu sehen sind. Ansonsten kann es leicht passieren, dass man die Linie zwischen den haltenden Walzen verpasst, die sich auf den nächsten 300 Metern häufen. Hier befindet sich die schwierigste Stelle der Folla, bei viel Wasser WW IV. Danach nehmen die Schwierigkeiten immer weiter ab, nun hat man Zeit die Natur zu genießen.

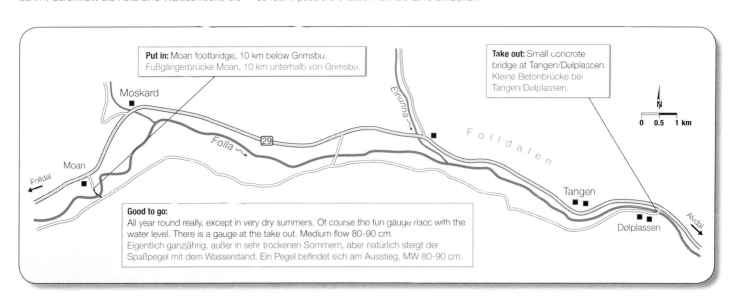

Put in: Moan footbridge, 10 km below Grimsbu.
Fußgängerbrücke Moan, 10 km unterhalb von Grimsbu.

Take out: Small concrete bridge at Tangen/Dølplassen.
Kleine Betonbrücke bei Tangen/Dølplassen.

Moskard

Einunna

Folla

29

Folldalen

0   0.5   1 km

Moan

Folldal

Tangen

Dølplassen

Alvdal

Good to go:
All year round really, except in very dry summers. Of course the fun gauge rises with the water level. There is a gauge at the take out. Medium flow 80-90 cm.
Eigentlich ganzjährig, außer in sehr trockenen Sommern, aber natürlich steigt der Spaßpegel mit dem Wasserstand. Ein Pegel befindet sich am Ausstieg, MW 80-90 cm.

Photos: ME

UNSETÅA

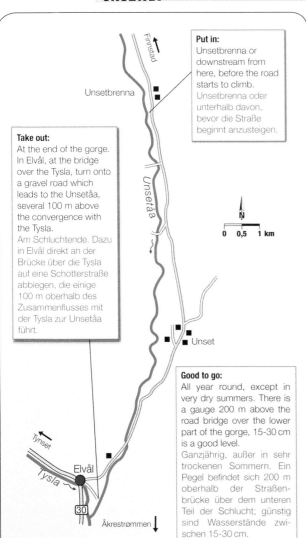

Put in:
Unsetbrenna or downstream from here, before the road starts to climb.
Unsetbrenna oder unterhalb davon, bevor die Straße beginnt anzusteigen.

Take out:
At the end of the gorge. In Elvål, at the bridge over the Tysla, turn onto a gravel road which leads to the Unsetåa, several 100 m above the convergence with the Tysla.
Am Schluchtende. Dazu in Elvål direkt an der Brücke über die Tysla auf eine Schotterstraße abbiegen, die einige 100 m oberhalb des Zusammenflusses mit der Tysla zur Unsetåa führt.

0   0,5   1 km

Good to go:
All year round, except in very dry summers. There is a gauge 200 m above the road bridge over the lower part of the gorge, 15-30 cm is a good level.
Ganzjährig, außer in sehr trockenen Sommern. Ein Pegel befindet sich 200 m oberhalb der Straßenbrücke über dem unteren Teil der Schlucht; günstig sind Wasserstände zwischen 15-30 cm.

The Unsetåa springs from the Finnstadsjøen, which is why it is called the Finnstadåa in its upper reaches. Or in other words, the Finnstadåa is called the Unsetåa in its lower section at Unset. Whatever the case may be, alongside the Tysla, it is the left and by far the bigger tributary to the Rena.

At the put in the water flows through pastures and meadows, where there is no sign of the pushy drops and rapids to come. But even these are fair and paddleable on sight, as long as it is not in flood. After each section there is a pool which offers enough time for rolls or rescues. The ravine never narrows to a deep gorge, so that scouting and portaging is possible everywhere, but can get to be quite hard work in some parts. If you should have to get off the river, you can always manage somehow to get back up to the road running high up above the left of the river.

The take out is about 1 kilometre after the bridge at the section by the first houses of Elvål. You can also get out at this bridge, but you miss running a few nice sections.

Tip: About 15 km above this section, after the release from the lake, the Finnstadåa thunders down several waterfalls. Worth checking out for waterfall fans!

CLASS: III - IV
LEVEL: 20 - 40 cumecs
LENGTH: 10 km
TIME: 2 - 4 h
SEASON: May - August

Die Unsetåa entspringt aus dem Finnstadsjøen und heißt deshalb in ihrem Oberlauf Finnstadåa. Oder anders gesagt: die Finnstadåa heißt in ihrem Unterlauf bei Unset Unsetåa. Wie dem auch sei, sie ist neben der Tysla der linke und deutlich größere Quellfluss der Rena.

Am Einstieg fließt sie durch Wiesen und Felder, noch deutet nichts auf die wuchtigen Stufen und Schwälle in der Schlucht hin. Aber auch die bleiben fair und auf Sicht fahrbar, wenn man nicht gerade Hochwasser hat. Nach jeder Stelle bietet ein Pool genügend Zeit zum Rollen oder Bergen. Die Felsschlucht verengt sich nirgends zur Klamm, sodass Besichtigen und Umtragen überall möglich bleibt, aber durchaus etwas mühsam werden kann. Bei einem eventuellen Fahrtabbruch bleibt die Straße, die links hoch über dem Fluss verläuft, immer irgendwie erreichbar.

Der Ausstieg ist etwa 1 Kilometer nach der Brücke an der Stelle bei den ersten Häusern von Elvål. Alternativ kann man auch schon direkt an der Brücke aussteigen, verpasst dann aber noch ein paar schöne Stellen.

Tipp: Etwa 15 km oberhalb der beschriebenen Strecke stürzt die Finnstadåa nach dem Seeausfluss über einige Wasserfälle. Erkundenswert für Wasserfallfans!

MISTRA: BIG GORGE

NICE BOULDER GARDENS IN A DEEP GORGE

Alongside the upper Atna, the Mistra is the most difficult river in Hedmark. After she has collected her cola coloured water in the headwaters of the highland moor, she thunders down a long, deep gorge to the valley of the Rena. The possibility of breaking off the run should not be seriously considered. It is vital to check the gauge first, and go to the rest area by the road about 4 kilometres above Åkrestrømmen. From here you see into gorge and get a look at one of the key rapids.

The first 5 kilometres are shallow and easy, WW II-III, you need a bit of water here. When the Renåa enters the Atna, not only the water volume increases, but also the level of difficulty. The river becomes more blocked, up to WW IV. After another 5 kilometres you can see the rest area by the 217, which signals the beginning of the actual gorge section.

CLASS: II - IV+ (V)
LEVEL: 10 - 20 cumecs
LENGTH: 19 km (10 km)
TIME: 3 - 6 h
SEASON: May - early August

Photo: GE

Die Mistra ist neben der oberen Atna der wohl schwerste Fluss der Hedmark. Nachdem sie in den Hochmoorregionen im Oberlauf ihr colafarbenes Wasser gesammelt hat, bricht sie in einer langen und tiefen Schlucht zum Tal der Rena durch. Einen Fahrtabbruch sollte man nicht ernsthaft in Erwägung ziehen. Unbedingt vorher den Pegel kontrollieren und einen Blick von einem großen Rastplatz an der Straße etwa 4 Kilometer oberhalb Åkrestrømmen in die Schlucht werfen, hier sieht man eine der Kernstellen.

Die ersten 5 Kilometer sind recht leicht und seicht, WW II-III, hier möchte man schon etwas Wasser haben. Ab der Mündung der Renåa steigt nicht nur die Wassermenge, auch die Schwierigkeiten klettern langsam nach oben. Es wird etwas verblockter, bis WW IV. Nach weiteren 5 Kilometern ist links oben der Rastplatz an der 217 sichtbar, hier beginnt die eigentliche Schluchtstrecke.

From a text by Manfred Eckert:
Edi experienced his own personal Mistra-disaster. His misfortune was the restless nature of the Queen: first a lengthy foreplay session, which he rashly used for some exhausting practice. Then the first highlight – and Edi was already in the drink. As he then made to retreat, Madame Mistra tempted him once more with some easy whitewater. And once she had him truly addicted with an inescapable gorge, she then pulled him to her breast. One roll after the other sucked the last energy reserves from poor Edmund. He begged for mercy, but in vain. Eventually the river dominatrix had had her full, and she showed pity, but Edi abstained the next day from a dance with the Crown Princess Setninga.

Aus einem Text von Manfred Eckert:
Edi erlebte sein ganz persönliches Mistra-De-saster. Sein Pech war der unstete Charakter der Königin: zuerst ein sehr langes Vorspiel, das er voreilig zum kräftezehrenden Üben nutzte. Dann ein erster Höhepunkt – und schon lag Edi im Bach. Als er daraufhin einen Rückzieher machen wollte, becircte ihn Madame Mistra wieder mit leichtem Wildwasser. Und erst als sie ihn mit einer ausweglosen Schlucht so richtig abhängig gemacht hatte, nahm sie sich Edi zur Brust. Eine Kenterung nach der anderen saugte auch die letzte Energie aus dem armen Edmund. Er flehte um Gnade, doch vergebens. Irgendwann hatte die Flussdomina zwar genug und erbarmte sich, Edi verzichtete am nächsten Tag trotz alledem auf die Kronprinzessin Setninga.

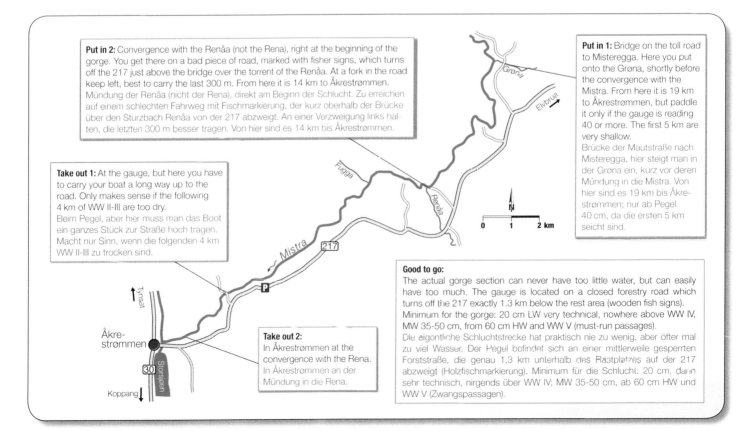

Put in 2: Convergence with the Renåa (not the Rena), right at the beginning of the gorge. You get there on a bad piece of road, marked with fisher signs, which turns off the 217 just above the bridge over the torrent of the Renåa. At a fork in the road keep left, best to carry the last 300 m. From here it is 14 km to Åkrestrømmen.
Mündung der Renåa (nicht der Rena), direkt am Beginn der Schlucht. Zu erreichen auf einem schlechten Fahrweg mit Fischmarkierung, der kurz oberhalb der Brücke über den Sturzbach Renåa von der 217 abzweigt. An einer Verzweigung links halten, die letzten 300 m besser tragen. Von hier sind es 14 km bis Åkrestrømmen.

Put in 1: Bridge on the toll road to Misteregga. Here you put onto the Grøna, shortly before the convergence with the Mistra. From here it is 19 km to Åkrestrømmen, but paddle it only if the gauge is reading 40 or more. The first 5 km are very shallow.
Brücke der Mautstraße nach Misteregga, hier steigt man in der Grøna ein, kurz vor deren Mündung in die Mistra. Von hier sind es 19 km bis Åkrestrømmen; nur ab Pegel 40 cm, da die ersten 5 km seicht sind.

Take out 1: At the gauge, but here you have to carry your boat a long way up to the road. Only makes sense if the following 4 km of WW II-III are too dry.
Beim Pegel, aber hier muss man das Boot ein ganzes Stück zur Straße hoch tragen. Macht nur Sinn, wenn die folgenden 4 km WW II-III zu trocken sind.

Take out 2:
In Åkrestrømmen at the convergence with the Rena.
In Åkrestrømmen an der Mündung in die Rena.

Good to go:
The actual gorge section can never have too little water, but can easily have too much. The gauge is located on a closed forestry road which turns off the 217 exactly 1.3 km below the rest area (wooden fish signs). Minimum for the gorge: 20 cm LW very technical, nowhere above WW IV, MW 35-50 cm, from 60 cm HW and WW V (must-run passages).
Die eigentliche Schluchtstrecke hat praktisch nie zu wenig, aber öfter mal zu viel Wasser. Der Pegel befindet sich an einer mittlerweile gesperrten Forststraße, die genau 1,3 km unterhalb des Rastplatzes auf der 217 abzweigt (Holzfischmarkierung). Minimum für die Schlucht: 20 cm, dann sehr technisch, nirgends über WW IV; MW 35-50 cm, ab 60 cm HW und WW V (Zwangspassagen).

Grøna
Elvbrua
Fugga
Renåa
Mistra
217
N
0 1 2 km
P
↑ Tynset
Åkre-strømmen
30
Storsjøen
Koppang ↓

TRYSILELVA: FEMUND RUN

A NICE RUN WITH BIG VOLUME IN SPRING

The Trysilelva's 500 kilometre long journey to the Swedish Lake Väner is more of a paradise for touring paddlers. The section which is of interest to whitewater paddlers is in the upper section, after the release from Lake Femund and various other small lakes. For the majority of its course, where it flows through Sweden, the Trysilelva is called the Klarälven. Just a note on the side: as is to be expected, the upper section of the Trysilelva is not in fact called the Trysilelva, but the Femundselva. Everything clear so far? Good, then let's go paddling!

CLASS:	**III+**
LEVEL:	**30 - 200 cumecs**
LENGTH:	**6 km**
TIME:	**2 - 3 h**
SEASON:	**May - August**

The Femund section is a short but classic big water trip on beautiful warm water. There are actually only four difficult sections, but each is very difficult to spot because of the high waves, and they also have the odd hole hidden up their sleeve. The most difficult section is the Elvbruafossen right before the take out. This can be easily scouted before putting on the river. In your first run on this section you never really feel all that comfortable, but the second time around everything gets better. Second run, twice the fun!

Tip: Hungry for more? »Glota« is a short 2.5 km section between Lake Femund and Lake Isteren, up to WW III+.

Der Trysilelva ist auf seiner fast 500 Kilometer langen Reise zum schwedischen Vänersee eher ein Paradies für Wanderpaddler. Der für Wildwasserpaddler interessante Teil befindet sich im Oberlauf, nach dem Ausfluss aus dem Femundsee sowie einigen kleineren Seen. Den größten Teil seiner Strecke, den der Trysilelva durch Schweden zurücklegt, wird er Klarälven genannt. Wie zu erwarten heißt der Trysilelva im Oberlauf Femundselva, aber das sei nur am Rande erwähnt. Alles klar? Gut, lasst uns paddeln gehen!

Der Femund-Abschnitt ist eine kurze, aber klassische Wuchtwassertour auf schönem warmem Wasser. Es gibt eigentlich nur vier schwierige Stellen, aber jede ist wegen der hohen Wellen unübersichtlich und hat noch dazu die eine oder andere versteckte Walze in petto. Die schwierigste Stelle ist der Elvbruafossen direkt vor dem Ausstieg, der sich schon vor dem Paddeln gut besichtigen lässt. Bei der ersten Fahrt fühlt man sich selten so richtig wohl, aber beim zweiten Mal wird alles besser: Second run, double fun!

Tipp: Mehr gefällig? »Gløta« ist eine 2,5 km kurze Wildwasserstrecke zwischen Femund- und Isterensee, bis WW III+.

Put in: About 2 km below Sølenstua, the road is right beside the river here.
Etwa 2 km unterhalb Sølenstua, die Straße ist hier direkt am Fluss.

Take out: Elvbrua, bridge on the 217.
Elvbrua, Brücke der 217.

Good to go: Actually all year round. For big water freaks: May and June provide the most water.
Eigentlich ganzjährig, für Wuchtwasserfans bei viel Wasser im Mai und Juni.

SJOA + CO

Daniel Herzig knows where he belongs - Sjoa playrun.

Sjoa - Daniel Herzig

SJOA

The paddling tradition of Norway is at its longest in the region of Oppland. This may be because this is a region which boasts countless whitewater gems between WW III-IV, but also possibly because of the WW V challenges which are hidden in between. We have split the Oppland region in two – into »Sjoa« and »Otta«. The Sjoa region will concern itself mostly with the Queen of the Norwegian whitewater rivers, the Sjoa, and her neighbouring subjects. However, rivers in the lower Gudbrandsdal, such as the Frya and the lower Lågen, shall also be granted our attention.

The Sjoa is THE classic in Norway. There are actually several classics, but only the Sjoa earns the title of »Super Classic Plus«. It offers almost 40 kilometres of concentrated paddling fun in the form of waves and holes, and quite simply is a must for any Norwegian holiday. Very close by you will find the waterfall classic Store Ula – or perhaps you would like to award the Veo a visit?

The Gudbrandsdålen is one of the highly populated main valleys in Norway, largely the result of cities like Lillehammer. Lillehammer hosted the 1994 winter Olympics, and has one of the most beautiful open air museums in Norway.

Oppland ist die Region Norwegens, in der die Paddeltradition am weitesten zurückreicht. Vielleicht, weil es sich hier um ein Gebiet handelt, das mit unzähligen Flussperlen zwischen WW III-IV auftrumpft, aber möglicherweise auch wegen der WW V Herausforderungen, die sich immer wieder dazwischen verstecken. Wir unterteilen die Region Oppland in »Sjoa« und »Otta«. Die Region Sjoa wird sich hauptsächlich mit der Königin der norwegischen Wildflüsse, der Sjoa, und den Flüssen in ihrer Umgebung beschäftigen. Aber auch den Flüssen im unteren Gudbrandsdal, wie der Frya und dem unteren Lågen, wird Aufmerksamkeit geschenkt.

Die Sjoa ist DER Klassiker in Norwegen. Es gibt ja einige Klassiker, aber nur der Sjoa gebührt das Prädikat »Oberklassiker«. Sie bietet fast 40 Kilometer geballten Paddelspaß in Form von Wellen und Walzen und gehört einfach zu jedem Norwegenurlaub. Ganz in der Nähe versteckt sich der Wasserfallklassiker Store Ula – oder vielleicht doch dem Veo einen Besuch abstatten?

Das Gudbrandsdålen ist eines der dicht besiedelten Haupttäler Norwegens, Städte wie Lillehammer tragen dazu bei. Lillehammer war 1994 Austragungsort der Winterolympiade und hat eines der schönsten Freilichtmuseen Norwegens.

SJOA FACTS

Character: Everything. From »open and pushy« to »steep and tight«.
Best time: You can always paddle here, but it is best in spring and summer. Many of the smaller creeks dry up in late summer, but you will always find an alternative.
Special remarks: Watch videos on the big screen at Strie Strømer.
Accommodation: Unofficial camp site on the Lågen down from the convergence of the Sjoa, in the Sjoa Elvepark, or in Sjoa directly on the Lågen or at the Hunderfossen dam.
Shops + kayak schools: • »Sjoa Kajakksenter« in Faukstad, Nedre Heidal, Phone: +47 900 66 222, www.kajakksenteret.no. Clinics and SRT 3 courses (Swiftwater Rescue Technician) .
• »Strie Strømmer Elvesport« in Bjølstadmo, Heidal, Phone: + 47 41 46 69, www.striestrommer.no. Strie Strømmer means something like »wild water« or »strong current«, and is just the right place to go for this very thing.

Charakter: Alles. Von »offen und wuchtig« bis »klein und steil«.
Beste Zeit: Paddeln kann man hier immer, allerdings am besten im Frühling und Sommer. Im Spätsommer trocknen einige Bächlein aus, es bleiben aber immer noch Alternativen.
Besonderheit: Bei Strie Strømer auf Leinwand Videos schauen.
Übernachtung: Wilder Campingplatz am Lågen unterhalb der Sjoamündung, am Sjoa Elvepark, am Campingplatz in Sjoa direkt am Lågen oder weiter unterhalb am Hunderfossen Staudamm.
Kajakschule + Shop: • »Sjoa Kajakksenter« in Faukstad, Nedre Heidal, Phone: +47 900 66 222, www.kajakksenteret.no, Kajakschule und SRT 3 Kurse (Swiftwater Rescue Technician).
• »Strie Strømmer Elvesport« in Bjølstadmo, Heidal, Phone: + 47 41 46 69, www.striestrommer.no. Strie Strømmer bedeutet so etwas wie »wildes Wasser« oder »starke Strömung«, und ist genau dafür der richtige Anlaufpunkt.

Flow phone / Pegeltelefon: (+47) 6123 4138

The good news is, there is a flow phone for the Sjoa. The bad news is, it is in Norwegian. For those of you able to speak Norwegian, the following table will be helpful:

Für die Sjoa gibt es ein Pegeltelefon, allerdings in Norwegisch. Wer der norwegischen Sprache mächtig ist, dem kann die folgende Tabelle helfen:

	Riddarspranget	Åsengjuvet	Playrun	Åmot
Low / Niedrig	< 351.15	< 351.15	< 351.15	< 351.00
High / Hoch	> 351.40	> 351.85	> 351.85	> 351.80

Kay-Arne from Strie Strømmer kayak shop

Rondane Nasjonalpark

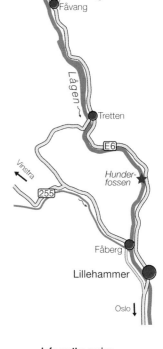

... and then I boofed that massive drop and ...

Info on the region
www.gudbrandsdalen.no
www.visitrondane.com

SJOA: STEINHOLET

OPEN AND RELAXED »SUNSHINE« WHITEWATER

The Sjoa is Norway's most popular river, and with good reason: 40 kilometres of crystal clear fun whitewater, spiked with dream waves and holes, and the odd challenge or two for the adrenalin junkies.

Steinholet is the upper most section, and also the easiest. Here the Sjoa meanders through an idyllic highland plain, the Murudalen. It is not the gradient of the river which is the centrepoint here, but rather the backdrop. This section is also recommended for beginners.

Tip: This run is perfect for beginners.

CLASS:	II - III
LEVEL:	15 - 50 cumecs
LENGTH:	6 km
TIME:	2 - 3 h
SEASON:	May - early August

Die Sjoa ist wohl der beliebteste Fluss Norwegens, und das zu Recht: Glasklares Spaßwildwasser auf 40 Kilometern, gespickt mit traumhaften Wellen und Walzen, und auch der ein oder anderen Herausforderung für Adrenalinjunkies.

Steinholet ist der oberste beschriebene Abschnitt, zudem der einfachste. Hier oben mäandert die Sjoa durch eine wunderschöne Hochebene, dem Murudalen. Nicht das Gefälle des Flusses steht hier im Mittelpunkt, sondern die Kulisse. Auch Anfängern ist dieser Abschnitt zu empfehlen.

Tipp: Dieser Abschnitt ist ideal für Anfänger.

Paddlerspranget:

Anything the knights can do, we can do too! It was exactly this thought which Olaf and Daniel had in mind as they dared the leap over the void before an awed crowd. Their initial elation at achieving the feat was soon replaced by a rather helpless grin at the sobering sight from the other side: the jump back is uphill! Correct! The jump back is considerably more difficult, particularly when it's slippery underfoot! Trapped, and with so many spectators! Luckily the lads had their life vests on, and were well equipped for the cold, wet trip home!

Was so ein Ritter kann, dass können wir auch! Genau diesen Gedankengang hatten Olaf und Daniel, als sie tollkühn vor breitem Publikum den Sprung über den Abgrund wagten. Ihre anfängliche Zufriedenheit über die vollbrachte Tat wurde schnell von einem ratlosen Grinsen abgelöst, der Blick zurück brachte Ernüchterung: Da geht es ja bergauf! Richtig, der Sprung zurück ist nämlich wesentlich schwieriger, vor allem bei glitschigem Boden. Gefangen – und das vor soviel Publikum! Glücklicherweise hatten die Jungs schon ihre Schwimmwesten an, um beim Rückweg dem kühlen Nass gewappnet zu sein.

Ridderspranget put in - Obsommer getting observed: What happens when they are sitting in a boat?

Herzig at the Ridderspranget waterfall. An interesting line.

SJOA: RIDDERSPRANGET

A FEW BIGGER RAPIDS WITH NICE WHITEWATER IN BETWEEN

According to legend, a knight once leapt over the Soja gorge directly above the put in, and so was able to escape his pursuers and save his beloved. The gorge is not very wide, at its narrowest a mere metre and a half across. Quite a warm up to our first section!

The gorge over which the daring knight jumped is in fact too pushy to paddle at normal flows, so its best to slide down the stone slab and into the torrent immediately below it. The slide which then follows immediately afterwards forms a strong towback at high flows, so have your throwbags at the ready!

After about 600 metres the water disappears at a horizon line – the Ridderspranget waterfall. It is best to put out on the right and take a look. The middle line is also paddled sometimes, scout from the left for this.

From here on make sure you do not paddle into anything blind: at the end of the next straight lies another waterfall in wait – do not miss the last eddy before it! The current flows very quickly into the first rapid, and just as quickly into the waterfall. Portage left or right!

The river flows on through a gorge which is a sporty challenge for the WW IV paddler, a treat for the WW V paddler. This gorge is very pushy, but fairly friendly as well. After several hundred metres the difficulties ease off somewhat, and the following kilometres offer heavenly waves and cataracts.

The next road bridge at the Nybrua Camp is a sign to be on your guard. You should end the tour here, unless you want to paddle the triple combo »Brurusti« which follows, WW V. After about another 300 metres the »Nedre Tråsåfossen« is announced by the power cables reaching over the river. Scout from the right, also WW V. The take out is 200 metres further downstream on the left.

| **CLASS:** III - IV (V, VII) |
| **LEVEL:** 15 - 40 cumecs |
| **LENGTH:** 10 km |
| **TIME:** 3 - 4 h |
| **SEASON:** May - August |

Tip: About 200 metres above the put in two waterfalls have been put there to haunt you. Surely runnable at the right flow.

Glaubt man der Sage, so sprang einst ein Ritter direkt oberhalb des Einstieges über die Sjoa-Klamm und konnte so seinen Verfolgern entkommen. Die Klamm ist hier nicht sehr breit, an seiner engsten Stelle nur eineinhalb Meter. Was für ein Auftakt zu unserer ersten Etappe.

Die Klamm, über die der tollkühne Ritter sprang um seine Liebste zu retten, ist bei normalem Wasserstand viel zu wuchtig für eine Befahrung, deshalb rutscht man besser erst dahinter über eine Platte direkt in die Fluten. Die sogleich folgende Rutsche bildet am Ausgang eine kräftige Walze – Wurfsäcke raus!

Nach ungefähr 600 Metern verschwindet das Wasser am Horizont, hier wartet der Ridderspranget-Wasserfall. Am besten rechts anlanden und besichtigen. Die mittlere Route wird auch gelegentlich gefahren, dafür von links besichtigen.

Von hier aus sollte man nicht weiter paddeln, als man schauen kann: Am Ende der folgenden Geraden lauert ein weiterer Wasserfall, vor dem man auf keinen Fall das letzte Kehrwasser verpassen sollte. Die Strömung zieht sehr schnell in den Eingangskatarakt, und genauso schnell in den folgenden Wasserfall. Links oder rechts umtragen!

Weiter geht es durch eine Schlucht, die sehr sportlich für den WW IV Paddler, aber ein Genuss für den WW V Paddler ist. Diese Schlucht ist zwar sehr wuchtig, aber trotzdem gutmütig. Nach einigen hundert Metern lassen die Schwierigkeiten nach, die folgenden Kilometer bieten herrliche Wellen und Katarakte.

Die nächste Straßenbrücke am Nybrua-Camp ist Zeichen zur Obacht. Hier sollte man die Fahrt beenden, will man die folgende Dreier-Kombination »Brurusti« nicht paddeln, WW V. Etwa 300 Meter danach wird der »Nedre Tråsåfossen« durch die Stromkabel über dem Fluss eingeleitet, rechts besichtigen, ebenfalls WW V. Nach weiteren 200 Metern folgt links der Ausstieg.

Tipp: Etwa 200 Meter oberhalb des Einstieges spuken noch zwei Wasserfälle, die beim richtigen Wasserstand sicherlich gehen.

Daniel Herzig on Ridderspranget section

»Brurusti« offers some fast technical lines.

Susanne Haug rocks Åsengjuvet

SJOA: ÅSENGJUVET

A NICE PLAYRUN IN AN AWESOME GORGE

The locals refer to the big gorge of the Sjoa as »Åsengjuvet«. Here the Sjoa digs itself deep into an amazing gorge, and nonetheless offers accessible whitewater. A feast for the eyes, and for the boat.

After an open, gentle warm up, the rapids get steadily more challenging as the Sjoa digs itself deeper into the ravine. Only in the middle is extreme caution required, and the section is difficult to recognize, coming after one of the uncountable right hand bends: in »The Gut« there have been several fatal accidents, particularly with rafting clients. At the end of this 300 metre long cataract there is a mean hole on the left which is almost impossible to escape without help. Stay hard right here.

The following bends now once more offer ample opportunity to play. You can succumb to the temptations of the wet and wild without fear of disaster, until the gorge suddenly opens up, and you are sadly at the end already.

Tip: At high water the Åsengjuvet is like the Zambezi without pools. The good thing about it: (almost) all the holes flush you out.

CLASS:	III - IV
LEVEL:	30 - 80 cumecs
LENGTH:	14 km
TIME:	3 - 5 h
SEASON:	May - August

Die Große Schlucht der Sjoa wird bei den Einheimischen »Åsengjuvet« genannt. Die Sjoa gräbt sich hier tief in diese wunderschöne Schlucht, und bietet trotzdem gut zugängliches Wildwasser. Ein Genuss für Auge und Boot.

Nach einem offenen, recht ruhigem Warm up werden die Stromschnellen immer anspruchsvoller, die Sjoa gräbt sich nun langsam in die Schlucht ein. Erhöhte Vorsicht ist lediglich in etwa der Mitte der Schlucht geboten, diese Stelle ist schwer zu erkennen und befindet sich nach einer der unzähligen Rechtskurven: Bei »The Gut« (WW IV) ereigneten sich schon einige tödliche Unfälle, insbesondere mit Raftingkunden. Am Ende dieses etwa 300 Meter langen Kataraktes lauert links ein gemeines Loch, welches ohne fremde Hilfe beinah nicht zu verlassen ist. Hier ganz rechts halten.

Die folgenden Kurven laden erneut zum Spielen ein, von nun an kann man unbeschwert dem rauschenden Nass verfallen. Bis die Schlucht plötzlich wieder aufmacht und man leider schon bald den Ausstieg erreicht.

Tipp: Bei Hochwasser ist Åsengjuvet wie der Sambesi ohne Pools. Das Gute dabei: (fast) alle Walzen spülen durch.

Watch out for »The Gut«

Photo: MN

SJOA: PLAYRUN   AN AWESOME PLAYRUN IN A VERY NICE GORGE

For the playrun the following rule applies: the more water the better! The surf waves then pop up like mushrooms out of the ground, and they sooner or later have you giving up before they do, simply out of a lack of fitness. That's why there is not really too much to say about this section – whether you're into surfing waves is a matter of personal preference. For the beginner the lengthy wave trains may seem a bit full on, but there are hardly any holes which have to be avoided.

Shortly before the end of this awesome gorge section a massive steel bridge reaches over the river, above which you will find the Faukstad wave. This is the scene of the Sjoa rodeo, and at the right water level, this wave is everyone's favourite. Shortly afterwards the right bank flattens out. There is a small drop here which forms a powerful hole on the right at high flows. The take out is about a hundred metres below this on the left.

CLASS: III - IV-
LEVEL: 30 - 100 cumecs
LENGTH: 6 km
TIME: 2 - 3 h
SEASON: May - August

Für den Playrun gilt: je mehr Wasser, desto geiler. Dann sprießen die Surfwellen wie Pilze aus dem Boden und lassen dich irgendwann aus Konditionsgründen vor ihnen kapitulieren. Deshalb gibt es zu diesem Abschnitt auch nicht viel zu sagen – die Wellen zu reiten, ist jedem seine Sache. Anfängern können die lang gezogenen Wellenzüge mächtig erscheinen, jedoch gibt es kaum Walzen, die es zu meiden gilt.

Kurz vor Ende der großartigen Schluchtstrecke posiert hoch über dem Fluss eine massive Stahlbrücke, etwas oberhalb befindet sich die Faukstad-Welle. Diese ist Schauplatz des Sjoa-Rodeos, und beim richtigen Wasserstand jedermanns Liebling. Kurz danach flacht das Ufer rechtsufrig ab. Dort befindet sich eine kleine Stufe, die bei hohem Wasserstand rechts eine kräftige Walze bildet. Etwa 100 Meter unterhalb erreicht man links den Ausstieg.

Tip: If you still haven't had enough you can paddle the following 4 km to the slalom section of the Sjoa Elvepark, WW II (III+).

Tipp: Wer noch nicht genug hat, kann noch die folgenden 4 km zur Slalomstrecke des »Sjoa Elveparks« weiterfahren, WW II (III+).

Herzig riding one of the waves on the playrun

✳ SJOA: ÅMOT

The lower section into the Lågen is known to the Norwegians as the Åmot. It offers fantastic whitewater, and used to be known as a WW V classic. Today it is paddled by those in the know in playboats, and even calling it a V- is almost a bit over the top.

Right after the put in the Sjoa winds through a short gorge. After the first left bend waits a hole, best to stay on the inside of the bend,

CLASS: IV - V-
LEVEL: 15 - 40 cumecs
LENGTH: 2 km
TIME: 1 - 2 h
SEASON: May - September

WW IV. After another 100 metres through a pushy gorge the slalom section starts, WW III+. The Junior World Championships were once held here, and since then the grounds have been managed by local paddlers, and used as a camping ground for paddlers. The slalom course is just as all slalom courses should be: wide, pushy, fast, and situated in idyllic surrounds.

About 600 metres after the wooden bridge at the end of the slalom section there is an S-bend

with an undercut at the exit. This is the beginning of the actual Åmot section. The gradient increases in a long cataract up to the next road bridge. After a few quiet metres there are two more sections, and before you know it you are out of the gorge. As soon as you see an island, the take out is on the left at a small wooden hut.

Tip: You can also paddle the next 2 km to the Lågen free-camping area and hope that the wave just downstream is going off!

Der untere Durchbruch in den Lågen wird von den Norwegern als Åmot bezeichnet. Er bietet wunderschönes Wildwasser und galt damals als WW V Klassiker. Heute wird er von Kennern auch gern im Spielboot befahren, ihn als WW V- zu bezeichnen ist schon fast etwas hoch gegriffen.

Gleich nach dem Einstieg windet sich die Sjoa durch eine kurze Schlucht. Nach der ersten Linkskurve wartet eine Walze, besser in der Innenkurve bleiben, WW IV. Nach weiteren 100 Metern durch eine wuchtige Klamm beginnt die Slalomstrecke, WW III+. Hier wurden schon die Junioren-Welt-

meisterschaften ausgetragen. Seitdem wird das Gelände von einheimischen Paddlern verwaltet und als Campingplatz für Paddler genutzt. Der Slalomparcours ist so, wie alle Slalomstrecken sein sollten: breit, wuchtig, schnell und in herrlicher Umgebung.

Etwa 600 Meter nach der Holzbrücke am Ende der Slalomstrecke folgt eine S-Kurve mit Unterspülung am Ausgang. Dies ist der Anfang des eigentlichen Åmot-Durchbruches. Das Gefälle nimmt in einem langen Katarakt bis zur nächsten

Straßenbrücke weiter zu. Nach einigen ruhigen Metern folgen zwei weitere Stellen, doch ehe man sich versieht, ist man schon wieder raus aus der Klamm. Sobald man eine Insel erspäht, liegt der Ausstieg auf der linken Seite bei einem kleinen Holzschuppen.

Tipp: Man kann noch die 2 km bis zum Lågen-Wildcamp weiterpaddeln und hoffen, dass die Welle kurz nach dem Zusammenfluss gut steht.

God bless the Norwegians!

In the Year of our Lord 2003 we had the opportunity to paddle »Åmot« with the two local matadors Flemming Schmidt and Morten Eilertsen. Had we been alone, the estimated 350 cumecs would have kept us off the river, but with such capable guides, who could say no? Lined up like lemmings, we followed Flemming, who neglected to mention that it had never been paddled at this flow until we were all in our boats with our spray decks on. His last piece of advice: »stay in the middle, and best not to take any eddies.« 10 minutes later, with an abnormally high adrenalin level pumping through our veins, we were kissing first solid ground once more, then Flemming's feet. God bless the Norwegians!

Gott hab sie selig, die Norweger!

Im Jahre 2003 hatten wir die Gelegenheit mit den Lokalmatadoren Flemming Schmidt und Morten Eilertsen »Åmot« zu paddeln. Geschätzte 350 Kubik hätten uns allein wohl abgehalten, aber bei so adäquaten Führern – wer kann da nein sagen? Aufgereiht wie die Lemminge folgten wir also Flemming, der uns erst nach dem Schließen unserer Spritzdecken verriet, Åmot bei soviel Wasser noch nie gefahren zu sein. Sein letzter Rat: »Immer mittig bleiben und besser keine Kehrwasser fahren«. Mit einem überdurchschnittlich hohen Anteil Adrenalin im Körper küssten wir 10 Minuten später am Ausstieg zuerst den Boden, dann Flemmings Füße. Gott hab sie selig, die Norweger!

Herzig and Obsommer enjoying the normal flow

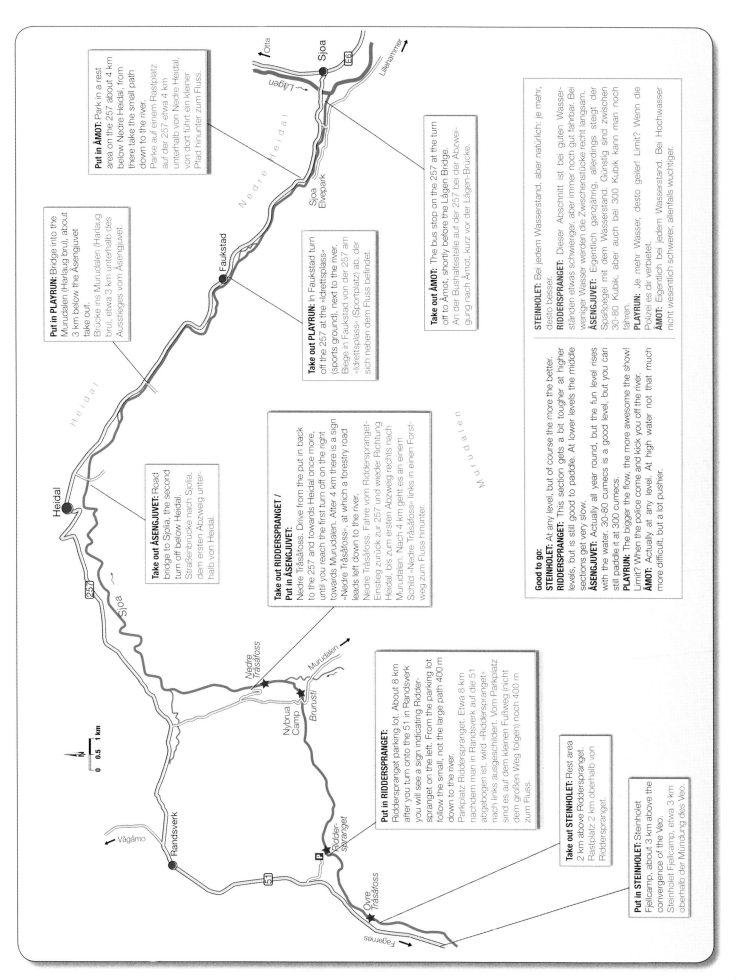

Put in ÅMOT: Park in a rest area on the 257 about 4 km below Nedre Heidal, from there take the small path down to the river.

Parke auf einem Rastplatz auf der 257 etwa 4 km unterhalb von Nedre Heidal, von dort führt ein kleiner Pfad hinunter zum Fluss.

Put in PLAYRUN: Bridge into the Murudalen (Harlaug bru), about 3 km below the Åsengjuvet take out.

Brücke ins Murudalen (Harlaug bru), etwa 3 km unterhalb des Ausstieges vom Åsengjuvet.

Take out PLAYRUN: In Faukstad turn off the 257 at the »Idrettsplass« (sports ground), next to the river. Biege in Faukstad auf die 257 »Idrettsplass« (Sportplatz) ab, der sich neben dem Fluss befindet.

Take out ÅMOT: The bus stop on the 257 at the turn off to Åmot, shortly before the Lågen Bridge.
An der Bushaltestelle auf der 257 bei der Abzweigung nach Åmot, kurz vor der Lågen-Brücke.

Take out ÅSENGJUVET: Road bridge to Sjolia, the second turn off below Heidal.
Straßenbrücke nach Sjolia, dem ersten Abzweig unterhalb von Heidal.

Take out RIDDERSPRANGET / Put in ÅSENGJUVET:
Nedre Tråsåfoss. Drive from the put in back to the 257 and towards Heidal once more, until you reach the first turn off on the right towards Murudalen. After 4 km there is a sign »Nedre Tråsåfoss«, at which a forestry road leads left down to the river.
Nedre Tråsåfoss. Fahre vom Riddderspranget-Einstieg zurück zur 257 und wieder Richtung Heidal, bis zum ersten Abzweig rechts nach Murudalen. Nach 4 km geht es an einem Schild »Nedre Tråsåfoss« links in einen Forstweg zum Fluss hinunter.

Put in RIDDERSPRANGET:
Ridderspranget parking lot. About 8 km after you turn onto the 51 in Randsverk you will see a sign indicating Ridderspranget on the left. From the parking lot follow the small, not the large path 400 m down to the river.
Parkplatz Ridderspranget. Etwa 8 km nachdem man in Randsverk auf die 51 abgebogen ist, wird »Ridderspranget« nach links ausgeschildert. Vom Parkplatz sind es auf dem kleinen Fußweg (nicht dem großen Weg folgen) noch 400 m zum Fluss.

Take out STEINHOLET: Rest area 2 km above Ridderspranget.
Rastplatz 2 km oberhalb von Ridderspranget.

Put in STEINHOLET: Steinholet Fjellcamp, about 3 km above the convergence of the Veo.
Steinholet Fjellcamp, etwa 3 km oberhalb der Mündung des Veo.

Good to go:
STEINHOLET: At any level, but of course the more the better.
RIDDERSPRANGET: This section gets a bit tougher at higher levels, but is still good to paddle. At lower levels the middle sections get very slow.
ÅSENGJUVET: Actually all year round, but the fun level rises with the water. 30-80 cumecs is a good level, but you can still paddle it at 300 cumecs.
PLAYRUN: The bigger the flow, the more awesome the show! Limit? When the police come and kick you off the river.
ÅMOT: Actually at any level. At high water not that much more difficult, but a lot pushier.

STEINHOLET: Bei jedem Wasserstand, aber natürlich: je mehr, desto besser.
RIDDERSPRANGET: Dieser Abschnitt ist bei guten Wasserständen etwas schwieriger, aber immer noch gut fahrbar. Bei weniger Wasser werden die Zwischenstücke recht langsam.
ÅSENGJUVET: Eigentlich ganzjährig, allerdings steigt der Spaßpegel mit dem Wasserstand. Günstig sind zwischen 30-80 Kubik, aber auch bei 300 Kubik kann man noch fahren.
PLAYRUN: Je mehr Wasser, desto geiler! Limit? Wenn die Polizei es dir verbietet.
ÅMOT: Eigentlich bei jedem Wasserstand. Bei Hochwasser nicht wesentlich schwerer, allenfalls wuchtiger.

LÅGEN: ROSTEN

A CLASSIC RUN

The Lågen in the Gudbrandsdal should not be confused with the Numedalslågen, even though they are of a similar size. For the most part it flows as a touring river, but does come up with short whitewater sections now and then. It is the biggest river feeding Lake Mjøsa, so even at this altitude it already has a respectable volume of water, thus Rosten can

CLASS: IV (V, VI/X)
LEVEL: 10 - 30 cumecs
LENGTH: 4 km
TIME: 2 - 3 h
SEASON: May - September

Der Lågen im Gud-brandsdal sollte nicht mit dem Numedalslågen im Süden verwechselt werden, auch wenn seine Größe ähnlich ist. Er fließt größtenteils als Wanderfluss dahin, wartet doch immer wieder mit kurzen Wildwasserstrecken auf. Als größter Zufluss des Mjøsa-Sees führt er auch hier oben schon eine respektable Wassermenge, so kann Rosten auch noch im Hochsommer gepaddelt werden.

still be paddled in high summer.

To begin with, the Lågen gets straight down to business and blasts through a racey blocked section which can be seen from the road. If the first metres are too much for you, don't bother paddling on. Afterwards the Lågen digs its way slowly into a small gorge, always close to the road, yet in difficult terrain. The highlight is a combination which should be scouted from the left bank, and is very difficult to portage. Here an athletic cataract

Gleich zu Beginn bläst der Lågen durch eine rassige Blockstrecke, die von der Straße einsehbar ist. Sind die ersten Meter zu viel für dich, fahre gar nicht erst weiter. Danach gräbt sich der Lågen langsam in eine kleine Schlucht, immer unmittelbar in der Nähe der Straße, jedoch teils in unwegsamen Gelände. Der Höhepunkt ist eine Kombination, die man sich vom linken Flussufer anschauen sollte, sie ist recht schwer zu umtragen. Hier bricht ein sportlicher Katarakt zu Tale, unmittelbar gefolgt

crashes down the valley, immediately followed by a waterfall with a strong towback.

After the cliffs have closed in on you in a rather threatening manner, things generally get easier. However, when you see a giant boulder on the right side, it is time to be on guard once more.

Tip: If the first 200 metres are too much for you, don't bother paddling on!

von einem rückläufigen Wasserfall.

Nachdem die Felswände bedrohlich näher gerückt sind, wird es im Allgemeinen leichter. Erspäht man allerdings einen riesigen Felsblock auf der rechten Seite, ist noch einmal Vorsicht geboten.

Tipp: Sind die ersten 200 Meter zu viel für dich, fahre gar nicht erst weiter!

Runnable at low water...

... but definetly worth a portage at higher levels

Photos: KD

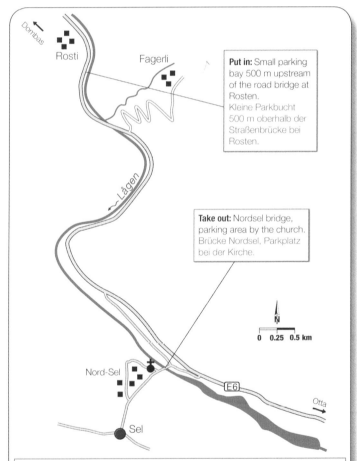

Put in: Small parking bay 500 m upstream of the road bridge at Rosten.
Kleine Parkbucht 500 m oberhalb der Straßenbrücke bei Rosten.

Take out: Nordsel bridge, parking area by the church.
Brücke Nordsel, Parkplatz bei der Kirche.

0   0.25   0.5 km

Good to go:
Rosten is also good to paddle with high water (25 cumecs and up), that's actually when the fun really starts. However, things do get more challenging then, and you should know where you have to go. Thanks to the flow from the Lågen you can still paddle here in high summer, however then only at moderate flow. You can get a good idea of the flow in the first 200 m after the put in.
Rosten geht auch bei viel Wasser (ab 25 Kubik), eigentlich macht es dann erst richtig Spaß. Allerdings wird es etwas anspruchsvoller und man sollte wissen, wo man wann hin muss. Dank der Wasserführung des Lågen kann man hier auch noch im Hochsommer paddeln, dann allerdings bei moderatem Wasserstand. Den Wasserstand kann man gut auf den ersten 200 m nach dem Einstieg abschätzen.

LÅGEN: HUNDERFOSS

A LOT OF WATER IN AN OPEN RIVERBED

On its long journey to Glomma, the Lågen here once more offers the whitewater paddler a chance to feel its power. Before it reaches Lake Mjøsa in Fåberg, waves and holes wait for big water fans, as long as the overflow from the dam is dishing out enough juice.

You only really need to be careful half way down the section: here the river makes a dog leg to the right, on the left a cliff face rises up. In the outside of the bend a serious hole lies growling at you, on the inside a boulder. Best to scout from the right beforehand. At high water you can also sneak down the right.

CLASS:	**III - IV**
LEVEL:	**50 - 500 cumecs**
LENGTH:	**6 km**
TIME:	**1 - 2 h**
SEASON:	**May - July**

Der Lågen bietet hier auf seiner langen Reise zur Glomma dem Wildwasserpaddler noch einmal Gelegenheit, seine Kraft zu spüren. Bevor er den Mjøsa-See in Fåberg erreicht, warten Wellen und Walzen auf Wuchtwasserfans, vorausgesetzt der Überlauf des Staudammes gibt ordentlich Wasser frei.

Vorsicht sei lediglich auf etwa der Hälfte der Strecke geboten: Hier knickt der Lågen nach rechts weg, links erhebt sich eine Felswand. In der Außenkurve brüllt eine ordentliche Walze, in der Innenkurve ein Felsblock, am besten vorher von rechts besichtigen. Bei viel Wasser kann man auch rechts sneaken.

Tip: The more water the better.
Tipp: Je mehr Wasser, desto besser.

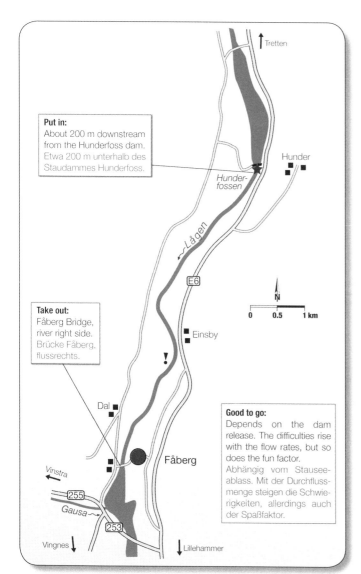

↑ Tretten

Put in:
About 200 m downstream from the Hunderfoss dam.
Etwa 200 m unterhalb des Staudammes Hunderfoss.

Hunder

Hunder-
fossen

Lågen

E6

N
0   0.5   1 km

Take out:
Fåberg Bridge, river right side.
Brücke Fåberg, flussrechts.

■ Einsby

!

Dal ■

Fåberg

Good to go:
Depends on the dam release. The difficulties rise with the flow rates, but so does the fun factor.
Abhängig vom Stauseeablass. Mit der Durchflussmenge steigen die Schwierigkeiten, allerdings auch der Spaßfaktor.

← Vinstra

255

Gausa

253

Vingnes ↓   ↓ Lillehammer

FRYA: GORGE

The Frya is fed by the Furusjøen and flows into the Lågen north of Ringebu. It flows through sometimes deep gorge sections, and even holds a (fair) must-run section in stall. Nonetheless, 98 percent of it can be run on sight. But beware: tree jams are a constant danger here.

Right at the put in by the old mill the Frya plays a trump in the form of a waterfall. This is paddleable, but has shallow water below. After that you have the chance to warm up on WW III water before entering the first canyon. The second canyon, which follows shortly afterwards, narrows down to a width of 2 metres in some parts. After that the difficulties range between WW III and IV. At the end of the third canyon there is a difficult right hand bend to paddle, with poor line of sight, WW IV+. It is best to hit it out to the left, and keep cool, there is a pool for swimming practice at the bottom.

At the weir before the unpaddleable gorge you have reached your destination. Take out on the right and carry 300 metres over the bridge to the small parking bay.

CLASS: IV (V-)
LEVEL: 10 - 15 cumecs
LENGTH: 15 km
TIME: 3 - 6 h
SEASON: late May - July

Die Frya wird vom Furusjøen gespeist und mündet nördlich von Ringebu in den Lågen. Sie durchfließt teilweise tiefe Schluchtstrecken und wartet sogar mit einer (fairen) Zwangspassage auf. Doch zu 98 Prozent geht alles auf Sicht, aber Vorsicht: Mit Baumhindernissen ist stets zu rechnen.

Gleich am Einstieg bei der alten Mühle trumpft die Frya mit einem Wasserfall auf, der zwar fahrbar ist, jedoch mit flachem Unterwasser auflauert. Danach hat man Gelegenheit, sich auf WW III warm zu fahren, bevor es in die erste Klamm geht. Die wenig später folgende zweite Klamm verengt sich bis auf 2 Meter. Die Schwierigkeiten schwanken im weiteren Verlauf zwischen WW III und IV. Am Ende der dritten Klamm muss eine schwierige Rechtskurve befahren werden, die nur schlecht eingesehen werden kann, WW IV+. Am besten nach links rausfahren und immer schön locker bleiben, ein Pool für Schwimmübungen folgt.

Am Wehr vor der unfahrbaren Klamm hat man sein Etappenziel erreicht. Rechts aussteigen und über die Brücke 300 Meter zur kleinen Parkbucht tragen.

Tip: Don't miss the take out!
Tipp: Nicht den Ausstieg verpassen!

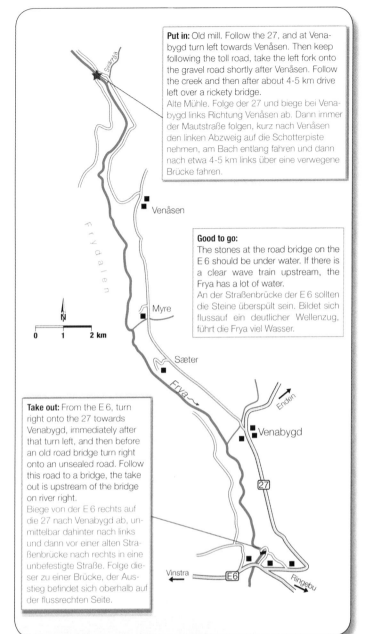

Put in: Old mill. Follow the 27, and at Venabygd turn left towards Venåsen. Then keep following the toll road, take the left fork onto the gravel road shortly after Venåsen. Follow the creek and then after about 4-5 km drive left over a rickety bridge.
Alte Mühle. Folge der 27 und biege bei Venabygd links Richtung Venåsen ab. Dann immer der Mautstraße folgen, kurz nach Venåsen den linken Abzweig auf die Schotterpiste nehmen, am Bach entlang fahren und dann nach etwa 4-5 km links über eine verwegene Brücke fahren.

Good to go:
The stones at the road bridge on the E 6 should be under water. If there is a clear wave train upstream, the Frya has a lot of water.
An der Straßenbrücke der E 6 sollten die Steine überspült sein. Bildet sich flussauf ein deutlicher Wellenzug, führt die Frya viel Wasser.

Take out: From the E 6, turn right onto the 27 towards Venabygd, immediately after that turn left, and then before an old road bridge turn right onto an unsealed road. Follow this road to a bridge, the take out is upstream of the bridge on river right.
Biege von der E 6 rechts auf die 27 nach Venabygd ab, unmittelbar dahinter nach links und dann vor einer alten Straßenbrücke nach rechts in eine unbefestigte Straße. Folge dieser zu einer Brücke, der Ausstieg befindet sich oberhalb auf der flussrechten Seite.

Photo: MN

VEO

The Veo flows far from the road through the Jotunheimen National Park. The water from Veobreen is diverted far up the valley, so a run is usually only possible in spring or after rainfall. Several drops are not that clean, nonetheless the Veo is a little treat.

At the very latest at the put in you will realize that Norwegian creeks can have rather extensive banks. As insignificant as the dis-tance from road to riverbed may seem, it still takes you half an hour to get down to it. And then follows – assuming you have a medium flow – a

CLASS: IV - V (VI, X)
LEVEL: 8 - 15 cumecs
LENGTH: 11 km
TIME: 4 - 6 h
SEASON: May - June

fairly slow start, which drags on for 2-3 kilometres, depending on which put in you choose.

The entrance to the gorge brings the hard labour to an end with pushy cataracts, and for a good 3 kilometres the Veo provides great whitewater with nice drops and tricky passages, around WW IV (V). The following short canyon is easy to portage around.

In the next 1.5 kilometres a series of cataracts, slides and recirculating drops line up one after another, forming the most difficult section of the Veo (WW V+). Here scouting is often necessary. The last part comes to a spectacular end with a tight and twisting double drop which is a feast for the eyes. However, thoughts of running it should only

be entertained at very low flows, if at all.

After that it opens up somewhat into a beautiful forest gorge and continues for another three lively kilometres (WW III-IV), until the last runnable drops in the entrance of the final gorge are reached. From above these look a lot less pushy than they actually feel in your boat. After this carry up on the left to the road. Warning, do not miss the take out.

Sebastian Gründler

Tip: At high flows the Voo probably gets pretty heavy and quite dangerous, better to try it first at somewhat lower flows, particularly as abandoning the run is practically impossible once you're on the river.

Der Veo fließt fernab der Straße durch den Jotunheimen National-park. Das Wasser des Veobreen wird weit oben abgeleitet, so ist eine Befahrung meist nur im Frühjahr und nach Regenfällen möglich. Einige Stellen sind etwas unsauber, trotzdem ist der Veo ein kleines Schmankerl.

Spätestens am Einstieg wird man merken, dass norwegische Bäche recht weitläufige Ufer haben können. So lächerlich nah das Flussbett vom Bomweg entfernt zu sein scheint, es dauert fast eine halbe Stunde bis man es endlich erreicht. Und dann folgt – einen mittleren Wasserstand vorausgesetzt – erst mal ein etwas zäher Start, der sich je nach gewähltem Einstieg über mindestens 2-3 Kilometer hinzieht.

Der Schluchteingang beendet die Schrappelei mit recht wuchtigen Katarakten, auf etwa 3 Kilometern bietet der Veo ansprechendes Wild-wasser mit schönen Stufen und trickreichen Passagen, um WW IV (V). Die folgende kurze Klamm lässt sich problemlos umtragen.

Auf den darauf folgenden 1,5 Kilometer reihen sich einige steile Katarakte, Rutschen und rückläufige Stufen aneinander, es ist die schwerste Strecke auf dem Veo (WW V+), die des Öfteren eine Be-sichtigung erforderlich macht. Spektakuläres Ende dieses Teilstücks ist eine verwinkelte Doppelstufe, welche schön anzusehen ist. Be-fahrungsgedanken dürften allerdings, wenn überhaupt, nur bei einem eher dürftigen Wasserstand aufkommen.

Danach wird die Schlucht etwas offener, in einer schön bewachse-nen Waldschlucht geht es zügig weitere 3 Kilometer dahin (WW III-IV), bis die noch fahrbaren Eingangsstufen der Schlussklamm erreicht sind, die von oben deutlich weniger wuchtig aussehen, als sie vom Boot aus erlebt werden. Direkt danach links hoch tragen und zur Stra-ße vorlaufen. Achtung, Ausstieg nicht verpassen!

Sebastian Gründler

Tipp: Bei zu hohem Wasserstand dürfte der Veo ziemlich heftig und gefährlich werden, lieber bei ein bisschen weniger antesten, zumal ein Abbruch der Fahrt quasi nicht möglich ist.

Photo: SG

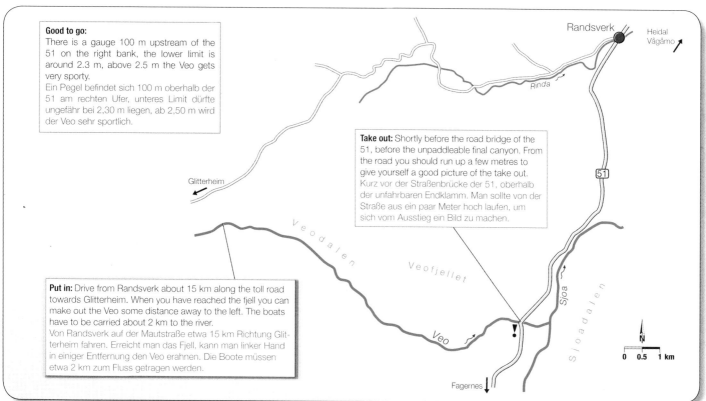

Good to go:
There is a gauge 100 m upstream of the 51 on the right bank, the lower limit is around 2.3 m, above 2.5 m the Veo gets very sporty.
Ein Pegel befindet sich 100 m oberhalb der 51 am rechten Ufer, unteres Limit dürfte ungefähr bei 2,30 m liegen, ab 2,50 m wird der Veo sehr sportlich.

Take out: Shortly before the road bridge of the 51, before the unpaddleable final canyon. From the road you should run up a few metres to give yourself a good picture of the take out.
Kurz vor der Straßenbrücke der 51, oberhalb der unfahrbaren Endklamm. Man sollte von der Straße aus ein paar Meter hoch laufen, um sich vom Ausstieg ein Bild zu machen.

Put in: Drive from Randsverk about 15 km along the toll road towards Glitterheim. When you have reached the fjell you can make out the Veo some distance away to the left. The boats have to be carried about 2 km to the river.
Von Randsverk auf der Mautstraße etwa 15 km Richtung Glit-terheim fahren. Erreicht man das Fjell, kann man linker Hand in einiger Entfernung den Veo erahnen. Die Boote müssen etwa 2 km zum Fluss getragen werden.

Randsverk

Heidal Vågåmo

Rinda

Glitterheim

51

Veodalen

Veofjellet

Sjoa

Sjoadalen

Veo

0   0.5   1 km

Fagernes

ULA

The Ula stands somewhat in the shadow of her headwaters, the Store Ula. The Ula maybe doesn't boast such impressive waterfalls as her big sister, but a trip here is certainly rewarded with great whitewater. The lower Ula is a short, tight section, with continuous rapids, sometimes over bedrock. The fun never stops, all the way to the take out at the lake.

CLASS:	**III**
LEVEL:	**10 - 15 cumecs**
LENGTH:	**3 km**
TIME:	**2 h**
SEASON:	**May - June**

Die Ula steht etwas im Schatten einer ihrer Quellflüsse, der Store Ula. Zwar kann die Ula hier unten nicht mit solch schönen Wasserfällen auftrumpfen, jedoch wird auch ein Abstecher hierhin mit flottem Wildwasser belohnt. Die untere Ula ist ein kurzer, enger Abschnitt, mit kontinuierlichen Stromschnellen, teils über Grundgestein. Der Spaß hält bis zum Ausstieg am See unentwegt an.

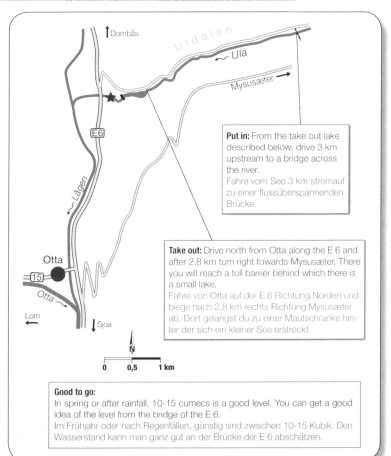

Put in: From the take out lake described below, drive 3 km upstream to a bridge across the river.
Fahre vom See 3 km stromauf zu einer flussüberspannenden Brücke.

Take out: Drive north from Otta along the E 6 and after 2.8 km turn right towards Mysusæter. There you will reach a toll barrier behind which there is a small lake.
Fahre von Otta auf der E 6 Richtung Norden und biege nach 2,8 km rechts Richtung Mysusæter ab. Dort gelangst du zu einer Mautschranke hinter der sich ein kleiner See erstreckt.

Good to go:
In spring or after rainfall, 10-15 cumecs is a good level. You can get a good idea of the level from the bridge of the E 6.
Im Frühjahr oder nach Regenfällen, günstig sind zwischen 10-15 Kubik. Den Wasserstand kann man ganz gut an der Brücke der E 6 abschätzen.

STORE ULA: WATERFALL RUN

The Store Ula is a typical highland creek which flows through the Rondane National Park. By reason of the waterfalls at the take out it is commonly referred to by Norwegians as »Dry Meadow Creek« but the kilometres which precede also have very worthwhile whitewater.

After the first tight section the river flows on with decreasing difficulty through an open river bed. After about 1 kilometre the large »Bruresløret« waterfall has to be portaged on the left. After that you are

CLASS:	**V**
LEVEL:	**5 - 10 cumecs**
LENGTH:	**4 km**
TIME:	**2 - 4 h**
SEASON:	**May - July**

carried into a small gorge with several drops and ledges. After 500 metres you reach a slide combination, whose 4 metre drop at the end is known as »Svabergfoss«. This is where the Ula Extreme Race is held.

Then follow a number of smaller drops, until you reach a foot bridge, and the 5 Ula waterfalls. These are easily scouted from the left bank. Take care at the fourth, the highest waterfall. In 2003 this was the scene of a tragic accident. An upcoming British paddler hit the kicker just below the ledge and landed flat in the almost green water – the result

was a serious spinal injury. We have no information as to whether he is able to walk again yet.

Photo: SG

Die Store Ula fließt als typischer Hochlandbach durch den Rondane Nationalpark. Sie wird aufgrund der Wasserfälle am Ausstieg gern als »Dry Meadow Creek« Norwegens bezeichnet, doch auch die Kilometer davor bieten lohnendes Wildwasser.

Nach der ersten Engstelle geht es mit abnehmenden Schwierigkeiten im offenen Flussbett weiter. Nach etwa einem Kilometer muss der große »Bruresløret« Wasserfall links umtragen werden, danach geht es in eine kleine Klamm mit einigen Abfällen und Schwellen. Nach 500 Metern gelangt

man zu einer Rutschenkombination, dessen Stufe am Ende »Svabergfoss« genannt wird. Hier wird das Ula-Extremrennen ausgetragen.

Es folgen noch ein paar Stellen, bis man eine Fußgängerbrücke und somit die fünf Wasserfälle erreicht. Diese sind vom linken Flussufer leicht einzusehen. Vorsicht beim vierten und höchsten Wasserfall, hier ereignete sich 2003 ein tragischer Unfall. Ein britischer Nachwuchspaddler erwischte den Kicker unterhalb der Kante und landete flach im beinah grünen Wasser – eine Verletzung der Wirbelsäule war die Folge. Ob er schon wieder laufen kann, ist uns nicht bekannt.

Put in: South of Otta turn off the E 6 towards Mysusæter, and fight your way up into the highlands. In Mysusæter take the left path, and at the next intersection turn right to a toll barrier. Continue over the plain to a car park at the end of the road, and from there carry the boats left to the river.

Biege südlich von Otta von der E 6 nach Mysusäter ab und kämpfe dich ins Hochland. Nimm in Mysusäter den linken Weg und biege bei der nächsten Kreuzung rechts zu einer Mautschranke ab. Von dort geht es weiter über die Hochebene zu einem Parkplatz am Ende der Straße. Von dort nach links die Boote zum Fluss tragen.

Take out: Drive back to the toll barrier, turn right and park at the hotel. From there follow the path down to the river on foot.

Fahre zurück zur Mautschranke, biege rechts ab und parke am Hotel. Von dort aus geht es zu Fuß auf einem Pfad hinunter zum Fluss.

Good to go:
As a reference point, the first waterfall at the take out. If the water curtain reaches across the whole width of the river, then the Ula is at high flow, if the water is falling in two individual streams, you have medium to low water.

Als Anhaltspunkt dient der erste Wasserfall am Ausstieg. Reicht der Wasservorhang über die gesamte Breite des Flusses, führt die Ula Hochwasser, fällt das Wasser in zwei einzelnen Strahlen hinab, handelt es sich um Mittelwasser bzw. Niedrigwasser.

Store Ula

Uldalen

Ula falls

Mysusæter

Otta

0   0.5   1 km

Obsommer doing the first descent of the 4th Ula fall back in 1995

Nico Langner enjoying the upper part

Photos: MN

Starting high up on the fjell: the Store Ula

STORY: STORE ULA   NICO LANGNER

THE RIVER OF ALL RIVERS

Years before planning my first trip to Norway, I listened eagerly to the stories about Norwegian rivers like the Sjoa, Rauma and especially about the Store Ula. Months before we finally left on our first trip to Norway, I started looking forward to paddling this river, since I prefer waterfalls and slides instead of big water and monster boils. My buddy Phil knew the Ula already and could tell us some stories about it. I simply went with the flow and looked forward with anticipation to the big day.

8:30 a.m. - at the Sjoa-camp: sleepless because I am so nervous, I crawl out of my sleeping bag and try to get mentally prepared for the Ula. Phil is still asleep. Hence, I decide to make breakfast.

9:20 a.m. - still at the Sjoa-camp: Phil finally wakes up, but before he can even say »good morning«, I shuffle him into the bus and off we go. Too bad for him, but as they say: »the early bird catches the worm.«

9:50 a.m. - we arrive at the toll booth: the cashiers are two beautiful blonds in tight jeans – after so much adrenalin, we almost forget our anxiety of paddling the river.

10:10 a.m. - at the put in: we get dressed quickly, get on the water and soon forget all about the blond girls. The landscape glitters breathtakingly against the sunlight. We're surrounded by moss and shrubs – no trees are to be seen anywhere. Too bad, since I feel like uprooting dozens of them right here and now.

DER FLUSS DER FLÜSSE

Schon Jahre vor meinem ersten Norwegenurlaub lauschte ich begeistert den Geschichten vom dortigen Wildwasser: von Sjoa, Rauma, und vor allem der Store Ula. Monate vor unserem Norwegenurlaub hatte ich mich auf diesen Fluss gefreut, denn Wasserfälle und Rutschen sind mir lieber als Wuchtwasser und Monsterpilze. Mein Freund Phil kennt die Ula und weiß einiges zu berichten. Ich lass es einfach auf mich zukommen und freue mich auf den kommenden Tag.

8:30 Uhr - Sjoa-Camp: Schlaflos vor Nervosität krieche ich aus dem Schlafsack, um mich auf die Ula vorzubereiten. Phil schläft noch. Naja, dann fange ich schon mal mit dem Frühstück an.

9:20 Uhr - noch immer am Sjoa-Camp: Phil wird wach, und noch ehe er »Guten Morgen« sagen kann, sitzt er ohne zu Frühstücken in meinem Bus. Pech gehabt – Morgenstund hat Gold im Mund!

9:50 Uhr - endlich an der Mautstelle: Zwei hübsche Blondinen kassieren hier die Maut, und zwar in knall-engen Jeans! Nach so viel Adrenalin schwindet die Aufregung vor dem Bach.

10:10 Uhr - am Einstieg: Im Handumdrehen sind wir umgezogen und auf dem Wasser und schon sind die Mädels wieder vergessen. Die Sonne lässt die Landschaft im Gegenlicht atemberaubend glitzern. Es wachsen nur Moose und Sträucher, es ist kein Baum weit und breit zu sehen. Und das gerade heute, wo ich mich doch fühle als ob ich sie zu

11:30 a.m. - at the steep part of the Ula: we walk along the passage to check out the lines. I can't wait any longer and decide to be the first to run the first slide. Those five slides are a real pleasure to paddle; only the one called »Against the Wall« requires caution so as not to hit the pillow on the right.

12:45 p.m. - the waterfalls: this time it's Phil who has ants in his pants and wants to paddle first. I watch the spectacle from the muddy shore. Phil catches the perfect line on the first fall and doesn't even get wet, same on the second waterfall. I'm quite impressed! He's now entering the third and highest fall. I can only see how he disappears over the ledge. It takes quite a while until he emerges again and something doesn't seem right. His boat is filled with water, his skirt has popped. In a slight state of panic, Phil tries to navigate his boat full of water to shore in front of a 16 metre fall! Thank god, Ulf is there with his throwbag and gets him on first try. Phil's now out of danger. Meanwhile, I am laughing my head off on shore. It was Phil who had been laughing about all those people who swam here. Now it was his turn.

1:05 p.m. - slightly amused I walk back to my boat, take a last look at the line, and get on the water. I double-check my skirt, will it stay on the cockpit? My worries are probably unnecessary; so far my skirt has never failed me. The height of the waterfall is now on my mind: should I boof or not? What happens if? Unanswered questions are swirling through my head. Just before reaching the ledge, I decide not to boof and land head first in the pool. At least I don't hurt myself. Now I still have two waterfalls ahead of me. The descent of the next one is perfect; I don't even get wet!

1:10 p.m. - in the eddy above the third fall: I'm still smiling at Phil's slight mishap. But I still have something ahead of me, so concentration is required! I am planning to boof like hell and vault out of the eddy. Somehow, my plan doesn't work out and I disappear deep in the pool. Everything around me is black and then… my legs get wet! I follow my instinct, exit the kayak and swim to the surface. Once again Ulf proves his accuracy with the throwbag and pulls me out of the water. Laughter greets me on shore: Phil's rolling on the ground. I can't help it but laugh myself. What can you do?

10:00 p.m. - back at the Sjoa-camp: everyone knows about our heroic »descent« and we are celebrated with due respect. Tonight, we'll have a few more beers than usual, but that's what they're there for!

Dutzenden ausreißen könnte.

11:30 Uhr - am Steilstück der Ula: Wir laufen die Strecke ab um die Linien auszumachen, ich kann es nicht abwarten und fahre die ersten Rutschen vor. Die fünf Rutschen kann man als reinen Genuss ansehen, nur bei der Rutsche mit dem Namen »Against the Wall« muss man zusehen nicht rechts ins Prallpolster zu schießen.

12:45 Uhr - die Wasserfälle: Diesmal hat Phil die Hummeln im Hintern und will unbedingt vorfahren, ich schaue mir das Spektakel vom matschigen Ufer aus an. Im ersten Fall erwischt Phil die Ideallinie und wird gar nicht erst nass, genauso im Zweiten. Ich bin beeindruckt! Jetzt fährt er in den dritten und höchsten Fall ein. Ich sehe nur wie er über die Kante verschwindet. Es dauert ganz schön lange bis er wieder auftaucht, irgendetwas scheint nicht zu stimmen: Phils Boot ist voll gelaufen, seine Spritzdecke offen. Panisch rudert er vor dem nächsten, 16 Meter hohen Wasserfall herum – mit vollem Boot! Gott sei Dank hat Ulf den Wurfsack zur Hand und trifft beim ersten Versuch, Phil ist gerettet. Ich halte mir während dessen den Bauch vor lachen: Hat doch Phil gerade noch Witze über die Anderen gemacht, die hier schwimmen mussten. Jetzt war auch er dran.

13:05 Uhr - noch etwas belustigt gehe ich zu meinem Boot, werfe noch einen Blick auf die Linie, und steige ein. Mein erster Check gilt der Spritzdecke, hält sie auf der Luke? Ich mache mir bestimmt nur unnötig Gedanken, schließlich ist sie noch nie aufgegangen. Auch die Höhe macht mir ein wenig Sorgen: Soll ich boofen oder nicht? Was wenn? Fragen über Fragen gehen mir durch den Kopf, die Antworten liegen noch im Dunkeln. Kurz vor der Kante beschließe ich nicht zu boofen – und lande kopfüber im Pool. Immerhin habe ich mir nicht weh getan, doch noch habe ich ja zwei Wasserfälle vor mir. Der nächste Fall klappt perfekt, ich werde noch nicht mal nass.

13:10 Uhr - im Kehrwasser vor dem dritten Fall: Ich muss grinsend an Phils Missgeschick denken. Aber ich habe ja noch was vor mir, also Konzentration! Ich nehme mir vor zu boofen was das Zeug hält und schwinge aus dem Kehrwasser. Aber irgendwie klappt mein Vorhaben nicht, ich werde tief im Gumpen versenkt. Alles ist schwarz und dann … meine Beine werden nass! Instinktiv steige ich aus und schwimme nach oben. Wieder einmal beweißt Ulf seine Zielsicherheit mit dem Wurfsack und zieht mich raus. Laut schallendes Gelächter begrüßt mich vom Ufer – Phil liegt am Boden. Ich kann nicht anders und lache mit. Was soll man machen?

22:00 Uhr - zurück am Sjoa Camp: Jeder weiß von unserer heldenhaften »Befahrung« und so werden wir dementsprechend gefeiert. An diesem Abend trinken wir ein paar Bier mehr als sonst, aber dafür ist es ja schließlich da!

NICO LANGNER 1980   www.nicolangner.com
Nico has more feeling for kayaking than some kayak clubs in total. The German Rodeo Champion loves to throw the ends of his playboat down, maybe because while playboating his skirt isn't as likely to pop.
Nico hat mehr Bootsgefühl im Popo als so mancher Paddelverein zusammen. Der Deutsche Rodeomeister schmeißt seine Enden am liebsten im Spielboot durch die Luft, vielleicht auch weil ihm dabei nicht so oft die Spritzdecke aufgeht.

OTTA + CO

Olaf Obsommer putting his paddle where it belongs.

Ottdalen at Billingen

OTTA

In this chapter we shall deal with the second part of Oppland. We'll concentrate on the tributaries of the Otta and the Lågen in the upper Gudbrandsdal, up to the convergence of the Otta. The rivers of this region differ somewhat in character from those of the Sjoa region: there are a number of whitewater gems up to WW IV, but these are almost outnumbered by the WW V challenges – some of which are in deep canyons.

The main river of the area, the Otta, flows north of the Jotunheimen into the Lågen, on the eastern edge of the Rondane Nasjonalparks. Sometimes forming lakes, sometimes down steep cataracts, the Otta collects its water from countless tributaries on its way to the small town of Otta. Halfway along its journey the Otta passes the town of Lom, which will enchant you with the old architecture of its houses, the Lom Stavkirke, and its long culinary tradition. South of Lom in the Jotunheimen Nasjonalpark, high up in the Visdalen, reign the highest peaks of Norway, the Glittertind (2472 metres) and Galdhøpiggen (2469 meters). Here you can hear the burble of the Bøvra, Leira and Visa, although only sections of the Bøvra are described here. West of Lom, towards Stryn, you will find the Skjøli, Ostri and Tora, small whitewater gems, which these days have been promoted to frequently-run whitewater classics.

You can find information on the glacial rivers Leira and Visa in the »Skandinavien Auslandsführer« (Scandinavian Guide) of the DKV (German Kayak Club). By reason of their character, neither of these rivers really seem particularly worthwhile to us, but could be interesting in high summer when there is not much water around elsewhere. Both flow close to the road, so you'll be able to check them out yourself. The nicest and most challenging whitewater is to be found in the lower gorge of the Visa, about 9 kilometres downriver from Spiterstulen. It is best to crash through the bush on river right to scout the section.

Mit dem zweiten Teil von Oppland befassen wir uns in diesem Kapitel. Hier werden die Zuflüsse der Otta und die des Lågen im oberen Gudbrandsdal bis zur Mündung der Otta abgehandelt. Das Gebiet unterscheidet sich etwas vom Charakter der Sjoa-Flüsse: es gibt einige Wildwasserperlen bis WW IV, aber fast noch mehr WW V Herausforderungen – zum Teil in tiefen Schluchten.

Der Hauptfluss des Gebietes, die Otta, erstreckt sich nördlich des Jotunheimen und mündet am östlichen Rande des »Rondane Nasjonalparks« in den Lågen. Teils seenartig, teils in steilen Abbrüchen sammelt sie durch unzählige Zuflüsse auf ihrem Weg zum Städtchen Otta ihr Wasser. Auf halber Strecke liegt das Örtchen Lom, das durch die alte Bauweise der Häuser, die Lom Stavkirke und durch eine lange Essenstradition verzaubert. Südlich von Lom im Jotunheimen Nasjonalpark, hoch oben im Visdalen, thronen Glittertind (2472 Meter) und Galdhøpiggen (2469 Meter), die höchsten Gipfel Norwegens. Hier rauschen Bøvra, Leira und Visa, von denen in diesem Buch allerdings nur die Etappen der Bøvra beschrieben sind. Westlich von Lom, Richtung Stryn, liegen Skjøli, Ostri und Tora, kleine Wildwasserperlen, die mittlerweile zu viel befahrenen Klassikern avanciert sind.

Informationen zu den Gletscherflüssen Leira und Visa findet man im Skandinavien Auslandsführer des DKV. Beide Flüsse erscheinen uns aufgrund ihres Charakters nicht wirklich lohnend, können aber gerade im Hochsommer bei Wassermangel bestimmt reizvoll sein. Die Flüsse verlaufen meist in Straßennähe, eine eigenständige Erkundung ist daher möglich. Das schönste und anspruchsvollste Wildwasser bietet wohl bei Niedrigwasser die Klamm der Visa etwa 9 Kilometer unterhalb Spiterstulen. Am besten flussrechts zur Besichtigung durchs Gebüsch kämpfen.

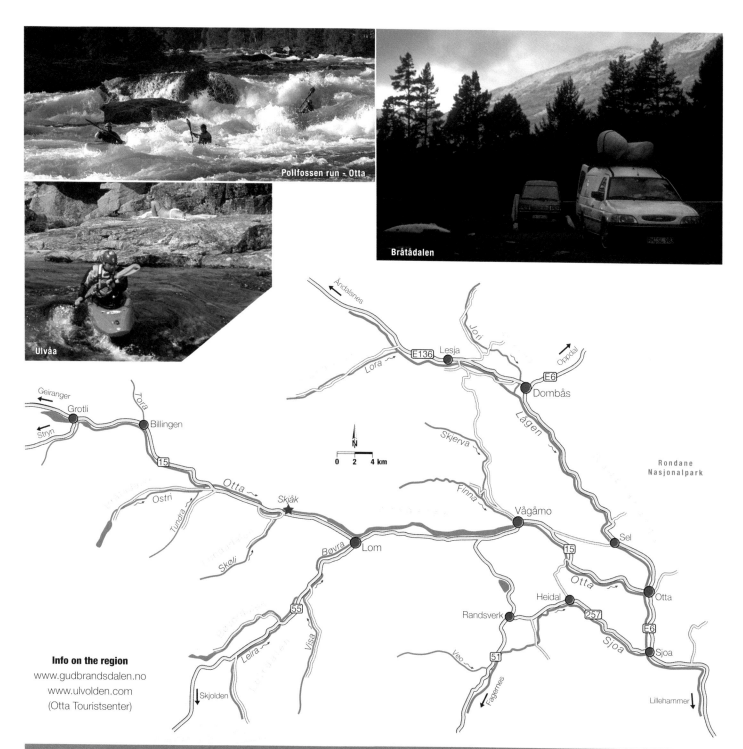

Pollfossen run - Otta

Bråtådalen

Ulvåa

Info on the region
www.gudbrandsdalen.no
www.ulvolden.com
(Otta Touristsenter)

OTTA FACTS

Character: Everything. From »open and pushy« to »steep and tight«. Mostly between WW IV-V. Only on some sections of the Otta, Lora and Jori are things somewhat more relaxed.

Best time: Spring until late summer. The glacial rivers flow into the late summer. The Tora, for example, cannot be paddled until its level drops in the late summer. However, some of the standard sections, such as Ostri, Jori and Rosten, are really only worth paddling at peak melt times in the early summer.

Special remarks: You'll find several glacial rivers which still run in high summer.

Accommodation: Storøya camping ground at Skjåk on the Otta.

Charakter: Alles. Von offen und wuchtig bis klein und steil. Meist zwischen WW IV-V, nur auf Teilstrecken von Otta, Lora und Jori geht es entspannter dahin.

Beste Zeit: Frühling bis Spätsommer. Die Gletscherbäche laufen bis in den Spätsommer hinein, die Tora beispielsweise geht erst bei wenig Wasser im Hochsommer. Zur Zeit der Hochschmelze im Frühsommer sind aber viele der Standardabschnitte, wie Ostri, Jori und Rosten, erst richtig lohnend.

Besonderheit: Hier gibt es einige Gletscherbäche, die auch im Hochsommer noch laufen.

Übernachtung: Storøya Camping bei Skjåk an der Otta.

OTTA: POLLFOSS RUN

SOME BIGGER RAPIDS IN AN OPEN RIVERBED

The Pollfoss run in the Billingsdalen is similar to the Numedalslågen before Dagali. It's a great run at medium flow (40-50 cumecs), but also paddleable at lower levels.

In the first 3.5 kilometres up to the convergence with the Tora, the difficulties get up to above WW IV. These two sections (WW V) are easily recognised, the edges of the drops are obvious.

After that things quieten down again, time to kick back. In the last kilometre before the Pollfossen the Otta cranks up the noise once more. The rapids can be scouted from the road and should be checked out before you put on. The last 500 metres up to the Pollfossen should only be run at low flows, under 25 cumecs.

CLASS: IV (V)
LEVEL: 9 km
LENGTH: 25 - 50 cumecs
TIME: 2 - 4 h
SEASON: late June - August

Der Pollfossen-Abschnitt im Billingsdalen ähnelt ein wenig dem Numedalslågen vor Dagali. Er ist sehr lohnend bei Mittelwasser (40-50 Kubik), aber auch fahrbar bei weniger.

Auf den ersten 3,5 Kilometern bis zur Mündung der Tora gehen die Schwierigkeiten zweimal über WW IV hinaus. Diese zwei Stellen (WW V) sind gut erkennbar, die Abrisskanten sind offensichtlich.

Danach wird es ruhiger, Zeit zum Lümmeln. Auf dem letzten Kilometer vor dem Pollfossen legt die Otta noch einmal richtig los. Die Katarakte sind von der Straße aus einsehbar und sollten schon vorher besichtigt werden. Die letzten 500 Meter bis zum Pollfossen sollten nur bei wenig Wasser, also unter 25 Kubik in Angriff genommen werden.

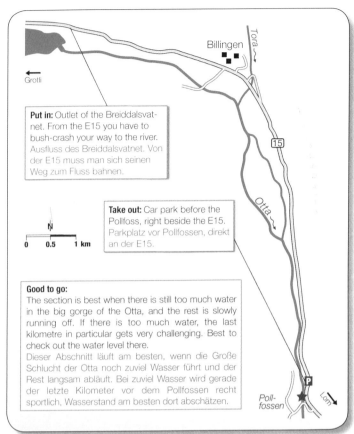

Put in: Outlet of the Breiddalsvatnet. From the E15 you have to bush-crash your way to the river. Ausfluss des Breiddalsvatnet. Von der E15 muss man sich seinen Weg zum Fluss bahnen.

Take out: Car park before the Pollfoss, right beside the E15. Parkplatz vor Pollfossen, direkt an der E15.

Good to go:
The section is best when there is still too much water in the big gorge of the Otta, and the rest is slowly running off. If there is too much water, the last kilometre in particular gets very challenging. Best to check out the water level there.
Dieser Abschnitt läuft am besten, wenn die Große Schlucht der Otta noch zuviel Wasser führt und der Rest langsam abläuft. Bei zuviel Wasser wird gerade der letzte Kilometer vor dem Pollfossen recht sportlich, Wasserstand am besten dort abschätzen.

Markus Hummel

OTTA: BIG GORGE

Above the Dønnfossen the Big Otta Gorge awaits adventurers. This short, very steep section, decorated with monster slides, has not been run very often, but those who do not mind dragging their boat through the bush will be well rewarded.

However, in 2005 the Hegebøttn Dam was completed, and the irony was complete: in the past the Big Gorge usually had too much water to be run, now it is diverted. At this stage we can not give any prognosis of when the gorge will have enough overflow from the dam to be runnable.

The diverted water will apparently be reintroduced above Dønnfoss, so the dam should not have too much effect on the flow of the rest of the Otta. As the dam is not intended as a reservoir, rather only as a regulator of the water level, the result could be a more consistent flow for the lower sections.

CLASS: V - VII
LEVEL: 20 - 25 cumecs
LENGTH: 4 km
TIME: 3 - 5 h
SEASON: July - September

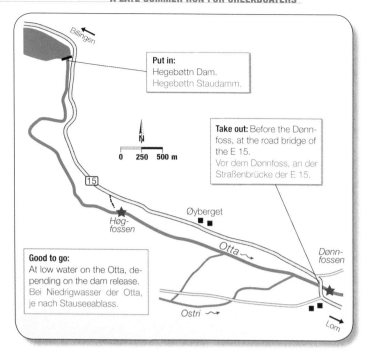

Put in:
Hegebøttn Dam.
Hegebøttn Staudamm.

Take out: Before the Dønn-foss, at the road bridge of the E 15.
Vor dem Dønnfoss, an der Straßenbrücke der E 15.

Good to go:
At low water on the Otta, depending on the dam release.
Bei Niedrigwasser der Otta, je nach Stauseeablass.

Oberhalb des Dønnfossen wartet die Große Schlucht der Otta auf Abenteurer. Dieser kurze und recht steile Abschnitt mit monströsen Rutschen wurde zwar noch nicht oft befahren, aber wer sich nicht grämt sein Boot auch mal ein paar Meter durch die Büsche zu zerren, wird hier trotzdem seinen Spaß haben.

Allerdings wurde direkt oberhalb der Schlucht 2005 der Hegebøttn Staudamm fertig gestellt und die Ironie des Schicksals schlägt um sich: früher hatte die Große Schlucht meist zuviel Wasser, heute wird es abgeleitet. Prognosen wann genügend Überlauf die Schlucht fahrbar macht, wollen wir nicht abgeben.

Das abgeleitete Wasser soll oberhalb des Dønnfoss wieder zugeführt werden, somit sollte sich der Staudamm nicht zu sehr auf die Reststrecke der Otta auswirken. Da der Staudamm nicht als Wasserspeicher, sondern lediglich als Regulator eingesetzt werden soll, könnte somit ein konstanterer Wasserdurchlauf für die unteren Strecken die Folge sein.

OTTA: FAMILY RUN   SUNSHINE WHITEWATER

The »family run« of the Otta is set in stunning landscape, with awesome waves and pumping eddies – but only at high flow. At low flow it is a very mellow trip, the beauty of the surrounds a feast for the senses. Particularly at medium flow, this section is perfect for beginners, or simply for the whole family.

CLASS: II
LEVEL: 40 - 100 cumecs
LENGTH: 6 km
TIME: 1 - 2 h
SEASON: May - September

Der »Family Run« der Otta ist ein landschaftlich hervorragender Abschnitt mit schönen Wellen und pulsierenden Kehrwässern – allerdings nur bei viel Wasser. Bei wenig Wasser geht es hier recht gelassen dahin, die schöne Landschaft bleibt natürlich erhalten. So ist dieser Abschnitt gerade bei moderatem Wasserstand perfekt für Anfänger, oder einfach für die ganze Familie.

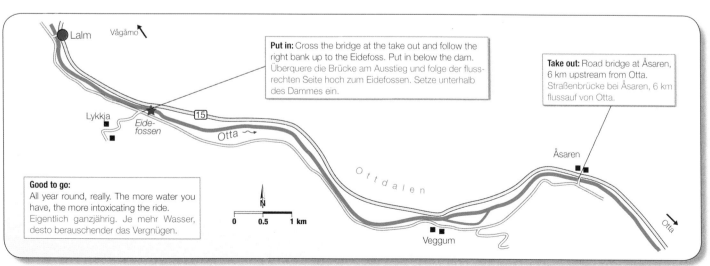

Put in: Cross the bridge at the take out and follow the right bank up to the Eidefoss. Put in below the dam.
Überquere die Brücke am Ausstieg und folge der fluss-rechten Seite hoch zum Eidefossen. Setze unterhalb des Dammes ein.

Take out: Road bridge at Åsaren, 6 km upstream from Otta.
Straßenbrücke bei Åsaren, 6 km flussauf von Otta.

Good to go:
All year round, really. The more water you have, the more intoxicating the ride.
Eigentlich ganzjährig. Je mehr Wasser, desto berauschender das Vergnügen.

BØVRA: UPPER

FLAT WATER ALTERNATING WITH STEEP RAPIDS

The Bøvra feeds into the Otta at Lom. It is itself not a glacial river, but the character of its lower reaches is largely determined by the Leira, the glacial tributary fed by the ice masses of Jotunheimen. In the upper section the water is still clear, and long quiet stretches alternate with drops and slides. The difficulties of the upper section are mostly around grade III-IV, with three sections WW IV-V. These can be easily inspected on the drive there.

The quiet water of the idyllic Dalsvatnet quickly flows into the first short gorge and shoots over a bedrock slide, after which the wall on the right is undercut. A long, open section leads to the low gorge, with a twisting drop and other nice sections. After the final jump (2-3 metres) the gorge opens up, and then numerous amusing slides accompany you all the way to the take out.

CLASS: III - IV (V-)
LEVEL: 8 - 20 cumecs
LENGTH: 7 km
TIME: 2 - 3 h
SEASON: May - September

Die Bøvra mündet bei Lom in die Otta. Sie ist zwar kein Gletscherfluss, ihr Unterlauf ist jedoch maßgeblich durch den Zufluss der Leira gekennzeichnet, die wiederum von den Eismassen des Jotunheimen gespeist wird. Auf der oberen Bøvra ist das Wasser noch klar, hier wechseln lange ruhige Passagen mit Stufen und rutschenartigen Abfällen. Die Schwierigkeiten des oberen Abschnittes liegen meist bei WW III-IV, mit drei Stellen WW IV-V, die gut bei der Anfahrt besichtigt werden können.

Das ruhige Wasser des idyllischen Dalsvatnet fließt schnell in die erste kurze Niederklamm und schießt über eine Grundgesteinsrutsche, danach ist rechts die Wand unterspült. Ein langer offener Abschnitt führt zur nächsten Niederklamm, mit einer verwinkelten Stufe und anderen interessanten Stellen. Nach dem Abschlusshüpfer (2-3 Meter) öffnet die Klamm, es folgen noch zahlreiche lustige Rutschen bis zum Ausstieg.

Tip: Rusta + Galdesand: The Rusta Gorge after the take out can be run at low water in August and September (gauge 90-100 cm). There are several WW-V-must-run sections, as well as a couple of siphons and undercuts, but it is worth it. Caution, there is a must-run section which can not scouted from your boat, but which absolutely must be scouted before you run it. It is advisable to go for a bush crash and scout the whole gorge before putting on. In combination with the following Galdesand Gorge this is a worthwhile but difficult trip.

Tipp: Rusta + Galdesand: Die Rusta-Schlucht nach dem Ausstieg ist bei Niederwasser im August und September möglich (Pegel 90-100 cm). Es warten einige WW-V-Zwangspassagen, auch ein paar Siphone und Unterspülungen, trotzdem ist sie lohnend. Achtung, eine vom Wasser aus uneinsehbare Zwangspassage muss vorher unbedingt besichtigt werden. Es empfiehlt sich die ganze Klamm erst durch die Büsche abzulaufen. In Kombination mit der Galdesand-Schlucht im Anschluss ein lohnender aber auch schwieriger Trip.

BØVRA: LOWER

ALTERNATES BETWEEN OPEN, FLAT SECTIONS AND NARROW GORGES

The glacial flow of the Leira makes its presence known on the lower section, here the Bøvra has noticeably more volume. After alternating between flat sections and a couple of cataracts, the Bøvra flows into a gorge. The edges of the drops to follow require inspection. After that things get a little easier, until you reach a drop which is undercut on the left. After further cataracts you reach a bridge where you will find a nasty waterfall. This should be portaged on the right. You then soon reach Lom without further major difficulty, where you will find the take out on the right above the drop. Caution: there have been several accidents here. Especially at high levels the water flows quickly into the waterfall. Have a good look at the take out before you put on.

Tip: Do not miss the take out!

CLASS: IV (X)
LEVEL: 40 - 80 cumecs
LENGTH: 7 km
TIME: 2 - 3 h
SEASON: May - September

The put in of the lower section

Photos: MN

Auf dem unteren Abschnitt macht sich das Gletscherwasser der Leira bemerkbar, hier hat die Bøvra an Volumen zugenommen. Nachdem sich Flachstücke und ein paar Katarakte abgewechselt haben, fließt die Bøvra in eine Klamm. Die nun folgenden Abrisskanten erfordern eine Besichtigung.

Danach lassen die Schwierigkeiten etwas nach, bis man an einen Abfall kommt, der links unterspült ist. Nach weiteren Katarakten folgt ein ekeliger Wasserfall an einer Brücke, der rechts umtragen werden sollte. Ohne weitere große Schwierigkeiten ist man nun bald in Lom, wo sich rechts vor dem

Abfall der Ausstieg befindet. Vorsicht: Hier ereigneten sich schon einige Unfälle, gerade bei viel Wasser zieht es schnell in den Abfall hinein. Also den Ausstieg vorher gut anschauen.

Tipp: Nicht den Ausstieg verpassen!

The upper part offers cool drop + pool

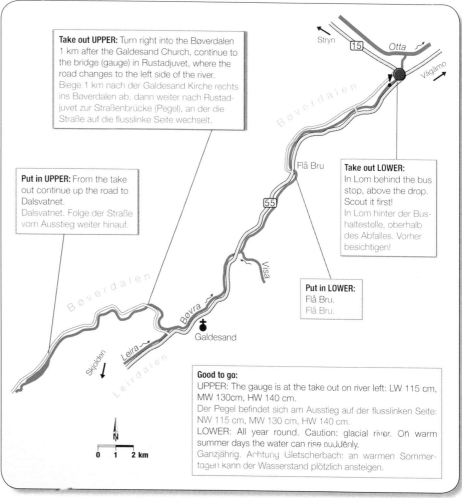

Take out UPPER: Turn right into the Bøverdalen 1 km after the Galdesand Church, continue to the bridge (gauge) in Rustadjuvet, where the road changes to the left side of the river.
Biege 1 km nach der Galdesand Kirche rechts ins Bøverdalen ab, dann weiter nach Rustadjuvet zur Straßenbrücke (Pegel), an der die Straße auf die flusslinke Seite wechselt.

Put in UPPER: From the take out continue up the road to Dalsvatnet.
Dalsvatnet. Folge der Straße vom Ausstieg weiter hinauf.

Take out LOWER:
In Lom behind the bus stop, above the drop. Scout it first!
In Lom hinter der Bushaltestelle, oberhalb des Abfalles. Vorher besichtigen!

Put in LOWER:
Flå Bru.
Flå Bru.

Stryn — 15 — Otta — Vågåmo

Bøverdalen

Flå Bru

55

Visa

Bøvra

Galdesand

Bøverdalen

Skjolden — Leira

Leirdalen

N
0 1 2 km

Good to go:
UPPER: The gauge is at the take out on river left: LW 115 cm, MW 130cm, HW 140 cm.
Der Pegel befindet sich am Ausstieg auf der flusslinken Seite: NW 115 cm, MW 130 cm, HW 140 cm.
LOWER: All year round. Caution: glacial river. On warm summer days the water can rise suddenly.
Ganzjährig. Achtung Gletscherbach: an warmen Sommertagen kann der Wasserstand plötzlich ansteigen.

Lake Liavatnet

✖ OSTRI: GORGE

A SHORT RUN THROUGH A CONTINUOUS CANYON

The Ostri (also known as the Åstre) and its headwaters spring from a magnificent highland valley in the foothills of the Jostedalsbreen. Unfortunately the most beautiful part of the valley is hidden behind the Liavatnet, the put in of our section. Nonetheless, the Ostri is well worthwhile, even if you don't get to see much of the landscape.

CLASS:	IV
LEVEL:	15 - 40 cumecs
LENGTH:	2 km
TIME:	1 - 2 h
SEASON:	May - August

Der Ostri (oder Åstre) und seine Quellflüsse entspringen in einem herrlichen Hochtal an den Ausläufern des Jostedalsbreen. Leider verbirgt sich der schönste Teil des Tales noch hinter dem Liavatnet, dem Einstieg zu unserer Etappe. Nichtsdestotrotz lohnt der Ostri allemal, auch wenn man von der Landschaft nicht viel zu

Shortly after its release from the dam, the Ostri digs itself quickly into a gorge. If you're not too sure, you should risk a peek over the edge of the gorge, and memorise the zig zag path through the obstacle course of stoppers: right - left - right - middle, or was it the other way around? At higher flows the Ostri gets more difficult and becomes one big non-stop roller coaster. Especially then,

sehen bekommt.

Der Ostri gräbt sich nach dem Ausfluss aus dem See schnell in eine Schlucht. Wer sich nicht sicher ist, sollte vorher mal einen Blick vom Schluchtrand riskieren und sich den Zickzackkurs durch den Walzenparcours merken: rechts - links - rechts - mittig, oder war es doch eine andere Reihenfolge? Bei viel Wasser wird der Ostri schwerer und ist eine durchgehende Achterbahn. Gerade dann

the hole 50 metres above the take out should be paid its due respect. Unfortunately the fun is already over when you get to the road bridge, so get in the car and give it another run!

Tip: Drive further up from Liavatnet and savour the peace and quiet of Norway. The slides at the end of the valley are not really worth doing.

soll der Walze 50 Meter oberhalb des Ausstieges gebührend Respekt gezollt werden. Leider ist der Spaß an der Straßenbrücke schon wieder vorbei, also schnell noch mal hoch fahren.

Tipp: Fahre vom Liavatnet weiter hinauf und genieße die Ruhe Norwegens. Die Rutschen am Talende sind aber nicht wirklich lohnend.

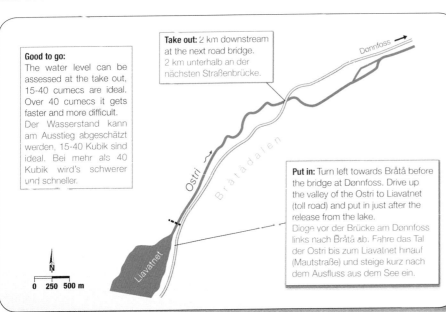

Good to go:
The water level can be assessed at the take out, 15-40 cumecs are ideal. Over 40 cumecs it gets faster and more difficult.
Der Wasserstand kann am Ausstieg abgeschätzt werden, 15-40 Kubik sind ideal. Bei mehr als 40 Kubik wird's schwerer und schneller.

Take out: 2 km downstream at the next road bridge.
2 km unterhalb an der nächsten Straßenbrücke.

Dønnfoss

Ostri

Bråtådalen

Liavatnet

0 250 500 m

Put in: Turn left towards Bråtå before the bridge at Dønnfoss. Drive up the valley of the Ostri to Liavatnet (toll road) and put in just after the release from the lake.
Diege vor der Brücke am Dønnfoss links nach Bråtå ab. Fahre das Tal der Ostri bis zum Liavatnet hinauf (Mautstraße) und steige kurz nach dem Ausfluss aus dem See ein.

SKJØLI

STEEP, FAST AND CONTINUOUS

The Skjøli in the Lundadalen is another classic, flowing into the Otta shortly before Skjåk. It descends fast and continuously, and slaps you about with unexpected holes around every other corner. It hammers blindly down the wide riverbed, and is a lot like a giant natural bob sled run. The Skjøli is definitely no place to be testing your limits, swimming here can have grave consequences (in every sense of the word). But for genuine kayak cowboys and cowgirls it is a treat, especially when you reach the bottom and have time to catch your breath again.

CLASS: IV - V
LEVEL: 15 - 25 cumecs
LENGTH: 4 km
TIME: 2 - 3 h
SEASON: June - August

After about the first third of the section, the most difficult cataract of the Skjøli runs right alongside the road. This can be scouted on the drive up. It is exactly 3.3 kilometres above the gravel pit. The short gorge about three quarters of the way down looks worse than it is, after that things get easier.

Tip: Don't forget to pay the toll for the Bomveg! The locals watch visitors closely, and it is not uncommon to be checked.
Survival tip: Don't swim!
Extra tip: In its short course, the upper Skjøli has great whitewater. For this section the boats have to be carried up about another kilometre from the put in of the standard section.

Photo: SG

Photo: KD

Der Skjøli im Lundadalen ist ein weiterer Klassiker, er mündet kurz vor Skjåk in die Otta. Schnell und stetig bricht er zu Tale, und ohrfeigt mit unverhofften Walzen hinter der nächsten Kurve. Er hämmert unübersichtlich durchs breite Flussbett und gleicht einer riesigen natürlichen Bobbahn. Der Skjøli ist definitiv kein Bach um seine Grenzen auszutesten, hier zu schwimmen, kann schlimme Konsequenzen haben. Für spritzdeckenfeste Paddler ist er aber ein Genuss, vor allem, wenn man unten angekommen ist und Zeit zum Luftholen hat.

Nach etwa einem Drittel der Strecke folgt der schwerste Katarakt des Skjøli direkt neben der Straße. Dieser kann schon beim Hochfahren besichtigt werden, er befindet sich genau 3,3 Kilometer oberhalb der Kiesgrube. Die kurze Schlucht nach etwa dreiviertel der Strecke sieht schlimmer aus als sie ist, danach lassen die Schwierigkeiten nach.

Tipp: Nicht vergessen die Maut für den Bomweg zu bezahlen! Die Anwohner passen hier sehr gut auf, Kontrollen sind keine Seltenheit.
Überlebens-Tipp: Nicht schwimmen!
Extra-Tipp: Der obere Skjøli bietet auf einem sehr kurzen Stück lohnendes Wildwasser. Dazu müssen die Boote vom Einstieg des Standardstückes etwa 1 Kilometer hoch getragen werden.

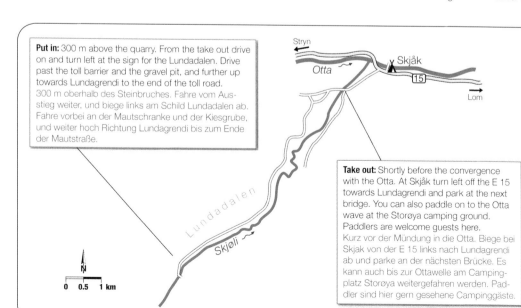

Put in: 300 m above the quarry. From the take out drive on and turn left at the sign for the Lundadalen. Drive past the toll barrier and the gravel pit, and further up towards Lundagrendi to the end of the toll road.
300 m oberhalb des Steinbruches. Fahre vom Ausstieg weiter, und biege links am Schild Lundadalen ab. Fahre vorbei an der Mautschranke und der Kiesgrube, und weiter hoch Richtung Lundagrendi bis zum Ende der Mautstraße.

Take out: Shortly before the convergence with the Otta. At Skjåk turn left off the E 15 towards Lundagrendi and park at the next bridge. You can also paddle on to the Otta wave at the Storøya camping ground. Paddlers are welcome guests here.
Kurz vor der Mündung in die Otta. Biege bei Skjak von der E 15 links nach Lundagrendi ab und parke an der nächsten Brücke. Es kann auch bis zur Ottawelle am Campingplatz Storøya weitergefahren werden. Paddler sind hier gern gesehene Campinggäste.

Good to go:
A high summer run that mostly has too much water during the spring snowmelt. There is a gauge at the end of the mini-gorge, before the toll barrier follow the path to the left down to the river. 1.15-1.5 m is a good level. But beware: the paddling world is divided on how the gauge should be properly read.
Ein Hochsommer-Run, der bei Hochschmelze im Frühjahr meist zuviel Wasser führt. Ein Pegel befindet sich am Ausgang der Miniklamm, einfach vor der Mautschranke links dem Weg zum Fluss folgen. Günstig sind zwischen 1,15-1,50 m. Aber Achtung: Die Paddlerwelt ist gespalten bei der korrekten Ablesung des Pegels.

Stryn
Otta
Skjåk
15
Lom
Lundadalen
Skjøli
0   0.5   1 km
N

TUNDRA: GORGE   *NORIBLE*

The Tundra is hidden high up in the Tundradalen. It is fast and blocked through and through, with mini-eddies, so is best enjoyed in a small group.

The first metres of the Tundra gurgle through open pasture with easy gradient. As soon as the cliffs come into sight, about 1 kilometre after the put in, you have reached the main attraction – a spectacular slide with a 3 metre drop at the end. Carved into the bedrock, it shoots the water into a lively little pool at the entrance to the gorge. Can be scouted and portaged on the left. Be careful on the steep, mossy banks – an easy place to slip and lose your footing.

From here you should walk down another 300 metres to look at the drop in the middle of the following gorge. After this furious prelude, the gorge opens up to be replaced with sheer cliff faces and small gravel banks at the foot of steep mossy slopes. The Tundra bounces on its lively way and gives you few breathers, instead continuous, steep but fair whitewater.

The take out above the next canyon must not be missed: it comes up suddenly in a long left hand bend. When you see the cliffs rising ahead of you, jump straight out of your boat. On the horizon the water disappears between smoothened rock walls into a blind inferno – don't go there! Better to work your way up the right bank until you get a look at the waterfalls. Then you walk up at right angles to the river to the road. After a good 15 minutes you're at the edge of the forest, sweating and grinning.

Ingrid Schlott

CLASS:	IV (V)
LEVEL:	5 - 10 cumecs
LENGTH:	4 km
TIME:	3 - 4 h
SEASON:	July - August

Die Tundra versteckt sich hoch oben im Tundradalen. Sie ist durchweg schnell und verblockt, mit Minikehrwässern, und ist somit am besten in einer kleinen Gruppe zu genießen.

Auf den ersten Metern gurgelt die Tundra mit angenehmem Gefälle durch eine offene Wiesenlandschaft. Sobald Felswände sichtbar werden, etwa 1 Kilometer nach dem Einstieg, erreicht man die Hauptattraktion, eine spektakuläre Rutsche mit 3-Meter-Stufe am Ausgang. Ins Grundgestein geschliffen, schickt sie das Wasser in einen quirligen Tumpf am Schluchteingang. Kann links besichtigt und umtragen werden. Vorsicht vor dem abschüssigen und mit Moosplatten versehenen Ufer – Rutschgefahr.

Man sollte von hier aus gleich 300 Meter weiterlaufen, um die Stufe in der Mitte der folgenden Klamm zu begutachten. Nach diesem furiosen Auftakt öffnet sich die Klamm, nun wechseln schiere Felswände mit schmalen Kiesbänken vor moosigen Steilhängen. Die Tundra springt munter weiter und lässt wenig Verschnaufpausen, sie bietet durchgehend steiles, aber faires Wildwasser.

Der Ausstieg oberhalb der nächsten Klamm darf nicht verpasst werden: er kommt abrupt in einer lang gezogenen Linkskurve. Wenn man am Ende die Felsen ansteigen sieht, hüpft man besser schnell aus dem Boot. Am Horizont verschwindet das Wasser zwischen glatt geschliffenen Felswänden in ein schwer einsehbares Inferno – don't go there! Besser flussrechts hoch arbeiten, bis man einen Blick auf die Wasserfälle erhascht. Dann läuft man rechtwinklig vom Fluss hinauf zur Straße. Nach gut 15 Minuten steht man schwitzend und grinsend am Waldrand.

Ingrid Schlott

Smile when you walk up to the car

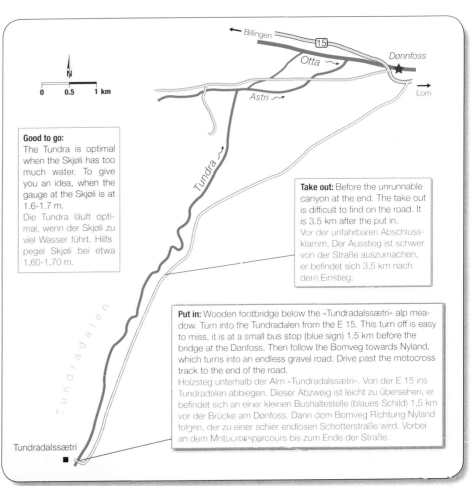

Good to go:
The Tundra is optimal when the Skjøli has too much water. To give you an idea, when the gauge at the Skjøli is at 1.6-1.7 m.
Die Tundra läuft optimal, wenn der Skjøli zu viel Wasser führt. Hilfspegel Skjøli bei etwa 1,60-1,70 m.

Take out: Before the unrunnable canyon at the end. The take out is difficult to find on the road. It is 3.5 km after the put in.
Vor der unfahrbaren Abschlussklamm. Der Ausstieg ist schwer von der Straße auszumachen, er befindet sich 3,5 km nach dem Einstieg.

Put in: Wooden footbridge below the »Tundradalssætri« alp meadow. Turn into the Tundradalen from the E 15. This turn off is easy to miss, it is at a small bus stop (blue sign) 1.5 km before the bridge at the Dønfoss. Then follow the Bomveg towards Nyland, which turns into an endless gravel road. Drive past the motocross track to the end of the road.
Holzsteg unterhalb der Alm »Tundradalssætri«. Von der E 15 ins Tundradalen abbiegen. Dieser Abzweig ist leicht zu übersehen, er befindet sich an einer kleinen Bushaltestelle (blaues Schild) 1,5 km vor der Brücke am Dønfoss. Dann dem Bomveg Richtung Nyland folgen, der zu einer schier endlosen Schotterstraße wird. Vorbei an dem Motocrossparcours bis zum Ende der Straße.

Tundradalssætri

TORA: TORA BORA

The Tora flows far from the road through the hidden Tordalen, so only the last metres of it are of interest to us. The Tora is a very steep creek here, with eight or more drops and slides, all one after the other: steep and deep. All the sections can be easily scouted.

The upper part of the Tora could be worth investigating, but there is no information available to date. So, get your tramping boots on and get going!

CLASS:	V
LEVEL:	5 - 10 cumecs
LENGTH:	800 m
TIME:	1 - 2 h
SEASON:	July - September

Die Tora fließt fernab der Straße durch das versteckte Tordalen und ist so für uns nur auf den letzten Metern interessant. Hier ist die Tora ein sehr steiler Bach, mit acht oder mehr aufeinander folgenden Abfällen und Rutschen: Steil ist geil. Alle Stellen sind einfach zu besichtigen.

Der obere Teil der Tora könnte eine Erkundung wert sein, Informationen liegen bis dato noch nicht vor. Also, Wanderschuhe ausgepackt und auf geht's!

My house, my river

Tipp: Wandere den linken Zufluss, die Store Frøysa, hinauf zum »Føystein«, und genieße den Blick über das Billingsdalen.

Tip: Tramp up the left tributary, the Store Frøysa, to the Føystein, and take in the view over the Billingsdalen.

Obsommer enjoying his walk back from the Store Frøysa

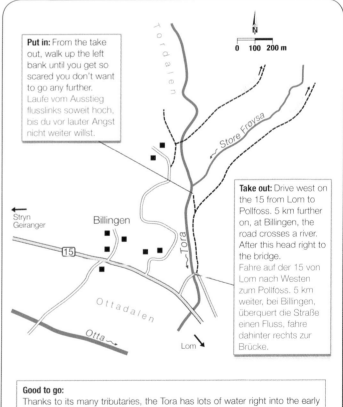

Put in: From the take out, walk up the left bank until you get so scared you don't want to go any further. Laufe vom Ausstieg flusslinks soweit hoch, bis du vor lauter Angst nicht weiter willst.

Stryn
Geiranger

Billingen

15

Tordalen

Store Frøysa

Tora

Ottadalen

Otta

Lom

Take out: Drive west on the 15 from Lom to Pollfoss. 5 km further on, at Billingen, the road crosses a river. After this head right to the bridge.
Fahre auf der 15 von Lom nach Westen zum Pollfoss. 5 km weiter, bei Billingen, überquert die Straße einen Fluss, fahre dahinter rechts zur Brücke.

Good to go:
Thanks to its many tributaries, the Tora has lots of water right into the early summer months. However for the lower section, a couple of cumecs are enough anyway. The level can be checked at the take out bridge.
Die Tora führt dank ihrer vielen Zuflüsse bis in den Frühsommer hinein viel Wasser. Für eine Befahrung des unteren Stückes reichen allerdings schon ein paar Kubik aus. Der Wasserstand kann an der Ausstiegsbrücke abgeschätzt werden.

The »Foystein«

Bernie Mauracher on number 1 ...

... and number 2

FINNA: LOWER CANYON

Unlike many Norwegian rivers, the Finna is extremely remote, has a virtually inescapable gorge, and brings with it a must-run WW V section! Those who feel up to the challenge are rewarded with an unforgettable whitewater adventure.

To get to the Finna you put into the Skjerva, and immediately get your wake-up call. When you reach the Finna after about a kilometre, there are several long rapids to be found in a canyon. A tight, steep bend to the right signals the start of the imminent challenging rapids. As soon as the left wall of the canyon gets high and vertical, take out on the right and scout the slot which follows. This is a potential pin spot, but can be portaged with some effort.

The following cataracts will also demand your undivided attention, until a couple of large blocks on the beach on the right bank signal the next spot to scout. To follow are countless awesome drops and cataracts, although the last section before the exit from the gorge is very challenging because it is so difficult to scout. The last kilometres to Vågåmo are spiked with iron reinforcements, so it's advisable to get out on the left after the gorge.

Tip: Make sure you're in good form!

CLASS:	IV - V (X)
LEVEL:	10 - 20 cumecs
LENGTH:	9 km
TIME:	3 - 5 h
SEASON:	June - July

Die Finna ist im Gegensatz zu vielen anderen Flüssen in Norwegen sehr ausgesetzt, dazu eine WW-V-Zwangspassage! Wer sich dieser Herausforderung gewachsen fühlt, wird belohnt mit einem nimmervergesslichen Wildwasser-Abenteuer.

Um zur Finna zu gelangen, setzt man in der Skjerva ein, und wird sofort wachgerüttelt. Erreicht man die Finna nach etwa einem Kilometer, führen einige lange Katarakte in eine Klamm. Eine enge, steile Rechtskurve läutet die kommenden erhöhten Schwierigkeiten ein. Sobald links die Felswände senkrecht ansteigen, rechts anlanden und den folgenden Schlitz anschauen. Dieser ist klemmgefährlich, er kann etwas umständlich umtragen werden.

Die folgenden Katarakte fordern weiter hohe Aufmerksamkeit, bis ein paar große Felsblöcke und ein Strand rechtsufrig die nächste Besichtigung ankündigen. Im Anschluss warten unzählige wunderschöne Stufen und Katarakte, wobei gerade die letzte Stelle vor dem Klammausgang recht anspruchsvoll ist, da sie nur schwer besichtigt werden kann. Die letzten Kilometer bis Vågåmo sind mit Stahlträgern gespickt, deshalb ist es empfehlenswert kurz nach der Klamm links auszusteigen.

Tipp: Sei in Topform!

Photo: BH

SKJERVA: UPPER

The Skjerva in the Slådalen is a fairly atypical river for Norway. From the fjell it digs its way deep down into an almost inaccessible gorge, and there gradually loses its gradient again. If you want to check out every section, bring lots of time with you. If you're an experienced eddy hopper, and are good at judging difficulties from your boat, the Skjerva will be one big intoxicating rush!

After the first 2 kilometres there is pretty much continuous whitewater, after which you reach a slot in the bed rock which can be scouted on the left. After that things stay fairly fast and furious, until a cliff on the right signals a steep S-bend, which is followed by a portage. 50 metres later you reach the take out on river left. Here you have to follow the creek bed up to the road.

Tip: UPPER UPPER: Above the put in the Skjerva flows through the beautiful Skjervedalen. This is well worth checking out, the whitewater is breathtaking here. However the boats have to be carried all the way up from the road. Best time: probably in late summer.

CLASS:	V (X)
LEVEL:	5 - 15 cumec
LENGTH:	5 km
TIME:	3 - 6 h
SEASON:	June - July

Die Skjerva im Slådalen ist für norwegische Verhältnisse ein etwas untypischer Bach. Sie gräbt sich vom Fjell tief in eine schwer zugängliche Schlucht und baut dort kontinuierlich ihr Gefälle ab. Wer jede Passage anschauen möchte, sollte viel Zeit mitbringen. Wer geübt ist im Kehrwasserfahren und Einschätzen der Schwierigkeit aus dem Boot, wird die Skjerva wie im Rausch erleben.

Nach den ersten 2 Kilometern mit recht kontinuierlichem Wildwasser kommt man an einen Grundgesteinsschlitz, den man von links besichtigt. Danach bleibt es schnell und anspruchsvoll, bis eine Klippe auf der rechten Seite eine steile S-Kurve ankündigt, auf die eine Umtragestelle folgt. 50 Meter dahinter erreicht man den Ausstieg auf der linken Seite. Dort musst du dem Bachbett hoch zur Schotterstraße folgen.

Tipp: UPPER UPPER: Oberhalb des Einstiegs fließt die Skjerva fernab der Straße durchs wunderschöne Skjervedalen. Eine Erkundung ist äußerst lohnend, das Wildwasser sieht atemberaubend aus. Allerdings müssen die Boote von der Straße die ganze Strecke hinauf getragen werden. Beste Zeit: Wahrscheinlich im Spätsommer.

SKJERVA: LOWER

STEEP AND CONTINUOUS WHITEWATER IN A DEEP GORGE

Photo: BH

Mariann Sæther

The second part of the Skjerva is by no means any less worthy than the upper section. It could even be said that the section after the portage is the nicest of the whole Skjerva.

The first rapids bring you to a couple of nasty cataracts which recently formed after a land slide. After a narrow slot you should portage right around the next steep cataract. After that you can delight in the constant slides and rapids over the next 4 kilometres – a real delight for any whitewater paddler. The take out is on the right at the road bridge.

Tip: Combine the lower Skjerva with the lower Finna canyon.

Der zweite Teil der Skjerva steht dem oberen Abschnitt in nichts nach, möglicherweise ist der Abschnitt nach der Umtragestelle sogar der schönste der gesamten Skjerva.

Die ersten Schwellen bringen dich zu ein paar ekeligen Katarakten, die nach einem Erdrutsch neu entstanden sind. Nach einem engen Schlitz sollte man den folgenden steilen Katarakt rechts umtragen. Nun kannst du die steigen Rutschen und Katarakte auf den nächsten 4 Kilometern genießen – ein Hochgenuss für jeden Wildwasserpaddler. Der Ausstieg befindet sich rechts an der Straßenbrücke.

Tip: Verbinde die untere Skjerva mit der unteren Finna Klamm.

CLASS:	IV - V (X)
LEVEL:	5 - 15 cumecs
LENGTH:	5 km
TIME:	3 - 6 h
SEASON:	June - July

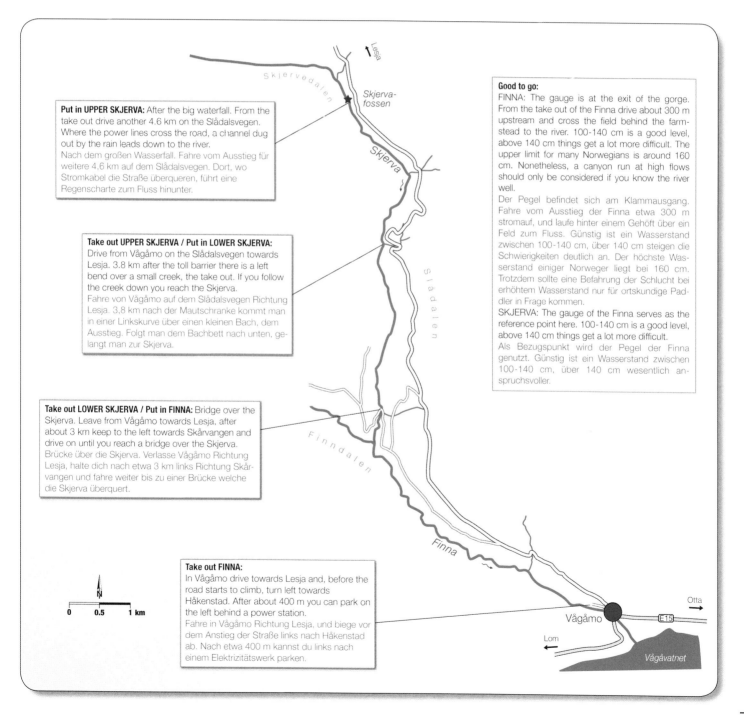

Put in UPPER SKJERVA: After the big waterfall. From the take out drive another 4.6 km on the Slådalsvegen. Where the power lines cross the road, a channel dug out by the rain leads down to the river.
Nach dem großen Wasserfall. Fahre vom Ausstieg für weitere 4,6 km auf dem Slådalsvegen. Dort, wo Stromkabel die Straße überqueren, führt eine Regenscharte zum Fluss hinunter.

Take out UPPER SKJERVA / Put in LOWER SKJERVA: Drive from Vågåmo on the Slådalsvegen towards Lesja. 3.8 km after the toll barrier there is a left bend over a small creek, the take out. If you follow the creek down you reach the Skjerva.
Fahre von Vågåmo auf dem Slådalsvegen Richtung Lesja. 3,8 km nach der Mautschranke kommt man in einer Linkskurve über einen kleinen Bach, dem Ausstieg. Folgt man dem Bachbett nach unten, gelangt man zur Skjerva.

Take out LOWER SKJERVA / Put in FINNA: Bridge over the Skjerva. Leave from Vågåmo towards Lesja, after about 3 km keep to the left towards Skårvangen and drive on until you reach a bridge over the Skjerva.
Brücke über die Skjerva. Verlasse Vågåmo Richtung Lesja, halte dich nach etwa 3 km links Richtung Skårvangen und fahre weiter bis zu einer Brücke welche die Skjerva überquert.

Take out FINNA: In Vågåmo drive towards Lesja and, before the road starts to climb, turn left towards Håkenstad. After about 400 m you can park on the left behind a power station.
Fahre in Vågåmo Richtung Lesja, und biege vor dem Anstieg der Straße links nach Håkenstad ab. Nach etwa 400 m kannst du links nach einem Elektrizitätswerk parken.

Good to go:
FINNA: The gauge is at the exit of the gorge. From the take out of the Finna drive about 300 m upstream and cross the field behind the farmstead to the river. 100-140 cm is a good level, above 140 cm things get a lot more difficult. The upper limit for many Norwegians is around 160 cm. Nonetheless, a canyon run at high flows should only be considered if you know the river well.
Der Pegel befindet sich am Klammausgang. Fahre vom Ausstieg der Finna etwa 300 m stromauf, und laufe hinter einem Gehöft über ein Feld zum Fluss. Günstig ist ein Wasserstand zwischen 100-140 cm, über 140 cm steigen die Schwierigkeiten deutlich an. Der höchste Wasserstand einiger Norweger liegt bei 160 cm. Trotzdem sollte eine Befahrung der Schlucht bei erhöhtem Wasserstand nur für ortskundige Paddler in Frage kommen.
SKJERVA: The gauge of the Finna serves as the reference point here. 100-140 cm is a good level, above 140 cm things get a lot more difficult.
Als Bezugspunkt wird der Pegel der Finna genutzt. Günstig ist ein Wasserstand zwischen 100-140 cm, über 140 cm wesentlich anspruchsvoller.

Lesja

Skjervedalen

Skjerva-fossen

Skjerva

Slådalen

Finndalen

Finna

N

0   0.5   1 km

Otta

Vågåmo

E15

Lom

Vågåvatnet

The first drop is worth a portage, for sure.

JORI: UPPER

STEEP RAPIDS IN BEAUTIFUL LANDSCAPE

The Jori flows through the beautiful, untamed Svartdalen, sometimes far removed from the road. With its crystal clear waters and magnificent cataracts, it enchants any paddler, whether you're a pleasure tourer or a hardcore drop addict.

The upper section is somewhat more challenging than the lower section, better suited for the drop pilots. It is sometimes described as being a bit dodgy, but there are enough clear lines – you just have to hit them!

After you have most likely carried around the entrance to the first section, you quickly reach a series of slides of all shapes and sizes. In a tight, difficult S-bend there are rocks below the surface on the right – caution. And in case you haven't noticed: the landscape is unbelievable!

CLASS: V
LEVEL: 10 cumecs
LENGTH: 6 km
TIME: 3 - 4 h
SEASON: late May - July

Der Jori fließt durch das wilde und wunderschöne Svartdalen teils fernab der Straße. Mit glasklarem Wasser und wunderschönen Katarakten verzaubert er jeden Paddler, egal ob Genussfahrer oder Vollblutstürzer.

Der obere Abschnitt ist etwas sportlicher als die untere Standardstrecke, er ist wohl eher was für Sturzbootfahrer. Er wird gelegentlich als etwas unsauber beschrieben, trotz alledem gibt es genügend saubere Linien – man muss sie nur treffen.

Nachdem man mit höchster Wahrscheinlichkeit den Eingang der ersten Stelle umhoben hat, kommt man schnell an eine Folge von Rutschen mit unterschiedlichster Würze. In einer engen und recht schwierigen S-Kurve befinden sich rechts schmerzliche Steine im Unterwasser, Vorsicht. Und falls es dir noch nicht aufgefallen ist: die Landschaft ist überwältigend!

Strohmeier: calm at the put in...

... but a rocket on the river.

JORI: LOWER

AWESOME FUN WHITEWATER, BEST AT HIGH FLOW

The take out at the road bridge.

The lower standard section of the Jori always has whitewater, first in an open canyon, then between steep walls. When the Jori is at high flow, you can enjoy big waves and holes in endless rapids, especially after the Grøna, a tributary from the left, generously donates its water as well.

About 1 kilometre after the put in there is a cataract with a river-wide hole at the end, not a bad idea to scout it first. The run continues with fun class III-IV whitewater up to the railway bridge shortly before the take out. The waterfall just before the E 136 road bridge has disappeared. Below and behind the bridge are three pushy rockslides which develop powerful holes at high flow. You should scout these on the way to the river.

Der untere Standardabschnitt des Jori birgt stetiges Wildwasser, anfangs in einer offenen Schlucht, später zwischen steilen Wänden. Gerade wenn der Jori viel Wasser führt, kann man die großen Wellen und Walzen über endlose Stromschnellen genießen, besonders nachdem die Grøna, ein linker Zufluss, dem Jori noch mehr Wasser schenkt.

Etwa 1 Kilometer nach dem Einstieg folgt ein Katarakt mit flussbreiter Walze am Ende, eventuell besichtigen. Im weiteren Verlauf geht es mit lustigem WW III-IV bis zur Eisenbahnbrücke kurz vor dem Ausstieg dahin. Der Wasserfall kurz vor der E 136 Straßenbrücke ist verschwunden. Unter und hinter der Brücke folgen drei wuchtige Felsrutschen, die bei viel Wasser kräftige Walzen bilden. Diese sollten schon bei der Anfahrt besichtigt werden.

CLASS:	**III - IV**
LEVEL:	**50 - 100 cumecs**
LENGTH:	**17 km**
TIME:	**3 - 4 h**
SEASON:	**May - July**

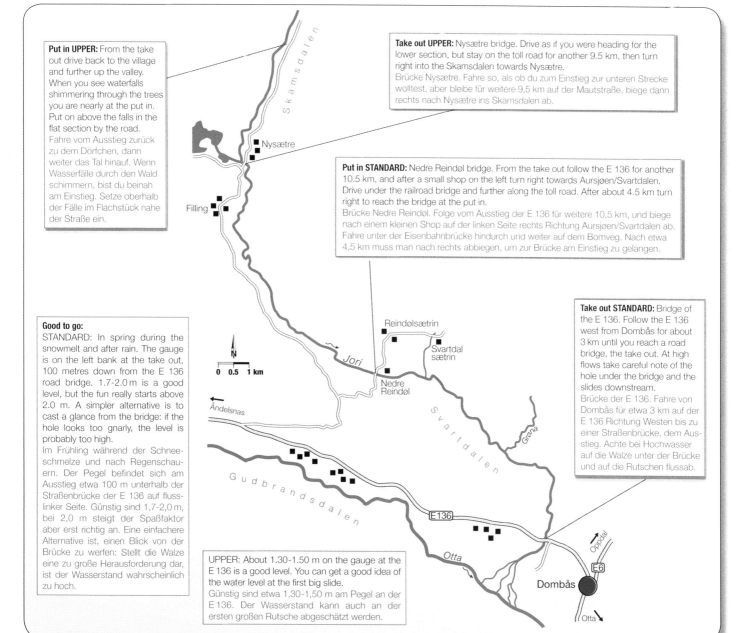

Put in UPPER: From the take out drive back to the village and further up the valley. When you see waterfalls shimmering through the trees you are nearly at the put in. Put on above the falls in the flat section by the road.
Fahre vom Ausstieg zurück zu dem Dörfchen, dann weiter das Tal hinauf. Wenn Wasserfälle durch den Wald schimmern, bist du beinah am Einstieg. Setze oberhalb der Fälle im Flachstück nahe der Straße ein.

Take out UPPER: Nysætre bridge. Drive as if you were heading for the lower section, but stay on the toll road for another 9.5 km, then turn right into the Skamsdalen towards Nysætre.
Brücke Nysætre. Fahre so, als ob du zum Einstieg zur unteren Strecke wolltest, aber bleibe für weitere 9,5 km auf der Mautstraße, biege dann rechts nach Nysætre ins Skamsdalen ab.

Put in STANDARD: Nedre Reindøl bridge. From the take out follow the E 136 for another 10.5 km, and after a small shop on the left turn right towards Aursjøen/Svartdalen. Drive under the railroad bridge and further along the toll road. After about 4.5 km turn right to reach the bridge at the put in.
Brücke Nedre Reindøl. Folge vom Ausstieg der E 136 für weitere 10,5 km, und biege nach einem kleinen Shop auf der linken Seite rechts Richtung Aursjøen/Svartdalen ab. Fahre unter der Eisenbahnbrücke hindurch und weiter auf dem Bomveg. Nach etwa 4,5 km muss man nach rechts abbiegen, um zur Brücke am Einstieg zu gelangen.

Good to go:
STANDARD: In spring during the snowmelt and after rain. The gauge is on the left bank at the take out, 100 metres down from the E 136 road bridge. 1.7-2.0 m is a good level, but the fun really starts above 2.0 m. A simpler alternative is to cast a glance from the bridge: if the hole looks too gnarly, the level is probably too high.
Im Frühling während der Schneeschmelze und nach Regenschauern. Der Pegel befindet sich am Ausstieg etwa 100 m unterhalb der Straßenbrücke der E 136 auf flusslinker Seite. Günstig sind 1,7-2,0 m, bei 2,0 m steigt der Spaßfaktor aber erst richtig an. Eine einfachere Alternative ist, einen Blick von der Brücke zu werfen: Stellt die Walze eine zu große Herausforderung dar, ist der Wasserstand wahrscheinlich zu hoch.

Take out STANDARD: Bridge of the E 136. Follow the E 136 west from Dombås for about 3 km until you reach a road bridge, the take out. At high flows take careful note of the hole under the bridge and the slides downstream.
Brücke der E 136. Fahre von Dombås für etwa 3 km auf der E 136 Richtung Westen bis zu einer Straßenbrücke, dem Ausstieg. Achte bei Hochwasser auf die Walze unter der Brücke und auf die Rutschen flussab.

UPPER: About 1.30-1.50 m on the gauge at the E 136 is a good level. You can get a good idea of the water level at the first big slide.
Günstig sind etwa 1,30-1,50 m am Pegel an der E 136. Der Wasserstand kann auch an der ersten großen Rutsche abgeschätzt werden.

Map labels: Skamsdalen · Nysætre · Filling · Reindølsætrin · Svartdal sætrin · Jori · Nedre Reindøl · Åndelsnas · Svartdalen · Grøna · Gudbrandsdalen · E 136 · Otta · Oppdal · E 6 · Dombås · Otta

0 0.5 1 km · N

EL BURRO: MATZE BRUSTMANN

blueandwhite

LORA

A WIDE OPEN RIVER WITH SOME LOW CANYONS

The Lora feeds into the Lågen below the Lesja-kogsvatnet. It flows through a wide river bed over athletic rapids, sometimes through long gorge sections, sometimes through the amazing landscape of the Lordalen.

CLASS:	**III - IV- (VI-)**
LEVEL:	**8 - 15 cumecs**
LENGTH:	**15 km**
TIME:	**4 - 6 h**
SEASON:	**May - late July**

About 2 kilometres after the put in you reach a small, easily accessible gorge at

Løstølen. This can be seen from the road, WW IV. After that the run gets easier for the next 4 kilometres, until you reach a 3 metre high, river wide drop under the road bridge in Rusti. Have a good look at this – you might want to portage it.

In the narrow gorge 2 kilometres downstream things get more difficult again, be careful here of undercuts. About 3 kilometres after the gorge the road comes back alongside the river. This is

a good place to get off. And don't miss the take out – 3 kilometres downstream are the impressive Lora Waterfalls.

Tip: When the standard section has good water, the Lorafoss is unpaddleable. It may be possible at low flows. Take out on the right beforehand and have a look at it. If you want to try your hand at it, get out at the lower bridge just before the bridge on the E 136.

Die Lora mündet unterhalb des Lesjakogsvatnet in den Lågen. Sie fließt im breiten Flussbett über sportliche Stromschnellen und Schwellen, teils durch längere Schluchtstrecken, teils durch die wunderschöne Landschaft des Lordalen.

Etwa 2 Kilometer nach dem Einstieg erreicht man eine kleine zugängliche Klamm bei Løstølen, die gut von der Straße aus besichtigt werden

kann, WW IV. Danach lassen die Schwierigkeiten für die nächsten 4 Kilometer nach, bis man zu einer flussbreiten, etwa 3 Meter hohen Schwelle unter der Straßenbrücke in Rusti kommt. Sorgsam besichtigen und gegebenenfalls umtragen.

In der recht engen Klamm 2 Kilometer unterhalb nehmen die Schwierigkeiten erneut zu, hier Vorsicht vor Unterspülungen. Etwa 3 Kilometer nach der Schlucht verläuft die Straße in Flussnähe, am

besten hier Aussteigen. Und nicht den Ausstieg verpassen, denn 3 Kilometer unterhalb befinden sich die beeindruckenden Lora-Wasserfälle.

Tipp: Der Lorafossen ist bei einem guten Wasserstand unfahrbar, bei weniger Wasser wird er eventuell fahrbar. Rechtzeitig davor rechts aussteigen und besichtigen. Wer den Lorafossen antesten möchte, steigt am besten an der unteren Brücke kurz vor der Brücke der E 136 aus.

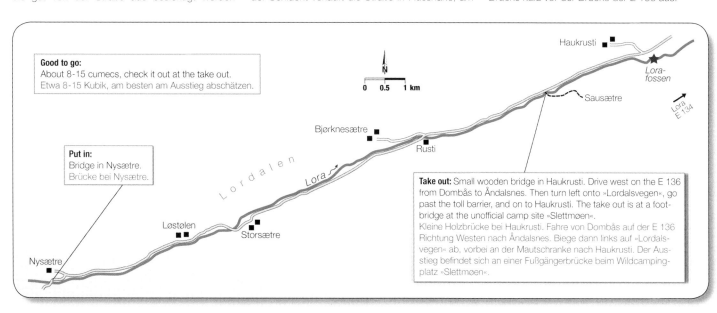

Good to go:
About 8-15 cumecs, check it out at the take out.
Etwa 8-15 Kubik, am besten am Ausstieg abschätzen.

Put in:
Bridge in Nysætre.
Brücke bei Nysætre.

Haukrusti

Lora-fossen

Sausætre

Lora E 134

Bjørknesætre

Rusti

Lordalen Lora

Løstølen

Storsætre

Nysætre

Take out: Small wooden bridge in Haukrusti. Drive west on the E 136 from Dombås to Åndalsnes. Then turn left onto »Lordalsvegen«, go past the toll barrier, and on to Haukrusti. The take out is at a footbridge at the unofficial camp site »Slettmøen«.
Kleine Holzbrücke bei Haukrusti. Fahre von Dombås auf der E 136 Richtung Westen nach Åndalsnes. Biege dann links auf »Lordalsvegen« ab, vorbei an der Mautschranke nach Haukrusti. Der Ausstieg befindet sich an einer Fußgängerbrücke beim Wildcamping-platz »Slettmøen«.

STORY: SKJERVA NILS KAGEL

CHEEK TO JOWL WITH THE »EVIL CORNER«

It seems possible. The rest of the group is more sceptical about the mission, but I ignore their doubts. I put in at the eddy a few metres above the ledge and wait for the signal to start.

A few moments later, I sprint out of the eddy and cut through the small hole on the right. As soon as I hit the main stream, I turn to the left and try to pick up as much speed as possible. Just as I had planned, I stay well left on the rock shelf. When I think I have reached the ledge, a ghost hand pulls me to the right. I slide sideways off the edge of the shelf and discover to my horror that I am about to boof the rest of it. I thrust myself forward with all my strength. No chance, I still land almost flat at the bottom. But instead of a hard landing, I get pulled down deep. My first roll fails. I can feel my boat getting pressed against the undercut wall. I let go of my paddle and pull myself up on the wall. Next thing I know I get pushed into the »corner« behind the fall. There is a small rock spur I can hold onto.

A glance upstream makes it immediately clear that my problems are just beginning. Without a paddle I have no chance whatsoever of making it over the one metre recirc. It is questionable whether it could even be done with a paddle. I can see through the spray that someone is swaying a rope in my direction. I get a hold of it and pull myself up with a rope clamp. But after a few metres, my rope clamp gets stuck and I am dangling over the undercut. Luckily, I manage to sway the rope until I get hold of a little ledge.

Here I am, once again, unable to move. The spray of the waterfall is constantly hitting me and, despite the sunshine, I start getting cold quite fast. I try moving my fingers so that they won't stiffen too much. Panic is spreading somewhere deep inside me. The minutes pass.

Then I see the rope swing in my direction again. This time a throw rope is tied to it, which comes from the other shore. I begin to understand their plan. Instead of hooking/clipping myself to the rope, I first tie the boat to it. But before I realize my mistake, both rope and boat disappear behind the curtain of water. I am left shivering on the ledge. I just missed my chance of getting out of here quickly.

After minutes of suspense, I see the rope being lowered once again. I click the throw bag to my lifejacket and mount a few metres on the climbing rope. Then I swing like Tarzan back and forth until I am downstream of the recirc and the undercut wall. I let go of the climbing rope and jump. Now it is all up to the land crew. Swimming over the next drop would be disastrous. I feel the rope of the throw bag tighten and get dragged through the water until I reach the shore. Shaking and totally whacked, I sit down on a rock.

AUF TUCHFÜHLUNG MIT DEM »BÖSEN ECK«

Das geht schon. Der Rest der Gruppe hat Zweifel, aber das ignoriere ich. Ich setze im Kehrwasser wenige Meter oberhalb der Abbruchkante ein und warte auf das Zeichen.

Mit voller Konzentration beschleunige ich mein Boot aus dem Kehrwasser heraus. Ein kräftiger Schlag und ich schneide die kleine Walze nach rechts an. Sobald ich mich im Hauptwasser befinde, drehe ich nach links und versuche möglichst viel Geschwindigkeit aufzunehmen. Wie geplant bleibe ich auf der Platte zunächst schön weit links. Aber als ich schon fast glaube die Fallkante erreicht zu haben, wird mein Boot wie von Geisterhand nach rechts geschoben. Ich rutsche seitlich über den Rand der Platte, werfe meinen Oberkörper mit voller Kraft nach vorn. Es nützt nichts – ich komme fast flach unten an! Der erwartete harte Aufprall bleibt jedoch aus, stattdessen werde ich tief versenkt. Die erste Rolle scheitert. Ich spüre, dass mein Boot an der unterspülten Felswand hängt, lasse das Paddel los und drücke mich mit den Händen an der Wand hoch. Im nächsten Moment werde ich in das Eck hinter dem Fall geschoben. An einem Felsvorsprung kann ich mich festhalten und aussteigen.

Ein Blick flussab macht deutlich, dass meine Schwierigkeiten gerade erst begonnen haben: auch mit einem Paddel würde ich es kaum über den meterlangen Rücklauf schaffen. Durch die Gischt sehe ich, wie jemand das Kletterseil in meine Richtung schwenkt. Mit einem beherzten Griff kann ich es fassen. Zunächst versuche ich es mit den Steigklemmen. Doch als ich einige Meter hoch gekommen bin, blockiert die untere Klemme: Ich hänge direkt über der Unterspülung fest. Glücklicherweise kann ich zurück auf den Felsabsatz pendeln, wo ich erneut festsitze. Ständig werde ich von der Gischt des Wasserfalls eingedeckt und obwohl die Sonne scheint, beginne ich allmählich auszukühlen. Ich versuche meine Finger zu bewegen. In meinem Kopf machte sich Panik breit. Nichts passiert, Minuten vergehen.

Dann sehe ich, wie sich das Kletterseil erneut in meine Richtung bewegt. An ihm ist ein Wurfsackseil befestigt, welches ans andere Ufer führt. Schnell wird mir klar, was die anderen vorhaben. Anstatt mich jedoch selber an das Seil zu hängen, befestige ich mein Boot daran. Ehe ich meinen Fehler erkenne, ruckt es am Seil und das Boot verschwindet hinter dem Wasservorhang. Ich bleibe fröstelnd zurück. Gerade habe ich die Chance vertan, hier schnell heraus zu kommen.

Nach Minuten der Ungewissheit sehe ich das Seil ein zweites Mal näher kommen. Diesmal weiß ich, was zu tun ist. Ich klinke das Wurfsackseil in meinen Brustgurt ein und steige einige Meter am Kletterseil empor. Dann pendele ich wie Tarzan an der Liane solange hin und her, bis ich mich unterhalb des Rücklaufes und der Unterspülung befinde – und lasse los. Weich lande ich im Tumpf des Wasserfalls. Jetzt hängt alles von der Landmannschaft ab, ein Schwimmer über die nächste Stufe hätte fatale Folgen. Ich spüre, wie sich das Wurfsackseil am Brustgurt strafft und ich durchs Wasser gezogen werde, dann habe ich das rettende Ufer erreicht. Bibbernd und völlig am Ende setze ich mich auf einen Felsen.

NILS KAGEL 1971
Nils loves testing his limits – and if necessary, he is also prepared to get in his boat alone for it. Can this be reconciled with work in a library, Dr. Kagel?
Nils liebt es seine Grenzen auszutesten – und wenn's sein muss, steigt er dazu auch allein ins Boot. Lässt sich das mit der Arbeit in einem Museum vereinbaren, Herr Dr. Kagel?

VOSS

Don Hölzl holding his breath for a moment - Jordalselvi.

Mauracher and Kagel

VOSS

Every sport has its Mecca. Extreme skiers go to Chamonix, free climbers to Yosemite Valley, mountain bikers to lake Garda. And whitewater paddlers? We would like to nominate the wee Norwegian town of Voss as the next cult sport centre. After all, films like »Mothership Connection« (Schäftlein) and »Sick Line« (Obsommer) have proven that it is here that you will find the highest concentration of paddleable waterfalls in all of Europe.

Voss is West Norway's best known winter sport region, but in summer it is also inundated by sport freaks – whether they be base jumpers, parachuters, climbers or mountain bikers. The high point of this outdoor frenzy is the annual Ekstremsportveko, at which bands such as »The Wailers« and »Salmonella Dub« also appear, just by the way.

In terms of paddling, the tours are almost exclusively up in the fifth grade, only on the Raundalselvi, Strondelvi and Tysselva will you find runs up to WW IV. But around Voss there are also a number of very inviting play spots.

About 100 kilometres from Voss is Bergen, the main city of western Norway, and the European City of Culture 2000. The wooden houses in Bergen (»Bryggen«), built by German traders in the time of the Hanseatic league, have been declared a UNESCO World Heritage Site. Why not make a small detour there?

Jeder Sport hat sein Mekka. Extreme Skifahrer pilgern nach Chamonix, Freikletterer ins Yosemite Valley, Mountainbiker zum Gardasee. Und Wildwasserpaddler? Wir schlagen das norwegische Städtchen Voss als neue Kultstätte vor. Schließlich haben Filme wie »Mothership Connection« (Schäftlein) und »Sick Line« (Obsommer) bewiesen, dass sich hier die höchste Konzentration fahrbarer Wasserfälle in ganz Europa befindet.

Voss ist Westnorwegens bekanntester Wintersportort, doch auch im Sommer tummeln sich hier Freizeitsportler in Scharen – ob Basejumper, Fallschirmspringer, Kletterer oder Mountainbiker. Höhepunkt des Outdoorgetummels ist die jährlich stattfindende Ekstremsportveko, bei der ganz nebenbei Bands wie »The Wailers« oder »Salmonella Dub« auftreten.

Paddeltechnisch bieten sich vornehmlich Touren im fünften Grad, lediglich auf Raundalselvi, Strondelvi und Tysselva finden sich Touren bis WW IV. Dafür bieten sich rund um Voss einige einladende Spielstellen.

Etwa 100 Kilometer entfernt von Voss liegt Bergen, die Hauptstadt Westnorwegens und Europäische Kulturstadt 2000. Die in der Hansezeit von deutschen Kaufleuten gebauten Holzhäuser in Bergen (»Bryggen«) wurden in die UNESCO-Liste des Weltkulturerbes aufgenommen. Warum auch nicht mal dahin einen Abstecher machen?

Photos: MN

Brown, Obsommer - Tysselva

Info on the region

www.alr.no
www.visitvoss.no
www.ekstremsportveko.com
www.visitbergen.com

Tvindefossen

Bergen

Eidfjord

Photo: DH

VOSS FACTS

Character: Steep and pushy, sometimes between slippery rock walls – a region for alpine specialists. But the Park + Play fan is also well served here.

Best time: Most of the smaller rivers, like the Brandsetelvi and the Urdlandselvi, run in spring or after rainfall. Several sections of the Raundalselvi do not start running until later, but for that keep on flowing into the high summer.

Special remarks: Mostly steep channels. Got your creekboat?

Accommodation: Taulen camping ground on the Strondelvi, at the Tvindefossen or left from the take out of the lower Myrkdalselvi.

Kayak shop: »Kajakkbua«, Evangerveien 57 in Voss, behind the Voss Sparebank. www.vossskiogsurf.com

Charakter: Wuchtig und steil, teils zwischen glitschigen Felswänden – ein Gebiet für Alpinisten. Doch auch der Park + Play Liebhaber wird bedient.

Beste Zeit: Die meisten der kleineren Bäche, wie Brandsetelvi und Urdlandselvi, laufen im Frühling oder nach Regenfällen. Einige Abschnitte der Raundalselvi gehen erst etwas später, dafür aber bis in den Hochsommer.

Besonderheit: Meist steile Rinnen. Creekboot dabei?

Übernachtung: Campingplatz Taulen an der Strondelvi, am Tvindefossen oder links vom Ausstieg der unteren Myrkdalselvi.

Kajakshop: »Kajakkbua«, Evangerveien 57 in Voss hinter der Voss Sparebank. www.vossskiogsurf.com

RAUNDALSELVI: UPPER (KLEIVELVI)

The Raundalselvi is the unchallenged showpiece of Voss. In its course through the Raundalen it brings one attraction after the other, two already in the first section: a 5 metre pleasure waterfall, and a 10 metre guts waterfall. Up here the Raundalselvi is actually still called the Kleivelvi. Flowing in from the left, it is the biggest headwater river feeding the Raundalselvi, but let's not spend too much time on that.

The agony of carrying the boats up pays off, the first kilometre down to the youth hostel offers magnificent whitewater, ending in a difficult slide. The course of the river continues with flat water alternating with more challenging sections. When the river divides make sure you take the right hand channel, on the left there is a monster towback with dangerous undercuts.

The unquestionable highlight awaits us at the take out: the »Nosebreaker« (also known as »Apocalypse now«) is a giant 10 metre waterfall, which turns slightly to the left. Whether run normally, boofed, upside down, backwards, or backwards and upside down, the Nosebreaker has been run in every possible fashion. It has also gathered all manner of injuries on its hit list: bruised ribs, ear aches and of course broken noses, to name a few. So please don't just bomb down it. Have a little think about your line beforehand. Best to sneak around the left of the rock at the entrance, then get back into the main current and let yourself get slightly covered by the curler. Paddle to the side, upper body forwards, and hey presto! You're at the bottom!

CLASS:	**V - VI**
LEVEL:	**8 - 20 cumecs**
LENGTH:	**12 km**
TIME:	**5 - 8 h**
SEASON:	**June - August**

Die Raundalselvi ist das unbestrittene Aushängeschild für Voss. Auf ihrem Lauf durch das Raundalen bringt sie immer wieder Attraktionen hervor, und schon zwei auf der obersten Etappe: einen 5-Meter-Genusswasserfall und einen 10-Meter-Mutwasserfall. Eigentlich heißt die Raundalselvi hier oben noch Kleivelvi, und ist der linke und größte Quellfluss der Raundalselvi, aber das soll uns nicht weiter interessieren.

Die Qualen beim Hochtragen der Boote lohnen sich, der erste Kilometer bis zur Jugendherberge bietet grandioses Wildwasser, welches mit einer schwierigen Rutsche endet. Im weiteren Verlauf wechseln ruhige Flachwasserpassagen mit anspruchsvollen Abschnitten. Bei einer Teilung sollte unbedingt der rechte Kanal erwischt werden, links lauert ein mächtiger Rücklauf mit gefährlichen Unterspülungen.

Der unbestrittene Höhepunkt wartet am Ausstieg: Der »Nosebreaker« (auch bekannt als »Apokalypse now«) ist ein mächtiger 10-Meter-Wasserfall, der sich etwas nach links eindreht. Ob normal, ob geboofed, ob kopfüber, rückwärts, oder rückwärts-kopfüber, der Nosebreaker wurde schon in allen möglichen Variationen befahren. Geprellte Rippen, Ohrenschmerzen und natürlich Nasenbeinbrüche stehen auf der Liste der Verletzungen. Also bitte nicht einfach nur runterstürzen, sondern schon vorher mal kurz über eine Linie nachdenken. Am besten um den Stein am Eingang links vorbei mogeln, dann in die Hauptströmung zurückkehren und sich von der Locke leicht eindecken lassen. Paddel zur Seite, Oberkörper nach vorne und schon ist man unten.

Photo: MN

Markus Hummel

Obsommer

Mr. Maus

Photo: MN

Notter

At the Nosebreaker do your helmet up good and tight, squeeze your nose peg a little tighter, and if necessary let go of your paddle – before your shoulder pops out.

RJUANDE

Kittelbreaker falls - Kagel

Herzig, Herzig, Herzig, Herzig ...

Nils Kagel scouting the tunnel

The tunnel - Tobi Pollinger

RAUNDALSELVI: FULL ON SECTION

This section holds extreme difficulties in store, and should absolutely not be attempted with too much water, because the passages are often only 3-5 metres wide, and there is a very strenuous portage to overcome.

The eddy for this is on the left, 20 metres before a threatening edge. The kayaks must first be carried up 15 metres, and then there is a 50 metre traverse before you can put on again. The portage takes about half an hour.

Then come several apparently harmless sections, but before the gorge opens up, there lies a low gorge in wait. This will tempt you to paddle through on sight, but resist this temptation. At the exit there is a recirculating drop with a dangerous undercut on the left wall. This has already swallowed several paddlers, thankfully without serious consequences to date. So please be on guard, and if necessary portage on the left. The take out in Reimegrend should be scouted beforehand, to ensure that you do not accidentally paddle the next section as well.

Tip: It's a good idea to combine this section with the upper section.

> **CLASS:** V - VI (X)
> **LEVEL:** 10 - 15 cumecs
> **LENGTH:** 1 km
> **TIME:** 1 - 2 h
> **SEASON:** late July - September

Dieser Abschnitt birgt hohe Schwierigkeiten und sollte auf keinen Fall bei zu viel Wasser gepaddelt werden, da die Durchfahrten oft nur 3-5 Meter breit sind. Zudem ist eine anstrengende Umtragung zu bewältigen.

Das dazugehörige Kehrwasser befindet sich links etwa 20 Meter vor einer bedrohlichen Abrisskante. Die Kajaks müssen erst 15 Meter hoch getragen werden, dann folgt eine 50 Meter Querung, bevor wieder eingebootet werden kann. Die Umtrage dauert etwa 30 Minuten.

Danach kommen einige unscheinbare Stellen, doch bevor sich die Schlucht öffnet, lauert eine Niederklamm. Man ist dazu verleitet, sie ohne Besichtigung zu durchstechen. Dies ist aber nicht ratsam, da im Ausgang eine Rücklaufstufe mit gefährlicher Unterspülung an der linken Wand ihr Unwesen treibt. Diese hat schon einige Paddler verschluckt, zum Glück bis dato ohne Folgen. Also bitte wachsam sein und gegebenenfalls links umtragen. Die Ausbootstelle in Reimegrend sollte vorher angeschaut werden, nicht das vor lauter Euphorie der nächste Abschnitt mitgepaddelt wird.

Tipp: Es bietet sich an, die Full on Section mit dem oberen Abschnitt zu verbinden.

RAUNDALSELVI: TRAIN STATION SECTION

OH MY GOD, A M-M-M-MUST-RUN!

This section is a true classic. With two small catches: a must run section at the beginning and a steep WW VII section half way down. F-f-f-first the m-m-m-must-run section: at its beginning, the Raundalselvi digs its way into a gorge, and gradually gets more and more difficult. At the point where the gorge grows into a ravine, and the Raundals-

CLASS: IV - V (VII)
LEVEL: 15 - 30 cumecs
LENGTH: 7 km
TIME: 3 - 5 h
SEASON: July - September

elvi bends to the left and into the unknown, you know you have reached the must-run section. Here you have three possibilities: hard right down the chicken line, full power boof right of centre, or down the left for a big beating and you can swim on from there. But no panic, you wouldn't be the first to swim and disappear around the corner. Luckily there is a quiet pool for your swimming practice which follows. What's more, there is a

world class rodeo hole with a pool and an eddy waiting for you. This hole has seen Olli Grau score more points in his creek boat than some rodeo stars at the world champs.

The steep section half way down can be portaged on the right. It has been run before, but this is more of a don't-try-this-at-home number. After this there are several fun sections to solve before you get to the take out bridge.

Dieser Abschnitt ist ein echter Klassiker. Mit zwei kleinen Haken: Eine Zwangspassage zu Beginn und einem WW-VI-Steilstück auf halber Strecke. ZZZur ZZZZZZwangspassage: Die Raundalselvi gräbt sich nach dem Start in eine Schlucht und steigert sich langsam. An dem Punkt, wo es klammartig wird und die Raundalselvi nach links ins Ungewis-

se abknickt, ist die Zwangspassage erreicht. Jetzt gibt es drei Möglichkeiten: ganz rechts die Chicken Line, rechts von der Mitte Vollgas-boofen, oder links aufmischen lassen und weiter schwimmen. Aber keine Panik, ihr wärt nicht die Ersten, die vor den Augen der Freunde schwimmend links um die Ecke verschwinden. Zum Glück folgt ein ruhiger Pool für Schwimmübungen. Außerdem wartet hier eine Weltklasse Rodeowalze, mit großem Pool und

Kehrwasser. Olli Grau hat mit seinem Creekboot in dieser Walze schon höher gepunktet als mancher Rodeostar auf der Weltmeisterschaft.

Das Steilstück auf halber Strecke wird rechts umtragen. Es wurde zwar schon befahren, das muss aber auch nicht sein. Danach hat man noch einige lustige Stellen zu absolvieren, bevor man die Ausstiegsbrücke erreicht.

Rumble in the jungle!

The m-m-must-run

Train station in Reimegrend

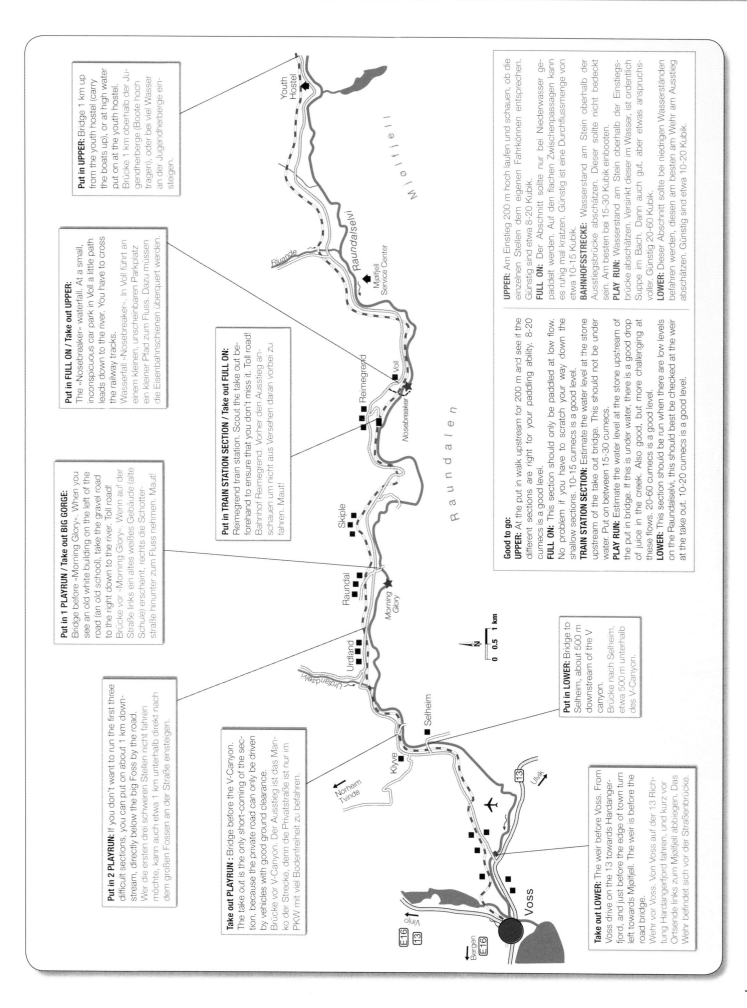

Put in UPPER: Bridge 1 km up from the youth hostel (carry the boats up), or at high water put on at the youth hostel. Brücke 1 km oberhalb der Jugendherberge (Boote hoch tragen), oder bei viel Wasser an der Jugendherberge einsteigen.

Put in FULL ON / Take out UPPER:
The »Nosebreaker« waterfall. At a small, inconspicuous car park in Voll a little path leads down to the river. You have to cross the railway tracks. Toll road!
Wasserfall »Nosebreaker«. In Voll führt an einem kleinen, unscheinbaren Parkplatz ein kleiner Pfad zum Fluss. Dazu müssen die Eisenbahnschienen überquert werden.

Put in 1 PLAYRUN / Take out BIG GORGE:
Bridge before »Morning Glory«. When you see an old white building on the left of the road (an old school), take the gravel road to the right down to the river. Toll road!
Brücke vor »Morning Glory«. Wenn auf der Straße links ein altes weißes Gebäude (alte Schule) erscheint, rechts die Schotterstraße hinunter zum Fluss nehmen. Maut!

Put in 2 PLAYRUN: If you don't want to run the first three difficult sections, you can put on about 1 km downstream, directly below the big Foss by the road.
Wer die ersten drei schweren Stellen nicht fahren möchte, kann auch etwa 1 km unterhalb direkt nach dem großen Fossen an der Straße einsteigen.

Put in TRAIN STATION SECTION / Take out FULL ON:
Reimegrend train station. Scout the take out beforehand to ensure that you don't miss it. Toll road!
Bahnhof Reimegrend. Vorher den Ausstieg anschauen, um nicht aus Versehen daran vorbei zu fahren. Maut!

Take out PLAYRUN: Bridge before the V-Canyon. The take out is the only short-coming of the section, because the private road can only be driven by vehicles with good ground clearance.
Brücke vor V-Canyon. Der Ausstieg ist das Manko der Strecke, denn die Privatstraße ist nur im PKW mit viel Bodenfreiheit zu befahren.

Put in LOWER: Bridge to Selheim, about 500 m downstream of the V canyon.
Brücke nach Selheim, etwa 500 m unterhalb des V-Canyon.

Take out LOWER: The weir before Voss. From Voss drive on the 13 towards Hardangerfjord, and just before the edge of town turn left towards Mjølfjell. The weir is before the road bridge.
Wehr vor Voss. Von Voss auf der 13 Richtung Hardangerfjord fahren, und kurz vor Ortsende links zum Mjølfjell abbiegen. Das Wehr befindet sich vor der Straßenbrücke.

Good to go:

UPPER: At the put in walk upstream for 200 m and see if the different sections are right for your paddling ability. 8-20 cumecs is a good level.

FULL ON: This section should only be paddled at low flow. No problem if you have to scratch your way down the shallow sections. 10-15 cumecs is a good level.

TRAIN STATION SECTION: Estimate the water level at the stone upstream of the take out bridge. This should not be under water. Put on between 15-30 cumecs.

PLAY RUN: Estimate the water level at the stone upstream of the put in bridge. If this is under water, there is a good drop of juice in the creek. Also good, but more challenging at these flows. 20-60 cumecs is a good level.

LOWER: This section should be run when there are low levels on the Raundalselvi; this should best be checked at the weir at the take out. 10-20 cumecs is a good level.

UPPER: Am Einstieg 200 m hoch laufen und schauen, ob die einzelnen Stellen dem eigenen Fahrkönnen entsprechen. Günstig sind etwa 8-20 Kubik.

FULL ON: Der Abschnitt sollte nur bei Niederwasser gepaddelt werden. Auf den flachen Zwischenpassagen kann es ruhig mal kratzen. Günstig ist eine Durchflussmenge von etwa 10-15 Kubik.

BAHNHOFSSTRECKE: Wasserstand am Stein oberhalb der Ausstiegsbrücke abschätzen. Dieser sollte nicht bedeckt sein. Am besten bei 15-30 Kubik einbooten.

PLAY RUN: Wasserstand am Stein oberhalb der Einstiegsbrücke abschätzen. Versinkt dieser im Wasser, ist ordentlich Suppe im Bach. Dann auch gut, aber etwas anspruchsvoller. Günstig 20-60 Kubik.

LOWER: Dieser Abschnitt sollte bei niedrigen Wasserständen befahren werden, diesen am besten am Wehr am Ausstieg abschätzen. Günstig sind etwa 10-20 Kubik.

Youth Hostel

Mjølfjell

Biuande

Raundalselvi

Mjølfjell Service Center

Voll

Reimegrend

Nosebreaker

Raundalen

Skiple

Raundal

Morning Glory

Urlandselvi

Urland

N
0 0.5 1 km

Selheim

Klyve

Norheim Tvinde

Ulvik

Voss

Vinjo

Bergen E16

E16
13

13

Shu-be-doo!

RAUNDALSELVI: URDLAND RUN (PLAYRUN)

AN AWESOME PLAYRUN WITH A FEW BIGGER RAPIDS

Crystal clear water, giant turquoise pools – the Raundalselvi offers dream whitewater here. You can see it from the road already, although it is easy to underestimate how pushy the water is. The playrun, also known as the Urdland run, is the easiest section of the Raundalselvi, and the brave can also turn up for duty in their play boats.

Morning Glory - Don Hölzl

After just 200 metres the first pushy cataract by the name of »Morning Glory« lies in wait, best to scout it beforehand from the left bank. The next foss in a left bend should be scouted from the right. Depending on the water level, you can either bomb down with the main current, or boof right over a 3 metre drop. Warning, the right wall below is undercut. Soon afterwards the Raundalselvi nears the road, and then you'll reach a 5 metre high foss with an old diversion on the right bank. It can be scouted, portaged, and run on the right. As an alternative, it is also possible to put on here.

Glasklares Wasser, riesige Pools mit türkis schimmerndem Wasser – die Raundalselvi formt hier Traumwildwasser. Das sieht man schon von der Straße aus, wobei man gerne die Wasserwucht unterschätzt. Der Playrun, oder auch Urdland Run, ist der leichteste Abschnitt der Raundalselvi. Sattelfeste Kollegen können hier auch im Spielboot antreten.

Schon nach 200 Metern lauert der erste wuchtige Katarakt Namens »Morning Glory«, am besten schon vorher von links besichtigen. Der nächste Fossen in einer Linkskurve sollte von rechts besichtigt werden. Je nach Wasserstand wird hier im Hauptwasser hinunter gebraten oder rechts über eine 3 Meter hohe Stufe geboofft. Achtung, die Wand unten rechts ist unterspült. Bald nähert sich

Then there is whitewater to be savoured and celebrated, and pools for collecting gear and paddlers. Shortly before the end there are two final treats – a 2 metre high drop, and a river-wide hole with questionable chances of escape. Scout and perhaps portage on the right.

After the following bridge, the take out, do not paddle on. Then comes the siphon gorge in the V-Canyon which can only be run at low water.

CLASS:	**III - IV (V)**
LEVEL:	**20 - 60 cumecs**
LENGTH:	**7 km**
TIME:	**3 h**
SEASON:	**May - September**

die Raundalselvi der Straße, es folgt ein etwa 5 Meter hoher Fossen mit alter Ableitung am rechten Ufer. Er kann rechts besichtigt, umtragen, oder befahren werden. Hier kann auch alternativ eingebootet werden.

Darauf folgt Wildwasser zum Genießen und Juchzen, mit großen Pools zum Sammeln. Kurz vor dem Ausstieg warten noch zwei Abschlusshäppchen: eine etwa 2 Meter hohe Stufe und gleich im Anschluss eine flussüberspannende Walze mit fraglichen Entkommenschancen. Rechts besichtigen und eventuell umtragen.

Von der folgenden Brücke, dem Ausstieg, keinesfalls weiterpaddeln, es folgt die nur bei Niedrigwasser fahrbare Siphonschlucht im V-Canyon.

Don Hölzl

RAUNDALSELVI: LOWER

POOL + DROP IN A NICE SCENERY

The lower Raundalselvi, up to just before Voss, is only a good choice at low water. It is not quite as spectacular as the upper sections, but a true technical treat. It is fairly remote, flows in parts through gorges, so there could be some must-run sections here. Especially at the beginning, you have no other choice but to paddle into the unknown. Best to keep left and hope you haven't misjudged the water level. What follows is the dream of every WW V fan. Because of one towback drop, the gorge before Voss should be checked out beforehand.

If you still haven't had enough you can also run the short gorge after the weir. Warning: steel girders in the river.

> **CLASS: V**
> **LEVEL: 10 - 20 cumecs**
> **LENGTH: 4 km**
> **TIME: 3 - 4 h**
> **SEASON: July - September**

You won't need much water for the lower section

Die untere Raundalselvi bis kurz vor Voss ist bei Niedrigwasser eine gute Wahl. Sie ist nicht ganz so spektakulär wie die oberen Strecken, aber dafür ein technisches Schmankerl. Sie ist etwas ausgesetzt und zum Teil klammartig, dadurch kann die eine oder andere Zwangspassage aufwarten. Vor allem nach dem Start bleibt keine Wahl, es muss ins Ungewisse gepaddelt werden. Dafür hält man sich am besten links und hofft, sich doch nicht mit dem Wasserstand verschätzt zu haben. Der weitere Verlauf ist ein Traum für jeden WW-V-Fan. Die Klamm vor Voss sollte wegen einer Rücklaufstufe erkundet werden.

Tipp: Wer immer noch nicht genug hat, kann auch noch die kurze Schlucht nach dem Wehr fahren. Vorsicht: Stahlträger im Fluss!

The gorge after the weir drop

URDLANDSELVI

STEEP AND SOMETIMES CONTINUOUS WHITEWATER WITH A NICE WATERFALL COMBO

The Urdlandselvi is a small tributary of the Raundalselvi. In the first kilometre up to the waterfall combination it offers drop + pool whitewater of the finest order. The double waterfall is the unquestionable highlight – first 7, then 6 metres of freefall!

For the rest of the section down to the take out, eddies are somewhat of a rarity. After the road bridge there is a nice drop, further on a mighty waterfall. You may know the giant slide further down from one of the Norway videos (Norgasmo).

CLASS:	V (VI)
LEVEL:	5 - 8 cumecs
LENGTH:	3 km
TIME:	2 - 3 h
SEASON:	May - July

Die Urdlandselvi ist ein kleiner Nebenbach der Raundalselvi. Sie bietet auf dem ersten Kilometer bis zur Wasserfallkombination Drop + Pool Wildwasser der Extraklasse. Der Doppelwasserfall ist der unbestrittene Höhepunkt – erst 7, dann 6 Meter Freiflug.

Auf der Reststrecke bis zum Ausstieg sind Kehrwasser rar. Nach der Straßenbrücke wartet noch eine schöne Stufe, etwas weiter ein prächtiger Wasserfall. Die Riesenrutsche weiter unten kennt man vielleicht aus einem der Norwegenvideos (Norgasmo).

Not too bad, duuude!

Jay Kincaid

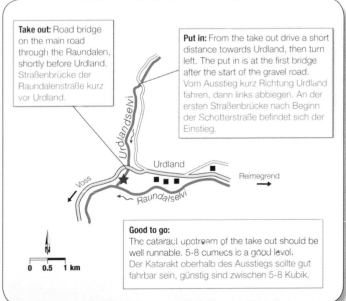

Take out: Road bridge on the main road through the Raundalen, shortly before Urdland. Straßenbrücke der Raundalenstraße kurz vor Urdland.

Put in: From the take out drive a short distance towards Urdland, then turn left. The put in is at the first bridge after the start of the gravel road. Vom Ausstieg kurz Richtung Urdland fahren, dann links abbiegen. An der ersten Straßenbrücke nach Beginn der Schotterstraße befindet sich der Einstieg.

Good to go:
The cataract upstream of the take out should be well runnable. 5-8 cumecs is a good level. Der Katarakt oberhalb des Ausstiegs sollte gut fahrbar sein, günstig sind zwischen 5-8 Kubik.

✳ STRONDELVI

The relatively short Strondelvi makes its way from the Oppheimsvatnet, along the E16, and then drowns in the Vangsvatnet at Voss. The Strondelvi is very popular with rafting companies and kayak schools, although only on the first part of our section. In the last 2 kilometres things get considerably more challenging.

On the first section up to the Taulen camp ground you can relax or cruise around in your playboat. By the way, it is on this section that you will find the Bus stop hole (see the chapter »Park + Play«), about 300 metres upstream of the bridge to the camp ground. Here you will always meet groups of paddlers from the kayak schools, the section is simply predestined for this.

However, the alarm bells go off as soon as you approach the road bridge of the E 16, where the road switches from river left to river right. In the 200 metres leading up to the bridge a WW IV cataract simmers away to itself, in which there is reportedly a siphon on the left hand side. Directly after the bridge seethes the unchallenged highlight of the Strondelvi, the Moneydrop. This furious looking waterfall is also known to the locals as »Aasbrekkgjelet«. You should have already cast an eye over the situation on the drive up. Shortly after the Moneydrop is a 3 metre drop, which does not have clean water in the main current, but which you can chicken run in the right channel. In the sections which follow there are sometimes hidden undercuts, so you should scout closely before running it. However actually only WW III-IV.

Why Moneydrop? It is not only fame and glory which move paddlers to great feats of heroism. A cash check can also work wonders. The Moneydrop has the annual »Ekstremsportveko« to thank for its name, in which the organisers would offer 300 dollars per run – and be relieved of several thousand dollars.

Die verhältnismäßig kurze Strondelvi bahnt sich ihren Weg vom Oppheimsvatnet entlang der E16 und ertrinkt dann in Voss im Vangsvatnet. Bei Raftingunternehmen und Kajakschulen ist die Strondelvi sehr beliebt, allerdings nur auf dem ersten Teilstück unseres Abschnittes. Auf den letzten 2 Kilometern wird es nämlich wesentlich anspruchsvoller.

Auf dem ersten Teilstück bis hin zum Campingplatz Taulen kann man sich entspannen oder im Spielboot rumcruisen. Auf diesem Abschnitt befindet sich übrigens auch das Bus-stop-hole (siehe Kapitel »Park+Play«), etwa 300 Meter oberhalb der Brücke zum Campingplatz. Hier wird man immer wieder Gruppen von Kajakschulen treffen, der Abschnitt ist dafür prädestiniert.

Die Alarmglocken läuten jedoch sobald man sich der Straßenbrücke der E16 nähert, also die Straße von flusslinks auf flussrechts wechselt. Auf den 200 Metern vor der Brücke köchelt ein WW IV Katarakt, in dem sich linker Hand ein Siphon verstecken soll. Direkt hinter der Brücke brodelt der unbestrittene Höhepunkt der Strondelvi, der Moneydrop. Dieser etwas grimmige Wasserfall wird von den Einheimischen auch als »Aasbrekkgjelet« bezeichnet. Man sollte schon bei der Anfahrt ein Auge auf die Situation vor Ort geworfen haben. Kurz nach dem Moneydrop folgt eine 3-Meter-Stufe, die im Hauptwasser unsauber ist, aber im rechten Kanal umfahren werden kann. In den folgenden Stellen lauern teilweise versteckte Unterspülungen, so sollte akribisch besichtigt werden. Jedoch eigentlich nur noch WW III-IV.

Warum bitte Moneydrop? Nicht nur Ruhm und Ehre bewegen Paddler zu Heldentaten, auch ein Barscheck kann allerhand bewirken. So verdankt der »Moneydrop« seinen Namen der alljährlich ausgetragenen »Ekstremsportveko«, bei der die Veranstalter 300 Dollar für jede Befahrung ausgelobt hatten – und einige 1000 Dollar loswurden.

CLASS:	II - IV/V+
LEVEL:	15 - 40 cumecs
LENGTH:	4 km / 2 km
TIME:	2 - 4 h
SEASON:	May - August

Photo: RS

Fresko Vujkow - Moneydrop

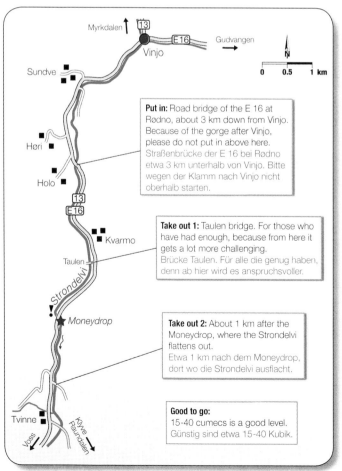

Put in: Road bridge of the E 16 at Rødno, about 3 km down from Vinjo. Because of the gorge after Vinjo, please do not put in above here.
Straßenbrücke der E 16 bei Rødno etwa 3 km unterhalb von Vinjo. Bitte wegen der Klamm nach Vinjo nicht oberhalb starten.

Take out 1: Taulen bridge. For those who have had enough, because from here it gets a lot more challenging.
Brücke Taulen. Für alle die genug haben, denn ab hier wird es anspruchsvoller.

Take out 2: About 1 km after the Moneydrop, where the Strondelvi flattens out.
Etwa 1 km nach dem Moneydrop, dort wo die Strondelvi ausflacht.

Good to go:
15-40 cumecs is a good level.
Günstig sind etwa 15-40 Kubik.

MYRKDALSELVI: UPPER

AN OPEN HIGHLAND RIVER WITH SOME NICE DROPS

The Myrkdalselvi is fed by the Vikafjell, and its upper section winds its way through classic highland landscape. This section has open drop + pool whitewater with several challenging sections, all of which appear in good time on the horizon, and are easy to scout.

Shortly before the take out there is a waterfall with a shallow landing. It gets paddled hard right again and again, and again and again it breaks ankles. After another cataract you reach the take out bridge.

CLASS: IV - V (VI)
LEVEL: 10 - 20 cumecs
LENGTH: 4 km
TIME: 2 - 3 h
SEASON: May - early July

Die Myrkdalselvi wird vom Vikafjell gespeist und schlängelt sich im Oberlauf durch ein klassisches Hochtal. Der obere Abschnitt bietet offenes Drop + Pool Wildwasser mit einigen anspruchsvollen Stellen, die alle offensichtlich am Horizont auftauchen und einfach zu besichtigen sind.

Kurz vor dem Ausstieg lauert ein Wasserfall mit flachem Unterwasser. Er wird immer wieder ganz rechts befahren, allerdings brechen auch immer wieder Knöchel. Nach einem weiteren Katarakt gelangt man zur Ausstiegsbrücke.

Strohmeier

MYRKDALSELVI: LOWER

A STEEP RUN WITH BIG SLIDES AND DROPS

For the lower section of the Myrkdalselvi you should bring lots of time with you for the constant scouting and safetying of the countless towbacks. But don't panic: the exceptional length and gradient of the slides usually has your boat going so fast that you drill through even impossible-looking towbacks. Just make sure you hold your breath long enough!

Already under the put in bridge the first drop awaits you, and that's just how it keeps going from there – steep downhill all the way. After about 500 metres you reach the most difficult section of the Myrkdalselvi, the so-called Triple Combo. At the entrance to the first drop the hole in the middle of the river should be paid its due respect, because at certain flows it forms a mean towback, and no one wants to swim the first slide. Nor the next two for that matter. If you don't want to paddle the Triple Combo portage it on the right. It is best to first carry up a bit, then across the fields and then back down through the bushes. Pessimists would call it »hard labour«, but »strenuous« actually covers it sufficiently.

About 1.5 kilometres further downstream you reach a 30 metre high waterfall which should be portaged on the right. If you don't want to end up smelling of cow dung and drains, do not use the little creek to climb back down. Instead walk down another 50 metres, but be careful. It is all very smooth and slippery. For your efforts, you will be rewarded with a dream slide after the waterfall.

CLASS: V - VI (X)
LEVEL: 8 - 15 cumecs
LENGTH: 3 km
TIME: 3 - 6 h
SEASON: July - August

Take out: Don't blatantly take up all the parking spaces in front of the small shop there!

Tip: Paddle the waterfall 100 metres below the take out as well, and carry back over the camp ground.

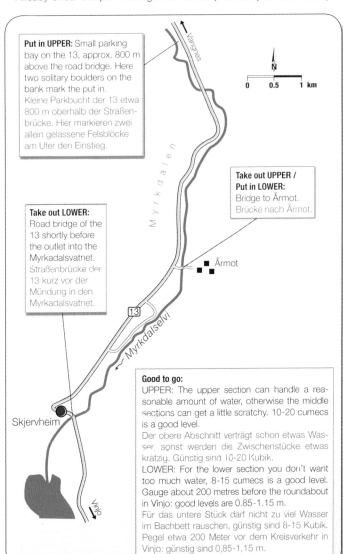

Put in UPPER: Small parking bay on the 13, approx. 800 m above the road bridge. Here two solitary boulders on the bank mark the put in.
Kleine Parkbucht der 13 etwa 800 m oberhalb der Straßenbrücke. Hier markieren zwei allein gelassene Felsblöcke am Ufer den Einstieg.

Take out LOWER: Road bridge of the 13 shortly before the outlet into the Myrkadalsvatnet.
Straßenbrücke der 13 kurz vor der Mündung in den Myrkadalsvatnet.

Take out UPPER / Put in LOWER: Bridge to Årmot.
Brücke nach Årmot.

Myrkdalen
Vangnes
Årmot
Myrkdalselvi
Skjervheim
Vinjo

Good to go:
UPPER: The upper section can handle a reasonable amount of water, otherwise the middle sections can get a little scratchy. 10-20 cumecs is a good level.
Der obere Abschnitt verträgt schon etwas Wasser, sonst werden die Zwischenstücke etwas kratzig. Günstig sind 10-20 Kubik.
LOWER: For the lower section you don't want too much water, 8-15 cumecs is a good level. Gauge about 200 metres before the roundabout in Vinjo: good levels are 0.85-1.15 m.
Für das untere Stück darf nicht zu viel Wasser im Bachbett rauschen, günstig sind 8-15 Kubik. Pegel etwa 200 Meter vor dem Kreisverkehr in Vinjo: günstig sind 0,85-1,15 m.

Daniel Herzig

Für den unteren Abschnitt der Myrkdalselvi sollte man viel Zeit mitbringen, zum ständigen Besichtigen und Sichern der unzähligen Rückläufe. Aber keine Panik: Meist ist das Boot durch die außerordentlichen Längen und Neigungen der Rutschen derart schnell, dass selbst augenscheinlich zu große Rückläufe durchbohrt werden. Nur bitte lange genug die Luft anhalten!

Schon unter der Einstiegsbrücke wartet die erste Stufe, und genau so geht es weiter: steil bergab. Nach etwa 500 Metern erreicht man die schwerste Stelle der Myrkdalselvi, die so genannte Dreier-Kombination. In der Einfahrt sollte einer Walze in Flussmitte gebührenden Respekt gezollt werden, da bei bestimmten Wasserständen ein gemeiner Rücklauf entsteht und wohl niemand gerne die erste Rutsche schwimmt – und auch nicht die nächsten beiden. Wer die Kombination nicht paddeln möchte, umträgt rechtsufrig. Am besten erst ein Stück nach oben, dann über die Wiesen queren und durch die Büsche wieder hinab. Pessimisten würden das Wort »mühselig« benutzen, »anstrengend« ist aber ausreichend.

Etwa 1,5 Kilometer unterhalb erreicht man einen 30 Meter hohen Wasserfall, der rechts umtragen werden sollte. Wer nicht nach Gülle und Kuhmist duften möchte, sollte auf keinen Fall durch den kleinen Bach hinunter steigen. Besser 50 Meter weiterlaufen, aber Vorsicht: es ist alles sehr glatt und rutschig. Dafür wird man nach dem Wasserfall mit einer Traumrutsche belohnt.

Ausstieg: Nicht gnadenlos den Parkplatz vor dem kleinen Lädchen zuparken!

Tipp: Noch den Wasserfall 100 Meter unterhalb des Ausstieges paddeln und über den Campingplatz zurücktragen.

Ron Fischer

Photos: MN

Triple combo - Mickey Abbott

Schäftlein, Ellard, Abbott

Ekstremsportveko 2003

BRANDSETELVI: COMPETITION RUN

A STEEP, LOW VOLUME CREEK WITH AWESOME SLIDES

The Brandsetelvi was only discovered a couple of years ago by local paddlers. It is a small creek which sheds its gradient in grand drops. These days an annual downriver race is held here, the »Voss Ekstremsportveko«, but quite apart from this, the section is enjoying ever increasing popularity.

Things get off to a furious start, and never really seem to slow down: right under the wooden bridge it makes a big downhill charge. Our Kiwi Nick Wimsett broke his shoulder on this slide. Please don't try this at home.

Not long afterwards you reach an impressive drop, which is best portaged over the rock slabs on the right. Absolutely top class slides and some not-always-fair drops keep the boredom at bay on the way to the next road bridge. From here things get a bit sketchy for a while until a monster slide announces the start of the race section. After the S is a tight double combo and a small slot, and there you are at the 5 metre waterfall already! You can either bomb over the kicker hard left (full flight time), or do a late boof in the middle. Then there is a racey block combination with a 2 metre jump, followed by the final slide with a grunty towback in front of the timber area. And for those of you who found it was all over a bit quickly: second run, double the fun!

Tip: Wear elbow pads!

> **CLASS:** IV - V (X)
> **LEVEL:** 5 - 10 cumecs
> **LENGTH:** 3 km
> **TIME:** 2 - 4 h
> **SEASON:** May - July

Die Brandsetelvi wurde erst vor ein paar Jahren von einheimischen Paddlern entdeckt. Sie ist ein recht kleiner Bach, der in grandiosen Abfällen sein Gefälle abbaut. Mittlerweile findet hier das alljährliche Abfahrtsrennen der »Voss Ekstremsportveko« statt, aber auch sonst erfreut sich die Brandsetelvi hoher Beliebtheit.

Die Action ist vom Start weg furios: gleich unter der Holzbrücke geht es steil bergab. Unser Kiwi Nick Wimsett brach sich an dieser Rutsche die Schulter, bitte macht es ihm nicht nach.

Bald darauf folgt ein imposanter Abbruch, den man besser schnell rechts über die Felsplatten umträgt. Rutschen der absoluten Extraklasse und nicht immer ganz saubere Stufen vertreiben die Langeweile auf dem Weg bis zur nächsten Straßenbrücke. Noch etwas hakelig geht es von dort aus weiter, bis eine fette Rutsche die Wettkampfstrecke einleitet. Nach diesem S folgen eine verzwickte Zweier-Kombination und ein kleiner Schlitz, und schon ist der 5-Meter-Wasserfall erreicht. Dieser kann ganz links aus voller Höhe, oder mittig verzögert gebooft werden (Neudeutsch: ganz links über den Kicker bomben oder mittig lateboofen). Es folgt eine rasante Blockkombination mit 2-Meter-Hupfer, dann die Abschlussrutsche mit fettem Rücklauf vor dem Holzplatz. Und wem alles zu schnell ging: Second run, double the fun!

Tipp: Ellbogenschoner nicht vergessen!

Andy Phillips

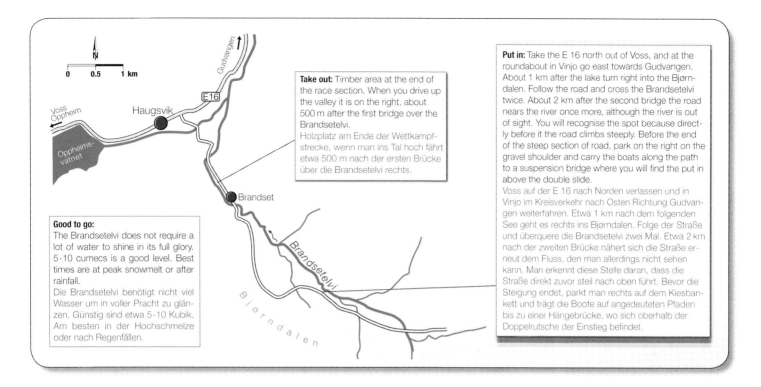

Take out: Timber area at the end of the race section. When you drive up the valley it is on the right, about 500 m after the first bridge over the Brandsetelvi.
Holzplatz am Ende der Wettkampfstrecke, wenn man ins Tal hoch fährt etwa 500 m nach der ersten Brücke über die Brandsetelvi rechts.

Put in: Take the E 16 north out of Voss, and at the roundabout in Vinjo go east towards Gudvangen. About 1 km after the lake turn right into the Bjørndalen. Follow the road and cross the Brandsetelvi twice. About 2 km after the second bridge the road nears the river once more, although the river is out of sight. You will recognise the spot because directly before it the road climbs steeply. Before the end of the steep section of road, park on the right on the gravel shoulder and carry the boats along the path to a suspension bridge where you will find the put in above the double slide.
Voss auf der E 16 nach Norden verlassen und in Vinjo im Kreisverkehr nach Osten Richtung Gudvangen weiterfahren. Etwa 1 km nach dem folgenden See geht es rechts ins Bjørndalen. Folge der Straße und überquere die Brandsetelvi zwei Mal. Etwa 2 km nach der zweiten Brücke nähert sich die Straße erneut dem Fluss, den man allerdings nicht sehen kann. Man erkennt diese Stelle daran, dass die Straße direkt zuvor steil nach oben führt. Bevor die Steigung endet, parkt man rechts auf dem Kiesbankett und trägt die Boote auf angedeuteten Pfaden bis zu einer Hängebrücke, wo sich oberhalb der Doppelrutsche der Einstieg befindet.

Good to go:
The Brandsetelvi does not require a lot of water to shine in its full glory. 5-10 cumecs is a good level. Best times are at peak snowmelt or after rainfall.
Die Brandsetelvi benötigt nicht viel Wasser um in voller Pracht zu glänzen. Günstig sind etwa 5-10 Kubik. Am besten in der Hochschmelze oder nach Regenfällen.

JORDALSELVI

A CLASSIC HIGHLAND POOL + DROP RIVER

The Jordalselvi flows through a romantic highland valley, miles from civilisation. At first sight it looks like a small meadow creek, which gurgles merrily through the prairie. Seen from the car, the water level can easily seem low or insufficient. But waiting for you are drops and slides which often have big juicy towbacks and stoppers, and here the water can get good and pushy.

In the first kilometres the Jordalselvi pummels down several slides and drops which are all easy to scout and portage. The highpoint of these first kilometres is a 4 metre waterfall which is best boofed to the left.

After the road switches to the river right there

| CLASS: III - V |
| LEVEL: 6 - 12 cumecs |
| LENGTH: 6 km |
| TIME: 3 - 5 h |
| SEASON: June - August |

is a rather bony section. After the next bridge the Jordalselvi starts to shake off some gradient once more, and you should exercise some caution at the drop in the low gorge.

After another 200 metres you'll find one of the most beautiful 10 metre waterfalls in the country: smooth approach, 2 seconds with your heart in your mouth, big pool. About 800 metres after the waterfall the Jordalselvi nears the road. Right before a 90° right bend there is a good take out (Take out 1), above this you can see a farmhouse.

You can also paddle on to the next road bridge. About 200 metres after the first take out the Jordalselvi chews its way into a gorge which holds some gnarly paddling in store. Especially at high flow things get very pushy and full on here.

Tip: The last gorge is only for very experienced paddlers.

Klatt blowing the line

Die Jordalselvi fließt fernab der Zivilisation in einem romantischen Hochtal. Auf den ersten Blick sieht sie wie ein kleiner Wiesenbach aus, der lustig durch die Prärie plätschert. So erscheint die Wassermenge, vom Auto aus betrachtet, schnell als gering oder nicht ausreichend. Doch es warten einige Stufen und Rutschen mit saftigen Rückläufen und Walzen auf ihre Eroberer, bei denen das vorhandene Wasser recht wuchtig werden kann.

Auf den ersten Kilometern bricht die Jordalselvi über einige Rutschen und Stufen zu Tale, die allesamt leicht zu besichtigen und gegebenenfalls zu umtragen sind. Als ein Höhepunkt der ersten Kilo-

meter ist ein 4-Meter-Wasserfall zu erwähnen, der am besten links geboofed wird.

Nachdem die Straße auf die flussrechte Seite gewechselt ist, folgt eine steinige Durststrecke. Erst ab der nächsten Brücke beginnt die Jordalselvi wieder ihr Gefälle abzuarbeiten, wobei gerade bei der Stufe in der kurzen Niederklamm Vorsicht angebracht ist.

Nach weiteren 200 Metern folgt einer der schönsten 10-Meter-Wasserfälle des Landes: ruhige Anfahrt, 2 Sekunden Magensausen, großer Pool. Etwa 800 Meter nach dem Wasserfall nähert sich die Jordalselvi der Straße – direkt vor einer

90-Grad-Rechtskurve befindet sich ein geeigneter Aussatzpunkt (Take out 1), oberhalb ist ein Bauernhof zu erspähen.

Man kann auch noch bis zur nächsten Straßenbrücke weiter fahren. Etwa 200 Meter nach dem ersten Ausstieg gräbt sich die Jordalselvi in eine Klamm, die mit erhöhten Schwierigkeiten wartet. Gerade bei hohen Wasserständen wird es hier sehr wuchtig.

Tipp: Die letzte Schlucht nur für sehr sichere Paddler!

The put in - Sebastian Gründler

Obsommer

The waterfall in the lower gorge - Erik Martinsen

Put in: Turn off the E 16 into the Jordalen and follow the gravel road through several tunnels up to the highland valley. After the third bridge continue on a toll road, until on the left you see the river widen to form a semi-lake, directly above is a small concrete bridge leading to a couple of isolated farmhouses. On the left a small path leads down to the Jordalselvi.

Biege von der E 16 ins Jordalen ab und folge der Schotterstraße durch einige Tunnel bis ins Hochtal. Nach der dritten Brücke geht es auf einem Bomweg weiter, bis man links eine seenartige Erweiterung und direkt oberhalb eine kleine Betonbrücke erkennen kann, die zu ein paar Einödhöfen führt. Links führt ein kleiner Feldweg hinunter zur Jordalselvi.

Nosi

Jordalselvi

waterfall

N

0   0.5   1 km

Take out 1: Heading up the valley, between the first and second bridge over the Jordalselvi, the river makes a 90° right hand bend and moves away from the road.

Zwischen der von unten ersten und zweiten Brücke über die Jordalselvi, der Fluss entfernt sich durch eine markante 90-Grad-Kurve von der Straße.

Take out 2: First bridge over the Jordalselvi, (when you come out of the tunnel, heading up the valley).

Erste Brücke über die Jordalselvi, (wenn man vom Tal her aus den Tunneln kommt.)

Jordalen

Jordalen

Gudvangen
Voss   E 16 ↓

Good to go:
The Jordalselvi can handle a bit of water, otherwise things can get a bit bony, and the landing from the waterfall too hard. 10 cumecs are good to have here. In the second part however, the lower gorge, make sure there is not too much water – better to have less than 10 cumecs.

Die Jordalselvi kann schon etwas Wasser vertragen, sonst werden die Zwischenstücke recht kratzig und der Aufprall am Wasserfall zu hart. Günstig sind hier etwa 10 Kubik. Im Zweiten Teil, also in der letzten Schlucht, sollte es aber definitiv nicht zu viel haben, besser weniger als 10 Kubik.

Obsommer

TEIGDALSELVI

STEEP RAPIDS, THE DOUBLE DROP AND FLAT WATER

The Teigdalselvi has earned its ominous reputation because of one waterfall: the infamous Double Drop. When you hear talk of the Norwegian Double Drop, they are talking about the Teigdalen Waterfall. If you have seen photos, you'll understand why. The rest of the Teigdalselvi stands somewhat in the shadow of this mighty waterfall, but nonetheless offers a fantastic whitewater experience.

CLASS: V - VI (X)
LEVEL: 6 - 12 cumecs
LENGTH: 12 km
TIME: 3 - 6 h
SEASON: May - June

In the upper reaches waits an unpaddleable rock-fall section, which is best portaged on the right. After that things go quiet for a short while, before the river plunges over the Notter Drop. The Notter Drop was first paddled by Andy Notter in 1999, and you can catch sight of it shining through the trees on the drive up. It is wise to have a look at it beforehand. The Teigdalselvi drops 10 metres into a narrow pool here, with an undercut rock on the right, and a mean exit. Before you reach the Double Drop there is then a 2 metre drop and a must-run 6 metre slide, WW V.

After the Double Drop you have kilometres of flat water, with the exception of two cataracts. After the flat water, however, the last kilometre turns the heat up for you once more. This last kilometre can be scouted from the road.

Tip: At high water huck the Double Drop only.

Die Teigdalselvi hat ihren ominösen Ruf aufgrund eines Wasserfalles: dem berüchtigten Double Drop. Spricht man vom norwegischen Double Drop, meint man den Teigdalen-Wasserfall. Wer Fotos gesehen hat, weiß warum. Der Rest der Teigdalselvi steht in einem großen Schatten, bietet dennoch ein wunderbares Wildwassererlebnis.

Im Oberlauf wartet eine Zwangspassage und eine unfahrbare Felssturzzone, die rechts am besten umtragen wird. Danach geht es kurz ruhig zu, bevor sich der Fluss wieder eingräbt und mit dem Notter-Drop aufwartet. Der Notter-Drop ist von Andy Notter 1999 erstbefahren worden, schon bei der Hochfahrt blitzt dieser Wasserfall zwischen den Büschen hindurch. Eine Besichtigung vorab ist ratsam. Die Teigdalselvi stürzt über 10 Meter in einen engen Pool mit einem unterspülten Stein flussrechts, die Ausfahrt ist gemein. Bis zum Double Drop folgen eine 2-Meter-Stufe und eine 6 Meter hohe Zwangsrutsche, WW V.

Nach dem Double-Drop ist bis auf zwei Katarakte kilometerlanges Flachwasserpaddeln angesagt, bevor es auf dem letzten Kilometer wieder zur Sache geht. Dieser besagte Kilometer kann von der Straße aus besichtigt werden.

Tipp: Bei viel Wasser nur den Double Drop hacken.

The Double Drop - Schäftlein

Allan Ellard on the must-run slide

Notter drop getting its name

Photo: MN

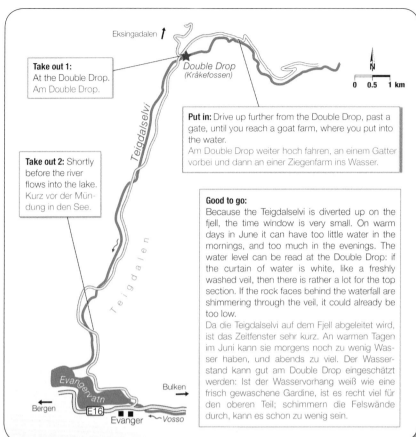

Eksingadalen ↑

Take out 1:
At the Double Drop.
Am Double Drop.

Double Drop
(Kråkefossen)

Put in: Drive up further from the Double Drop, past a gate, until you reach a goat farm, where you put into the water.
Am Double Drop weiter hoch fahren, an einem Gatter vorbei und dann an einer Ziegenfarm ins Wasser.

Take out 2: Shortly before the river flows into the lake. Kurz vor der Mündung in den See.

Teigdalselvi

Teigdalen

Good to go:
Because the Teigdalselvi is diverted up on the fjell, the time window is very small. On warm days in June it can have too little water in the mornings, and too much in the evenings. The water level can be read at the Double Drop: if the curtain of water is white, like a freshly washed veil, then there is rather a lot for the top section. If the rock faces behind the waterfall are shimmering through the veil, it could already be too low.
Da die Teigdalselvi auf dem Fjell abgeleitet wird, ist das Zeitfenster sehr kurz. An warmen Tagen im Juni kann sie morgens noch zu wenig Wasser haben, und abends zu viel. Der Wasserstand kann gut am Double Drop eingeschätzt werden: Ist der Wasservorhang weiß wie eine frisch gewaschene Gardine, ist es recht viel für den oberen Teil; schimmern die Felswände durch, kann es schon zu wenig sein.

Evangervatn

Bergen ←

Evanger

E16

Bulken →

← Vosso

0   0.5   1 km

N

The Lake to Lake Combo - Obsommer

EKSINGADALEN: PARK + HUCK SPECIAL

A PARK + HUCK FEAST: BIG SLIDES, BIG DROPS

The Eksingadalen is for film freaks and testosterone bombers only. You will find here a couple of true park + huck classics which have already appeared in a couple of kayak videos. What more can the park + huck fan ask for?

The **upper section:** here it looks like California. After the monster slide behind the Askjellsvatnet comes a 1.5 kilometre long bedrock dream. Just one thing – where is the water?

The **Lake to Lake Combo** is a must in the Eksingadalen, you spot it as soon as you drive over from the Teigdalen. A mother of a slide into a pool, followed by another slide, going into a 5 metre drop straight into the lake. The whole thing has a vertical drop of about 20 metres, at low water the ride is a little bumpy.

Sometime after that there are **two mighty waterfalls.** The first is definitely unpaddleable,

the second simply high – about 25 metres! It's not enough to get you the world record, but for impressing the girls it'll do the trick anytime!

About 25 minutes paddling downstream from the Lake to Lake section, the **Schnellaelva** trickles its way down from the right. This was made famous by Mike Abbott's ginormous airtime in our »Sick Line 3« film. Here three monster slides wait patiently for their guests: extreme rock sliding!

Das Eksingadalen ist nur für videogeile Testosteronbomber zu empfehlen. Hier findet man ein paar echte Park + Huck Klassiker, die schon in einigen der Kajakvideos vertreten waren. Was will der Park + Huck Fan mehr?

Der **Oberlauf:** Hier sieht es aus wie in Kalifornien. Nach der Monsterrutsche hinter dem Askjellsvatnet folgt ein etwa 1,5 Kilometer langer Traum aus

Grundgestein. Bloß wo ist das Wasser?

Die **Lake to Lake Combo** ist ein MUSS im Eksingadalen, man erspäht sie sofort, wenn man vom Teigdalen hinüberfährt. Eine fette Rutsche in einen Pool mit anschlie-

CLASS:	V - VII
LEVEL:	20 - 50 cumecs
LENGTH:	not much
TIME:	as long as it takes
SEASON:	May - June

ßender Rutsche, die in einen 5 Meter hohen Abfall übergeht, der direkt in den See plumpst. Das ganze macht etwa 20 Meter Höhenunterschied, bei wenig Wasser ist es etwas hoppelig.

Irgendwann danach folgen **zwei mächtige Wasserfälle:** Der Erste ist definitiv unfahrbar, der Zweite einfach nur hoch, etwa 25 Meter. Den Weltrekord kann man sich damit zwar nicht mehr holen, aber um die Mädels zu beeindrucken, reicht es allemal.

Ungefähr 25 Minuten Fahrt vom Lake to Lake flussab plätschert von rechts die **Schnellaelva** zu Tale. Diese ist bekannt geworden durch den mächtigen Sprung von Mike Abbott in unserem »Sick Line 3«. Hier warten 3 Monsterrutschen auf ihren Berutscher: Extreme Rocksliding!

Good to go: Getting the right water level in the Eksingadalen is a test of the patience, or rather a pure question of luck. Most of the water is diverted right at the top, so very little actually reaches the bottom. For most of the sections you generally need a lot of water, so when everything else is in flood, head for the Eksingadal! Only the Lake to Lake Combo runs also at low water.

Im Eksingadalen den richtigen Wasserstand abzupassen, ist eine Geduldsprobe, oder besser gesagt, reine Glückssache. Ganz oben wird das meiste Wasser abgeleitet, dementsprechend wenig kommt unten an. Für die einzelnen Stellen benötigt man in der Regel viel Wasser. Also am besten ins Eksingadalen fahren, wenn alles andere überläuft. Nur die Lake to Lake Combo geht auch bei weniger Wasser.

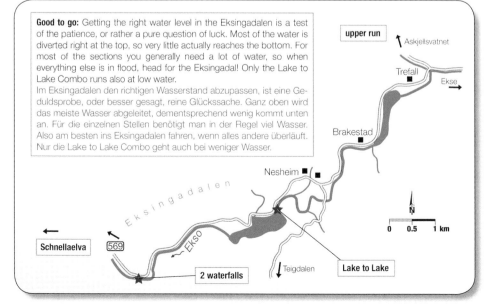

TYSSELVA

Even if the photos and Ben Brown's story (p. 166) scare most paddlers off, the Tysselva is in fact a creek for all paddlers. Sound strange? It's true! The Tysselva is for the most part a »Forest and Field« creek, and only comes at you in big drops very occasionally. The largest concentration of extreme difficulties comes right at the end, shortly before it flows into the Bolstadfjorden, but by then most paddlers are long gone.

In its upper reaches the Tysselva winds its way from lake to lake, slides here and there over rock slabs, easing through untouched natural landscape. But don't nod off: when the river disappears over a horizon line into a yawning void, it's time to get out of the boat and take a look.

After a picturesque lake with its banks enshrouded in reeds, the Tyss divides in two, and this can almost go unnoticed. The smaller right channel is definitely unpaddleable, the larger left channel ends in a double waterfall. The left outlet from the lake flows into a swift wavy section, so make sure you get out in good time.

Sometime later there is a short low gorge, which may even be paddleable. Best to portage on the right, and then to compensate, do a flatwater sprint across the lake. Thereafter come a number of small drops, until the river disappears over the horizon once more, laying the world at your feet. Here you are at the brink of the steep section into the fjord. You should now carry along the left bank to the bridge. If the dirt road isn't navigable by car, you can carry on along the right bank, and take the track which crosses the fjord to the E 16.

Tip: Photo-mad waterfall junkies can try the steep section into the fjord.

CLASS:	III - IV (VI/VII)
LEVEL:	10 - 15 cumecs
LENGTH:	6 km (7 km)
TIME:	4 - 6 h
SEASON:	May - July

Auch wenn die Fotos und Ben Browns Ausführungen den Normalpaddler in erster Linie abschrecken, ist die Tysselva doch ein Bach für jedermann. Klingt komisch? Ist aber wahr. Denn die Tysselva ist in erster Linie ein »Wald- und Wiesenbach«, der nur hin und wieder sein Gefälle in großen Fossen abbaut. Die höchste Ansammlung von Extremschwierigkeiten befindet sich am Schluss, kurz vor der Mündung ins Bolstadfjorden. Doch da hat man sich in der Regel schon längst aus dem Staub gemacht.

In ihrem oberen Verlauf schlängelt sich die Tysselva von See zu See, rutscht hier und da über Felsplatten, und führt an unberührter Natur vorbei. Ein Fest für die Sinne. Aber nicht einschlafen: Verschwindet der Fluss am Horizont und erzeugt gähnende Lehre, raus aus dem Boot und ange-

schaut.

Nach einem See mit herrlichem Schilfufer teilt sich die Tyss fast unmerklich in zwei Kanäle. Der kleinere rechte Kanal ist definitiv unfahrbar, der größere Linke endet in einem Doppelwasserfall. Der linke Ausfluss aus dem See strömt recht flott und wellig dahin, rechtzeitig aussteigen.

Irgendwann folgt eine kurze Niederklamm, die vielleicht sogar fahrbar ist. Am besten rechts umtragen und danach zum Ausgleich über den See einen Flachwassersprint fahren. Bald danach folgen einige kleinere Abfälle, bis der Fluss am Horizont verschwindet und einem die Welt zu Füßen liegt. Hier steht man an der Kante zum unteren Steilstück ins Fjord. Man sollte nun links am Fluss bis zur Brücke tragen. Ist die Dirtroad mit dem Auto nicht befahrbar, kann man auch

am flussrechten Ufer weiter tragen, und den Weg übers Fjord zur E 16 antreten.

Tipp: Alle fotogeilen Wasserfallproleten können sich am unteren Steilstück ins Fjord versuchen.

Ben about to touch down in the fjord

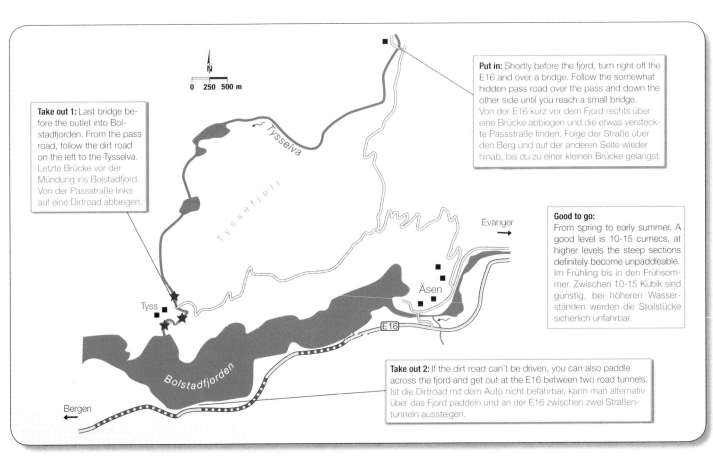

Put in: Shortly before the fjord, turn right off the E16 and over a bridge. Follow the somewhat hidden pass road over the pass and down the other side until you reach a small bridge.
Von der E16 kurz vor dem Fjord rechts über eine Brücke abbiegen und die etwas versteckte Passstraße finden. Folge der Straße über den Berg und auf der anderen Seite wieder hinab, bis du zu einer kleinen Brücke gelangst.

Take out 1: Last bridge before the outlet into Bolstadfjorden. From the pass road, follow the dirt road on the left to the Tysselva.
Letzte Brücke vor der Mündung ins Bolstadfjord. Von der Passstraße links auf eine Dirtroad abbiegen.

Good to go:
From spring to early summer. A good level is 10-15 cumecs, at higher levels the steep sections definitely become unpaddleable.
Im Frühling bis in den Frühsommer. Zwischen 10-15 Kubik sind günstig, bei höheren Wasserständen werden die Steilstücke sicherlich unfahrbar.

Take out 2: If the dirt road can't be driven, you can also paddle across the fjord and get out at the E16 between two road tunnels.
Ist die Dirtroad mit dem Auto nicht befahrbar, kann man alternativ über das Fjord paddeln und an der E16 zwischen zwei Straßentunneln aussteigen.

Schäftlein

STORY: TYSSELVA   BEN BROWN

CAN THE TYSSELVA BE BEATEN?

»Looks like it's good to go!« These were Olaf's words as he walked into Mikey Abbott and Allan Ellard's apartment in Voss. He and Jens had spent the afternoon scouting the hills above Voss for a possible first descent - and it sounded like they had come up with the goods.

The following morning, Arnd, Matze, and myself were led by Olaf and Jens to the put in of the Tysselva. Like the put in to any first descent, nervous anticipation of what lay ahead hung in the air. The first few kilometres of whitewater were pretty mellow; nice clean slides broken up by alpine lakes where all you had to do was to paddle straight across. Our hearts first started beating as the river split into two channels and disappeared behind the horizon line. A quick scout revealed that the right side was unrunnable and the left was marginal at best. The line involved boofing an 8 metre drop sideways into a 30 cm deep pool. Arnd stepped up to the mark and had a solid line; the bar had been set, it looked as though it would be an exciting day!

After a few more kilometres of fun whitewater, ominous grey clouds rolled in. The weather began to set in, so we tried to push on. But what now lay ahead of us looked like the end of the world. After spending an hour or so nervously plodding along the river, we decided to leave the boats overnight and return the following day when the light conditions would hopefully be more conducive to filming.

After a long, wet hike out to the car and a restless night we returned the next morning to see if we could knock off the Tysselva. The first drop brought us to our knees; the landing was too rocky and we had

IST DIE TYSSELVA ZU KNACKEN?

»Könnte gehen!« waren Olafs Worte, als er in Mike Abbott und Allan Ellards Wohnung in Voss trat. Er und Jens hatten den Nachmittag damit verbracht die hintersten Ecken um Voss nach neuen Bächen abzugrasen – und es hörte sich an als hätten sie gute Neuigkeiten.

Am nächsten Morgen wurden Arnd, Matze und ich zum Einstieg geführt; wie vor jedem neuen Fluss lag leichte Anspannung in der Luft. Doch die ersten Kilometer gestalteten sich recht ruhig – auf saubere kleine Rutschen folgten kurze Seen, bei denen es lediglich geradeaus zu paddeln galt. Das erste Herzklopfen kam, als sich die Tysselva in zwei Kanäle teilte und am Horizont verschwand. Der rechte Arm stellte sich schnell als Unfahrbar heraus, der Linke warf ein großes Fragezeichen in den Raum. Hier müsste man schräg einen 8 Meter Fall boofen, um in einem 30 Zentimeter tiefen Pool zu landen. Arnd wollte es wissen und legte eine klare Linie vor – die Messlatte war gelegt, es schien ein aufregender Tag zu werden!

Nach weiteren Kilometern mit lockerem Wildwasser zogen die ersten Wolken auf. Das Wetter schlug um, also versuchten wir uns zu beeilen. Doch was nun vor uns lag, sah von oben aus wie das Ende der Welt. Nach einer Stunde nervösem Rumgestapfe am Ufer entschieden wir uns die Boote über Nacht liegen zu lassen und am nächsten Morgen zurückzukehren, um dann die hoffentlich besseren Lichtverhältnisse zum Filmen zu nutzen.

Trotz der langen Wanderung zum Auto und einer schlaflosen Nacht kamen wir am nächsten Morgen frohen Mutes zurück, um uns mit der Tysselva zu messen. Doch schon der erste Fall zwang uns in die Knie.

Matze Brustmann just after headbutting his cockpit rim

»Mama, mama - guess what we just did?«

to portage. But then Jens set the ball rolling running the first slide of the day. His line was clean, the footage was sick, it was game on! The next waterfall seemed too painful to paddle, but the slide that followed was one of the biggest, most spectacular slides any of us had even seen – and it was runnable! Matze ran it first hitting a sweet line. When everyone had had their turn and satisfied their appetite, it was time to head downstream and see what else the Tysselva had to offer. A short section of tight technical rapids was now on the menu. For the dessert, gravity had come up with something really special: a clean 13 metre waterfall. Jens decided that he wanted his name to this one and hucked his meat off hitting yet another clean line. The rest of the team followed with a few anxious moments as Matze hit his face on his cockpit rim on landing with a loud noise, Arnd over-boofed and landed on the stern and I was thrown off line and pioneered a new route – way too close to the rocks! With little aches and pains and adrenaline pumping through our veins, we had to admit that the Tysselva was living up to Norwegian standards.

At this point, the character of the river changed, gaining a lot more gradient and becoming almost completely unrunnable. The final section of whitewater was an enormous cascading fall with several channels dropping straight into the fjord. At least the last drop of the right channel was runnable, although it was only a trickle of water. A half hour paddle across the fjord to the vehicle on the opposite shore signalled the end of our little journey. It had taken two days but everyone was stoked with the quality of the whitewater that the Tysselva had offered. A few Red Bulls to celebrate and recharge and it was time to head North in search of more of Norway's whitewater gems!

Das Unterwasser schien zu unsauber, wir mussten umtragen. Danach brachte Jens den Ball zum rollen, als er die erste Rutsche fuhr. Seine Linie war sauber, die ersten Aufnahmen im Kasten – die Spiele waren eröffnet! Der nächste Wasserfall erschien zu schmerzhaft zum Paddeln, doch die dann folgende Rutsche war eine der größten und spektakulärsten Rutschen die wir je gesehen hatten – und sie war machbar: Matze fuhr als Erster, und erwischte die perfekte Route. Nachdem jeder seinen ersten Appetit an diesem schmackhaften Happen gestillt hatte, war es Zeit weiter flussab zu schnuppern. Ein paar verblockte Meter standen nun auf der Speisekarte, erst zum Nachtisch hatte sich die Erdanziehungskraft wieder etwas Besonderes ausgedacht: Einen sauberen 13 Meter hohen Wasserfall. Jens wollte hier seinen Namen verewigt haben und bombte gleich mal vor. Der Rest des Teams tat es ihm gleich, allerdings stieg der Adrenalinpegel dabei etwas an: Matze donnerte bei der Landung mit seinem Helm gegen den Süllrand, Arnd überboofte und landete mit dem Heck zuerst, und ich eröffnete aus Versehen eine neue Route – verdammt nah an den Felsen entlang! Mit kleinen Wehwehchen und jeder Menge Adrenalin im Blut mussten wir feststellen, dass die Tysselva voll aufgetischt hatte.

Und genau hier veränderte sich die Tysselva und präsentierte sich wesentlich steiler und fast komplett unfahrbar. Die Abschlusspassage fällt in mehreren Kanälen dirckt ins Fjord, zumindest der letzte Fall des rechten Kanals war fahrbar, wenn auch nur wenig Wasser hinunterlief. Eine halbe Stunde Flachwasser paddeln zur entgegengesetzten Seite signalisierte das Ende unserer kleinen Reise. Es hatte uns zwei Tage gekostet, aber jeder war gestoked von Tysselva. Ein paar Red Bull zum feiern und auftanken und schon war es Zeit weiterzudüsen, auf der Suche nach weiteren norwegischen Wildwasserperlen.

BEN BROWN 1978 *www.benbrown.co.nz*
Kiwi who set out to discover the world. In New Zealand, you can finish university with 21; so for the last years, the Red Bull team member used his free time to travel through Africa, Europe and the US.
Ein Kiwi der auszog die Welt zu bereisen. In Neuseeland kann man schon mit 21 Jahren sein Studium zu Ende bringen, und so nutzte der Red Bull Teamfahrer in den letzten Jahren seine Freiheit um Afrika, Europa und die USA unsicher zu machen.

Schäftlein

Obsommer

Yeah! - Schäftlein

SOGN OG FJORDANE

Jølstravatnet

Sanddalsvatnet

SOGN OG FJORDANE

With its fjord landscape, Sogn og Fjordane is a sight to behold. And it's no surprise, it is here that the mighty Sognefjord pushes its way through the land. At 204 kilometres it is not only the longest fjord in Norway, but with a depth of 1300 metres also the deepest. Its walls climb to a height of 1000 metres above sea level, but in the flatter areas small fruit tree plantations still grow, thanks to the mild climate.

This is also the home of the Jostedalsbreen, Norway's largest glacier. With a length of almost 90 kilometres and a width of up to 35 kilometres, the Jostedalsbreen covers an enormous area of land – only very few mountain peaks manage to push up through this massive carpet of ice. This giant ice cube feeds rivers like the Jostedøla and the Sumelvi with constant water flow up into the high summer.

But Sogn og Fjordane is not only a feast for the eyes. It also heeds the beck and call of the boater's soul: whether it is easier whitewater on the Sumelvi, nice fun runs on the Jølstra and Storeelva, or the waterfall spectacle of the Sogndalselva – here all paddlers will find what they are looking for. This chapter is very short, but very diverse, and well worth your while.

Sogn og Fjordane beeindruckt durch eine wunderschöne Fjordlandschaft. Wen wundert es, presst sich doch hier der Sognefjord durchs Land, welcher mit 204 Kilometern nicht nur der längste, sondern mit 1300 Metern auch der tiefste Fjord Norwegens ist. Die Seitenhänge steigen bis zu 1000 Meter über den Meeresspiegel an, trotzdem erstrecken sich an den abgeflachten Hängen dank des milden Klimas hie und da kleine Obstbaumplantagen.

Norwegens größter Gletscher, der Jostedalsbreen, ist hier beheimatet. Mit fast 90 Kilometern Länge und einer Breite von bis zu 35 Kilometern bedeckt er eine riesige Landfläche – nur wenige Bergspitzen schaffen es aus diesem Eisteppich emporzuragen. Dieser Eisbrocken beschert Flüssen wie Jostedøla und Sumelvi bis in den Hochsommer einen stetigen Wasserlauf.

Sogn og Fjordane ist nicht nur dem Auge ein Vergnügen, auch die Bootfahrerseele wird bedient: Ob leichtes Wildwasser auf der Sumelvi, schöne Genussruns wie Jølstra und Storeelva, oder das Wasserfallspektakel der Sogndalselva – hier wird jeder fündig. Dieses Kapitel ist zwar recht kurz, jedoch äußerst lohnend und abwechslungsreich.

SOGN OG FJORDANE FACTS

Character: Rivers with good flow in mostly open terrain, from WW I-V+, it's all there! Play runs, waterfalls and pushy high volume monsters.
Best time: Spring to early summer, glacial rivers like the Jostedøla and the Sumelvi up until high summer.
Special remarks: Warning: Gyro is on the prowl! Sogndalselva is a salmon river, Smeddalselvi (Lærdalselvi) is affected. Disinfection: ask at the local petrol stations for help, or disinfect by using chlorine.
Accommodation: Camp ground on the right of where the Sogndalselva flows into the fjord.

Charakter: Wasserreiche Flüsse in meist offenem Gelände, von WW I-V+ ist alles da: Spielbäche, Wasserfälle und Wuchtwassermonster.
Beste Zeit: Frühling bis Frühsommer, Gletscherbäche wie Jostedøla und Sumolvi bis in den Hochsommer.
Besonderheit: Achtung: Der Gyro geht um! Die Sogndalselva ist ein Lachsfluss, die Smeddalselvi (Lærdalselvi) obendrein infiziert. Desinfektion: An der Tankstelle nachfragen oder eigenständig mir Chlor.
Übernachtung: Campingplatz rechts der Mündung der Sogndalselva ins Fjord.

Info on the region

www.fjordinfo.no
www.stryn-sommerski.no
www.jostedal.com
www.alr.no

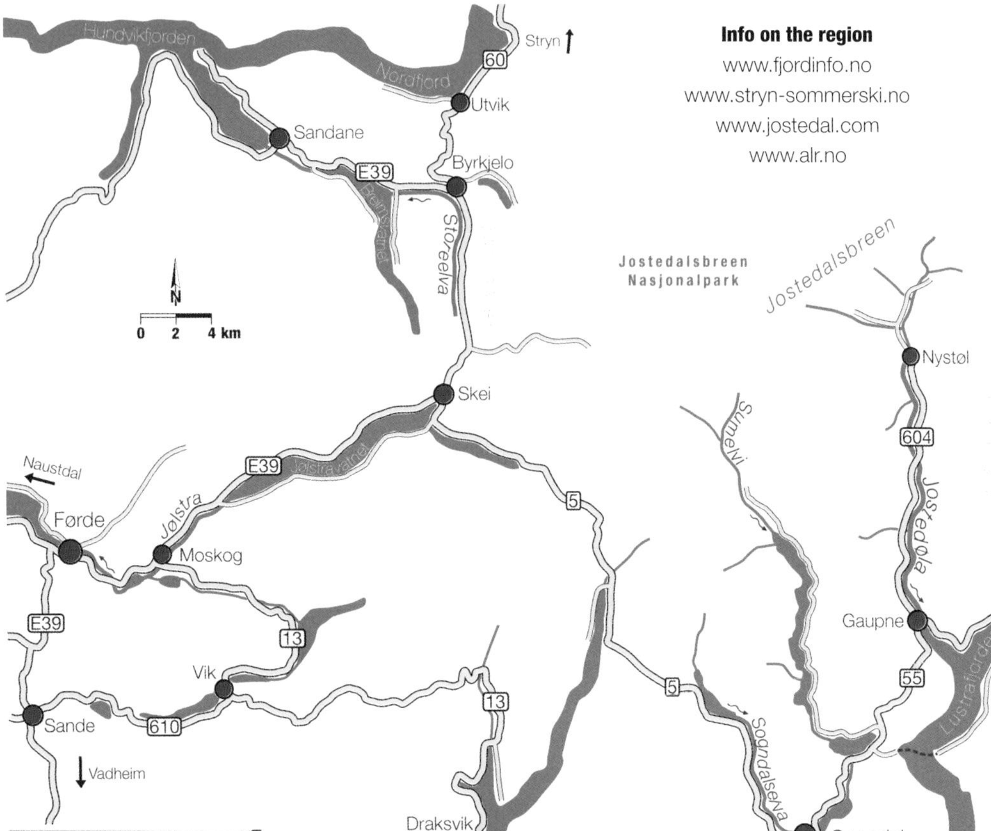
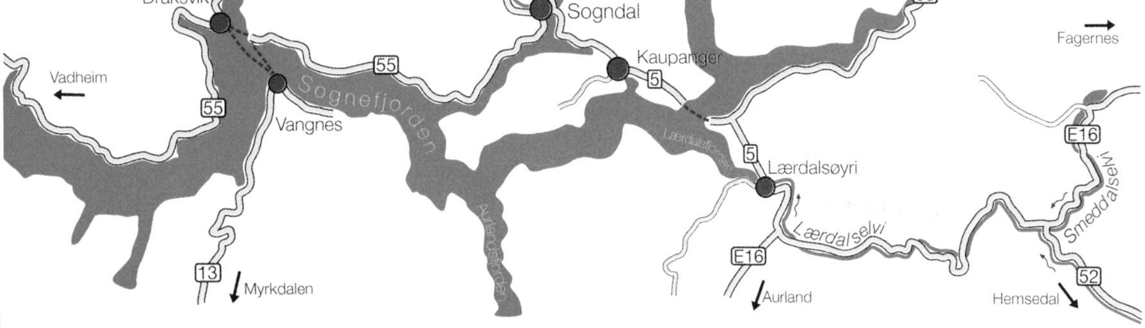
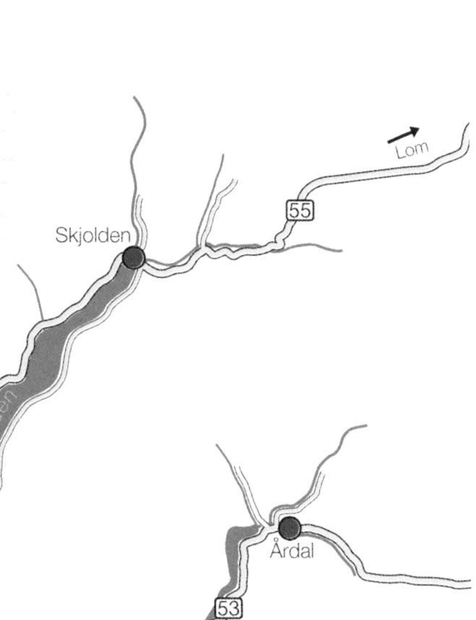
Hundvikfjorden
Nordfjord
Stryn
60
Utvik
Sandane
E39
Byrkjelo
Storeelva
N
0 2 4 km
Jostedalsbreen
Nasjonalpark
Jostedalsbreen
Nystøl
Skei
Naustdal
E39
Jølstravatnet
Jølstra
Førde
Moskog
5
604
Jostedøla
Sumelvi
Lom
55
Skjolden
Gaupne
Lustrafjorden
E39
13
Vik
5
55
Sande
610
13
Vadheim
Sogndalselva
Årdal
53
Draksvik
Sogndal
Fagernes
Kaupanger
55
Vadheim
5
55
Sognefjorden
Vangnes
Lærdalsfjorden
E16
5
Lærdalsøyri
Smeddalselvi
Aurlandsfjorden
Lærdalselvi
E16
52
13
Myrkdalen
Aurland
Hemsedal

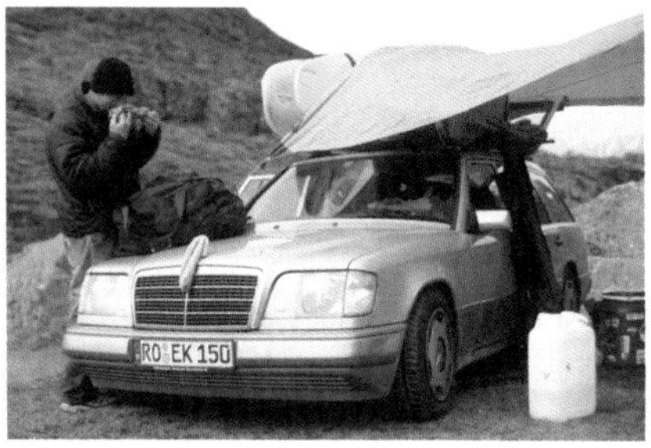
RO EK 150

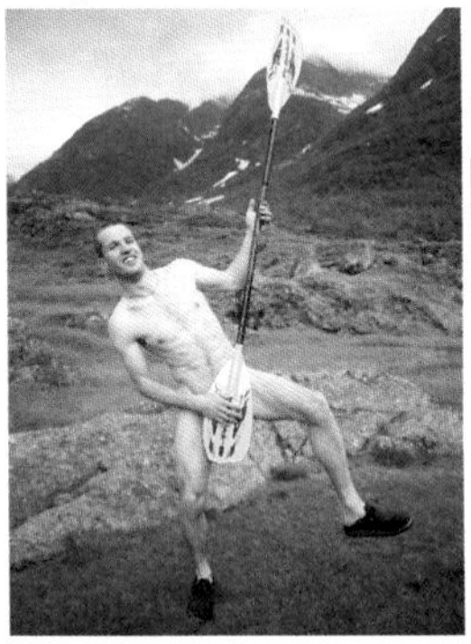

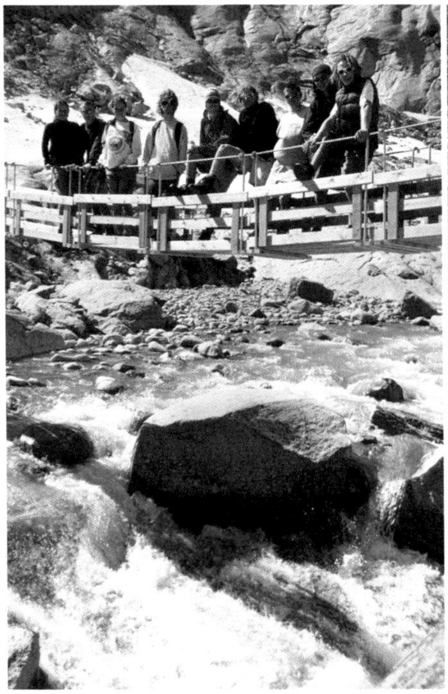

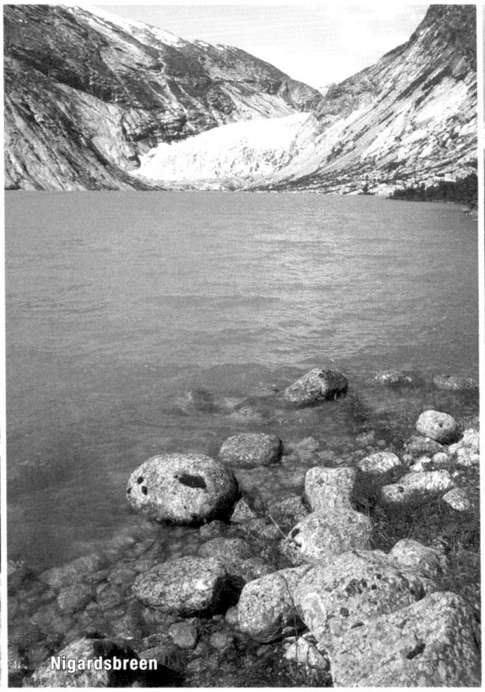
Nigårdsbreen

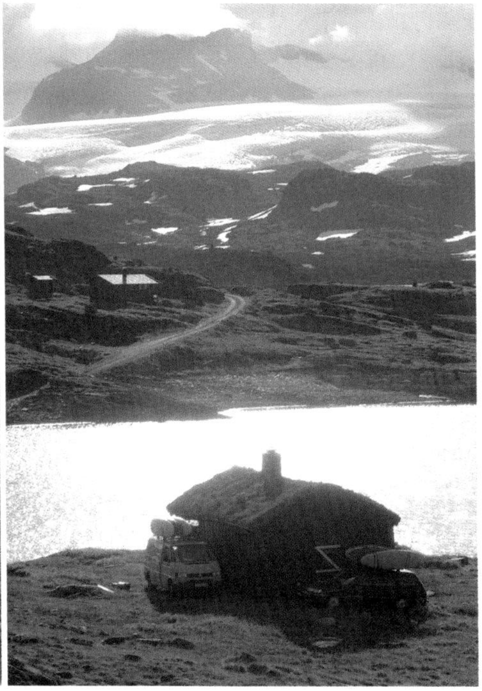

SMEDDALSELVI: UPPER

A DROP + POOL SUPER SWEET AWESOME DUDE DREAM RIVER

At this point we should actually be describing the Lærdalselvi. For years there was no doubt in our minds that we would be describing the Lærdalselvi at this point. We had always chosen to ignore the fact that, up to the convergence of the Mørkedøla, the Lærdalselvi is actually called the Smeddalselvi. However when we decided, on account of the salmon problem, not to describe the lower section of the Lærdalselvi, (that is to say from the convergence of the Mørkedøla), we found that there was in fact not much left of the Lærdalselvi to describe. Conclusion: the document was changed to a description of the Smeddalselvi, and the Lærdalselvi was put into retirement. But since it is actually only the name which has been changed, we are able to live with this, can wave farewell to the Lærdalselvi, and

CLASS: V - VI
LEVEL: 10 - 20 cumecs
LENGTH: 5 km
TIME: 4 - 6 h
SEASON: June - July

are delighted to present the Smeddalselvi, which is now one of the crowning glories of Sogn og Fjordane. In a word: if you are looking for non-stop problems, you've come to the right place! All the sections have in fact already been mastered, but shouldering your boat here a couple of times need be no cause for shame. You're off the hook!

500 metres after the lake you reach the first siphon, which should be portaged on the right. The siphon can be recognised as follows: after the first difficulties the Smeddalselvi collects its thoughts once more in a pool. The cataract which follows flows under a large rock after about 50 metres. 3 metres before the siphon is an eddy on the right. The gradient of the cataract is moderate, the difficulty around WW III-IV.

The second siphon follows after another 300

metres. Caution, it is difficult to recognise! Exit on the right and portage. From around 20 cumecs and up the siphons can no longer be recognised, be extremely careful.

After that you have dream whitewater, including a beautiful 3 metre waterfall with a serious tow-back, which is rather difficult to boof. There is a tricky drop in the last low gorge which has already invited a number of paddlers to an involuntary swim session. Those who portage the difficult entry on the right can see to the end of the low gorge, and can easily forget the ledge before the pool. From here it looks as though the last cataract flows into the pool without a drop – but it doesn't. The best line is hard left, a clean boof is a must. For the remaining kilometre to the road bridge you can relax once more.

Eigentlich sollte an dieser Stelle die Lærdalselvi beschrieben werden. Jahrelang bestand auch gar kein Zweifel daran, dass an dieser Stelle die Lærdalselvi beschrieben werden würde. Wir wollten immer ignorieren, dass der Oberlauf der Lærdalselvi bis hin zur Mündung der Mørkedøla eigentlich Smeddalselvi hieß. Als wir uns aber entschlossen, den unteren Teil der Lærdalselvi, also ab der Mündung der Mørkedøla, aufgrund der Lachsproblematik nicht zu beschreiben, blieb von der Lærdalselvi nicht mehr viel übrig. Fazit: Das Dokument wurde in Smeddalselvi geändert und die Lærdalselvi ging in Rente. Da sich aber eigentlich nur der Name ändert, können wir damit leben, winken zum Abschied und freuen uns nun auf die Smeddalselvi, denn nun ist sie einer der Höhepunkte in Sogn og Fjordane. Lange Rede, kurzer Sinn: Wer Schwierigkeiten am Fließband sucht, wird genau hier fündig. Es wurden zwar schon alle Stellen gemeistert, aber auch wer sein Kajak ein paar Mal schultert, ist gewiss kein schlechter Mensch. Glück gehabt!

Etwa 500 Meter nach dem See erreicht man den ersten Siphon, der rechts umhoben werden sollte. Erkannt wird der Siphon wie folgt: Nach den ersten Schwierigkeiten sammelt sich die Smeddalselvi kurz in einem Pool. Der folgende Katarakt strömt nach etwa 50 Meter unter einen großen Stein. 3 Meter vor dem Siphon ist rechts ein Kehrwasser. Das Gefälle in dem Katarakt ist mäßig, die Schwierigkeiten liegen bei WW III-IV.

Der zweite Siphon folgt nach weiteren 300 Metern. Vorsicht, er ist schwer zu erkennen! Rechts aussteigen und umtragen. Ab ungefähr 20 Kubik sind die zwei Siphons nicht mehr zu erkennen, Vorsicht.

Danach folgt traumhaftes Wildwasser mit einem wunderschönen 3-Meter-Wasserfall, der sehr rückläufig und etwas schwierig zu boofen ist. Eine tückische Stelle befindet sich in der letzten

Niederklamm, sie hat schon vielen Paddlern zu einem unfreiwilligen Schwimmer verholfen. Wer den schwierigen Eingang rechts umträgt, kann bis ans Ende der Niederklamm sehen und vergisst dabei leicht die letzte Kante vor dem Pool. Dort sieht es

so aus, als ob der letzte Katarakt ohne Stufe in den Pool läuft – tut er aber nicht. Die beste Linie befindet sich ganz links, ein sauberer Boof ist Pflicht. Auf dem restlichen Kilometer bis zur Straßenbrücke kann man sich wieder Entspannen.

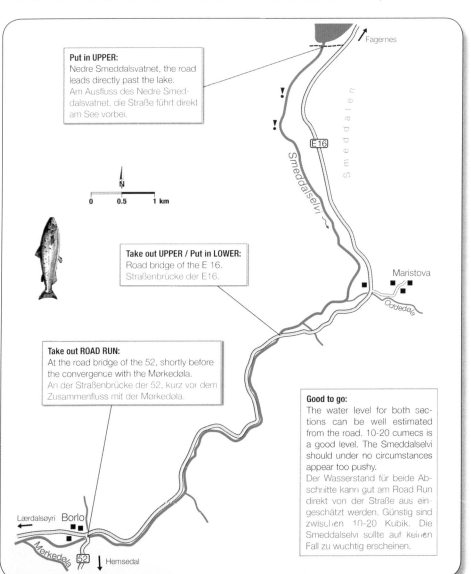

Put in UPPER:
Nedre Smeddalsvatnet, the road leads directly past the lake.
Am Ausfluss des Nedre Smeddalsvatnet, die Straße führt direkt am See vorbei.

Fagernes

Smeddalen

E 16

Smeddalselvi

Maristova

Oddedøla

Take out UPPER / Put in LOWER:
Road bridge of the E 16.
Straßenbrücke der E16.

Take out ROAD RUN:
At the road bridge of the 52, shortly before the convergence with the Mørkedøla.
An der Straßenbrücke der 52, kurz vor dem Zusammenfluss mit der Mørkedøla.

Lærdalsøyri Borlo

Mørkedøla

52 Hemsedal

Good to go:
The water level for both sections can be well estimated from the road. 10-20 cumecs is a good level. The Smeddalselvi should under no circumstances appear too pushy.
Der Wasserstand für beide Abschnitte kann gut am Road Run direkt von der Straße aus eingeschätzt werden. Günstig sind zwischen 10-20 Kubik. Die Smeddalselvi sollte auf keinen Fall zu wuchtig erscheinen.

SMEDDALSELVI: ROAD RUN   A RUN NEXT TO THE ROAD

The Road Run of the Smeddalselvi is much more difficult and much nicer than it appears from the road. First impressions can indeed be misleading.

CLASS: V (VI)
LEVEL: 10 - 20 cumecs
LENGTH: 6 km
TIME: 2 - 4 h
SEASON: June - July

All the difficult sections can be well scouted from river right. The WW VI drop about 500 metres before the take out has already been paddled, but is also easily portaged on the right. It is also possible to end the trip at a bus stop here.

Warning: The lower section of the Smeddalselvi, the Lærdalselvi, looks very tempting, but should not be paddled because of the anglers (private revier!).

Der Road Run der Smeddalselvi ist viel schwieriger und schöner als er von der Straße aus erscheint. Der erste Eindruck ist eben doch nicht immer der Richtige. Alle Schwierigkeiten können von der flussrechten Seite gut angeschaut werden. Die Vier-Stelle etwa 500 Meter vor dem Ausstieg ist auch schon bekagelt worden, jedoch auch problemlos rechts zu umtragen. Es besteht auch die Möglichkeit hier an einer Bushaltestelle die Fahrt zu beenden.

Achtung: Der Unterlauf der Smeddalselvi, die Lærdalselvi, sieht zwar toll aus, sollte jedoch aufgrund der Angler (Privatstege!) nicht gepaddelt werden.

Photos: SG

Ulrich Kittelberger

Zip-a-dee-doo-dah!

SOGNDALSELVA: UPPER

A NICE CONTINUOUS RUN IN A GORGE

The Sogndalselva flows out of the Dalavatnet, and at Sogndal flows into the Sogndalsfjorden, a branch of the mighty Sognfjorden.

For a number of WW V pleasure paddlers, the upper section of the Sogndalselva is the high point of the Norway trip. If you can remember the lines through the countless slides and cataracts you are in for a whitewater experience of the highest order – getting out of your boat is virtually never necessary. However, all the difficult sections can be well scouted.

But woe betide he who is the victim of rising water: from 20 cumecs upwards this section becomes a veritable motorway, and the eddies disappear fast. The Sogndalselva is then a full on, very dangerous ride.

Tip: Up to the headwaters and try the Langdalselva. Steep for freaks!

CLASS: IV - V
LEVEL: 10 - 15 cumecs
LENGTH: 5 km
TIME: 2 - 4 h
SEASON: June - July

Die Sogndalselva entspringt aus dem Dalavatnet und mündet bei Sogndal ins Sogndalsfjorden, einem Nebenarm des mächtigen Sognfjorden.

Für einige WW-V-Genusspaddler ist der Oberlauf der Sogndalselva der Höhepunkt einer Norwegenreise. Kann man sich sogar noch an die Linien durch die endlose Rutschen und Katarakte erinnern, erlebt man einen Wildwasserrausch der Superlative – aussteigen wird beinah unnötig. Alle schweren Stellen können jedoch gut besichtigt werden.

Aber wehe wenn der Wasserstand steigt: ab 20 Kubik wird dieser Abschnitt zu einer Autobahn und die Kehrwässer verschwinden schnell. Dann ist die Sogndalselva ein heißer und sehr gefährlicher Ritt.

Tipp: Auf zu den Quellflüssen und die Langdalselva versuchen. Steil ist Geil!

Ron Fischer

Lukas Wielatt

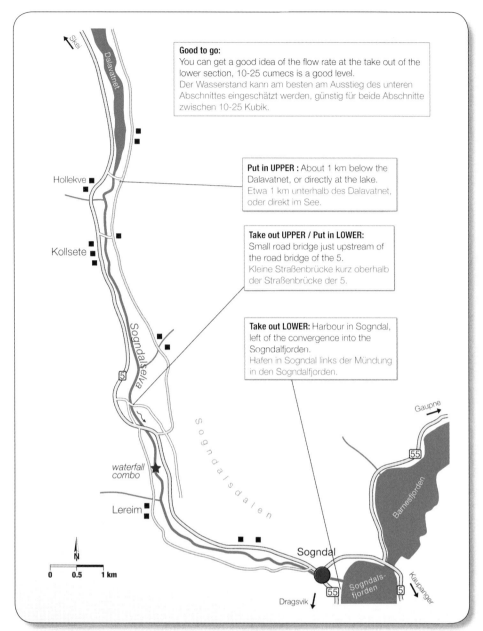

Good to go:
You can get a good idea of the flow rate at the take out of the lower section, 10-25 cumecs is a good level.
Der Wasserstand kann am besten am Ausstieg des unteren Abschnittes eingeschätzt werden, günstig für beide Abschnitte zwischen 10-25 Kubik.

Put in UPPER : About 1 km below the Dalavatnet, or directly at the lake.
Etwa 1 km unterhalb des Dalavatnet, oder direkt im See.

Take out UPPER / Put in LOWER:
Small road bridge just upstream of the road bridge of the 5.
Kleine Straßenbrücke kurz oberhalb der Straßenbrücke der 5.

Take out LOWER: Harbour in Sogndal, left of the convergence into the Sogndalfjorden.
Hafen in Sogndal links der Mündung in den Sogndalfjorden.

Team Prijon having fun

SOGNDALSELVA: WATERFALL RUN

A RUN WITH AN AWESOME WATERFALL COMBO

The upper Sogndalselva was already conquered at the end of the eighties, but there was nothing but dark rumours to be heard regarding the lower section. The legend of a triple waterfall combo with a freefall of up to 20 metres seemed to scare every pioneer off. For a long time nobody made the effort to take a closer look at this section. Then in 1998 we dared an attempt, and were rewarded with one of the most amazing waterfall combinations of any universe you care to name. (What? How? There is only one universe?) See also the short story by Olli Grau on page 184. Except for the waterfalls, however, the lower

CLASS:	V (VI-X)
LEVEL:	10 - 25 cumecs
LENGTH:	5 km
TIME:	3 - 5 h
SEASON:	June - July

Die obere Sogndalselva wurde schon Ende der Achtziger bezwungen, über die untere hingegen brodelte nur die Gerüchteküche. Der Mythos einer dreifachen Wasserfallkombi mit Fallhöhen bis zu 20 Metern schreckte wohl alle Pioniere ab. Lange machte sich niemand die Mühe den Abschnitt genauer unter die Lupe zu nehmen. 1998 wagten wir einen Versuch und wurden mit einer der tollsten Wasserfallkombinationen aller Universen belohnt (Was? Wie? Es gibt nur ein Universum?). Siehe auch die Kurzgeschichte von Olli Grau auf Seite 184. Die Untere ist allerdings, bis auf die Wasserfälle, etwas unsauber und kantiger als das obere Teilstück.

Sogndalselva is somewhat unclean and sharper-edged than the upper section.

The first kilometres leading up to the waterfalls should be approached with care, as road works have left sharp rocks strewn through the river bed. One inconspicuous section should be scouted closely, as all the water disappears under a rock slab. There has already been one pin at this spot! But don't be scared off, and take good care, and you will be guaranteed the ultimate waterfall experience! In fact, you reach the waterfalls a mere 700 metres after putting on. If you want to have a look at it before putting on, you will need to follow the road on river right, then cross the fields and bushbash a bit to get down to the river.

Der erste Kilometer bis zu den Wasserfällen sollte vorsichtig angegangen werden, da durch Straßenbauarbeiten scharfe Steine im Fluss verteilt sind. Eine unscheinbare Stelle sollte genau besichtigt werden, da das ganze Wasser unter eine Platte zieht. An dieser Stelle gab es schon einen Stecker! Aber lasst euch nicht abschrecken und seid schön vorsichtig, dann ist der ultimative Wasserfallgenuss garantiert. Die Wasserfälle erreicht man etwa 700 Meter nach dem Einstieg. Will man schon vor dem Paddeln einen Blick darauf werfen, muss man der flussrechten Straße folgen und sich über Wiesen und ein kurzes Waldstück zum Fluss durchschlagen.

Nach den Wasserfällen erreicht man bald eine

After the waterfalls you soon reach an unpaddleable drop, which has in fact already been kagelled, but which is also easy to portage on the right. Numerous drops and slides then carry you to the fjord. The long slide at the salmon steps can be paddled, despite the iron girders river right at the exit. At the last drop you must check whether the anglers are there trying their luck. If this is the case, it is best to portage well around them, or politely ask if they would mind you running it. The anglers pay a lot of money for the pursuit of their prey.

»The waterfalls of the Sogndalselva are a gift from God: you simply need to close your spray deck and bomb down.« Thomas Fink, Rheinfall conqueror

Unfahrbare, die zwar schon bekagelt wurde, jedoch auch einfach rechts umtragen werden kann. Bis in den Fjord folgen noch zahlreiche Stufen und Rutschen. Die lange Rutsche an der Fischtreppe kann trotz der Eisenteile flussrechts am Ausgang gepaddelt werden. An der letzten Stelle vor dem Fjord muss man sicher gehen, dass keine Angler Ihr Glück versuchen. Wenn dem so ist, besser weiträumig umtragen oder höflich fragen, ob einer Befahrung etwas im Wege stehe. Die Angler zahlen sehr viel Geld für ihre Jagd nach den Fischen.

»Die Wasserfälle der Sogndalselva sind ein Geschenk Gottes: Da muss man einfach die Spritzdecke zu machen und runterstechen.« Thomas Fink, Rheinfall-Bezwinger

Photo: MA

Sogndalsfjorden at Sogndal

Olli Grau

The weir drop on the lower section

JOSTEDØLA: UPPER CANYONS

A BIG VOLUME GLACIER RIVER

The Jostedøla, also known as the Jostedalselva, with its numerous head-waters, drains the east of the Jostedalsbreen and reaches the Sognefjord at Gaupne. She's big, as cold as ice, and a force to be reckoned with, especially in the summer months. Her character changes frequently from »open and flat« to »steep and tight«.

In the two gorges above Gjerde you really get to make the acquaintance of the Jostedøla, and from that moment on one is either friend or foe. Once you're in your boat, the dimensions of the Jostedøla are made clear in no un-certain terms, so have a good look at her first, and decide whether you could ever befriend this ferocious »God-this-is-cold-I-think-I'm-dying-of-hypothermia« beast

In the deep gorge scouting and safetying is very important, but not always easy, so you should plan plenty of time. You should scout the whole of the first gorge from the left bank before running it. The holes do not look so impressive from the edge of the gorge, but be warned – everything is massive! You should also scout closely between the two road tunnels, otherwise the river-wide monster hole will devour anything and everything that doesn't hit the teeny-weeny tongue left of middle. But beware: at certain flows the monster shows its tongue no more, just rabid foam.

CLASS: V
LEVEL: 20 - 50 cumecs
LENGTH: 4 km
TIME: 3 - 5 h
SEASON: July - September

»*Some holes are a paddler-devouring monster that, once it has you, never lets you out of its claws again.*« From AKC Tip

Tip: Dress warmly!

Die Jostedøla, oder auch Jostedalselva, entwässert mit mehreren Quellflüs-sen den Osten des Jostedalsbreen und erreicht das Sognefjord bei Gaupne. Sie ist groß, eiskalt und mächtig – gerade in den Sommermonaten. Der Fluss-charakter wechselt häufig von »offen und flach« zu »eng und steil«.

In den zwei Schluchten oberhalb von Gjerde lernt man die Jostedøla richtig kennen, hier gibt es nur Freund oder Feind. Sitzt man einmal im Boot, wer-den einem die Dimensionen der Jostedøla extrem nahe gelegt, also schon

The glacial archway of the Nigardsbreen - Obsommer 1995

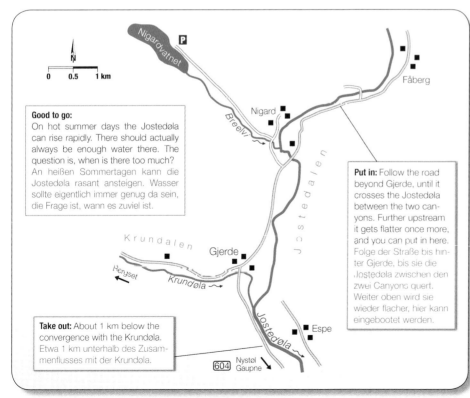

Good to go:
On hot summer days the Jostedøla can rise rapidly. There should actually always be enough water there. The question is, when is there too much?
An heißen Sommertagen kann die Jostedøla rasant ansteigen. Wasser sollte eigentlich immer genug da sein, die Frage ist, wann es zuviel ist.

Put in: Follow the road beyond Gjerde, until it crosses the Jostedøla between the two can-yons. Further upstream it gets flatter once more, and you can put in here.
Folge der Straße bis hin-ter Gjerde, bis sie die Jostedøla zwischen den zwei Canyons quert. Weiter oben wird sie wieder flacher, hier kann eingebootet werden.

Take out: About 1 km below the convergence with the Krundøla.
Etwa 1 km unterhalb des Zusam-menflusses mit der Krundøla.

vorher gut besichtigen, und sich überlegen, ob man mit diesem »Man-ist-das-kalt-ich-glaub-ich-sterbe-Wässerchen« überhaupt je Freund werden kann.

In den klammartigen Schluchten ist sichern und besichtigen sehr wichtig, allerdings auch nicht so einfach, also sollte etwas Zeit eingeplant werden. Die erste Schlucht wird am besten schon vor einer Befahrung linksufrig abgelau-fen. Die Walzen schauen vom Schluchtrand nicht so beeindrucken aus, aber seid gewarnt – alles ist gewaltig. Auch zwischen den beiden Straßentunneln sollte genau geschaut werden, da ein flussbreites Walzenmonster sonst jeden verschlingt, der nicht die klitzekleine Zunge links der Mitte nutzt. Doch Obacht, bei bestimmten Wasserständen zeigt das Monster keine Zunge mehr, sondern nur schäumendes Weiß.

»*So manche Walze ist ein paddlerverschlingen-des Monster, das einen nicht mehr aus den Klauen lässt*«. Originaltext AKC Tip

Tipp: Warm anziehen!

SUMELVI: SCENIC RUN

The Sumelvi drains the Austerdalsbreen, a run off of the Jostedalsbreen. It flows through a valley parallel to the Jostedøla, completely isolated from the rest of the world. It is not the whitewater which makes a descent worthwhile, rather the breathtaking backdrop. The aura of the valley permeates your body like x-rays, and fills you with elation: up here the World is still just as it should be. A trip here is something for sunny days, with unlimited visibility to the surrounding mountains and glaciers.

CLASS: I - II (IV/V)
LEVEL: 5 km
LENGTH: 15 - 25 cumecs
TIME: 2 h
SEASON: May - September

Warning: We didn't paddle the Sumelvi, the cold rain scared us prudes off. Nonetheless we would like to recommend this river. The description is based on reconnaissance made from the road.

From the put in, the Sumelvi sets off with a sprightly gait, to shortly receive additional flow from the Langedalsbreen. After about 1 kilometre you reach a short gorge (WW IV), which you will have surely discovered on the drive up. After that she hums her way through the landscape once more, allowing time to savour the surrounds. About 1 kilometre before the take out lies a short interruption in wait, you could actually end the trip here as well. In any case, end the trip at the very latest before the next short low gorge at the toll station.

Die Sumelvi entwässert den Austerdalsbreen, einen Ausläufer des Jostedalsbreen. Sie fließt durch ein Paralleltal der Jostedøla, völlig abgeschieden vom Rest der Welt. Es ist nicht das Wildwasser welches eine Befahrung lohnend macht, sondern einfach die atemberaubende Kulisse. Die Aura des Tales durchdringt den Körper wie Röntgenstrahlen und vermittelt ein erhabenes Gefühl: Hier oben ist die Welt noch in Ordnung. Eine Befahrung ist was für sonnige Tage, mit ungetrübtem Blick auf die angrenzenden Berge und Gletscher.

Achtung: Wir sind die Sumelvi nicht gepaddelt, der kalte Regen hielt uns Warmduscher ab. Dennoch wollen wir diesen Fluss empfehlen. Die folgende Beschreibung basiert auf Erkundungen von der Straße:

Die Sumelvi fließt vom Einstieg munter dahin, um kurze Zeit später Zuschusswasser vom Langedalsbreen zu erhalten. Nach etwa einem Kilometer erreicht man eine kurze Niederklamm (WW IV), die man sicherlich schon bei der Anfahrt entdeckt hat. Danach summt sie weiter durch die Landschaft und lässt Zeit, die Aussicht zu genießen. Etwa 1 Kilometer vor dem Ausstieg lauert ein kurzer Abbruch, eigentlich kann auch schon hier die Fahrt beendet werden. Auf jeden Fall aber vor der nächsten kurzen Niederklamm an der Mautstation.

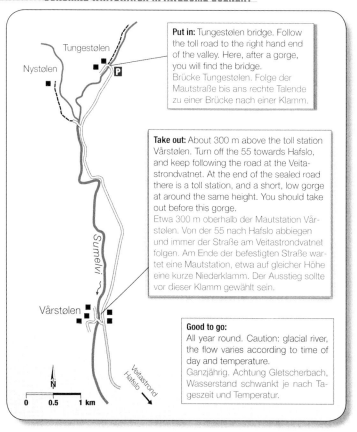

Put in: Tungestølen bridge. Follow the toll road to the right hand end of the valley. Here, after a gorge, you will find the bridge.
Brücke Tungestølen. Folge der Mautstraße bis ans rechte Talende zu einer Brücke nach einer Klamm.

Take out: About 300 m above the toll station Vårstølen. Turn off the 55 towards Hafslo, and keep following the road at the Veitastrondvatnet. At the end of the sealed road there is a toll station, and a short, low gorge at around the same height. You should take out before this gorge.
Etwa 300 m oberhalb der Mautstation Vårstølen. Von der 55 nach Hafslo abbiegen und immer der Straße am Veitastrondvatnet folgen. Am Ende der befestigten Straße wartet eine Mautstation, etwa auf gleicher Höhe eine kurze Niederklamm. Der Ausstieg sollte vor dieser Klamm gewählt sein.

Good to go:
All year round. Caution: glacial river, the flow varies according to time of day and temperature.
Ganzjährig. Achtung Gletscherbach, Wasserstand schwankt je nach Tageszeit und Temperatur.

Just by the way: it's 11.30 pm

JØLSTRA

The Jølstra is a must for fun paddlers who like surfing waves and getting vertical in eddy lines. The rapids are up to 300 metres long, and in between there are quiet sections. The difficult sections are almost always possible to scout from the road which runs along the right of the river.

CLASS: III - IV+ (V-)
LEVEL: 30 - 60 cumecs
LENGTH: 8 km / 10 km
TIME: 2 - 4 h
SEASON: May - September

This racey, pushy, slightly blocked run starts in the Jølstravatnet. After about 2.5 kilometres, at Kvammen, you reach a striking left bend. The Jølstra divides here, and in the left channel there is a life threatening towback. If your line is wide enough in the outside of the bend, you should be on the safe side. The section can be seen from the road, and should be scouted before the run.

The next 5 kilometres catapult you into a parallel whitewater dimension, but beware: when the Jølstra then flows away from the road and disappears into the forest, there is a towback which needs to be scouted from the left. The last eddy to scout from is directly in front of the drop. The following 200 metres can be mastered with a big bag of courage and a long neck. If you're not too keen to try your luck, scout beforehand from the right.

The first take out point is at a small parking bay about 150 metres before the Stakallefoss. The Jølstra flows directly beside the road here, the edge of the foss can be seen in the distance. If you've still got extra energy to burn off, you can portage around the Stakallefoss on the left and put into the outlet of the power station. As a reward for your efforts you will be granted three nice, pushy slides which come after the next road bridge (gauge). These can be scouted from the gravel road on river left before you run them. A little later the Huldrefoss crashes into the Jølstra from the left and has proven itself to be a fitting take out point. You can take out on river right at the school opposite the Huldrefoss.

Tip: For those who simply cannot live without a bit of WW V-VI in their day, an attempt at the Stakallefoss can be recommended. For this foss the gauge should be reading at least 180 cm.

Für alle Genusspaddler, die gerne Wellen surfen und sich in Verschneidungslinien in die Vertikale beamen, ist die Jølstra ein Muss. Die Strom-schnellen sind bis zu 300 Meter lang, dazwischen liegen ruhige Passagen. Die Schwierigkeiten sind fast immer von der rechts nebenher laufenden Straße einsehbar.

Der Jølstravatnet ist der Start dieser rasanten Fahrt mit wuchtigem und leicht verblocktem Wild-wasser. Nach etwa 2,5 Kilometern erreicht man kurz vor Kvammen eine Stufe an einer markanten Linkskurve. Hier teilt sich die Jølstra, im linken Kanal lauert ein lebensgefährlicher Rücklauf. Wer seine Linie weit genug rechts in der Außenkurve wählt, ist auf der sicheren Seite. Diese Stelle ist von der Straße zu erkennen und sollte besser schon vor dem Paddeln erkundet werden.

Die nächsten 5 Kilometer katapultieren dich in ein Wildwasser-Paralleluniversum, doch dann Ob-acht: Entfernt sich die Jølstra von der Straße und verschwindet im Wald, muss eine Rücklaufstufe von links angeschaut werden. Das letzte Kehr-wasser zum Besichtigen ist direkt vor der Kante. Die 200 Meter im Anschluss können mit Mut und gestreckter Haltung gemeistert werden. Wer sich nicht auf sein Glück verlassen möchte, schaut lieber schon vorher nach dem Rechten.

Die erste Ausstiegsmöglichkeit befindet sich an einer kleinen Straßenbucht etwa 150 Meter vor dem Stakallefossen. Die Jølstra fließt hier direkt neben der Straße, die Abrisskante des Fossen ist in der Ferne zu sehen. Wer noch überschüssige Kraftreserven abbauen muss, kann den Stakalle-fossen links umtragen und im Kraftwerksausfluss einbooten. Als Belohnung für die Mühe warten nach der nächsten Straßenbrücke (Pegel) drei schöne und wuchtige Rutschen. Diese können vor

einer Befahrung von der flusslinken Schotterstraße besichtigt werden. Der Huldrefossen stürzt etwas später von links in die Jølstra und erweist sich als gebührender Ausstieg. Man kann flussrechts an der Schule gegenüber dem Huldrefossen aus-booten.

Tipp: Wer ohne WW V-VI nicht in Frieden leben kann, soll sich am Stakallefossen versuchen. Für eine Befahrung des Fossen sollte der Pegel min-destens 180 cm markieren.

Put in:
Outlet of the Jølstravatnet.
Ausfluss des Jølstravatnet.

Take out 2:
At the school in Mo, oppo-site the Huldrefoss.
An der Schule in Mo gegen-über dem Huldrefossen.

Take out 1: Parking bay on the E 39, shortly before the Stakallefoss.
Straßenbucht der E 39 kurz vor dem Stakallefossen.

Good to go:
The gauge is on the river left side of the road bridge on the 13, direction Dragsvik. Minimum 140 cm, at 160 cm and above you can reckon with a faster, pushier run.
Der Pegel befindet sich an der flusslinken Seite unterhalb der Straßenbrücke der 13 Richtung Dragsvik. Minimum 140 cm, ab 160 cm steigende Wasserwucht und Fließgeschwindigkeit.

The outlet of the Jølstravatnet...

... and the following 100 metres

Chicken line - Klatt

STOREELVA: LOWER

A LOT OF WAVES WITH A FEW GRADE V- DROPS IN BETWEEN

For us the lower section of the Storeelva before the Breimsvatnet is of interest. Here she will enchant you with a magical put in at the outflow from a lake, the take out at the inflow into the next lake, and mind blowing waves in between which invite you to a session of endless surfing, spinning and air time. There are also four difficult cataracts and a weir, all of which can easily be portaged.

For the first 2 kilometres the Storeelva flows calmly, until it reaches a difficult cataract directly before the gauge bridge. It is recommendable to take out on the left and scout, and this is also a possible alternative for putting on. Up until the next WW V section you can now show your style in the waves and holes. Then there are two WW V-slides, followed by a weir. All three sections can be scouted and portaged on the left. The last V- section is a left bend directly after a bridge. At a gauge reading of 180 cm and above, you can paddle around this in the left channel. Otherwise take out on the left directly after the bridge, and cross to river right to scout. Warning: after the bridge the current flows strongly into a pile of rocks. After this the Storeelva flows without further major difficulties into the Breimsvatnet. After the convergence paddle right to the harbour.

Die Storeelva ist für uns auf ihrem Unterlauf kurz vor dem Breimsvatnet interessant. Hier verzaubert sie mit einem tollen Ein- und Ausstieg im See, dazwischen mit berauschenden Wellen, die zum Meilensurfen, Kreiseln und Luftsprüngen einladen. Es lauern vier schwere Katarakte und ein Wehr, allesamt können einfach umtragen werden.

Auf den ersten 2 Kilometern fließt die Storeelva ruhig dahin, bevor ein schwerer Katarakt direkt vor der Pegelbrücke des Paddlers Aufmerksamkeit fordert. Es empfiehlt sich linksufrig anzulanden und zu besichtigen, hier kann auch alternativ eingebootet werden. Bis zum nächsten Fünfer kann in Wellen und Walzen gestylt werden. Dann folgen zwei WW V- Rutschen, anschließend ein Wehr. Alle drei Stellen können ebenfalls von links einfach erkundet und umtragen werden. Die letzte V- Stelle ist eine Linkskurve direkt nach einer Brücke. Ab Pegel 180 cm kann diese Stelle im linken Kanal umfahren werden. Sonst direkt nach der Brücke links ausbooten und zum Anschauen zur rechten Seite wechseln. Achtung: Die Strömung zieht nach der Brücke kräftig auf einen Steinverhau. Anschließend strömt die Storeelva ohne nennenswerte Schwierigkeiten in den Breimsvatnet. Nach der Mündung rechts zum Hafen paddeln.

CLASS:	III - IV- (V)
LEVEL:	25 - 60 cumecs
LENGTH:	7.5 km (5 km)
TIME:	2 - 3 h
SEASON:	May - August

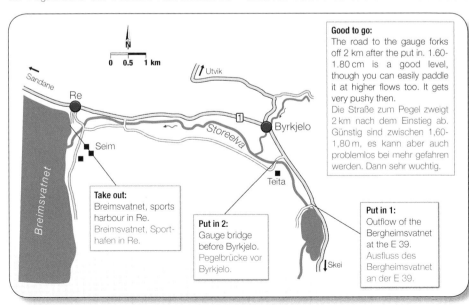

Good to go:
The road to the gauge forks off 2 km after the put in. 1.60-1.80 cm is a good level, though you can easily paddle it at higher flows too. It gets very pushy then.
Die Straße zum Pegel zweigt 2 km nach dem Einstieg ab. Günstig sind zwischen 1,60-1,80 m, es kann aber auch problemlos bei mehr gefahren werden. Dann sehr wuchtig.

Take out:
Breimsvatnet, sports harbour in Re.
Breimsvatnet, Sport-hafen in Re.

Put in 2:
Gauge bridge before Byrkjelo.
Pegelbrücke vor Byrkjelo.

Put in 1:
Outflow of the Bergheimsvatnet at the E 39.
Ausfluss des Bergheimsvatnet an der E 39.

Sandane
Re
Seim
Breimsvatnet
Storeelva
Utvik
Byrkjelo
Teita
Skei

Don Hölzl

STORY: SOGNDALSELVA OLLI GRAU

LOVE AT FIRST SIGHT

Falling in love is always exciting. Through the eyes of a lover, every moment seems richer and more intense. And the first true love is something you will remember for the rest of your life. My first kayaking trip to Norway stuck in my memory just like that: it was love at first sight. In Norway, the rivers are bigger, pushier, but also more forgiving than what we're used to in the Alps. During a first visit to the country of abundant whitewater, you're bound to undergo a metamorphosis: you learn to differentiate between »spectacular« and »lethal« drops. At the end, intense memories of life-shaping experiences with powerful rivers and foamy holes remain. In such a country of superlatives, a first descent or the discovery of an unknown waterfall or section of a river is a pivotal experience.

It was in July 1998 that I made my first trip to Norway. We had done most of the classic runs and were searching for new territory. With the patience of saints and a youthful spirit, we explored all the potential rivers north of the Sognefjord hoping to discover some unknown creek or unheard of tributary. Unfortunately, we didn't find anything of interest. Consequently we were looking forward all the more to running the Sogndalselva. Olaf had already done its headwaters and declared the run another must-do classic. But this standard section was to become a mere prologue to it all. Between the bridge at the take-out and the estuary mouth, there was a small stretch left that had not yet been run. Chief Commissioner Ulrich Kittelberger once reported a 20 metre waterfall in this lower section.

Our initial efforts to scout the river revealed neither unrunnable drops nor other nasties of any kind. The last 2 kilometres before the village were riddled with amazing slides and drops. Similar to the Laerdalselvi, paved fish ladders were built into the river. Scary looking rods stick out of the steps, however they never seem to get in the way. During the first third of the section, the river flows away from the road and towards the bottom of the valley. This was the only possible stretch where a waterfall might be hidden. A gorge-like structure of the creekbed seemed unlikely here, thus we decided sponateously to put in.

After a few fun class four warm-up rapids, we soon reached the »blind corner«. And indeed: all of a sudden we faced a ledge with spray at the bottom hole mounting over the top of the ledge. This is so very characteristic of Norway! After the first fleeting inspection from the shore, our unbridled exhilaration burst forth from our chests in primal cries of joy. Embedded in polished granite and hidden in a rock dome, three big-volume waterfalls were waiting for us, one after the other. They varied between seven and ten meters and were draped with lime-green ferns and deciduous trees. The pools were big enough in the eyes of kayakers to venture a descent, but small enough to call the consecutive falls a combo. Overwhelmed by this discovery, we decided to end the run and come back the next day to take advantage of the morning light to film and take photographs.

We don't actually know if it was the first descent ever or not, but it doesn't matter. We came and explored this unknown river section like great explorers and we discovered world-class whitewater. This particular combo of waterfalls has now become one of the must-do classics and is to be seen in numerous kayak movies and magazines that portray the Sogndalselva. The only sad consequence of our first official descent is that today no one will have that initial experience of running this waterfall combo as »virgin territory«, feeling the butterflies – and experiencing love at first sight.

MEIN ERSTES MAL

Das erste Mal: Es ist spannend, es ist intensiv und es bleibt ein Leben lang in Erinnerung. Auch meine erste Kajakreise nach Norwegen wird mir mein Leben lang in Erinnerung bleiben. Alles ist größer, wuchtiger aber auch gutmütiger als wir es in den Alpen gewohnt sind. Während des ersten Besuchs im Land der zehntausend Wildflüsse durchlebt man eine Metamorphose, und lernt spektakulär von gefährlich zu unterscheiden. Zurück bleiben tiefe Erinnerungen und intensive Erlebnisse von der Verschmelzung mit kraftvollen Fossen und schäumenden Walzen. Im Land solcher Superlative als »Erster« einen Wasserfall oder Flussabschnitt zu entdecken und auch zu befahren, ist ein initiales Erlebnis.

Als wir im Juli 1998, meinem ersten Urlaub in Norwegen, die meisten Klassiker abgehakt hatten, waren wir auf der Suche nach Neuem. Mit Engelsgeduld und jugendlichem Optimismus klapperten wir eine Woche lang potentielle Flüsse nördlich des Sognefjords ab, spekulierten auf ungefahrene Fossen und unentdeckte Seitenbäche. Leider fand sich nichts Interessantes. So fieberten wir umso mehr auf die Sogndalselva, deren Oberlauf Olaf schon befahren hatte und als weiteren Klassiker ankündigte. Doch die Standardstrecke sollte nur der Prolog sein. Von der Ausstiegsbrücke bis zur Mündung ins Meer direkt in der Kleinstadt Sogndal waren noch ein paar Kilometer Strecke und einige Höhenmeter unbefahren. Oberkomissar Ulrich Kittelberger berichtete einst von 20 Meter Wasserfällen, dort am Unterlauf.

Unsere ersten Bemühungen die Strecke zu erkunden, wiesen weder auf unfahrbare Fossen noch auf einen fiesen Flusscharakter hin. Die letzten 2 Kilometer im Ortsgebiet sind gespickt mit tollen Rutschen und Stufen. Dort wurden ähnlich wie auf der Lærdalselvi Fischtreppen betoniert, deren hervorstehende Armiereisen zwar unappetitlich aussehen, aber nie im Weg sind. Im oberen Drittel der Flussstrecke verläuft die Straße weg vom Talgrund, dort war der einzige Bereich in dem sich noch Wasserfälle verstecken könnten. Eine klammartige Verengung des Bachbettes war nicht zu vermuten, so entschieden wir uns schnell für einen Befahrungsversuch.

Nach ein paar lustigen Aufwärmkatarakten im vierten Grad erreichten wir schnell einen »Blind Corner«, tatsächlich: Abrisskante und, eben so typisch für Norwegen, Gischt aus dem Unterwasser bis über die Abrisskante. Nach der ersten flüchtigen Beurteilung vom Ufer aus war unsere Begeisterung nur durch inbrünstige Jubelschreie auszuhalten. Der Felsendom versteckt eine Gerade mit drei unmittelbar aufeinander folgenden, wuchtigen und fahrbaren Wasserfällen zwischen sieben und zehn Meter; eingebettet in zu Glanz poliertem Granit, von oben mit grünen Laubbäumen und Farn behangen. Die Gumpen sind gerade groß genug um die Szenerie aus der Kajakperspektive genießen zu können, aber klein genug um den Dom als Wasserfallkombination gelten zu lassen. Überwältigt von diesem Schatz entschlossen wir uns die Fahrt abzubrechen, und am nächsten Morgen bei idealen Lichtverhältnissen zurück zu kehren, zu filmen und zu fotografieren was das Zeug hält.

Wir wissen nicht, ob es eine Erstbefahrung war oder nicht, das spielt auch keine Rolle. Wir kamen und erkundeten wie die Ersten und fanden Weltklasse-Wildwasser. Die Wasserfallkombination ist heute zum Klassiker avanciert, unzählige Kajakvideos und Magazine zeigen Bilder der Sogndalselva. Die traurige Konsequenz unserer Befahrung ist nur, dass wahrscheinlich niemand mehr die Freude des Entdeckers spürt und die Wasserfälle wie ein »Erster« fahren wird.

OLLI GRAU 1974 *www.olligrau.de*

Olli was world champion in 1995 and has since been travelling the rivers of the world. He has written books such as »Rodeo Boating« and »Whitewater Kayaking« and has immense know-how in whitewater. Norway is still one of his favourite stomping grounds in the world, and his experience on the Sogndal may very well have had a part in it.

Olli wurde 1995 Rodeo-Weltmeister und ist seitdem auf Flüssen in aller Welt unterwegs. Der Wahl-Bayer schrieb Bücher wie »Richtig Rodeofahren« und »Besser Wildwasserfahren« und hat ein riesiges Know-How zum Thema Wildwasser. Norwegen zählt zu seinen Lieblingsrevieren weltweit, die Erlebnisse im Sogndal werden wohl einen Beitrag dazu geliefert haben.

MØRE OG ROMSDAL

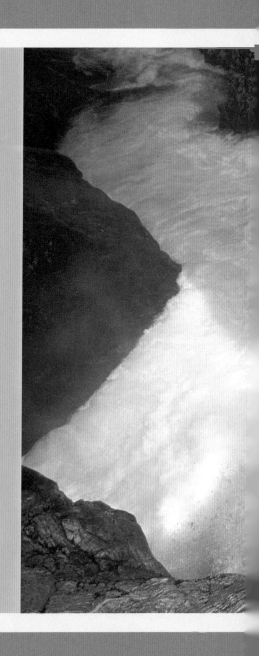

Olaf Obsommer running the must-run on lower Langedalselva.

Hellesyltfossen

MØRE OG ROMSDAL

Møre og Romsdal covers the north of Norway's Fjordland, and thus (how could it be any other way?) offers fascinating fjord landscape to admire. The Geirangerfjord, with its »Seven Sisters«, the »Trollstigen« and the Romsdal are not only popular stop-off points for the average tourist, but are also of interest to us paddlers, because you will find here fabulous rivers in the immediate vicinity. To run all the different sections you will certainly have to cross a number of fjords with the ferries, so your itinerary should be well planned.

Mention names like Rauma, Valldøla or Ulvåa to any Norway connoisseur, and he'll immediately prick his ears up. But have you ever heard of the Stordalselva, Langedalselva and Horndøla? They are easily just as worthwhile, if not even bett… agh! Enough of all the talk! Just go there!

The difficulties are mostly around the WW V mark, only on the Valldøla, Ulvåa, Asbjørnsåe and Embla will you find easier sections.

Møre og Romsdal umfasst den Norden Fjordnorwegens, und somit, wie sollte es anders sein, gibt es hier faszinierende Fjordlandschaften zu bestaunen. Der Geirangerfjord mit seinen »Sieben Schwestern«, die »Trollstigen« und das Romsdal sind nicht nur beliebte Haltepunkte für den Normaltouristen, auch uns Paddler dürfen sie interessieren, schließlich befinden sich grandiose Flüsse in unmittelbarer Nähe. Um alle Abschnitte zu fahren, wird man sicher einige Fjorde per Fähre überbrücken müssen. Also sollte die Fahrtroute gut geplant sein.

Flussnamen wie Rauma, Valldøla oder Ulvåa lassen jeden Norwegenkenner sofort aufhorchen. Doch schon mal von Stordalselva, Langedalselva und Horndøla gehört? Die sind mindestens genauso lohnend, wenn nicht noch bes... aber wozu die lange Rede? Hinfahren!

Die Schwierigkeiten liegen vermehrt im WW V Bereich, nur auf Valldøla, Ulvåa, Asbjørnsåe und Embla finden sich auch leichtere Abschnitte.

Rauma kommune

Photo: SG

Geirangerfjord

Info on the region
www.geiranger.no
www.visitmolde.com
www.goldenroute.com

VANN ORINGEN I ELVA KAN OKE **UTEN VARSEL** TAFJORD KRAFT PRODUKSJON AS

Stordalselva - Mauracher

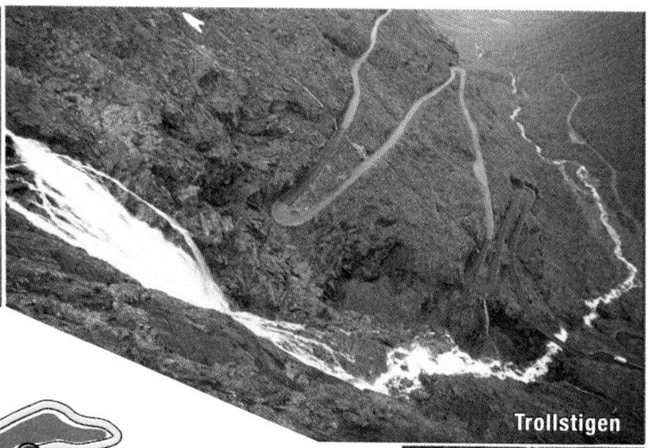

Trollstigen

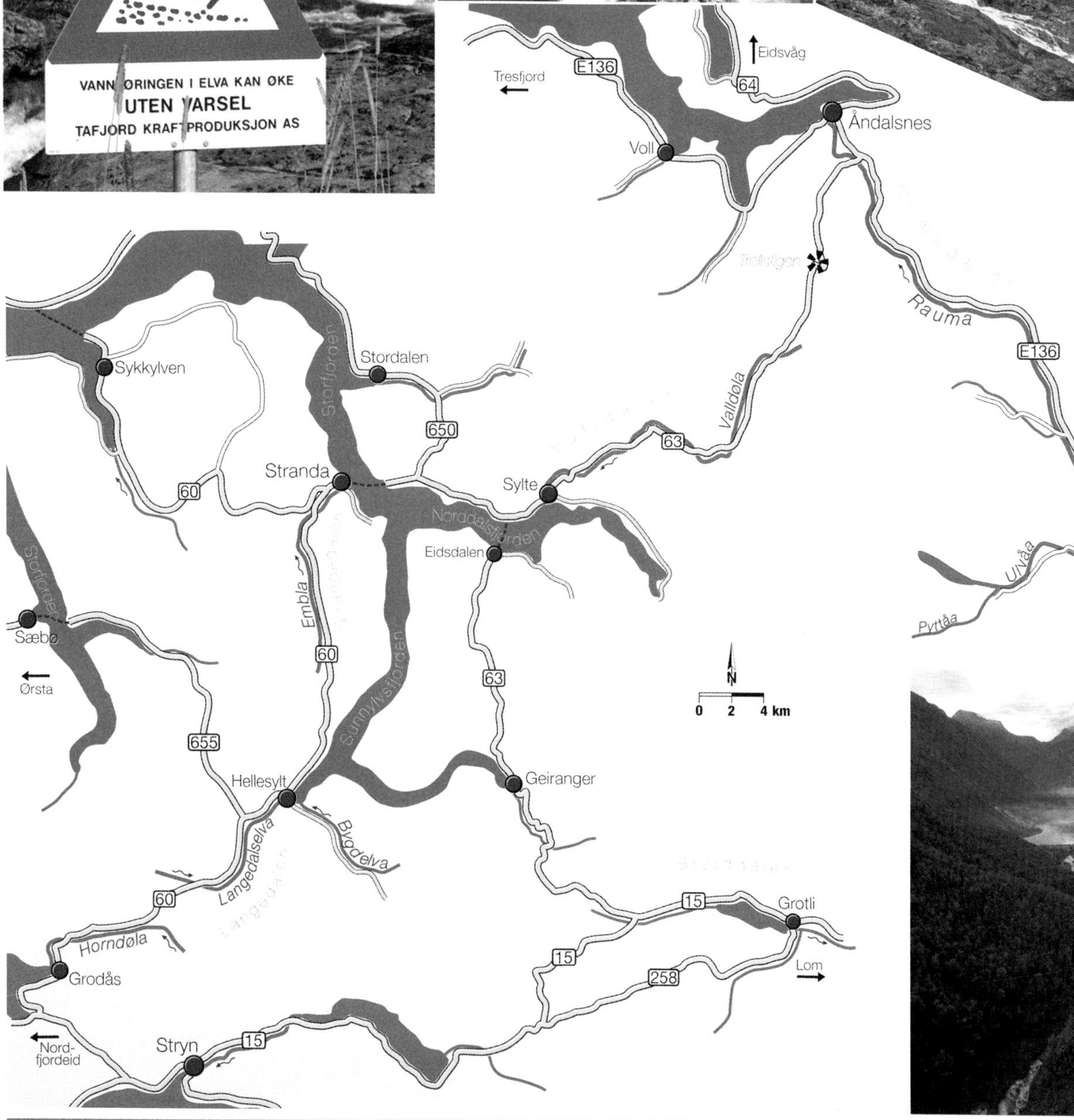

Geiranger

MØRE OG ROMSDAL FACTS

Character: Diverse whitewater, from the fives to be savoured, to the pseudo-sixes, with a couple of easy class three sections.

Best time: Spring to summer, the lower Rauma and the lower Ulvåa not until they have low water in the late summer. In high summer the rivers in the west are mostly dry.

Special remarks: Warning: Gyro is on the prowl. Embla, Stordalselva and Bygdelva are salmon rivers, Rauma is affected! Disinfection: at the Åndalsnes camping ground or the Trollvegen camping ground.

Accommodation: Camp ground in Hellesylt on the Bygdelva. In Sylte, at the convergence of the Valldøla, or at the put in of the middle section.

Charakter: Abwechslungsreiches Wildwasser vom Genussfünfer bis zum Pseudosechser, mit ein paar einfachen Dreier-Strecken.

Beste Zeit: Frühling bis Sommer, untere Rauma und untere Ulvåa erst bei Niedrigwasser im Spätsommer. Im Hochsommer sind die Bäche im Westen in der Regel trocken.

Besonderheit: Achtung: Der Gyro geht um. Bygdelva, Embla, Stordalselva sind Lachsflüsse, die Rauma ist infiziert! Desinfektion: Åndalsnes oder Trollvegen Camping.

Übernachtung: Campingplatz in Hellesylt an der Bygdelva. In Sylte an der Mündung der Valldøla oder am Einstieg zum mittleren Abschnitt.

RAUMA: UPPER

STEEP DROP + POOL ADVENTURE

The Rauma is popular not only with paddlers, but also with fishermen and tour coach tourists. Especially in the lower reaches of its almost 70 kilometre journey, it offers breathtaking scenery, the Romsdal passing between two mountain ranges and along the famous Troll Walls.

The upper section of the Rauma does not offer quite such spectacular scenery, but in exchange provides impressive whitewater – which isn't such a bad thing. Between the numerous drops and slides you'll almost always discover small pools, which make scouting and portaging a breeze. The Rauma has been pronounced the »super-duper-absolute-must-run-again-favourite« by many a paddler. What more is there to say?

CLASS:	IV - V
LEVEL:	8 - 15 cumecs
LENGTH:	4 km
TIME:	3 - 5 h
SEASON:	May - August

Die Rauma erfreut sich nicht nur bei Paddlern größter Beliebtheit, auch Angler und Reisebustouristen erfreuen sich an ihr. Gerade im unteren Verlauf ihrer fast 70 Kilometer langen Reise bezaubert sie mit atemberaubender Kulisse, das Romsdal gräbt sich hier tief zwischen die angrenzenden Gebirgszüge und passiert die berühmten Trollwände.

Der obere Abschnitt der Rauma liegt in nicht ganz so beeindruckender Kulisse, bietet dafür aber eindrucksvolles Wildwasser – was ja auch nicht schlecht ist. Zwischen den vielen tollen Abfällen und Rutschen erstrecken sich fast immer kleine Pools, die ein Besichtigen und Umtragen einfach machen. Die Rauma wird von vielen Paddlern als »Lieblingssuper-hyper-unbedingt-nochmal-Bach« betitelt. Mehr gibt es da wohl nicht zu sagen.

Tip: Second run, twice the fun.

»Little Huka falls« - Hummel

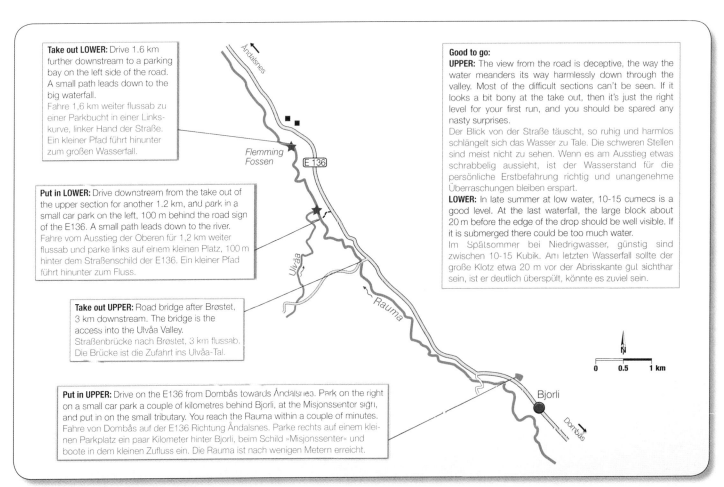

Take out LOWER: Drive 1.6 km further downstream to a parking bay on the left side of the road. A small path leads down to the big waterfall.
Fahre 1,6 km weiter flussab zu einer Parkbucht in einer Linkskurve, linker Hand der Straße. Ein kleiner Pfad führt hinunter zum großen Wasserfall.

Put in LOWER: Drive downstream from the take out of the upper section for another 1.2 km, and park in a small car park on the left, 100 m behind the road sign of the E136. A small path leads down to the river.
Fahre vom Ausstieg der Oberen für 1,2 km weiter flussab und parke links auf einem kleinen Platz, 100 m hinter dem Straßenschild der E136. Ein kleiner Pfad führt hinunter zum Fluss.

Take out UPPER: Road bridge after Brøstet, 3 km downstream. The bridge is the access into the Ulvåa Valley.
Straßenbrücke nach Brøstet, 3 km flussab. Die Brücke ist die Zufahrt ins Ulvåa-Tal.

Put in UPPER: Drive on the E136 from Dombås towards Åndalsnes. Park on the right on a small car park a couple of kilometres behind Bjorli, at the Misjonssentor sign, and put in on the small tributary. You reach the Rauma within a couple of minutes.
Fahre von Dombås auf der E136 Richtung Åndalsnes. Parke rechts auf einem kleinen Parkplatz ein paar Kilometer hinter Bjorli, beim Schild »Misjonssenter« und boote in dem kleinen Zufluss ein. Die Rauma ist nach wenigen Metern erreicht.

Åndalsnes
Flemming Fossen
E 136
Ulvåa
Rauma
Bjorli
Dombås

0   0.5   1 km

Good to go:
UPPER: The view from the road is deceptive, the way the water meanders its way harmlessly down through the valley. Most of the difficult sections can't be seen. If it looks a bit bony at the take out, then it's just the right level for your first run, and you should be spared any nasty surprises.
Der Blick von der Straße täuscht, so ruhig und harmlos schlängelt sich das Wasser zu Tale. Die schweren Stellen sind meist nicht zu sehen. Wenn es am Ausstieg etwas schrabbelig aussieht, ist der Wasserstand für die persönliche Erstbefahrung richtig und unangenehme Überraschungen bleiben erspart.
LOWER: In late summer at low water, 10-15 cumecs is a good level. At the last waterfall, the large block about 20 m before the edge of the drop should be well visible. If it is submerged there could be too much water.
Im Spätsommer bei Niedrigwasser, günstig sind zwischen 10-15 Kubik. Am letzten Wasserfall sollte der große Klotz etwa 20 m vor der Abrisskante gut sichtbar sein, ist er deutlich überspült, könnte es zuviel sein.

RAUMA: LOWER

AN EVEN STEEPER AND BIGGER POOL + DROP ADVENTURE

The lower section of the Rauma is only for true blue drop junkies. Without a local guide, this short section can demand a great deal of your time. Since Olli Grau, Manuel Arnu and Olaf Obsommer were here in the summer of 1999, the »bottom section« has enjoyed increased popularity.

At the put in, right before the first steep slide, the right arm of the Ulvåa splashes into the Rauma in the form of a small waterfall. A few hundred metres downstream and several sizes bigger, the left arm thunders down a monster slide into the Rauma, adding another good shot of water. In dazzling backlight this is a true spectacle of nature, which loses significance only on account of the 7 metre waterfall right in front of your bow.

CLASS:	V - VI (VII)
LEVEL:	10 - 15 cumecs
LENGTH:	2 km
TIME:	4 - 6 h
SEASON:	late July - September

And so the Rauma roars down the valley, over massive slides and drops – mostly fair, but almost always very full on. Scouting the individual sections is vital, a description is difficult, but the lines are mostly pretty clear. However there is one section I should warn you about: a giant slide with a 3 meter auto-boof. This little baby needs to be paddled just right. The window for a clean landing in the pool is only a few metres wide, left and right are rock slabs. Two paddlers broke their backs here in the summer of 2003 – and they were both sure of hitting the window.

The last waterfall at the take out has also cost a few ribs, although it has not been run often. The more water the better. More something to gaze at in wonder. Warning: if you paddle the last waterfall, you have to paddle on another 500 metres to the next bridge. After the big pool the river bends to the right and into a cataract which was the scene of a fatal accident.

Tip: Don't break your nose on the first drop!

Der untere Abschnitt der Rauma ist nur was für waschechte Stürzer. Ein kurzer Abschnitt, der ohne einen ortskundigen Begleiter reichlich Zeit in Anspruch nehmen kann. Seitdem Olli Grau, Manuel Arnu und Olaf Obsommer im Sommer 1999 hier unterwegs waren, erfreut sich die »Untere« erhöhter Beliebtheit.

Am Einstieg, direkt an der ersten steilen Rutsche, plätschert der rechte Arm der Ulvåa als kleiner Wasserfall in die Rauma. Wesentlich mächtiger donnert hingegen der linke Arm über eine Monsterrutsche wenige hundert Meter flussab hinzu, und bringt noch mal ordentlich Zuschusswasser. Im gleißenden Gegenlicht ein echtes Naturspektakel, welches lediglich durch den 7-Meter-Wasserfall vor dem eigenen Bug unwichtig erscheint.

Und so donnert sie zu Tale, die Rauma, über riesige Rutschen und Stufen – meistens fair, doch fast immer *full on*. Die Erkundung der einzelnen Stellen ist unerlässlich, eine Erklärung schwierig und die Routen meist klar. Gewarnt sei lediglich vor einer Stelle: eine riesige Rutsche mit abschließendem 3-Meter-Autoboof will sehr sauber gefahren werden. Bei der Landung hat man ein Fenster mit sauberem Unterwasser von wenigen Metern zu erwischen, rechts und links lauert eine Platte. Hier haben sich im Sommer 2003 zwei Paddler den Rücken gebrochen – und auch sie waren sich sicher das Fenster zu treffen.

Der letzte Wasserfall am Ausstieg hat schon einige Rippen gefordert, trotzdem er noch nicht oft befahren wurde. Je mehr Wasser, desto besser. Eher was zum Betrachten und Staunen. Achtung: Wer den letzten Wasserfall fährt, muss anschließend etwa 500 Meter bis zur nächsten Brücke weiterfahren. Nach dem großen Pool folgt in der Rechtskurve ein Katarakt, hier ereignete sich ein tödlicher Unfall.

Tipp: Nicht die Nase am ersten Wasserfall brechen!

Ulvåa meets Rauma - Herzig

Daniel Herzig

Photo: MN

Ulvåa meets Rauma - Jobst Hahn

Team Hamburg running »The slide«

ULVÅA: STANDARD

NICE OPEN WHITEWATER IN A BEAUTIFUL VALLEY

In this beautiful valley the Ulvåa offers superb whitewater, alternating between big slides and holes, and flatwater in between. A very entertaining section, provided it's roaring loud and clear in the river bed.

CLASS:	**III - IV (V)**
LEVEL:	**20 - 60 cumecs**
LENGTH:	**8 km**
TIME:	**3 - 4 h**
SEASON:	**June - August**

The first blocked cataract grumbles directly under the Puttbua, beware of undercuts! 300 metres on you reach the Ulvåa, and after another kilometre, the high point of the day – the long slide on the Kabbebrua. You can get a look at this on the drive to the river. About 200 metres after the T-intersection you reach another gate at a small wooden bridge. Another 100 metres beyond this a path to the Kabbebrua leads away to the right.

As the river continues its course, constantly changing between magnificent rapids and flat sections, the Ulvåa provides ample time to savour the landscape. Exaltation is guaranteed at the get out!

Tip: For those who still have excessive energy to burn off, it is possible to paddle on to an old pedestrian bridge, but only at low levels! There is a 3 metre drop and a number of nice rapids. After the bridge walk about another 200 metres through the trees up to the road.

Die Ulvåa bietet in diesem wunderschönen Hochtal traumhaftes Wildwasser, auf dem sich große Rutschen und Walzen mit Flachstücken abwechseln. Ein sehr unterhaltsamer Abschnitt, vorausgesetzt es rauscht lauthals im Bachbett.

Gleich unter der Puttbua grummelt der erste verblockte Katarakt, Achtung Unterspülungen! 300 Meter weiter erreicht man die Ulvåa, nach einem weiteren Kilometer den Höhepunkt des Tages, die lange Rutsche an der Kabbebrua. Diese kann schon bei der Anfahrt besichtigt werden: Etwa 200 Meter nach der T-Kreuzung gelangt man an einer kleinen Holzbrücke erneut an ein Tor, etwa 100 Meter dahinter geht rechts ein Fußweg zur Kabbebrua.

Im weiteren Verlauf wechseln sich wunderschöne Katarakte und Flachstücke ab, die Ulvåa lässt also immer wieder Zeit die Landschaft zu genießen. Ein erhabenes Gefühl am Ausstieg ist garantiert.

Tipp: Wer noch überschüssige Energie loswerden muss, kann bis zu einer alten Fußgängerbrücke weiterfahren, aber nur bei wenig Wasser! Es folgen eine 3-Meter-Stufe und einige schöne Katarakte. Laufe etwa 200 Meter nach der Brücke durch den Wald hinauf zur Straße.

KABBEBRUA
Framskøt bru restaurert 1993-94

Take out PYTTÅA / Put in ULVÅA STANDARD:
At the Puttbua. From the take out of the Ulvåa standard section drive up the valley until you reach a T-intersection. To the right you can see a bridge, take the road on the left. After another 2 km you reach the Puttbua, the bridge reaching over the Pyttåa, on the right. With an off-road vehicle you can take the left path and fight your way up to the Pyttåa. Otherwise dismount here.
An der Puttbua. Fahre das Tal vom Ausstieg der Ulvåa Standard-strecke weiter hinauf, bis zu einer T-Kreuzung. Rechts erspäht man eine Brücke, wähle die linke Straße. Nach weiteren 2 km erreicht man rechter Hand eine Brücke über die Pyttåa, die Puttbua. Mit einem geländegängigen Wagen kann man sich auf dem linken Weg die Pyttåa weiter hoch kämpfen, ansonsten hier einsteigen.

Take out ULVÅA STANDARD / Put in LOW WATER RUN: Bridge in Nedre Brøstet. Drive from the take out of the upper Rauma further into the Brøstdalen, to the settlement of Brøstet. Here you will find a toll station, behind which is the take out bridge.
Brücke Nedre Brøstet. Fahre vom Ausstieg der oberen Rauma weiter ins Brøstdalen, bis zur Siedlung Brøstet. Dort gelangst du zu einer Mautstation, kurz dahinter zur Ausstiegsbrücke.

Put in PYTTÅA: The boats have to be carried from the Puttbua, the put in for the Ulvåa. Cross the bridge, then carry up the tramping path on river left for about 4 km. At the latest put in at the outlet of the small lake.
Ab der Puttbua, dem Einstieg zur Ulvåa, müssen die Boote getragen werden. Die Brücke queren und dann den Wanderweg flusslinks etwa 4 km hoch tragen. Spätestens an dem kleinen See, am besten an dessen Ausfluss kann man starten.

Take out LOW WATER RUN: At the latest where the Asbjørnsåe flows into the Ulvåa, blessing it with a giant Foss.
Spätestens an der Mündung der Asbjørnsåe, die als riesiger Wasserfall von rechts die Ulvåa beglückt.

Åndalsnes

E 136

Rauma

Dombås

Nedre Brøstet

Brøstet

Asbjørnsåe

Ulvåa

Brøstdalen

Ulvådalen

Kabbebrua

Pyttåa

Pyttbudalen

N

0   0.5   1 km

Good to go:
PYTTÅA: Mostly from May to the end of July, good between 10 and 15 cumecs. The Ulvåa should also be running at a good level to paddle. At high levels the Pyttåa quickly becomes a lot more difficult.
Meist von Mai bis Ende Juli, günstig zwischen 10 und 15 Kubik. Die Ulvåa sollte auf jeden Fall auch gut fahrbar sein. Bei viel Wasser wird die Pyttåa schnell schwerer.
ULLVÅA STANDARD: Above the take out the current should be flowing swiftly. If lots of rocks are visible in the middle of the river the flat sections become very hard work. 20-60 cumecs is a good level.
Oberhalb des Ausstieges sollte die Strömung eine flotte Geschwindigkeit haben. Sind viele Steine in der Flussmitte sichtbar, werden die flachen Zwischenstücke recht zäh. Günstig sind zwischen 20-60 Kubik.
ULLVÅA LOW WATER RUN: At low water on the Ulvåa in late summer, 10-15 cumecs is a good level. Above the put in bridge you should find rocks in the river bed.
Bei Niedrigwasser der Ulvåa im Spätsommer, hier will man eigentlich nicht mehr als 10-15 Kubik. Oberhalb der Einstiegsbrücke sollte man Steine im Bachbett entdecken.

Daniel Herzig

ULVÅA: LOW WATER RUN

THE PERFECT ALTERNATIVE WHEN THERE IS NO WATER AROUND

The lower section of the Ulvåa is a good option when there is not enough water for the standard section. The Ulvåa becomes considerably tighter and steeper here, with a number of nice drops and slides.

About 300 metres after the put in, a 3 metre drop will bring a smile to your face, and this is followed by further rapids and drops. Take care at the suspension bridge, the second take out of the standard section. At high water levels the water flows to the left and under a rock, no problem at low levels.

After a short low gorge (scout from the left), and another rock passage, you come to an absolute monster slide. Please do not accidentally bomb down this – it would hurt a lot! Best to portage it on the left or right. After another 300 metres is the take out at the waterfall where the Asbjørnsåe flows into the Ulvåa with a giant foss. Here walk up to the left to the road. Do not miss the take out (is actually very difficult to miss!), the following siphon-gorge is not terribly runnable.

Tip: On the last kilometre, up to the convergence with the Rauma, there are a number of slides and drops, some of which are real gems. For this put in at the next road bridge.

CLASS:	IV - V
LEVEL:	10 - 15 cumecs
LENGTH:	2.5 km
TIME:	3 - 4 h
SEASON:	July - September

Der untere Abschnitt der Ulvåa bietet sich bei zu niedrigen Wasserständen für das obere Standardstück an. Hier wird die Ulvåa deutlich enger und steiler, es warten einige schöne Stufen und Rutschen.

Etwa 300 Meter nach dem Einstieg macht dir eine 3-Meter-Stufe eine Freude, es folgen weitere Katarakte und Abfälle. Vorsicht an einer Hängebrücke, dem zweiten Ausstieg des Standardstückes. Hier zieht bei viel Wasser die Strömung links unter einem Stein hindurch, bei wenig Wasser kein Problem.

Nach einer kurzen Niederklamm (links besichtigen) kommt man nach einem weiteren Felskanal an eine riesige Monsterrutsche. Bitte nicht aus Versehen runterbomben, das würde wehtun. Besser rechts oder links umtragen. Der Ausstieg folgt nach weiteren 300 Metern am Mündungswasserfall der Asbjørnsåe, hier muss man links zur Straße hoch laufen. Ausstieg nicht verpassen (kann man eigentlich nicht), die folgende Siphon-Klamm ist eher unfahrbar.

Tipp: Auf dem letzten Kilometer bis zum Durchbruch in die Rauma warten noch einige teils sehr schöne Rutschen und Abfälle. Dazu an der nächsten Straßenbrücke starten.

The first drop after the portage - Thomas Motz

Photo: MN

Olaf Obsommer and Michi Neumann

At the Puttbua - Mr. Maus

PYTTÅA

The Pyttåa, also known as the Puttåa, flows through the isolated Pyttbudalen in spectacular highland scenery.

Nice wave sections alternate with drops and rapids, only a few sections get up to WW V. Worthy of mention is one cataract with an undercut at the exit of the rapid, and the sections before and after the Puttbua. With a lot of water, from around 20 cumecs, some of the holes and towbacks get very big, paddle it then only with local knowledge.

CLASS: III - V
LEVEL: 7 - 15 cumecs
LENGTH: 4 km
TIME: 2 - 4 h
SEASON: May - early July

Tip: Paddle the Ulvåa too!

Die Pyttåa, oder auch Puttåa, fließt durch das abgeschiedene Pyttbudalen in einer wundervollen Hochlandschaft.

Schöne Schwallstrecken wechseln ab mit Stufen und Katarakten, nur wenige Stellen steigern sich auf WW V. Erwähnt sei ein Katarakt mit Unterspülung am Ausgang, und die Stellen vor und unter der Puttbua. Bei viel Wasser, ab etwa 20 Kubik, werden einige Walzen und Rückläufe recht groß, dann nur noch mit Ortskundigen fahren.

Tipp: Die Ulvåa gleich mitpaddeln!

Map: p.194
Karte: S.194

ASBJØRNSÅE

A MELLOW HIGHLAND RUN WITH A SCARY FERRY AT THE TAKE OUT

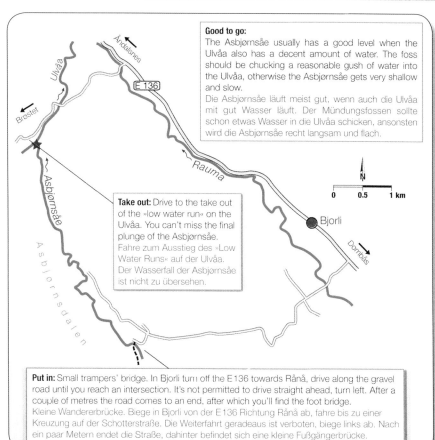

Good to go:
The Asbjørnsåe usually has a good level when the Ulvåa also has a decent amount of water. The foss should be chucking a reasonable gush of water into the Ulvåa, otherwise the Asbjørnsåe gets very shallow and slow.
Die Asbjørnsåe läuft meist gut, wenn auch die Ulvåa mit gut Wasser läuft. Der Mündungsfossen sollte schon etwas Wasser in die Ulvåa schicken, ansonsten wird die Asbjørnsåe recht langsam und flach.

Take out: Drive to the take out of the »low water run« on the Ulvåa. You can't miss the final plunge of the Asbjørnsåe.
Fahre zum Ausstieg des »Low Water Runs« auf der Ulvåa. Der Wasserfall der Asbjørnsåe ist nicht zu übersehen.

Put in: Small trampers' bridge. In Bjorli turn off the E 136 towards Rånå, drive along the gravel road until you reach an intersection. It's not permitted to drive straight ahead, turn left. After a couple of metres the road comes to an end, after which you'll find the foot bridge.
Kleine Wandererbrücke. Biege in Bjorli von der E 136 Richtung Rånå ab, fahre bis zu einer Kreuzung auf der Schotterstraße. Die Weiterfahrt geradeaus ist verboten, biege links ab. Nach ein paar Metern endet die Straße, dahinter befindet sich eine kleine Fußgängerbrücke.

The Asbjørnsåe flows into the Ulvåa with a giant foss which has everyone reaching for their camera. Before its convergence with the Ulvåa, it weaves its way through magnificent highlands.

After the put in the Asbjørnsåe gradually takes on energy, but even at high flow the difficulties are never more than WW III. However, when the river disappears at a horizon line, caution is required. The first unpaddleable rapids here lead into the Foss into the Ulvåa. Take out on the left and scramble down to the Ulvåa. Because the car is on the other side of the river, you now need to ferry across. When the Ulvåa has a lot of water the current here flows rapidly into the next Foss. This is no place for beginners! Best to scout it before undertaking the run.

CLASS: I - II+
LEVEL: 4 km
LENGTH: 5 - 15 cumecs
TIME: 2 - 3 h
SEASON: June - late July

Die Asbjørnsåe mündet in einem gewaltigen Fossen in die Ulvåa, und lockt damit jedem den Fotoapparat aus der Tasche. Vor ihrer Mündung durchkämmt sie eine tolle Hochebene.

Nach dem Einstieg steigert sie sich langsam, die Schwierigkeiten liegen bei viel Wasser zum Ende hin maximal bei WW III. Verschwindet der Fluss allerdings am Horizont, ist Vorsicht geboten. Die ersten unfahrbaren Katarakte leiten den Mündungsfossen ein. Hier muss man links aussteigen, runter zur Ulvåa kraxeln und zur anderen Talseite queren. Führt diese viel Wasser, zieht es recht zügig in den nächsten Fossen. Nix für Anfänger! Am besten schon vor der Fahrt besichtigen.

VALLDØLA: UPPER

AWESOME DROP + POOL WHITEWATER IN FANTASTIC LANDSCAPE

Every Norway holidaymaker should have driven the famous Trollstigen with their car, and have paddled the Valldøla with their boat. No problem, these are easily combined, as the road to the Trollstigen follows the Valldøla. The difficult sections line up like cars in a traffic jam, to which is added a mysterious sense of the apocalypse, when the surrounding mountains are enshrouded in clouds.

The Valldøla is a real feast for

CLASS:	IV - V (VI, X)
LEVEL:	8 - 15 cumecs
LENGTH:	3 km
TIME:	3 - 5 h
SEASON:	June - early August

every WW V- paddler. The drop + pool character serves each section on a golden platter, soft music echoes from the mountains, the clear water makes an excellent replacement for the red wine. Too much of the red wine makes for powerful towbacks, too little leaves the countless slides thirsty. Whatever your taste, the Valldøla satisfies every appetite. All sections are easy to scout, too many details here would spoil the fun!

It is also possible to get off the river at a small concrete bridge 300 metres before the rest area.

There is a classy drop directly beneath the bridge. The drops which then follow are not everyone's cup of tea. But at the very latest, when the Litlelangdalselva flows into the Valldøla on river left, it's time to call it a day. The mini gorge and the monster slide which follow are for viewing purposes only, even if the waterfall has been run at very low flow.

Tip: Don't miss the take out!

Die berühmten Trollstigen sollte jeder Norwegenurlauber mit seinem Auto gefahren, und die Valldøla mit seinem Boot gepaddelt sein. Kein Problem, lässt sich beides gut verbinden, da die Straße zu den Trollstigen die Valldøla begleitet. Die Schwierigkeiten reihen sich aneinander wie Autos bei einem Stau, hinzu kommt eine mysteriöse Endzeitstimmung, falls die umliegenden Berge in den Wolken hängen.

Die Valldøla ist ein Festschmaus für jeden

Wildwasser V-Paddler: Durch den Drop + Pool Charakter werden alle Stellen mundgerecht auf dem Tablett serviert, leise Musik tönt von den Bergen, das klare Wasser ersetzt den Rotwein. Zuviel Rotwein erzeugt hie und da kräftige Rückläufe, zu wenig lässt auf den unzähligen Rutschen dürsteln. Wie dem auch sei, die Valldøla stopft alle Mäuler. Alle Stellen sind einfach zu erkunden, zu viele Einzelheiten würden den Spaß hemmen.

Es kann auch schon an einem kleinen Betonsteg 300 Meter vor dem Rastplatz ausgestiegen

werden, unter dem sich eine tolle Stufe befindet. Die folgenden Stellen sind nicht jedermanns Sache. Aber spätestens wenn die Litlelangdalselva von flusslinks in die Valldøla mündet, ist Endstation. Die folgende Miniklamm und die anschließende Monsterrutsche sind nur was fürs Auge, auch wenn der Wasserfall schon bei ganz wenig Wasser befahren wurde.

Tipp: Nicht den Ausstieg verpassen!

Toni Drinnenberg

Mauracher + Kagel

VALLDØLA: MIDDLE

There are few greater pleasures than paddling the middle section of the Valldøla with unexpected sunshine. It offers fantastic whitewater fun in the finest of landscapes. Only in one section do the difficulties reach above WW IV: about 1 kilometre after the road switches to the river right side there is a low gorge. Here awaits the »Triple Offermann«, a recirculating drop which has already caused no end of excitement in the paddling world. But no worries, the drop can also be paddled without capsizing, and if you do flip, the pool is big enough to catch a whole football team of swimmers! After that things quieten down again.

So why the name »Triple Offermann«? In the middle of the nineties the Valldøla was paddled by three valiant paddlers. When the horizon appeared before them, only two were able to squeeze into the saving eddy before the drop. For the third paddler, Volker Offermann, there was no room left, and he paddled the drop sight unseen, and backwards. The other two watched his beating, and subsequent swim, from above. In a rage Volker carried his kayak back up to dare a second descent: no luck again, the towback had him for breakfast. All good things come in threes, they say, so minutes later Volker sat once again above the drop, ready to try his luck a third time. This time he rolled already in the wave above the drop, and so plunged upside down into the towback. No two ways about it – he swam again. Since then our dear Volker has had to bear burden of being the patron saint of the »Triple Offermann«. Bad luck!

Tip: Find your line through the »Gudbrandsjuvet« 3 km below the take out, and send a »foamy« down to test it.

CLASS:	III - IV (V-)
LEVEL:	20 - 40 cumecs
LENGTH:	6 km
TIME:	2 - 3 h
SEASON:	May - July

Gerade bei unerwartetem Sonnenschein gibt es kein schöneres Erlebnis als die mittlere Valldøla zu paddeln. Sie bietet offenes Spaßwildwasser in ehrwürdiger Kulisse. Lediglich an einer Stelle steigen die Schwierigkeiten über den vierten Grad: Etwa 1 Kilometer nachdem die Straße auf die flussrechte Seite gewechselt ist, folgt eine kurze Niederklamm. Hier wartet der »Dreifache Offermann«, eine rückläufige Stufe, die schon für jede Menge Aufruhr in der Paddlerwelt gesorgt hat. Aber keine Sorge, der Abfall kann auch ohne Kenterung gepaddelt werden und wenn doch mit, dann reicht der folgende Pool um eine ganze schwimmende Fußballmannschaft aufzufangen. Danach wird es wieder ruhig.

Warum bitteschön »Dreifacher Offermann«? Mitte der Neunziger befuhren drei wackere Paddler die Valldøla. Als eine Abrisskante am Horizont erschien, konnten sich lediglich zwei in das rettende Kehrwasser direkt vor der Kante retten – für den Dritten, Volker Offermann, war kein Platz mehr, er fuhr den Abfall rückwärts und ungesehen. Die anderen sahen von oben zu wie er aufgemischt wurde und anschließend kraulte. Wut entbrannt trug Volker sein Kajak wieder hinauf und wagte eine zweite Fahrt: Kein Glück, der Rücklauf fraß ihn erneut. Alle guten Dinge sind drei und so saß er wenige Minuten später erneut vor der Abrisskante und forderte sein Glück heraus. Diesmal kenterte er schon in der Locke vor dem Abfall und stürzte kopfüber in den Rücklauf. Wie sollte es anders kommen – er schwamm erneut. Seitdem muss unser Volker nun als Namenspatron für den »Dreifachen Offermann« herhalten. Pech gehabt.

Tipp: Finde deine Linie durch den »Gudbrandsjuvet« 3 km unterhalb des Ausstieges und schicke einen Foamie durch zum testen.

VALLDØLA: FAMILY SECTION

The lower section of the Valldøla is the perfect family sunshine trip. The local rafting companies also know this, so you may chance to meet the odd rubber boat floating down. But no panic, even at peak season the lower Valldøla is nowhere near as busy as the Imster gorge on the Inn. The road is always close to the river.

Der untere Abschnitt der Valldøla ist der perfekte Familien-Sonnenschein-Trip. Dies wissen auch die hiesigen Raftingunternehmen, und so kann einem hier schon mal das ein oder andere Gummiboot über den Weg schwimmen. Aber keine Panik, so hoch frequentiert wie die Imster Schlucht des Inn ist die untere Valldøla auch zur Hochsaison nicht. Die Straße verläuft immer in Flussnähe.

CLASS:	I - II (III)
LEVEL:	20 - 50 cumecs
LENGTH:	10 km
TIME:	2 - 3 h
SEASON:	May - early July

Good to go:
UPPER: The upper section can actually handle a good serving of water, as it flows mostly through open terrain. The slides and cataracts are then nicer and faster, but the holes and towbacks are also bigger.
Die Obere verträgt eigentlich schon einen ordentlichen Schluck Wasser, da sie fast immer im offenen Gelände zu Gange ist. Dann sind die Rutschen und Katarakte wesentlich schöner und schneller, allerdings wachsen auch Walzen und Rückläufe.
MIDDLE: Here too you can feel free to fill your glasses to the brim, the fun level rises with the water level!
Hier darf gut eingeschenkt sein, der Spaßpegel steigt mit dem Wasserstand.
FAMILY: Theoretically, this section should be paddleable all year round. However, it's most fun at high water, so the best season is probably from May to July, depending on how much snow the sun can convince to melt.
Dieser Abschnitt ist, rein theoretisch, das ganze Jahr fahrbar. Allerdings macht er bei viel Wasser am meisten Spaß, so ist die beste Saison wahrscheinlich von Mai bis Juli, je nachdem wie viel Schnee die Sonne zum schmelzen überreden kann.

Put in UPPER: 300 m above the road bridge of the 63.
300 m oberhalb der Straßenbrücke (Byksebrua) der 63.

Take out FAMILY: Bridge of the 63, shortly before it flows into the Norddalsfjord.
Brücke der 63, kurz vor der Mündung ins Norddalsfjord.

Put in FAMILY: Holsbrua. From the take out, follow the 63 upstream for about 10 km.
Holsbrua. Folge der 63 vom Ausstieg etwa 10 km flussaufwärts.

Take out UPPER: Rest area at the convergence of the Litlelangdalselva.
Rastplatz an der Mündung der Litlelangdalselva.

Take out MIDDLE: Derelict bridge about 3 km before »Gudbrandsjuvet«. This is just below a road bridge (turn off), a giant boulder in the middle of the river is a reliable marker for the take out.
Zerfallende Brücke etwa 3 km vor dem »Gudbrandsjuvet«. Diese befindet sich kurz unterhalb einer Straßenbrücke (Abzweig), ein riesiger Felsklotz in Flussmitte markiert den Ausstieg sehr verlässlich.

Put in MIDDLE: Camping area »Langdal«. The turn off to here is about 2 km down from the take out of the upper section.
Wildcampingplatz »Langdal«. Der Abzweig hierzu befindet sich etwa 2 km unterhalb des Ausstiegs der oberen Strecke.

Trollstigen Åndalsnes →

Grønning →

Berli

Hol

Valldalen

Valldøla

Valldal

Uri

Stranda ←

Sylte

Fjøra

Norddalsfjorden

Langdal

Valldalen

Valldøla

Grønningselva

Berli ←

Grønning

Litlelangdalselva

N

0   0.5   1 km

Obsommer running the must-run in the first gorge - Stordalselva

STORDALSELVA

SUPERB RUN WITH SUPERB DROPS

To prevent mix-ups, we will refer to the Storeelva in Møre og Romsdal simply as the Stordalselva. What? Sorry? Exactly! There is another Storeelva near the Jølstra. Why are we telling you all this? To avoid confusion when reading the maps.

The Stordalselva rages down the valley over bedrock, sometimes in open terrain, sometimes between rock massifs. For the not-so-bold paddler, the second put in is recommended, as portaging in the first gorge is not always easy. All the sections have been paddled, but not all at the same flow.

After only 300 metres you're into the gorge already. For starters a 7 metre waterfall frolics down, then a double drop. After another 100 metres the Stordalselva makes a slight bend to the right, and then follow two towback drops. After that the gorge opens up somewhat, and portaging becomes easier. It is best to scout the first gorge from river right before getting on, because at high flows individual sections can develop strong towbacks. However the bank is rough and difficult to walk.

After approximately 500 metres a slide with a kicker comes rather unexpectedly, and is difficult to recognise from the water. Scout from the right. The next right bend should be no problem, thereafter follow several sections which are not to be taken lightly. In particular, a double combination shortly before the second put in puts the life back into the party!

About 200 metres after the second put in there is a powerful slide, shortly thereafter a waterfall. Scout both from the right. After the wooden bridge do not miss the eddy on the left, the S-bend which follows is there to test your mettle. Shortly afterwards there is a drop with towback in a low gorge, best to portage on the right. Right up to the take out there are a number of bedrock slides and drops to drain the last reserves of energy from your arms.

CLASS:	V - VI (X)
LEVEL:	8 - 15 cumecs
LENGTH:	6 km (3 km)
TIME:	5 - 7 h
SEASON:	late June - August

Klatt

Tip: Do not paddle the first gorge if the level is too high.
Tipp: Nicht bei zu viel Wasser in die erste Schlucht einfahren.

Um Verwechslungen zu vermeiden, nennen wir die Storeelva in Møre og Romsdal einfach Stordalselva. Wie? Was? Ja genau, es gibt noch eine Storeelva, und zwar in Sogn og Fjordane in der Nähe der Jølstra. Warum erzählen wir so was? Um Verwirrungen beim Karten studieren zu vermeiden.

Die Stordalselva braust über Grundgestein zu Tale, teils in offenem Gelände, teils zwischen bedrohenden Felsmassen. Für nervenschwache Fahrer ist der zweite Einstieg zu empfehlen, da ein Umtragen in der ersten Schlucht nicht immer einfach ist. Es wurden schon alle Stellen gefahren, allerdings nicht alle bei demselben Wasserstand.

Schon 300 Meter nach Start geht's in die Schlucht. Zu Beginn frohlockt ein 7-Meter-Wasserfall, dann eine Doppelstufe. Nach weiteren 100 Metern knickt die Stordalselva leicht nach rechts ab, es folgen zwei rückläufige Stellen. Danach macht die Schlucht etwas auf, umtragen wird etwas leichter. Diese erste Schlucht sollte am besten schon vor der Fahrt von rechts erkundet werden, da bei zu hohem Wasserstand die einzelnen Stellen schnell sehr rückläufig werden können. Allerdings ist das Ufer recht unwegsam.

Nach etwa 500 Metern kommt unverhofft eine Rutsche mit Kicker, die schwer vom Wasser aus erkennbar ist. Von rechts besichtigen. Die folgende Rechtskurve sollte kein Problem sein. Es folgen noch einige hochachtungsvolle Stellen, insbesondere die Doppelkombination kurz vor dem zweiten Einstieg bringt wieder Leben in die Bude.

Etwa 200 Meter nach dem zweiten Einstieg folgt eine kräftige Rutsche, kurz danach ein Wasserfall. Beide rechts besichtigen. Nach einer Holzbrücke sollte auf keinen Fall das linke Kehrwasser verpasst werden, die folgende S-Kurve hat es in sich. Bald danach folgt eine sehr rückläufige Stufe in einer Niederklamm, besser rechts umtragen. Bis zum Ausstieg kommen noch einige Grundgesteinsrutschen und Abfälle, die dir die Kraft endgültig aus den Armen saugen.

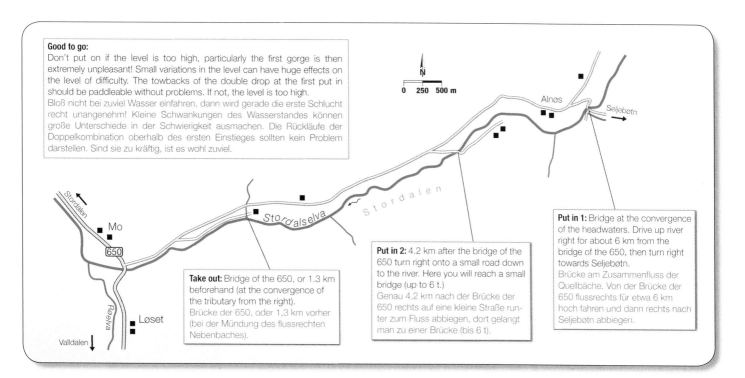

Good to go:
Don't put on if the level is too high, particularly the first gorge is then extremely unpleasant! Small variations in the level can have huge effects on the level of difficulty. The towbacks of the double drop at the first put in should be paddleable without problems. If not, the level is too high.
Bloß nicht bei zuviel Wasser einfahren, dann wird gerade die erste Schlucht recht unangenehm! Kleine Schwankungen des Wasserstandes können große Unterschiede in der Schwierigkeit ausmachen. Die Rückläufe der Doppelkombination oberhalb des ersten Einstieges sollten kein Problem darstellen. Sind sie zu kräftig, ist es wohl zuviel.

0   250   500 m

Alnøs

Seljebøtn

Stordalen

Stordalselva

Stordalen

Mo

650

Rødelva

Løset

Valldalen

Take out: Bridge of the 650, or 1.3 km beforehand (at the convergence of the tributary from the right).
Brücke der 650, oder 1,3 km vorher (bei der Mündung des flussrechten Nebenbaches).

Put in 2: 4.2 km after the bridge of the 650 turn right onto a small road down to the river. Here you will reach a small bridge (up to 6 t.)
Genau 4,2 km nach der Brücke der 650 rechts auf eine kleine Straße runter zum Fluss abbiegen, dort gelangt man zu einer Brücke (bis 6 t).

Put in 1: Bridge at the convergence of the headwaters. Drive up river right for about 6 km from the bridge of the 650, then turn right towards Seljebøtn.
Brücke am Zusammenfluss der Quellbäche. Von der Brücke der 650 flussrechts für etwa 6 km hoch fahren und dann rechts nach Seljebøtn abbiegen.

EMBLA

The Embla flows through the Strandadalen and into the Norddalsfjorden in Stranda, after which it is popularly known as the Strandaelva. We trust our map of the area, which calls it the Embla. There are two put ins to choose from, depending on the water level. If there is enough water for the first put in, the second section gets very pushy. It is always possible to eddy out before the difficult sections, but there should be no doubt in your mind about catching the last eddy.

Shortly after the first put in the Embla rears its head and provides 300 metres of adrenaline. Here you need to portage a 5 metre waterfall on the left. There is then a difficult section (WW V-) before a bridge, about 2 kilometres before the road bridge of the 60, the second put in. Aside from that, the Embla does not really offer much for adrenaline junkies in this section, although it does come recommended, especially at 20+ cumecs, where it offers nice WW III+ whitewater.

After the second put in the adrenaline withdrawal is at an end: two bedrock combinations awaken the first butterflies in your stomach, before the following gorge then pushes your pulse up over 180. But no panic, somehow you always seem to find an eddy of salvation just above the next drop. All sections can be scouted or guesstimated. The exit of the gorge in Stranda should be viewed before a run, and the road bridge to Opshaugsvik is just the ticket for this. You should also scout the section which follows, as the current continues to flow swiftly. The adventure finishes with a fitting take out in the harbour of Stranda.

Tip: Check your email in the library in Stranda.

CLASS:	II - V (X)
LEVEL:	15 - 20 cumecs
LENGTH:	10 km / 4 km
TIME:	3 - 4 h
SEASON:	May - late June

Die Embla fließt durchs Strandadalen und mündet in Stranda ins Norddalsfjorden, demnach wird sie gern als Strandaelva bezeichnet. Wir vertrauen unserer Karte, diese sagt Embla. Es bieten sich zwei Einstiege an, je nach Wasserstand: Ist es für das erste Stück genug Wasser, wird es im zweiten Abschnitt recht wuchtig. Es ist immer möglich vor den Schwierigkeiten anzulanden, nur sollte der Mut das letzte Kehrwasser anzusteuern nicht fehlen.

Kurz nach dem ersten Einstieg bäumt sich die Embla auf und sorgt auf 300 Metern für Spannung. Hier muss ein 5-Meter-Wasserfall links umtragen werden. Es folgt noch eine schwere Stelle (WW V-) vor einer Brücke, etwa 2 Kilometer vor der Straßenbrücke der 60, dem zweiten Einstieg. Ansonsten ist die Embla hier nichts für Adrenalinjunkies. Nichtsdestotrotz ist diese Strecke zu empfehlen, gerade bei mehr als 20 Kubik, dann WW III+.

Ab dem zweiten Einstieg hat der harte Entzug ein Ende: Zwei Grundgesteinskombinationen sorgen für das erste Kribbeln, bevor in der folgenden Klamm der Puls auf 180 schnellt. Aber keine Panik, irgendwie taucht vor der nächsten Kante immer wieder ein rettendes Kehrwasser auf. Alle Stellen können besichtigt oder erahnt werden. Der Klammausgang in Stranda sollte vor einer Befahrung besichtigt werden, dort überspannt die Straßenbrücke nach Opshaugsvik das Geschehen. Ebenso sollte die Stelle im Anschluss besichtigt werden, denn die Strömung zieht zügig weiter. Ein gebührender Ausstieg im Hafen von Stranda rundet das Abenteuer ab.

Tipp: In der Bibliothek Emails checken.

The drop at the bridge to Opshaugsvik

Take out: Harbour in Stranda.
Hafen in Stranda.

Put in 2: Road bridge of the 60, about 4 km before Stranda. Straßenbrücke der 60 etwa 4 km vor Stranda. Ab hier anspruchsvoller!

Put in 1: Parking bay 10 km before Stranda, there take the fork with the wooden bridge. Straßenbucht 10 km vor Stranda, dort Abzweig mit Holzbrücke.

Good to go:
The first put in should only be chosen at high water levels, the lower section should also be ok at lower flows.
Der erste Einstieg sollte nur bei viel Wasser gewählt werden, der untere Abschnitt auch/erst bei weniger.

BYGDELVA: RACE COURSE
A SHORT PARK + HUCK RUN

Simon Strohmeier

We were on a trip with Deb Pinniger and Cheesy Robertson in Norway, filming a road movie for BBC Wales. Where could we take such a crew, under time pressure, to get enough footage as quickly as possible? Enter Flemming Schmidt to the rescue! At that time Flemming was living with his family in Hellesylt, and he told us of an extremely short, but absolutely worthwhile homerun: the Bygdelva. This the right tributary into the Sunnylvsfjord at Hellesylt.

Admittedly, the section we describe here really belongs in the park + huck category. Nonetheless it comes highly recommended! 200 metres which can easily be paddled ten times in a row. The section is easy to reach, stress-free, and all the lines are obvious.

For those who haven't had enough, you can then drive around the 800 metre diversion race, and attack the three WW V+ sections into the fjord. All the sections can be seen from the road.

Bonustrack: just the 800 metre diversion in between is missing. Basically, there are three must-run WW VI sections which, with enough overflow from the weir, should not be left out. But be careful: after the exit from the gorge do not overlook the unpaddleable waterfall. The section under the bridge to the power station could produce a Don-Quixote situation so make sure you get your line right!

CLASS:	IV - VI (X)
LEVEL:	10 - 15 cumecs
LENGTH:	200 m (1 km)
TIME:	2 - 3 h
SEASON:	middle May - July

Photo: KD

Barbara Winter

Wir waren mit Deb Pinniger und Cheesy Robertson in Norwegen unterwegs um einen Roadmovie für BBC Wales abzudrehen. Wohin mit so einer Gruppe, um unter Zeitdruck rechtzeitig genügend Filmmaterial zu sammeln? Flemming Schmidt, unsere Rettung! Flemming lebte zu dieser Zeit mit seiner Familie in Hellesylt und berichtete von seinem extrem kurzen, doch lohnenden Homerun, der Bygdelva. Diese ist der rechte Zufluss ins Sunnylvsfjord bei Hellesylt.

Zugegeben, der beschriebene Abschnitt gehört wohl eher in die Park + Huck Liga, nichtsdestotrotz möchten wir ihn empfehlen. 200 Meter, die problemlos zehn Mal gepaddelt werden können. Dieser Abschnitt ist leicht zugänglich und stressfrei, die Linien sind offensichtlich.

Wem das nicht genug ist, der kann die folgenden 800 Meter Ableitung umfahren und die drei WW V+ Stellen ins Fjord meistern. Alle Stellen sind von der Straße aus zu sehen.

Bonustrack: Fehlen nur die 800 Meter Ableitung dazwischen. Im Grunde handelt es sich um drei Zwangsstellen, WW VI, die bei ausreichend Überlauf des Wehres nicht ausgelassen werden sollten. Doch Vorsicht: Nach dem Ausgang aus der Klamm sollte der unfahrbare Wasserfall nicht übersehen werden. Die Stelle unter der Brücke zum Kraftwerk könnte eine Don-Quijote-Situation ergeben, also bitte genau fahren!

Daniel Herzig

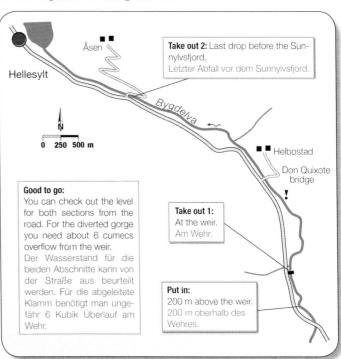

Hellesylt

Åsen

Take out 2: Last drop before the Sunnylvsfjord.
Letzter Abfall vor dem Sunnylvsfjord.

Bygdelva

Helbostad

Don Quixote bridge

N

0   250   500 m

Good to go:
You can check out the level for both sections from the road. For the diverted gorge you need about 6 cumecs overflow from the weir.
Der Wasserstand für die beiden Abschnitte kann von der Straße aus beurteilt werden. Für die abgeleitete Klamm benötigt man ungefähr 6 Kubik Überlauf am Wehr.

Take out 1:
At the weir.
Am Wehr.

Put in:
200 m above the weir.
200 m oberhalb des Wehres.

LANGEDALSELVA: FLEMMINGS HOMERUN

Flemming is indeed worthy of envy: not only one, but two homeruns he could call his own. The Langedalselva is a real surprise treat, with slides and fine drop combos, up to 3 metres high.

The first drop, the Gråttefossen, is directly upstream of the road bridge and can be seen from the car, but a closer examination is recommended. The Norwegian Benjamin Hjort got pulled into the cave behind the waterfall and took three attempts to dive out from behind it. The approach and the boof are trickier than they appear, so set up good safety.

After about 800 metres is an unpaddleable drop which should be portaged on the left or right. As you drive in you can see it as a shimmering white wall through the trees. Right after this a nice three metre boof fills your heart with joy, but in your euphoria you should not forget the second difficult section: the current flows into a twisting slide with a brutal towback at the end. Flemming was once relieved of his boat on a solo run here. All he can remember is being washed up on the bank at some stage, with boat and paddle. So unless you crave a similar experience, portage on the left, or bring a reliable throw-bag crew with you. Then the Langedalselva nears the road once more. The trip can then be ended on the right before the bridge, or at the drop after the bridge.

CLASS: IV - V- (V, X)
LEVEL: 10 - 15 cumecs
LENGTH: 4 km
TIME: 2 - 3 h
SEASON: May - July

Zu beneiden ist der Flemming: nicht nur einen Homerun, sondern zwei konnte er sein Eigen nennen. Die Langedalselva überrascht mit Rutschen und feinen Kombinationen von Stufen bis zu 3 Meter Höhe.

Die erste schwere Stufe, der Gråttefossen, ist direkt oberhalb von der Straßenbrücke aus dem Auto zu erblicken, eine genauere Untersuchung ist sinnvoll. So ist der Norweger Benjamin Hjort bei einer Befahrung in die Höhle hinter den Fall gezogen worden, für das Raustauchen benötigte er drei Anläufe. Anfahrt und Boof sind trickreicher als es den Anschein hat, also bitte gut absichern!

Nach etwa 800 Metern folgt eine unfahrbare Stufe, die links oder rechts umtragen werden sollte. Schon bei der Anfahrt schimmert diese Stelle als weiße Wand durch den Wald. Direkt im Anschluss erfreut ein schöner 3-Meter-Boof das Herz, doch vor lauter Aufregung sollte die zweite schwere Stelle nicht vergessen werden: Die Strömung zieht in eine verwinkelte Rutsche mit heftigem Rücklauf am Ausgang. Flemming ist in diesem Rücklauf bei einer Solobefahrung seines Bootes entledigt worden. Er kann sich nur noch daran erinnern, dass er irgendwann samt Paddel und Kajak ans Ufer gespült wurde. Wer nicht nach ähnlichen Erlebnissen lechzt, sollte links umtragen, oder zuverlässige Wurfsackwerfer mitbringen. Danach nähert sich die Langedalselva wieder der Straße. Die Tour kann rechts vor der nächsten Brücke beendet werden, oder am Abfall nach der Brücke.

Tip: The following gorge, up to the steep section, should only be attempted at low water. Extremely difficult whitewater and a must-run waterfall are guaranteed. Only for true junkies!

Tipp: Die folgende Klamm bis zum Steilstück sollte nur bei Niedrigwasser versucht werden. Schwerstes Wildwasser und ein Zwangswasserfall sind gewiss. Nur für Freunde des Extremsports!

Olaf Obsommer

Photo: SG

Nils Kagel

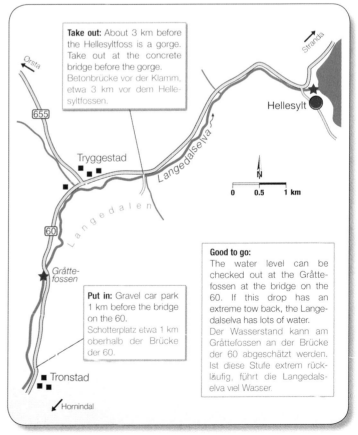

Take out: About 3 km before the Hellesyltfoss is a gorge. Take out at the concrete bridge before the gorge. Betonbrücke vor der Klamm, etwa 3 km vor dem Hellesyltfossen.

Put in: Gravel car park 1 km before the bridge on the 60. Schotterplatz etwa 1 km oberhalb der Brücke der 60.

Good to go:
The water level can be checked out at the Gråttefossen at the bridge on the 60. If this drop has an extreme tow back, the Langedalselva has lots of water. Der Wasserstand kann am Gråttefossen an der Brücke der 60 abgeschätzt werden. Ist diese Stufe extrem rückläufig, führt die Langedalselva viel Wasser.

Orsta

655

Tryggestad

L a n g e d a l e n

60

Gråtte-fossen

Tronstad

Hornindal

Stranda

Hellesylt

Langedalselva

N

0   0.5   1 km

HORNDØLA — A WHITEWATER GEM WITH AWESOME SLIDES AND DROPS

Anecdote: If you're looking for the last eddy, take a leaf out of Stefan Renner's book. Stefan found himself in the boily pool above the double waterfall at the entrance to the gorge – a place almost impossible to escape without outside help. Luckily his girlfriend (!) was able to pull him out with a rope, otherwise he would probably still be recirculating at the bottom of the falls right now. But it was all in vain, because after minute examination of the waterfall he went and ran it anyway!

Anekdote: Wer auf der Suche nach dem letzten Kehrwasser ist, kann sich ein Beispiel an Stefan Renner nehmen: Stefan fand sich in dem Tumpf vor dem Doppelwasserfall am Klammeingang wieder, dessen Verlassen ohne fremde Hilfe so gut wie unmöglich ist. Zum Glück konnte ihn seine Freundin (!) dann am Seil aus dem Tumpf bergen, sonst würde er vielleicht heute noch seine Runden dort drehen. Die Mühen waren allerdings umsonst, denn nach eingängiger Besichtigung wurde der Wasserfall von ihm befahren.

Tipp: Nach dem Ausstieg gräbt sich die Horndøla über Grundgestein bis in den Hornindalsvatnet. Dieser Abschnitt wartet noch auf seine Helden.

The motto of the Horndøla: inconspicuous but exquisite. It follows the 60 in the opposite direction to the Langedalselva, and has a lot to offer before it drowns in the Hornindalsvatnet!

Right after the put in two WW IV sections await you, and the Horndøla then hastens to rush you to the next difficulties. There is a gorge with magnificent whitewater (IV-V) and several big towbacks. Before the slides and drops there is always a saving eddy to stop and scout. After the gorge the valley opens up, though the Horndøla continues to treat paddlers to an array of bed rock slides and drops. The difficulties get up to WW V, and can all be portaged.

When you see the roof of a hall on the left, make sure you put out on the left. The Horndøla divides here, and this is the first take out. Shortly afterwards, the main right arm flows into a gorge. The double waterfall at the entry into the gorge should be portaged on the left, and you should put on again as soon as possible. At high flows you can paddle around the waterfall in the left arm, but you then have to take out left 100 metres later and portage the next section. Your toils are rewarded with an awesome slide into the exit of the gorge. Loads more great whitewater all the way to the second take out.

Tip: After the take out the Horndøla digs its way over bed rock down into the Hornindalsvatnet. This section is still waiting for its heroes to come along.

CLASS:	**IV - VI (X)**
LEVEL:	**10 - 15 cumecs**
LENGTH:	**6 km**
TIME:	**3 - 4 h**
SEASON:	**May - early July**

»Unscheinbar aber fein« ist das Motto der Horndøla. Sie folgt der 60 entgegengesetzt zur Langedalselva, also Richtung Westen. Bevor sie im Hornindalsvatnet ersäuft, hat sie noch richtig was zu bieten.

Direkt nach dem Start lauern zwei WW IV Stellen, bis zu den nächsten Schwierigkeiten strömt die Horndøla flott dahin. Es folgt eine Schlucht mit wunderbarem Wildwasser (IV-V) und einigen kräftigen Rückläufen. Vor den Rutschen und Stufen ist immer ein rettendes Kehrwasser zum Anhalten und Besichtigen. Nach der Schlucht öffnet sich das Tal, wobei die Horndøla den Paddler weiterhin mit Grundgesteinsrutschen und Stufen beglückt. Die Schwierigkeiten steigern sich auf WW V, und

können alle problemlos umtragen werden.

Wenn links das Dach einer Halle zu sehen ist, unbedingt links halten und anlanden, die Horndøla teilt sich hier. Es ist die erste Ausstiegsmöglichkeit erreicht, kurz danach führt der rechte Hauptarm in eine Klamm. Den Doppelwasserfall am Eingang der Klamm sollte man links umtragen, und baldmöglichst wieder einbooten. Bei viel Wasser kann der Eingangswasserfall im linken Arm umfahren werden. Aber auch hier muss man nach 100 Metern links ausbooten und die folgende Stelle umtragen. Belohnt werden die Mühen mit einer tollen Rutsche des Seitenarms in den Klammausgang. Bis zum zweiten Ausstieg ist weiterhin spritziges Wildwasser geboten.

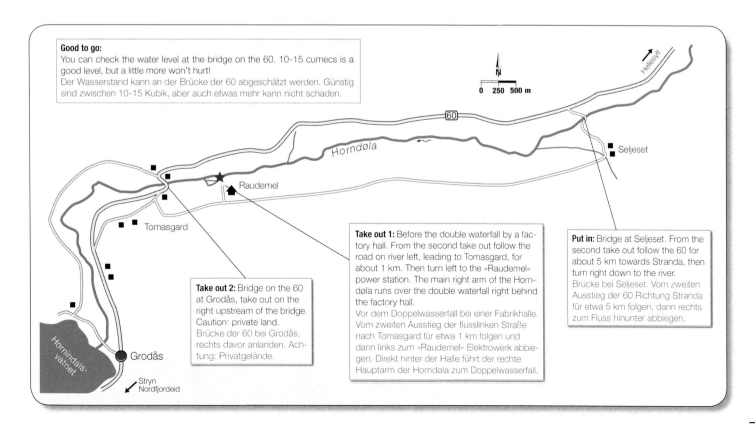

Good to go:
You can check the water level at the bridge on the 60. 10-15 cumecs is a good level, but a little more won't hurt!
Der Wasserstand kann an der Brücke der 60 abgeschätzt werden. Günstig sind zwischen 10-15 Kubik, aber auch etwas mehr kann nicht schaden.

Horndøla

Seljeset

Raudemel

Tomasgard

Take out 1: Before the double waterfall by a factory hall. From the second take out follow the road on river left, leading to Tomasgard, for about 1 km. Then turn left to the »Raudemel« power station. The main right arm of the Horndøla runs over the double waterfall right behind the factory hall.
Vor dem Doppelwasserfall bei einer Fabrikhalle. Vom zweiten Ausstieg der flusslinken Straße nach Tomasgard für etwa 1 km folgen und dann links zum »Raudemel« Elektrowerk abbiegen. Direkt hinter der Halle führt der rechte Hauptarm der Horndøla zum Doppelwasserfall.

Put in: Bridge at Seljeset. From the second take out follow the 60 for about 5 km towards Stranda, then turn right down to the river.
Brücke bei Seljeset. Vom zweiten Ausstieg der 60 Richtung Stranda für etwa 5 km folgen, dann rechts zum Fluss hinunter abbiegen.

Take out 2: Bridge on the 60 at Grodås, take out on the right upstream of the bridge. Caution: private land.
Brücke der 60 bei Grodås, rechts davor anlanden. Achtung: Privatgelände.

Hornindals-vatnet

Grodås

Stryn Nordfjordeid

Nils Kagel taking a minute to breathe

STORY: RAUMA   MARIANN SÆTHER

A NORMAL DAY ON THE RAUMA

I could feel the butterflies swirling around in my stomach as I walked down to the put in of the lower Rauma with my boat on my shoulder. Today would be the day of my first descent of this river. If only there weren't all those stories spooking around in my head. It seemed as though the Rauma had some good surprises in store for every group paddling it.

When I reached the put in, which is also the first difficult drop, I held my breath for a second, overwhelmed by the river's stunning beauty: here at the put in, the right channel of the Ulvåa cascades into the Rauma in the form of a waterfall, creating quite a little spectacle of nature. But it was time to go kayaking, so I grabbed my throw bag and followed Morten and Flemming to scout the first drop. It turned out to be high and steep, but a fair slide into a deep pool.

After both of them had hit a clean line, it was my turn. As I dropped over the edge, I remembered Morton's words: »Put your paddle to the side, so it won't break on impact!« Two seconds later, I rolled up in the pool – my paddle was alright, but my nose was bleeding! The paddle had hit me right between the eyes, but luckily I got away with a minor cut. Morten taped it up and off we went to run the next waterfall.

After a few slick boofs, we walked the following two slides due to the high water level. The next highlight was »The Slide«, the most famous rapid on the Lower Rauma. While running the shuttle earlier in the day, I had glimpsed it from the road and immediately told Flemming with a high

EIN GANZ NORMALER TAG AUF DER RAUMA

Die Schmetterlinge in meinem Bauch spielten verrückt, als ich mit meinem Boot auf der Schulter den Pfad zur unteren Rauma hinabstieg. Heute also sollte sie stattfinden, meine persönliche Erstbefahrung. Wären da nicht all die Geschichten über dieses Mysterium, die in meinem Kopf herumspukten. Es scheint als hätte die Rauma hier für jede Gruppe eine kleine Überraschung parat.

Als ich den Einstieg und somit die erste schwierige Stelle erreicht hatte, musste ich innehalten, die beeindruckende Schönheit des Flusses überwältigte mich für einen kurzen Moment: Hier direkt am Einstieg fällt der erste Arm der Ulvåa in die Rauma und bildet ein kleines Naturspektakel. Aber es war Zeit sich ums Paddeln zu kümmern, also schnappte ich meinen Wurfsack und folgte Morten und Flemming zum Besichtigen. Was sich mir offenbarte, war eine sehr hohe und steile, aber faire Rutsche in einen riesigen Pool.

Nachdem beide eine solide Linie vorgelegt hatten, war ich nun an der Reihe. An der Abrisskante hatte ich noch Mortens Worte in den Ohren: »Nimm das Paddel zur Seite, sonst kann es beim Aufprall brechen!« Zwei Sekunden später rollte ich im Pool hoch – mit einem intakten Paddel, aber mit blutiger Nase! Ich hatte mir das Paddel genau zwischen die Augen gehauen, aber glücklicher Weise war es nur eine kleine Platzwunde. Morten klebte die Wunde fix wieder zusammen, und schon ging es weiter zum nächsten Wasserfall.

pitched voice that I would certainly NOT be running that slide. It looked huge, even from the road. The idea of running it just seemed ridiculous. Flemming on the other hand smiled and said nothing.

Finally standing beside it, I realized why Flemming had reacted that way. It is almost impossible to miss the line and, to top it off: there is a 3 metre auto-boof in the middle of the 100 metre long slide. The entrance is about three metres wide, but the end about a hundred. We all arrived at the bottom wearing a wide smile. Nevertheless, I was starting to feel exhausted – maybe not so much physically, but mentally.

We had one more drop to go until we reached the take out. But just when you think you're done, there is this one last waterfall. For most paddlers the question of should or shouldn't doesn't even arise. The waterfall is monstrous! But Flemming had answered that question before and he was probably the only one to have positive feelings about it. Today, he felt like it again. After all, the water was high and therefore just right for his mission. The entrance slide to the water-fall seems like an unsolvable riddle to most. Flemming came out of it backwards, but managed at least to catch an eddy before the fall. He rested a second and then paddled toward the lip. To see him drop 20 metres and disappear in the water was incredible. Never had I seen anything like this run before and it simply blew my mind.

Now, two years later, I have paddled the lower Rauma numerous times. It strikes me as one of the most beautiful and breathtaking runs ever. Its combination of drops and the pure natural beauty make me drive hours after work just to paddle there. Writing this text, I have two

Flemming Schmidt Photo: DA

black eyes and a cut on my nose. It was that first drop again that got me when I least expected it. Two years have passed since I received my first lesson about respect – now it was time to refresh my memory. It was just another normal day on the Rauma.

Nach ein paar Flugeinheiten am Wasserfall umtrugen wir die nächsten zwei Rutschen, denn dafür brauste für unseren Geschmack zu viel Wasser im Flussbett. Der nächste Höhepunkt folgte dann etwas später, als wir die wohl bekannteste Stelle der unteren Rauma erreichten, die einfach nur »Die Rutsche« genannt wird. Beim Umsetzen des Autos hatte ich von weit oben einen Blick auf die Riesenrutsche erhascht und sofort lauthals beschlossen dieses Ding nie im Leben zu fahren. Schon von der Straße sah die Rutsche gewaltig aus – die Idee dort runterzupaddeln, schien mir wie ein Hirngespinst. Flemming hingegen hatte dazu gar nichts gesagt und nur gegrinst.

Als wir nun unten standen, wusste ich warum Flemming so reagiert hatte. Die Linie ist offensichtlich und fast nicht zu verfehlen, und der Autoboof in der Mitte der Rutsche schreit nach einem Freiflug. Die Einfahrt ist nur etwa 3 Meter breit, der Ausgang fast hundert. Jeder von uns kam mit einem breiten Grinsen unten an, das Herz bis zu den Ohren schlagend. Trotzdem fühlte ich mich jetzt erschöpft – nicht mal so sehr körperlich, eher mental.

Nun war es nicht mehr weit und so hatten wir kurze Zeit später den Ausstieg erreicht. Aber gerade wenn man denkt man hat es geschafft, blinkt einem der letzte Wasserfall ins Auge. Für die meisten Paddler ist es keine Frage ob oder ob nicht, denn es ist ein Monster! Flemming hatte die Frage für sich schon mal beantwortet, wahrscheinlich war er sogar der Erste der je eine positive Antwort aus seinem Bauch bekommen hatte. Heute war ihm mal wieder danach, schließlich war der Wasserstand hoch und somit optimal für eine Befahrung. Allein die Eingangsrutsche zum Wasserfall stellt für viele ein unlösbares Problem dar: Flemming kam zwar rückwärts dort heraus, konnte aber noch ein Kehrwasser vor dem Fall erwischen. Kurze Pause – und schon dropte er über die nächste Abrisskante. Es war ein unbeschreibliches Gefühl zu sehen, wie Flemming nach 20 Metern Freiflug im Unterwasser verschwand. Ich war noch nie bei der Befahrung eines solchen Monsters dabei, und es zog mir regelrecht die Schuhe aus.

Mittlerweile, zwei Jahre später, bin ich die untere Rauma schon oft gefahren. Es ist einer der wunderschönsten und atemberaubendsten Abschnitte weltweit. Die Kombination der einzelnen Stellen und deren Schönheit lassen mich manchmal nach der Arbeit noch ein paar Stunden Autofahrt in Kauf nehmen, nur um dort zu paddeln. Während ich diesen Text schreibe, quälen mich zwei blaue Augen und eine kleine Platzwunde dazwischen. Der erste Drop der Unteren Rauma hat mich mal wieder erwischt, und zwar als ich es am wenigsten erwartet hatte. Zwei Jahre nachdem mir meine erste Unterrichtsstunde in Sachen Respekt erteilt worden war, wurde es wohl wieder Zeit mich erneut zu erinnern. Es war mal wieder ein ganz normaler Tag auf der unteren Rauma.

MARIANN SÆTHER 1980 www.mariannsaether.com

Mariann has accomplished the step from a promising young gun to a distinguished and experienced paddling star. And as if by chance, she calls Norway home. No matter if it is freestyle kayaking or hard-core creeking, Mariann belongs to the top paddlers. She enjoys her Kavu Day with her friends Flemming Schmidt and Morten Eilertsen – on the Rauma of course! Thanks to her sponsors: Dagger, Werner, IR, System X, Palm, Olden.

Mariann hat sich von der Nachwuchspaddlerin zur profilierten und routinierten Größe im Kajakrummel gemausert – und ist ganz zufällig in Norwegen beheimatet. Ob Rodeo oder Wildwasser im Grenzbereich, Mariann ist vorne mit dabei. Ihren Kavu Day genießt Mariann am liebsten mit ihren Freunden Flemming Schmidt und Morten Eilertsen – natürlich auf der Rauma!

SØR-TRØNDELAG

Kagel and Mauracher just wanna run the slot again - Gråura section, Driva.

A place to be

SØR-TRØNDELAG

The past of both Trøndelag regions is spiked with Norwegian history. They say that if you took all the Trøndelag history out of the history books, you would be left with nothing but the covers. If you took the Driva out of this river guide, a piece of whitewater history would also be missing.

In the middle ages, Trøndelag was the seat of power in Norway, the historical capital city of Trondheim was the centre point of the goings-on. However, these days Oppdal is of much greater interest to us, for this is the home ground of local matador Tore Meirik who, on the next pages, is going to share with us some of his secret tips. Numerous remarkable rivers lie hidden in Sør-Trøndelag (South-Trøndelag), most of which, aside from the lower Fora and the Rafting Section of the Driva, start at grade four and work their up.

The Drivdalen and Gauldalen are the most interesting main valleys for us, most of the rivers described flow into either the Driva or the Gaula. Thus you can quickly and easily reach the tributaries. The Forra marks the northern-most point of our Norwegian odyssey, north of here lies yet uncharted terrain. Anyone for a little expedition?

Die Vergangenheit der beiden Trøndelag-Regionen ist gespickt mit norwegischer Geschichte. Man sagt, dass nur der Umschlag der Geschichtsbücher zurückbleiben würde, wenn man alles was Trøndelag betrifft aus ihnen herausnehme. Nehme man die Driva aus diesem Flussführer heraus, würde ein Stück Wildwassergeschichte fehlen.

Im Mittelalter war Trøndelag das Machtzentrum Norwegens, in der historischen Hauptstadt Trondheim konzentrierte sich das Geschehen. Für uns jedoch ist heutzutage Oppdal viel interessanter, denn hier lebt Lokalmatador Tore Meirik, der uns auf den nächsten Seiten einige seiner Geheimtipps verraten wird. In Sør-Trøndelag (Süd-Trøndelag) verstecken sich eine Vielzahl bemerkenswerter Flüsse, abgesehen von der unteren Fora und dem Rafting Abschnitt auf der Driva, meist vom vierten Schwierigkeitsgrad an aufwärts.

Das Drivdalen und Gauldalen stellen die für uns interessanten Haupttäler dar, viele der beschriebenen Bäche münden in Driva und Gaula. So sind die Nebenbäche schnell erreicht. Die Forra markiert den nördlichsten Punkt unserer Norwegenreise, nördlich von hier erstreckt sich für uns noch unbekanntes Terrain. Kleine Expedition gefällig?

»Vertical Playground« in Oppdal

Tore Meirik (1979) has been kayaking since 1996, and has visited most parts of Norway with his boat. He has also been lucky enough to notch up a couple of first descents around the country. He and Benjamin Hjort put together a little »Trøndelag River Guide« a few years ago. Many thanks to his sponsors: Robson, Noname and Vertical Playground.

Tore Meirik (1979) sitzt seit 1996 im Boot, und war mit diesem schon in fast allen Ecken Norwegens unterwegs. Einige Erstbefahrungen gehen auf sein Konto, ebenso ein kurzer Trøndelag-Flussführer, den er zusammen mit Benjamin Hjort erarbeitete. Vielen Dank an seine Sponsoren: Robson, Noname und Vertical Playground.

Info on the region

www.trondelag.com
www.trondheim.com
www.oppdal.com
www.sunndal-aktivum.no
www.surnadal-turist.no
www.gaula.no

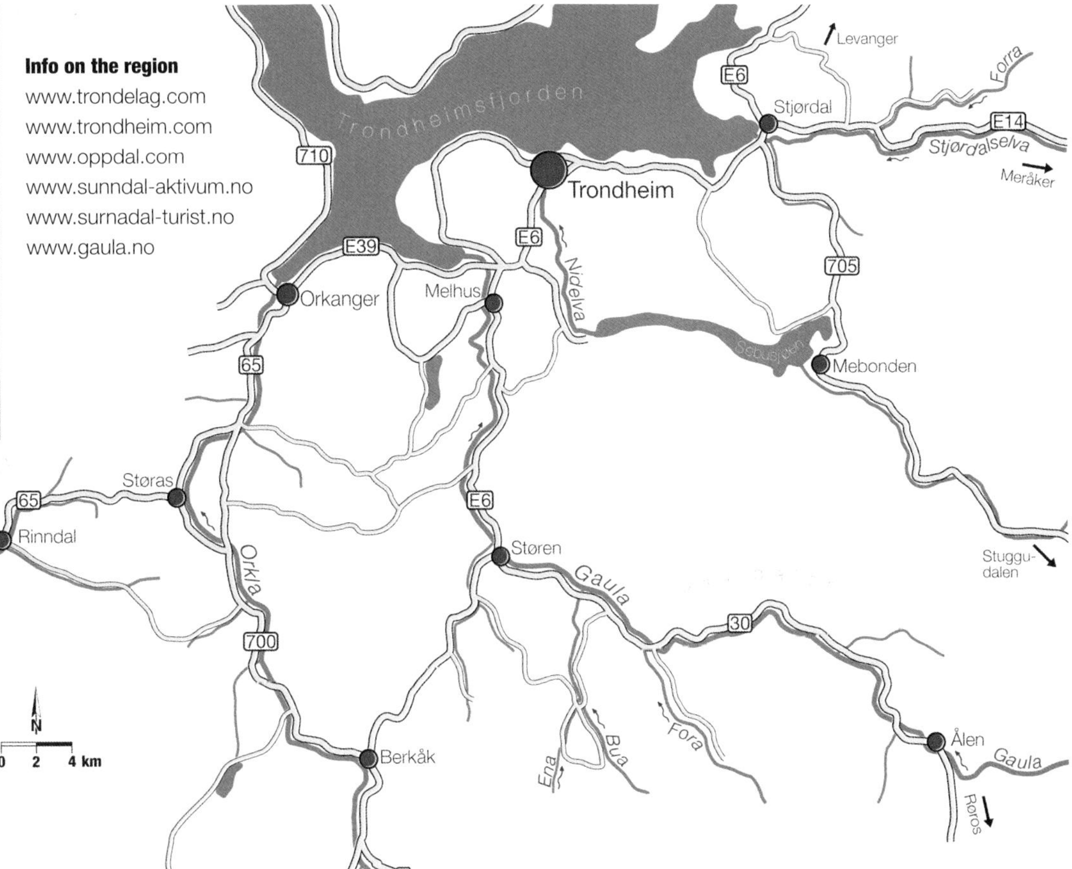

Olli Grau - Driva

Disinfection!

SØR-TRØNDELAG FACTS

Character: Mostly beautiful steep creeks between WW IV-V, also several easier sections on the Driva and Fora.

Best time: Spring to summer, the classics such as the Gråura canyon and the Bua gorge run until high summer.

Special remarks: In most of the tributaries of the Gaula the levels rise and fall very quickly after rainfall. Beware: Gyro is on the prowl! At the Shell petrol station in Oppdal you can disinfect your boat around the clock for free.

Accommodation: You will find camping grounds all around Oppdal and at the take out of the Gråura section of the Driva.

Kayak shop: The employees of the outdoor store Vertical Playground (Auneveien 4, Oppdal, www.vpg.no) are happy to give further information on the area. From the large roundabout in Oppdal simply follow the 70 for a short distance to the hotel »Nor«.

Charakter: Vor allem wunderschöne Sturzbäche zwischen WW IV-V, auch einige leichtere Abschnitte auf Driva und Fora.

Beste Zeit: Frühling bis Sommer, die Klassiker wie die Gråura-Schlucht und die Bua-Klamm bis in den Hochsommer.

Besonderheit: Bei den meisten Nebenbächen der Gaula steigt und fällt das Wasser nach Regenfällen sehr schnell. Achtung: Der Gyro geht um! In Oppdal kann man sein Boot kostenlos und rund um die Uhr an der Shell Tankstelle in Oppdal desinfizieren.

Übernachtung: Campingplätze befinden sich rund um Oppdal und am Ausstieg des Gråura-Abschnittes der Driva.

Kajakshop: Die Mitarbeiter des Outdoorladen Vertical Playground (www.vpg.no, Auneveien 4, Oppdal) liefern gern weitere Informationen zur Region. Einfach vom großen Kreisverkehr in Oppdal kurz der 70 zum Hotel »Nor« folgen.

DRIVA: UPPER

A LITTLE BIT OF EVERYTHING, INCLUDING AWESOME STEEP RAPIDS

The Driva flows out of the Døvrefjell, east of the Snøhetta Peak, and initially follows the E6. In Oppdal it turns away to the west into the Sunndalen, to reach the fjord in Sunndalsøra. Almost all of the 120 kilometres can be paddled, we are going to pick out the four main sections.

On the upper section the Driva offers steep whitewater between WW IV and V, with quiet sections in between. There are three larger sections, and numerous smaller cataracts. Steep, but not »super full on«. Scouting is almost always necessary, but never difficult. Breaking off the trip is always possible, the road is never far from the river. The most difficult section is the first slide/drop right after Kongsvoll.

CLASS: IV - V
LEVEL: 15 - 20 cumecs
LENGTH: 7 km
TIME: 2 - 4 h
SEASON: early June - July

Tip: Below Hesthåggån you will find the Magalaupet Gorge. Caution, it is very short, but very mean!

Trond Finseth

Die Driva entspringt am Døvrefjell östlich der Snøhetta Gipfel und begleitet anfangs die E 6. In Oppdal knickt sie nach Westen ins Sunndalen ab, um in Sunndalsøra das Fjord zu erreichen. Von den 120 Flusskilometern sind fast alle fahrbar, wir werden uns die vier wesentlichen Abschnitte rauspicken.

Auf dem oberen Abschnitt bietet die Driva steiles Wildwasser zwischen dem vierten und fünften Grad, dazwischen liegen ruhige Abschnitte. Es folgen drei größere Stellen und viele kleine Katarakte – steil, aber nicht »super krass«. Vorheriges Besichtigen ist fast immer nötig, aber nie schwierig. Ein Fahrtabbruch ist jederzeit möglich, die Straße

verläuft immer in Flussnähe. Die schwierigste Stelle ist der erste rutschenähnliche Abfall direkt hinter Kongsvoll.

Tipp: Unterhalb von Hesthåggån erstreckt sich die Magalaupet-Schlucht, Vorsicht. Diese ist sehr kurz, aber auch sehr fies.

Roger Løkken

DRIVA: RAFTING TRIP

MELLOW PLAYBOATING IN BEAUTIFUL SCENERY

This section can be paddled as long as the eddies aren't frozen over. Several defined cataracts in a low gorge lead to a small, river-wide drop, then to a road bridge, the Vika Bru.

Dieser Abschnitt ist paddelbar solange kein Eis die Kehrwässer versperrt. Einige definierte Katarakte in einer niedrigen Klamm führen zu einem kleinen flussbreiten Abfall, anschließend zu einer Straßenbrücke, der Vika Bru. Danach

After that there are short, low gorges with boily currents, which carry the paddler to another, somewhat bigger drop. Then the difficulties ease off a bit. In the last low gorge a couple

folgen kurze Niederklammen mit quirligen Strömungen, die den Paddler zu einem weiteren, etwas mächtigeren Abfall bringen. Anschließend lassen die Schwierigkeiten nach. Es warten noch ein paar kleinere

of smaller rapids await you, until you reach the take out on the right at the end of the gorge.

Stromschnellen in der letzten Niederklamm, bis man am Klammende rechts den Ausstieg erreicht.

CLASS:	II - III (III+)
LEVEL:	40 - 80 cumecs
LENGTH:	12 km
TIME:	2 - 4 h
SEASON:	May - September

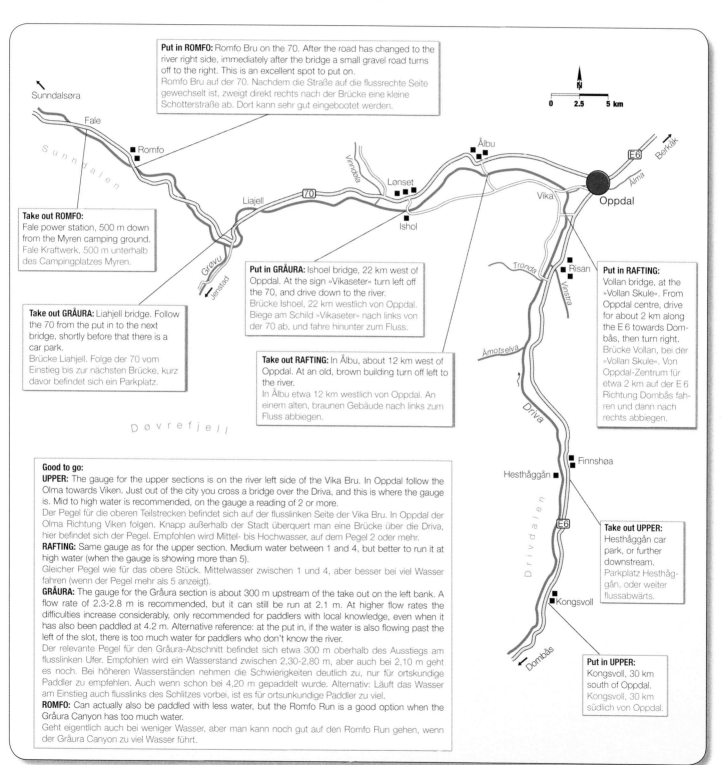

Put in ROMFO: Romfo Bru on the 70. After the road has changed to the river right side, immediately after the bridge a small gravel road turns off to the right. This is an excellent spot to put on.
Romfo Bru auf der 70. Nachdem die Straße auf die flussrechte Seite gewechselt ist, zweigt direkt rechts nach der Brücke eine kleine Schotterstraße ab. Dort kann sehr gut eingebootet werden.

Take out ROMFO: Fale power station, 500 m down from the Myren camping ground.
Fale Kraftwerk, 500 m unterhalb des Campingplatzes Myren.

Put in GRÅURA: Ishoel bridge, 22 km west of Oppdal. At the sign »Vikaseter« turn left off the 70, and drive down to the river.
Brücke Ishoel, 22 km westlich von Oppdal. Biege am Schild »Vikaseter« nach links von der 70 ab, und fahre hinunter zum Fluss.

Take out GRÅURA: Liahjell bridge. Follow the 70 from the put in to the next bridge, shortly before that there is a car park.
Brücke Liahjell. Folge der 70 vom Einstieg bis zur nächsten Brücke, kurz davor befindet sich ein Parkplatz.

Take out RAFTING: In Ålbu, about 12 km west of Oppdal. At an old, brown building turn off left to the river.
In Ålbu etwa 12 km westlich von Oppdal. An einem alten, braunen Gebäude nach links zum Fluss abbiegen.

Put in RAFTING: Vollan bridge, at the »Vollan Skule«. From Oppdal centre, drive for about 2 km along the E 6 towards Dombås, then turn right.
Brücke Vollan, bei der »Vollan Skule«. Von Oppdal-Zentrum für etwa 2 km auf der E 6 Richtung Dombås fahren und dann nach rechts abbiegen.

Take out UPPER: Hesthåggån car park, or further downstream.
Parkplatz Hesthåggån, oder weiter flussabwärts.

Put in UPPER: Kongsvoll, 30 km south of Oppdal.
Kongsvoll, 30 km südlich von Oppdal.

Good to go:
UPPER: The gauge for the upper sections is on the river left side of the Vika Bru. In Oppdal follow the Olma towards Viken. Just out of the city you cross a bridge over the Driva, and this is where the gauge is. Mid to high water is recommended, on the gauge a reading of 2 or more.
Der Pegel für die oberen Teilstrecken befindet sich auf der flusslinken Seite der Vika Bru. In Oppdal der Olma Richtung Viken folgen. Knapp außerhalb der Stadt überquert man eine Brücke über die Driva, hier befindet sich der Pegel. Empfohlen wird Mittel- bis Hochwasser, auf dem Pegel 2 oder mehr.
RAFTING: Same gauge as for the upper section. Medium water between 1 and 4, but better to run it at high water (when the gauge is showing more than 5).
Gleicher Pegel wie für das obere Stück. Mittelwasser zwischen 1 und 4, aber besser bei viel Wasser fahren (wenn der Pegel mehr als 5 anzeigt).
GRÅURA: The gauge for the Gråura section is about 300 m upstream of the take out on the left bank. A flow rate of 2.3-2.8 m is recommended, but it can still be run at 2.1 m. At higher flow rates the difficulties increase considerably, only recommended for paddlers with local knowledge, even when it has also been paddled at 4.2 m. Alternative reference: at the put in, if the water is also flowing past the left of the slot, there is too much water for paddlers who don't know the river.
Der relevante Pegel für den Gråura-Abschnitt befindet sich etwa 300 m oberhalb des Ausstiegs am flusslinken Ufer. Empfohlen wird ein Wasserstand zwischen 2,30-2,80 m, aber auch bei 2,10 m geht es noch. Bei höheren Wasserständen nehmen die Schwierigkeiten deutlich zu, nur für ortskundige Paddler zu empfehlen. Auch wenn schon bei 4,20 m gepaddelt wurde. Alternativ: Läuft das Wasser am Einstieg auch flusslinks des Schlitzes vorbei, ist es für ortsunkundige Paddler zu viel.
ROMFO: Can actually also be paddled with less water, but the Romfo Run is a good option when the Gråura Canyon has too much water.
Geht eigentlich auch bei weniger Wasser, aber man kann noch gut auf den Romfo Run gehen, wenn der Gråura Canyon zu viel Wasser führt.

DRIVA: GRÅURA

NICE DROP + POOL RAPIDS IN A BIG GORGE

The Gråura Gorge is the unchallenged highlight of the Driva. When it was paddled for the first time in the 70's, it was considered one of the most difficult sections in the country. Today it has become well known as a breathtaking gorge section, with world class whitewater and surrounds. Here the Driva digs itself as far as 250 metres down between the rock masses.

The challenges here are almost all around grade IV, there are no (real) portage sections, perhaps above a gauge level of 2.90 metres.

CLASS:	IV (V-)
LEVEL:	30 - 60 cumecs
LENGTH:	13 km
TIME:	3 - 5 h
SEASON:	May - September

However, scouting and safetying of the sections is not always easy, particularly at higher flows. In addition, the river flows far from the nearest road, so this section should absolutely be taken seriously, despite the many descents it enjoys.

About 2 kilometres after putting in you enter the gorge. From above, the entrance rapid looks worse than it actually is: approach from the right, stay in the middle, and watch out the hole at the bottom on the left. Somewhat later a small wooden bridge stretches over the gorge. The following towback drop can be scouted from the right. After that the gorge opens up and becomes quieter again.

However, powerful cataracts continue to escort you down at regular intervals, particularly towards the end of the gorge.

It will take an experienced team between 2 and 3 hours to get down the 13 kilometre long section, the record held by the Norwegian Erik Vognild is 1 hour, 1 minute and 23 seconds. How fast are you?

Tip: Feel like a bit of variety? At the put in there is a climbing garden.

DieGråura-Schlucht ist der unbestrittene Höhepunkt der Driva. Als sie in den Siebziger Jahren zum ersten Mal befahren wurde, galt sie als eine der schwersten Strecken des Landes. Heute ist dieser Abschnitt als wunderschöne Schluchtstrecke bekannt, mit Natur und Wildwasser der Weltklasse. Bis zu 250 Meter tief gräbt sich die Driva hier zwischen die Felsmassen.

Die Schwierigkeiten bewegen sich fast durchweg im vierten Grad, es gibt (eigentlich) keine Umtragestellen, eventuell ab einem Pegel von 2,90 Meter. Allerdings ist ein Besichtigen und Sichern der einzelnen Stellen nicht immer ganz einfach, gerade bei höheren Wasserständen. Hinzu kommt, dass die Straße weit über dem Fluss verläuft, also sollte diese Strecke trotz der vielen Befahrungen Ernst genommen werden.

Etwa 2 Kilometer nach dem Einstieg geht es in eine Klamm hinein. Der Eingangskatarakt sieht von oben schlimmer aus als er ist: von rechts anfahren, dann mittig bleiben, aufpassen auf die Walze unten links. Etwas später überspannt eine kleine Holzbrücke die Klamm. Die Rücklaufstufe im Anschluss kann von rechts besichtigt werden.

Danach macht die Klamm auf und es wird ruhiger. Es folgen aber immer wieder kräftigere Katarakte, gerade wenn es dem Ende zugeht.

Die 13 Kilometer lange Strecke wird ein erfahrenes Team zwischen zwei und drei Stunden kosten. Der Rekord des Norwegers Per Erik Vognild liegt bei 1 Stunde, 1 Minute und 23 Sekunden. Wie schnell bist du?

Tipp: Abwechslung gefällig? Am Einstieg befindet sich ein Klettergarten.

Nils Kagel

Bernie Mauracher

One of the last rapids of Gråura - Jobst Hahn

DRIVA: ROMFO   A SHORT WARM UP RUN

The Romfo section is ideal as a warm up, or as a Plan B at high water. Both river banks are very accessible, the lines through the cataracts easy to recognise, so there is not much to say.

Das Romfo Teilstück ist ideal zum einfahren, oder als Auswegstrecke bei Hochwasser. Die Flussufer sind beidseitig recht gut begehbar, die Linien durch die Katarakte sind leicht zu erkennen – deswegen gibt es nichts zu sagen.

CLASS:	III - IV
LEVEL:	4 km
LENGTH:	30 - 80 cumecs
TIME:	1 - 2 h
SEASON:	May - July

The first rapid of Gråura - Olli Grau

TRONDA: TWITCH SECTION   EXTREMELY STEEP AND NARROW SLOT-BOATING

The Tronda is an extremely steep, extremely short, and extremely tight tributary of the Driva. Only for true-blue waterfall heroes! This Kamikaze creek is similar to Dry Meadow Creek in California, but the Tronda is considerably narrower. What we're talking about here are ten clean waterfalls and slides, from 1 to 9 metres in height, which add up to 50 metres of vertical drop over 200 metres!

Take a good look at the Tronda, go hucking, and then put your boat back on the roof. But warning: the pool after the highest drop has changed. Is it still deep enough?

Tip: Check the Tronda river on Eric Link's movie »Twitch«.

CLASS:	V
LEVEL:	200 m
LENGTH:	2 - 3 cumecs
TIME:	5 min - 1 h
SEASON:	July - September

Die Tronda ist ein extrem steiler, extrem kurzer und extrem enger Nebenbach der Driva. Nur was für waschechte Wasserfallhelden! Dieser Sturzbach ähnelt dem Dry Meadow Creek in Kalifornien, doch ist die Tronda wesentlich schmaler. Es handelt sich um zehn saubere Wasserfälle und Rutschen, von 1 bis 9 Meter Höhe – das macht 50 Meter Gefälle auf 200 Metern!

Schau dir die Tronda gut an, geh stürzen, und lade die Boote wieder aufs Dach. Aber Vorsicht: Der Pool nach dem höchsten Abfall hat sich verändert. Ist er noch tief genug?

Tip: Auf dem Video »Twitch« von Eric Link gibt's die Tronda zu sehen.

Photo: RK

Trygve Sande from VPG

Tore Meirik

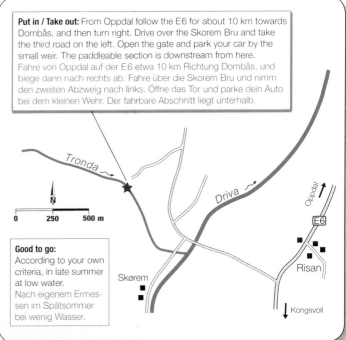

Photo: RK

Put in / Take out: From Oppdal follow the E6 for about 10 km towards Dombås, and then turn right. Drive over the Skorem Bru and take the third road on the left. Open the gate and park your car by the small weir. The paddleable section is downstream from here.

Fahre von Oppdal auf der E6 etwa 10 km Richtung Dombås, und biege dann nach rechts ab. Fahre über die Skorem Bru und nimm den zweiten Abzweig nach links. Öffne das Tor und parke dein Auto bei dem kleinen Wehr. Der fahrbare Abschnitt liegt unterhalb.

Tronda

Driva

Oppdal

E6

Risan

Skørem

Kongsvoll

0   250   500 m

Good to go:
According to your own criteria, in late summer at low water.
Nach eigenem Ermessen im Spätsommer bei wenig Wasser.

GRØVU: UPPER

BEAUTIFUL, STEEP RAPIDS IN BEAUTIFUL SURROUNDS

The Grøvu flows into the Driva at Gjøra in the Sunndalen, and consists of two interesting sections. In between these two is a rather mysterious, very steep section.

The cataracts of the upper Grøvu offer continuous but very nice whitewater. If the sun is shining, the water sparkles blue, and the spectacular surrounds are a sight to behold. A fantastic 5 metre waterfall in the small gorge above the car park is the highlight of this trip. Further downstream there is a portage section which is not easy to recognise. Carry around on the left.

Der Grøvu mündet im Sunndalen bei Gjøra in die Driva und besteht aus zwei interessanten Teilstrecken. Dazwischen verbirgt sich ein etwas mysteriöser, sehr steiler Abschnitt.

Die Katarakte des oberen Grøvu bieten stetiges, doch sehr schönes Wildwasser. Scheint die Sonne, schimmert das Wasser bläulich und die wunderschöne Landschaft zeigt ihre wahre Pracht. Ein toller 5 Meter-Wasserfall in der kleinen Klamm oberhalb des Parkplatzes ist der Höhepunkt dieser Etappe. Weiter stromab folgt eine Umtragestelle, die nicht einfach zu erkennen ist. Links umtragen.

CLASS: IV - V (VI)
LEVEL: 15 - 25 cumecs
LENGTH: 5 km
TIME: 2 - 4 h
SEASON: May - early September

Tip: Buy a map for the area!
Tipp: Kaufe eine Landkarte für dieses Gebiet!

Photo: SG

The first drops after the put in

GRØVU: LOWER

STEEP, FAST, CONTINUOUS

Tyler Curtis + Kjell Sandemshaugen

The lower Grøvu probably boasts Norway's most beautiful put in, though it is not only for this that it is so popular. In the Aamodtan Gorge several waterfalls thunder down into the Grøvu and form quite a little spectacle of nature.

The lower section flows through a stunning gorge section, with beautiful cataracts in an impressive backdrop. It is a little like the Skjøli in character. The

most difficult cataracts lie far from the road, which is why they should not be underestimated. The difficulties follow one another continuously, so take it nice and slowly, particularly if you are in a large group. There have already been fatal accidents on the Grøvu: a sturdy roll is mandatory, he who swims is in a world of pain!

CLASS:	IV (V)
LEVEL:	20 - 30 cumecs
LENGTH:	4 km
TIME:	2 - 3 h
SEASON:	late May - August

Der untere Grøvu hat den wahrscheinlich schönsten Einstieg Norwegens, doch ist nicht nur deshalb sehr beliebt. In der Aamodtan-Schlucht stürzen mehrere Wasserfälle in den Grøvu und bilden ein kleines Naturspektakel.

Der untere Abschnitt durchfließt eine wunderschöne Klammstrecke, mit tollen Katarakten in beeindruckender Kulisse. Vom Charakter ähnelt er etwas dem Skjøli. Die schwersten Katarakte liegen fernab der Straße, gerade deshalb sollten sie nicht unterschätzt werden. Die Schwierigkeiten folgen recht kontinuierlich aufeinander, also immer schön langsam, gerade in großen Gruppen. Es gab auf dem Grøvu schon tödliche Unfälle: Die Rolle ist Pflicht – wer schwimmt, hat ein Problem!

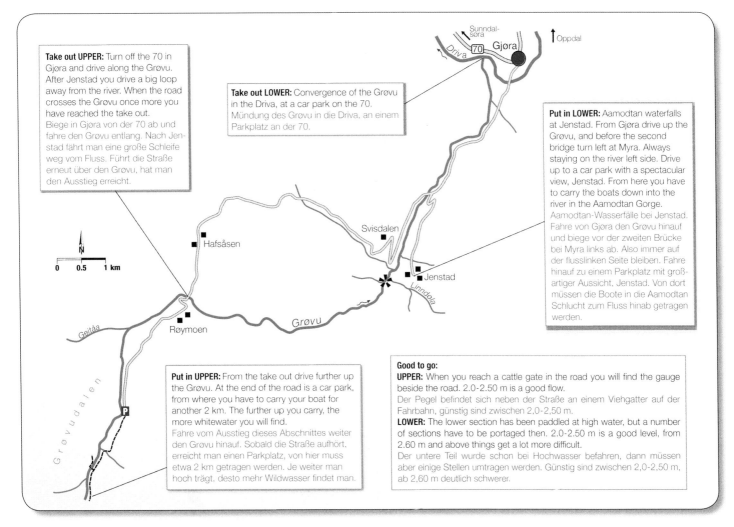

Take out UPPER: Turn off the 70 in Gjøra and drive along the Grøvu. After Jenstad you drive a big loop away from the river. When the road crosses the Grøvu once more you have reached the take out.
Biege in Gjøra von der 70 ab und fahre den Grøvu entlang. Nach Jenstad fährt man eine große Schleife weg vom Fluss. Führt die Straße erneut über den Grøvu, hat man den Ausstieg erreicht.

Take out LOWER: Convergence of the Grøvu in the Driva, at a car park on the 70.
Mündung des Grøvu in die Driva, an einem Parkplatz an der 70.

Put in LOWER: Aamodtan waterfalls at Jenstad. From Gjøra drive up the Grøvu, and before the second bridge turn left at Myra. Always staying on the river left side. Drive up to a car park with a spectacular view, Jenstad. From here you have to carry the boats down into the river in the Aamodtan Gorge.
Aamodtan-Wasserfälle bei Jenstad. Fahre von Gjøra den Grøvu hinauf und biege vor der zweiten Brücke bei Myra links ab. Also immer auf der flusslinken Seite bleiben. Fahre hinauf zu einem Parkplatz mit großartiger Aussicht, Jenstad. Von dort müssen die Boote in die Aamodtan Schlucht zum Fluss hinab getragen werden.

Sunndalsøra

Gjøra

Oppdal

Driva

Svisdalen

Hafsåsen

Jenstad

Linndøla

Røymoen

Grøvu

Geitåa

Grøvudalen

N

0   0.5   1 km

P

Put in UPPER: From the take out drive further up the Grøvu. At the end of the road is a car park, from where you have to carry your boat for another 2 km. The further up you carry, the more whitewater you will find.
Fahre vom Ausstieg dieses Abschnittes weiter den Grøvu hinauf. Sobald die Straße aufhört, erreicht man einen Parkplatz, von hier muss etwa 2 km getragen werden. Je weiter man hoch trägt, desto mehr Wildwasser findet man.

Good to go:
UPPER: When you reach a cattle gate in the road you will find the gauge beside the road. 2.0-2.50 m is a good flow.
Der Pegel befindet sich neben der Straße an einem Viehgatter auf der Fahrbahn, günstig sind zwischen 2,0-2,50 m.
LOWER: The lower section has been paddled at high water, but a number of sections have to be portaged then. 2.0-2.50 m is a good level, from 2.60 m and above things get a lot more difficult.
Der untere Teil wurde schon bei Hochwasser befahren, dann müssen aber einige Stellen umtragen werden. Günstig sind zwischen 2,0-2,50 m, ab 2,60 m deutlich schwerer.

TOÅA

A NICE GRADE IV RUN IN A REMOTE VALLEY

The Toåa, also known as the Todalselva, is a wee pearl hidden in the beautiful, somewhat remote Todalen. It flows out of the Tovatnet in Trollheimen, and is a very popular salmon river – a 21 kilogram Salmon was once caught here! Only anglers and hikers stray this far up, because they know how beautiful it is.

The Toåa offers quite continuous whitewater and nicely formed cataracts. Scouting and portaging is never a problem. Pretty much everything is well runnable, only the double drop in the last third really requires closer examination. Make sure you don't miss the take out before the two waterfalls, the Talgøyfossen.

CLASS: IV (V-)
LEVEL: 3 km
LENGTH: 8 - 15 cumecs
TIME: 2 - 3 h
SEASON: May - early July

Tip: When the weather is nasty you can rent a room at the Kårvatn Farm. The owner there is paddler-friendly. *www.kaarvatn.no*

Die Toåa, oder auch Todalselva, ist eine kleine versteckte Perle im wunderschönen, etwas abgelegenen Todalen. Sie entspringt dem Tovatnet in Trollheimen und ist ein sehr beliebter Lachsfluss – selbst ein 21 Kilogramm Lachs wurde hier schon gefangen. Nur Angler und Wanderer verirren sich hier hoch, denn die wissen wie schön es ist.

Die Toåa bietet recht kontinuierliches Wildwasser und schön geformte Katarakte. Besichtigen und Umtragen der Stellen stellt nie ein Problem dar. Im Grunde ist alles gut fahrbar, lediglich eine Doppelstufe im letzten Drittel sollte genauer unter die Lupe genommen werden. Der Ausstieg vor den zwei Wasserfällen, dem Talgøyfossen, sollte auf keinen Fall verpasst werden.

Tipp: In der Kårvatn Farm kann man bei schlechtem Wetter ein Zimmer mieten. Der Chef des Hauses ist Paddler gut gesonnen. *www.kaarvatn.no*

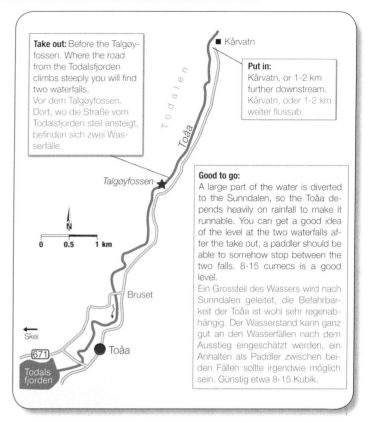

Take out: Before the Talgøyfossen. Where the road from the Todalsfjorden climbs steeply you will find two waterfalls.
Vor dem Talgøyfossen. Dort, wo die Straße vom Todalsfjorden steil ansteigt, befinden sich zwei Wasserfälle.

Put in:
Kårvatn, or 1-2 km further downstream.
Kårvatn, oder 1-2 km weiter flussab.

Good to go:
A large part of the water is diverted to the Sunndalen, so the Toåa depends heavily on rainfall to make it runnable. You can get a good idea of the level at the two waterfalls after the take out, a paddler should be able to somehow stop between the two falls. 8-15 cumecs is a good level.
Ein Grossteil des Wassers wird nach Sunndalen geleitet, die Befahrbarkeit der Toåa ist wohl sehr regenabhängig. Der Wasserstand kann ganz gut an den Wasserfällen nach dem Ausstieg eingeschätzt werden, ein Anhalten als Paddler zwischen beiden Fällen sollte irgendwie möglich sein. Günstig etwa 8-15 Kubik.

VINDØLA: GORGE

A DEEP GORGE WITH GREAT WHITEWATER

The Vindøla is a tributary of the Surna in the Surnadalen, and is often confused with the Vindøla in the Sunndalen, which flows into the Driva. It flows through a deep gorge, and this section could be termed something of an adventure creek. A trip here is very strenuous, the banks are often difficult to move around on.

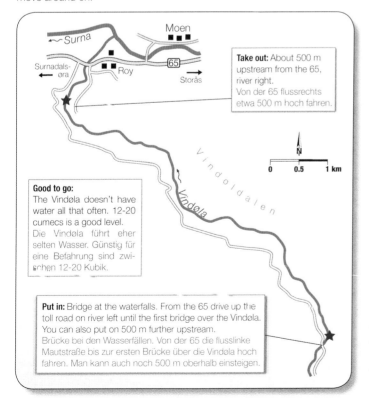

Take out: About 500 m upstream from the 65, river right.
Von der 65 flussrechts etwa 500 m hoch fahren.

Good to go:
The Vindøla doesn't have water all that often. 12-20 cumecs is a good level.
Die Vindøla führt eher selten Wasser. Günstig für eine Befahrung sind zwischen 12-20 Kubik.

Put in: Bridge at the waterfalls. From the 65 drive up the toll road on river left until the first bridge over the Vindøla. You can also put on 500 m further upstream.
Brücke bei den Wasserfällen. Von der 65 die flusslinke Mautstraße bis zur ersten Brücke über die Vindøla hoch fahren. Man kann auch noch 500 m oberhalb einsteigen.

If you want to portage the waterfalls at the put in, you will have to then abseil down to the river on the left bank. Then you have open cataracts. After about half of the trip you reach the first unrunnable section. Then there is a 3 metre river-wide drop with an unclean landing. It is difficult to scout. Best approach is to boof the edge two thirds from river left (i.e. right of centre), and not to think of anything bad happening.

After the gorge there is a waterfall with a difficult approach, about 7 metres high. Shortly afterwards you reach a good take out, about 600 metres before the convergence.

Tip: Paddlers are rather unpopular here, so always wear a friendly smile!

CLASS: IV - V (X)
LEVEL: 6 km
LENGTH: 12 - 20 cumecs
TIME: 3 - 5 h
SEASON: June - July

Die Vindøla ist ein Nebenbach der Surna im Surnadalen und wird gern mit der Vindøla im Sunndalen verwechselt, die in die Driva mündet. Sie fließt durch eine tiefe Schlucht, man könnte diesen Abschnitt als Abenteuerbach bezeichnen. Eine Befahrung ist recht mühsam, die Ufer sind oft nur schwer begehbar.

Wer die Wasserfälle am Einstieg umtragen will, muss ein paar Meter danach flusslinks zum Fluss runterseilen. Es folgen offene Katarakte. Nach etwa der Hälfte der Strecke erreicht man die erste unfahrbare Stelle. Danach folgt eine 3-Meter-Stufe über die gesamte Flussbreite, allerdings mit unsauberem Unterwasser. Schwer zu besichtigen. Am besten am Ende des rechten Drittels hinunterboofen (von rechts gesehen!), also etwas rechts von der Mitte – und an nichts Schlimmes denken.

Nach der Schlucht folgt ein Wasserfall mit schwieriger Anfahrt, etwa 7 Meter hoch. Kurz danach erreicht man einen guten Ausstieg, etwa 600 Meter vor der Mündung.

Tipp: Paddler sind hier irgendwie unbeliebt, also immer freundlich lächeln!

GAULA: UPPER

The Gaula winds its way casually through the Gauladalen, and only offers interesting whitewater in its upper reaches. But here too, cataracts and waterfalls, all steep and pushy, are relieved by flat quiet sections in between. In this way you get a nice rest in between each section. Scouting is easy, but portaging can sometimes be rather strenuous. All of the sections have been run, but for this you need a good safety team, and plenty of time. Nonetheless, the upper Gaula comes highly recommended.

CLASS: IV - V
LEVEL: 25 - 40 cumecs
LENGTH: 3 km
TIME: 2 - 4 h
SEASON: May - September

Tip: From the put in you can drive further up the valley, there you will find several more sections.

Die Gaula schlendert recht gelassen durch das Gauldalen und bietet nur in ihrem Oberlauf für Paddler interessantes Wildwasser. Aber auch hier oben wechseln die Katarakte und Wasserfälle, alle steil und wuchtig, mit ruhigen Flachstücken ab. So ist nach jeder Stelle eine Ruhepause vergönnt. Das Besichtigen ist recht einfach, allerdings kann ein Umtragen hin und wieder anstrengend sein. Es wurden schon alle Stellen befahren, dazu braucht man aber eine gute Sicherungsmannschaft und etwas Zeit. Trotzdem ist die obere Gaula nur zu empfehlen.

Tipp: Man kann vom Einstieg auch weiter flussaufwärts fahren, es folgen noch einige Abbrüche.

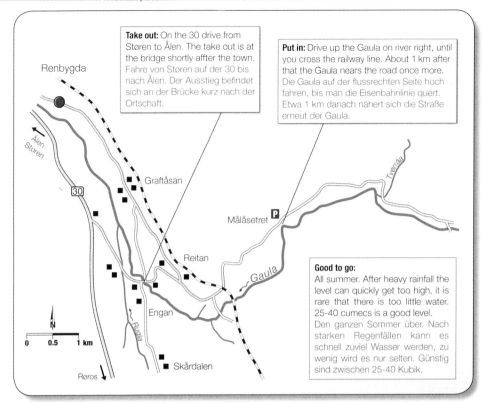

Take out: On the 30 drive from Støren to Ålen. The take out is at the bridge shortly after the town. Fahre von Støren auf der 30 bis nach Ålen. Der Ausstieg befindet sich an der Brücke kurz nach der Ortschaft.

Put in: Drive up the Gaula on river right, until you cross the railway line. About 1 km after that the Gaula nears the road once more. Die Gaula auf der flussrechten Seite hoch fahren, bis man die Eisenbahnlinie quert. Etwa 1 km danach nähert sich die Straße erneut der Gaula.

Good to go: All summer. After heavy rainfall the level can quickly get too high, it is rare that there is too little water. 25-40 cumecs is a good level. Den ganzen Sommer über. Nach starken Regenfällen kann es schnell zuviel Wasser werden, zu wenig wird es nur selten. Günstig sind zwischen 25-40 Kubik.

BUA: CANYON

The Bua converges with the lower section of the Gaula, and flows through the beautiful Gaudalen. The gorge of the Bua is a true classic, with beautiful cataracts between steep rock faces. The first descenders in the 70's required seven attempts to paddle the whole section – hard labour! Thank you!

Shortly after the start there is a drop combination, up to WW V. After about 2 kilometres the convergence of the Ena signals the »point of no return«, from here we're off down the gorge. Scouting the gorge is, however, very easy, even though none of the sections (actually) needs to be portaged. But, breaking off the trip is virtually possible, so do not forget to take a split paddle with you.

After the gorge you reach the Bua Bru. The last 4 kilometres after that are open again, and can be seen from the road.

Tip: The last 4 kilometres after the gorge are also good to paddle at high water. For this you can put on at the Bua Bru.

CLASS: III - IV+ (V)
LEVEL: 10 - 25 cumecs
LENGTH: 16 km
TIME: 3 - 4 h
SEASON: May - September

Die Bua mündet in den Unterlauf der Gaula, sie fließt durch das schöne Budalen. Die Klamm der Bua ist ein echter Klassiker, mit schönen Katarakten zwischen steilen Felswänden. Die Erstbefahrer benötigten in den Siebziger Jahren sieben Anläufe um die gesamte Strecke zu befahren – Knochenarbeit. Danke!

Kurz nach dem Start wartet eine Stufenkombination, bis WW V. Nach etwa 2 Kilometern signalisiert die Mündung der Ena den »Point of no return«, nun geht es in die Klamm. Ein Besichtigen in der Klamm ist trotzdem recht einfach, auch wenn (eigentlich) keine Stelle umtragen werden muss. Allerdings ist ein Fahrtabbruch so gut wie unmöglich, also sollte auf keinen Fall das Ersatzpaddel vergessen werden.

Nach der Klamm erreicht man die Bua Bru. Die letzen 4 Kilometer danach sind dann wieder offen und von der Straße aus sichtbar.

Tipp: Die letzen 4 Kilometer nach der Klamm sind auch bei viel Wasser gut fahrbar. Dazu kann man an der Bua Bru starten.

Manuel Arnu

Photo: MN

ENA: UPPER + MIDDLE DESCRIBED AS ONE

Take out BUA:
Road bridge of the 30.
Straßenbrücke der 30.

Good to go BUA:
In the summer months. Check out the water level at the take out bridge: If the left hand concrete foot of the bridge is underwater, best not to get on. If the water is about 10 cm below it, you've got a good medium flow.
In den Sommermonaten. Wasserstand am besten an der Ausstiegsbrücke einschätzen: Ist der flusslinke Betonsockel der Brücke mit Wasser bedeckt, besser nicht einsteigen. Liegt das Wasser etwa 10 cm darunter, handelt es sich um gutes Mittelwasser.

Take out ENA: From Budal follow the Ena on river left. The first bridge over the Ena is in Budal, keep driving straight ahead. The take out is at the next bridge.
Folge der Ena von Budal flusslinks. Bei Budal liegt die erste Brücke über die Ena, fahre weiter geradeaus. Der Ausstieg befindet sich an der nächsten Brücke.

Put in BUA:
Bridge at Enodden.
Brücke bei Enodden.

Put in ENA: From the take out follow the road upstream, and whenever the road splits stay close to the river. Cross a bridge and continue along the private gravel road (and pay the toll!). About 3 km after the bridge you will see a steep slide combination, here the boats must be carried down to the river.
Folge der Straße vom Ausstieg weiter flussauf, wenn die Straße sich teilt immer in Flussnähe bleiben. Überquere eine Brücke und folge weiter der privaten Schotterpiste (und bezahle die Maut!). Etwa 3 km nach der Brücke erspäht man eine steile Rutschenkombination, hier müssen die Boote zum Fluss hinunter getragen werden.

Good to go ENA:
In spring and after rainfall. The Ena can be run at high and low flows, 10-15 cumecs is a good level.
Im Frühling und nach Regenfällen. Die Ena kann sowohl bei viel, als auch bei wenig Wasser gefahren werden, günstig sind etwa 10-15 Kubik.

(Map labels: Støren, Kjellbrua, Gaula, 30, Kotsøy, Sørlia, Bua Bru, Buset, Røros, Storrød, Bua, Budalen, E6, Soknedal, Enodden, Budal, Enlian, Ena, Budalsdalen, Storlilia, Moaløkka, Endalen, Enmoen. Scale: 0 0.5 1 km. N compass.)

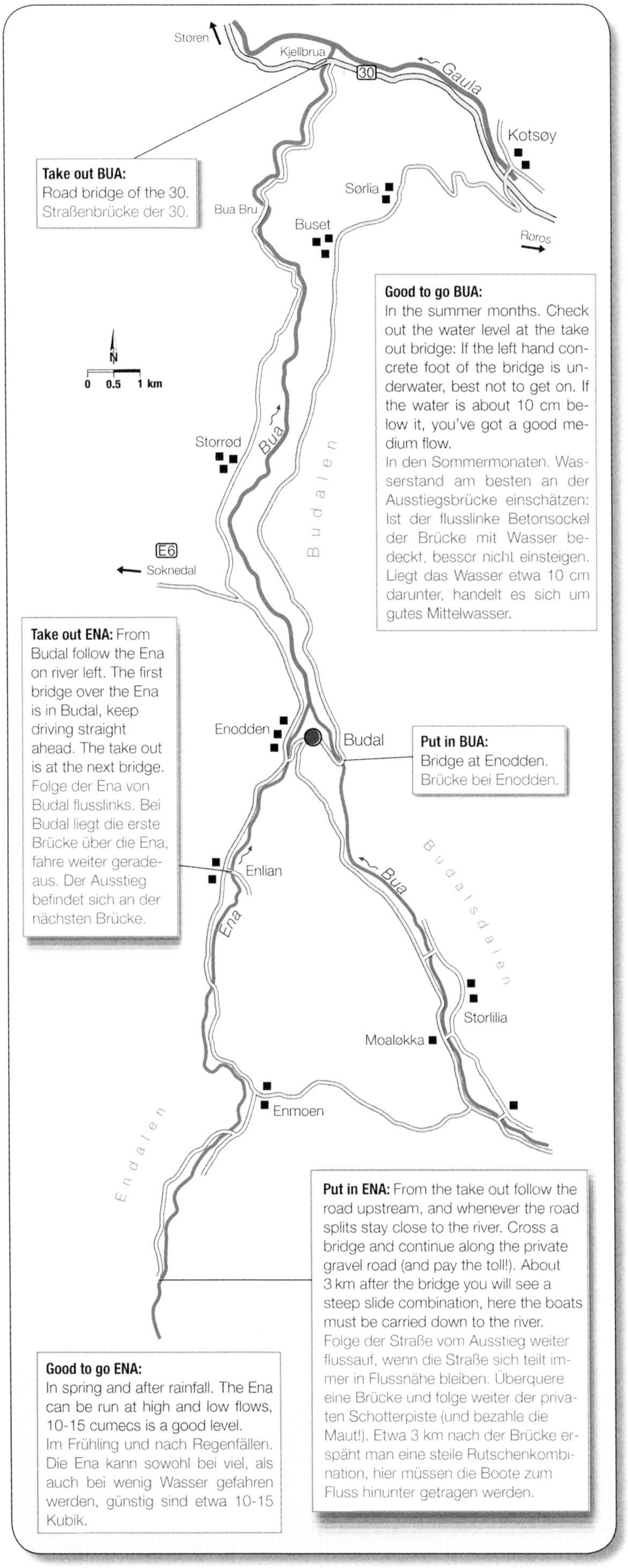

The Ena is a left tributary to the Bua and flows through fascinating open landscape. It offers an awesome, steep cataract and a couple of smaller waterfalls and drops. All sections are easy to scout and portage, and are always followed by pools to collect gear and paddlers. This makes the Ena ideal for paddlers who want to gradually work their way up above grade four.

The further you drive up the valley, the more whitewater you will find. The most difficult sections come right at the beginning. Everything has already been paddled, but the difficulty of the individual sections depends on the water level.

The Ena can be paddled at high and low flows, according to personal taste. Of course the holes and towbacks get more powerful as the water level increases, but this does not deter the experienced paddler.

> **CLASS:** III - IV+ (V-)
> **LEVEL:** 9 km
> **LENGTH:** 5 - 15 cumecs
> **TIME:** 2 - 4 h
> **SEASON:** May - July

Tip: The very steep lower section of the Ena is also runnable, but you then have to continue the trip through the Bua Gorge.

Die Ena ist ein linker Nebenfluss der Bua und fließt durch eine offene, sehr reizvolle Landschaft. Sie bietet ziemlich geile und steile Katarakte und ein paar kleinere Wasserfälle und Stufen. Alle Stellen sind sehr einfach zu Besichtigen und zu Umtragen, danach folgen immer ruhige Pools zum Sammeln. Das macht die Ena ideal für Paddler, die sich langsam über den vierten Grad steigern wollen.

Je weiter man das Tal hoch fährt, je mehr Wildwasser wird man finden. Die schwersten Stellen kommen gleich zu Beginn. Es wurde schon alles befahren, die Befahrbarkeit der einzelnen Stellen hängt aber vom Wasserstand ab.

Die Ena kann sowohl bei viel, als auch bei wenig Wasser befahren werden, je nach persönlichem Geschmack. Natürlich werden die Walzen und Rückläufe mit steigender Wasserwucht etwas kräftiger, aber das macht dem erfahrenen Paddler nicht viel aus.

Tipp: Auch der sehr steile untere Abschnitt der Ena ist fahrbar, allerdings muss die Fahrt dann durch die Bua-Klamm fortgesetzt werden.

Photo: MN

Manuel Arnu

TY WARP
Transcendent Paddle Design

www.tywarp.com

Ty Warp GmbH

Nico Langner
Samerstrasse 53 A
83122 Samerberg
Germany

info@tywarp.com
Tel.: +49 (0) 8032 707310
Fax: +49 (0) 8032 989554

FORA (FORDA): LOWER

The Fora flows through the stunning Forddalen, and is a tributary to the Gaula. Its upper reaches as far as Volden are also worthwhile (WW II-IV), but here we shall concentrate on the lower section.

In Fløttan carry the boats down to the river – but ask the farmer first! About 300 metres after putting on you will reach a tight section which should be scouted, as should the drop at Kosberg. About 2 kilometres further down a couple of powerful holes put the brakes on, but you can paddle around these to the left.

Tip: Above the gorge, between Volden and Fløttan, there is also nice whitewater to be found.

A NICE RUN

Die Fora durchkämmt das wunderschöne Fordtalen, sie ist ein Nebenfluss der Gaula. Auch ihr Oberlauf bis Volden ist lohnend (WW II-IV), wir wollen uns jedoch auf den Unterlauf beschränken.

Die Boote müssen in Fløttan zum Bach hinunter getragen werden. Erst den Bauern fragen! Etwa 300 Meter nach dem Start folgt eine Engstelle die besichtigt werden sollte, ebenso die Schwelle auf Höhe Kosberg. Etwa 2 Kilometer unterhalb bremsen noch ein paar kräftige Walzen, die aber links umfahren werden können.

Tipp: Oberhalb der Schlucht zwischen Volden und Fløttan befindet sich auch noch schönes Wildwasser.

CLASS:	III - IV
LEVEL:	5 km
LENGTH:	15 - 30 cumecs
TIME:	2 - 3 h
SEASON:	May - June

Take out: At the last bridge in Singsås, shortly before the convergence with the Gaula. An der letzten Brücke bei Singsås kurz vor der Mündung in die Gaula.

Good to go:
The level rises and falls very quickly after rainfall. Otherwise the snowmelt in spring should provide the necessary goodies. 1.80 m is a good level on the gauge, minimum is 1.60 m.
Das Wasser steigt und fällt nach Regenfällen sehr schnell. Ansonsten im Frühjahr zur Schneeschmelze. Günstig sind 1,80 m oder mehr am Pegel, Minimum 1,60 m.

Put in: In Fløttan there is a large farm with a white and a yellow house on it, next to which a small path leads down to the river. Please ask the farmer for permission before using the path.
In Fløttan führt bei einem großen Bauernhof mit einem weißen und einem gelben Haus ein kleiner Weg hinunter zum Fluss. Aber vorher den Bauern um Erlaubnis fragen!

The gorge between Volden and Fløttan:
»Have heard rumors about the gorge above Fløttan. Some people have paddled it, I heard a few stories, but nobody could tell me the right things. A friend of mine had a really bad time there, and just mentioned a 30 metre fall to me. I don't really know more yet.« Benjamin Hjort via email

FORRA STEEP AND SERIOUS, BUT SERIOUSLY FUN

The Forra never ceases to amaze me. The cataracts are all very steep, and as the highlight you can expect a clean 6 metre waterfall. With the exception of one section, everything has already been paddled, although some are actually best portaged. Every section should be scouted, so bring some time and some muesli bars with you.

The first 2 kilometres are the easiest. As soon as you reach a mighty waterfall, you have reached the »point of no return«. From here the difficulties increase to WW V, and leaving the gorge is virtually impossible. The waterfall has already been run, but there is really no shame in portaging it on the left.

Be on the lookout for the portage section 4 kilometres downstream. After that comes the beautiful 6 metre waterfall, which is then quickly forgotten once more, thanks to the 200 metres of world class whitewater which then follow.

Tip: Do lots of scouting, and look forward to the waterfall!

CLASS:	V
LEVEL:	10 - 20 cumecs
LENGTH:	6 km
TIME:	3 - 6 h
SEASON:	June - early September

Photo: KH

Die Forra versetzt mich immer wieder ins Staunen. Die Katarakte sind durchweg recht steil, und als Höhepunkt wartet ein sauberer 6-Meter-Wasserfall. Es wurden bis auf eine Stelle alle schon befahren, auch wenn die ein oder andere besser umtragen werden sollte. Jede Stelle muss besichtigt werden, also bringe etwas Zeit und einen Müsli-Riegel mit.

Die ersten 2 Kilometer sind die leichtesten. Sobald man einen mächtigen Wasserfall erreicht, ist man am »Point of no return«. Ab hier steigen die Schwierigkeiten auf WW V, zudem wird ein Verlassen der Schlucht praktisch unmöglich. Der Wasserfall wurde schon befahren, es ist aber wirklich keine Schande ihn auf der linken Seite zu umtragen.

Achte auf die Umtragestelle etwa 4 Kilometer unterhalb. Danach folgt der schöne 6-Meter-Fall, der dank der folgenden 200 Metern Weltklasse-Wildwasser schnell in Vergessenheit gerät.

Tipp: Schau dir die Stellen genau an und freu dich auf den Wasserfall!

Put in: Elgvadet. Drive north along the E6 from Trondheim and in Stjørdal turn onto the E14 towards Sweden. At the sign for Forradal turn left and follow the road to Vigdenes, the take out. Keep following the road, cross the bridge over the Vigda, and continue for about 5 km on the forest road until you reach Elgvadet. Here the road nears the Forra.
Elgvadet. Fahre von Trondheim auf der E6 Richtung Norden und biege bei Stjørdal auf die E14 Richtung Schweden ab. Biege beim Schild Forradal links ab und folge der Straße bis Vigdenes, dem Ausstieg. Folge weiterhin der Straße, überquere die Brücke der Vigda, bis du nach etwa 5 km auf der Forststraße Elgvadet erreichst. Hier nähert sich die Straße der Forra erneut.

Take out:
Vigdenes, at the convergence of the Vigda.
Vigdenes, an der Mündung der Vigda.

Good to go:
Almost always. However, at peak melt times in spring the level can quickly get too high, in Autumn it will need some rain. It is best to check the flow at the take out: when a small rock splits the last drop into two clear channels, the water level should be about right. When the last drop looks rather mean and nasty, best to exercise caution.
Fast immer. Bei der Hochschmelze im Frühling wird es jedoch schnell zuviel, im Herbst wird sie etwas Regen brauchen. Am besten den Wasserstand am Ausstieg einschätzen: Wenn ein kleiner Fels die letzte Stelle deutlich in zwei Kanäle teilt, sollte der Wasserstand stimmen. Sieht die letzte Stelle ziemlich gemein und eklig aus, sei besser vorsichtig.

Benjamin Hjort

Morten Eilertsen

Photos: DA

STORY: TOUGH AS BOOTS FRESKO VUJKOW

TOUGH AS BOOTS

»Blow until the light goes on!« ordered the stout policewoman. I didn't dare to defy a lady of her stature. But let's start with the beginning of the story.

After a beautiful day on the Bua River, Bernie, Till and I made ourselves as comfortable as we could in the small parking lot as we discussed the adventures of the day. But scores of passing cars kept disturbing the tranquility of our campsite, a seemingly strange occurrence at such a late hour and on such a small road? But we perservered, made some food, and tried to get some much needed R+R. But the cars packed with teenagers kept driving past! We quickly came to the conclusion that there had to be a party around here somewhere. So we got out of our sleeping bags and into fresh clothes while shaving quickly and putting on some aftershave. Finally we were all good to go… three nice, peaceful kayakers in our old '84 VW Passat waiting for the next speeding Volvo to start our pursuit. The headlights in our rear-view mirror bode good prey. When the car passed us, we started driving. But before our party-van could even reach second gear, the taillight of our victim had long disappeared behind the next bend. Oh well, at least the cloud of dust they left behind was easy enough to follow.

We kept on driving until we got to the local community hall, where a party was already raging. What could the occasion be? We had no idea so we made some inquiries. It turned out that over the weekend the junior boys and girls soccer matches were taking place. So we decided to try to blend in with the crowds of wild dancing teens. As the evening progressed, a young girl offered to fill us in on the local traditions. The night before the game, the girl's team will start drinking at home or on the village square before heading to the community hall, where you get about half a litre of beer for five Euros. Despite the fact that most parents were right there working either as chaperones or behind the bar, they didn't seem to worry the least about their consumptive offspring. When I expressed my concern about the alarming state of a red-haired girl, her dad replied with a weary smile: »A bucket should be enough.« Meanwhile Till was carried off by a girl into the nearest tree-house. Bernie and I couldn't imagine how there would be a game next morning at all. Late at night, we returned back to our camp. On our way back, we ended up at a road block on the bridge close to Enodden, the put in of the Bua. A stout policewoman greeted us. Luckily, since we're model athletes, we didn't have anything to worry about. Well, to be honest, the alcohol at the community hall was way too expensive anyway. With the same scores on our driver's licences as before, we waved good bye to the police and headed to bed. The next morning, we couldn't refrain from watching the game – and to our big surprise, the girls kicked butt. Norwegians truely are as tough as boots!

HART IM NEHMEN

»Blow until the light goes on!«, meinte die Politesse. Bei ihrer Statur, mache ich auch keine Anstalten ihr zu widersprechen. Aber fangen wir mal von vorne an.

Nach einem guten Tag auf der Bua machten wir – Bernie, Till und ich – es uns in einer Parkbucht gemütlich und ließen die erlebten Abenteuer noch einmal Revue passieren. Immer wieder stören Autos die Ruhe unseres kleinen Lagers – zu so später Stunde auf dieser kleinen Straße? Hm, seltsam. Erstmal essen, in Ruhe verdauen und schla… – schon wieder Autos, randvoll mit Jugendlichen! Ganz klar, da muss eine Party im Gange sein! Also raus aus den Schlafsäcken, frische Klamotten an, schnell rasiert und edle Düfte aufgetragen. Da sitzen wir, drei nette, friedfertige Wassersportler in unserem alten VW Passat Baujahr 84 und warten auf den nächsten tiefer gelegten Volvo um die Verfolgung aufzunehmen. Die Scheinwerfer im Rückspiegel verheißen fette Beute: Doch ehe unser Partymobil den zweiten Gang erreicht hatte, waren die Rücklichter unserer Opfer schon hinter der nächsten Kurve verschwunden. Na ja, aber zumindest war es nicht schwer der Staubwolke zu folgen.

In der Gemeindehalle ging schon richtig die Post ab. Grund für die Feier? Am Wochenende sind die Spiele der Junioren-Fußballmannschaften, Jungs wie Mädels. Also schnell unters Volk gemischt und mitgetanzt. Eines der Mädels klärte uns mal auf: Die Damenmannschaft macht erst ein kollektives Besäufnis daheim oder auf dem Dorfplatz, bevor sie in der Gemeindehalle ungefähr fünf Euro für'n halben Liter Bier ausgeben. Obwohl die meisten Eltern als Security oder an der Theke arbeiten, also hautnah am Ort des Geschehens dabei sind, machen sie sich keine Sorgen um ihren Nachwuchs. Auf meine Bedenken über den Zustand der kleinen Rothaarigen bekam ich von ihrem Vater nur ein müdes Lächeln: »A bucket should be enough« meinte er nur. (»Ein Eimer sollte reichen«). Till wurde von einem Mädel ins nächste Baumhaus verschleppt, und Bernie und ich konnten uns gar nicht vorstellen, wie Morgen überhaupt ein Spiel zustande kommen sollte. Daher machten wir uns mit einem müden Lächeln auf den Weg zurück ins Camp. Und prompt fuhren wir geradewegs in eine Alkoholkontrolle auf der Brücke bei Enodden, dem Einstieg der Bua. Wir als Vorzeigeathleten hatten ja nix zu befürchten, und außerdem ist Alkohol hier einfach zu teuer.

Natürlich konnten wir es uns am nächsten Morgen nicht entgehen lassen die Spiele anzugucken – und siehe da, die Mädels pflügten den Rasen mit Grätschen um, als wäre es ihr hauseigener Acker. Die Norweger sind wirklich in jeder Hinsicht hart im nehmen!

FRESKO VUJKOW 1977

Fresko is an enfant terrible in the German whitewater scene. Mainly because he always says what he thinks – straight out and offhand. Other than that, he is one of the nicest paddlers you can encounter on the river and he is always game for a laugh.
Fresko ist ein Enfant terrible der deutschen Wildwasserszene. Und eigentlich nur deshalb, weil er immer sagt was er denkt – dies allerdings sehr direkt und ohne Umwege. Ansonsten ist er einer der freundlichsten Paddler die man auf dem Bach treffen kann, und für jeden Spaß zu haben.

PARK + PLAY

PLAYSPOTS IN NORWAY

In Norway you will find, besides the countless whitewater rivers, a huge variety of playspots which can be easily reached by car. Here is a small selection:

In Norwegen findet man neben unzähligen Wildflüssen auch eine Vielzahl von Spielstellen, die problemlos mit dem Auto erreichbar sind. Hier eine kleine Auswahl:

1) SARPSBORG [OSLO]

What? Giant wave at the right level.
Where? Near Oslo on the Glomma. Follow the E6 from Oslo towards Sarpsborg. When you cross the large bridge over the Glomma you can see it already. Drive up river left.
When? When the Glomma has about 1000 cumecs. It is best to check on the net first: www.GLB.no, under Solbergfoss.
Special remarks? Beware of the anglers!

Was? Riesenwelle bei richtigem Wasserstand.
Wo? Bei Oslo auf der Glomma. Von Oslo nach Sarpsborg auf der E6 fahren. Passiert man die große Brücke über die Glomma, kann man sie schon sehen. Flusslinks hoch fahren.
Wann? Wenn die Glomma hier etwa 1000 Kubik führt. Am besten vorher im Netz nachschauen: www.GLB.no, unter Solbergfoss.
Besonderheit? Achtung vor Anglern.

2) GRETTEFOSSEN [TELEMARK]

What? Big wave or small hole, depending on the flow.
Where? On the Numedalslågen at Svene, about 16 kilometres north of Kongsberg. The playspot is directly below the road bridge of the 40.
When? At normal flows the hole is a little downstream of the bridge, at high flow the big wave is directly under the bridge.

Was? Große Welle oder kleine Walze, je nach Wasserstand.
Wo? Auf dem Numedalslågen bei Svene, etwa

The Don

16 Kilometer nördlich von Kongsberg. Die Spielstelle befindet sich direkt unterhalb der Straßenbrücke der 40.
Wann? Bei Normalwasser steht die Walze etwas unterhalb der Brücke, bei Hochwasser die große Welle direkt unter der Brücke.

3) SANGFOSSEN [HEDMARK]

What? Little wave train with a big eddy, perfect for beginners.
Where? On the Trysilelva at Trysil. From Trysil drive for about 18 kilometres towards Sweden, then turn right onto a forest track (about 1 kilometre after the Grotoya bridge). Behind the little peninsula there is a nice wave train.
When? All year round really. However, at high flows in May the wave can flatten out. At very low flows in high summer the first wave can turn into a nice hole.
Special remarks? Mosquitoes!
Tip: About 700 metres downstream, 100 metres after the dam, there is a very powerful hole with a nice shoulder on river left. However the eddy is very small, and at high flows it disappears altogether.

Was? Kleiner Wellenzug mit großem Kehrwasser, perfekt für Anfänger.
Wo? Auf dem Trysilelva bei Trysil. Von Trysil etwa 18 Kilometer Richtung Schweden fahren und dann rechts auf einen Waldweg zum Fluss abbiegen (etwa 1 Kilometer hinter der Grotoya Brücke). Hinter der kleinen Halbinsel befindet sich ein schöner Wellenzug.
Wann? Eigentlich ganzjährig. Bei hohen Wasserständen im Mai kann die Welle aber ausflachen. Bei sehr niedrigen Wasserständen im Hochsommer wird aus der ersten Welle eine schöne Walze.

Sjoa

Besonderheit? Mücken!
Tipp: Etwa 700 Meter unterhalb, 100 Meter nach dem Damm, befindet sich auf der flusslinken Seite eine sehr kräftige Walze mit einer netten Schulter. Allerdings ist das Kehrwasser recht klein, und bei viel Wasser gar nicht mehr da.

4) FAUKSTAD WAVE [SJOA]

What? Fast wave with a powerful foam pile.
Where? On the Sjoa in Faukstad. Fight your way down to the river at the »Sjoa Kajakksenter«.
When? At medium flows on Sjoa. www.GLB.no
Special remarks? This wave is the scene of the legendary Sjoa Festival.

Was? Schnelle Welle mit kräftigem Schaumberg.
Wo? Auf der Sjoa in Faukstad. Am »Sjoa Kajakksenter« zum Fluss hinterkämpfen.
Wann? Bei Mittelwasser der Sjoa. www.GLB.no
Besonderheit? Diese Welle ist Schauplatz des legendären Sjoa-Festivals.

Photos: MK

Klatt in 1998 - Sangfossen

5) SKJÅK EURO WAVE   [OTTA]

What? Fast wave with a fat hole.
Where? On the Otta at Skjåk, just below the convergence of the Skjøli. Turn off the E 15 towards the Storøya Camping Ground and park before the bridge.
When? All year round really. The quality varies with the water level. Caution: new dam at Hegebottn!

Was? Schnelle Welle mit dicker Walze.
Wo? Auf der Otta bei Skjåk, kurz unterhalb der Mündung des Skjøli. Von der E 15 zum Storøya-Campingplatz abbiegen und vor der Brücke parken.
Wann? Eigentlich ganzjährig. Qualität variiert mit Wasserstand. Achtung: Neuer Staudamm bei Hegebottn!

Markus Hummel - Skjåk

6) BULKEN   [VOSS]

What? A wide, long wave with a hole mid-river.
Where? At Bulken on the Vosso, at the outlet of the Vangsvatnet. Follow the E 16 to the west from Voss. The wave is below the bus stop directly before a bridge.
When? When the tributaries of the Vangsvatnet are at high flow the wave can quickly flatten out, with too little water it gets thirsty. You will find a link under *www.vosskajakkklubb.com*: Vosso: 130-155 cumecs.

Was? Eine breite und lang gezogene Welle mit Walze in Flussmitte.
Wo? Bei Bulken auf dem Vosso, am Ausfluss des Vangsvatnet. Von Voss der E 16 Richtung Westen folgen. Die Welle befindet sich unterhalb der Bushaltestelle direkt vor einer Brücke.
Wann? Bei hohen Wasserständen der Zuflüsse des Vangsvatnet läuft die Welle schnell zu flach hinaus, bei zu wenig Wasser verdurstet sie. Auf *www.vosskajakkklubb.com* befindet sich ein Link: Vosso: 130-155 Kubik.

7) FLAGE HOLE   [VOSS]

What? Nice, gentle hole for relaxed playing.
Where? Near Voss on the Vosso. The hole is by the E 16 exactly 1.1 kilometres after Bulken. You can park at the entrance to a small private road and then make your way to the river. Warning: private land: limited parking space!
When? Anytime really, don't you think? Under *www.vosskajakkklubb.com* there is a link: Vosso: 80-170 cumecs.
Special remarks: Right after the hole there is a rather nasty drop which you wouldn't really want to run in your play boat. You need a quick roll, so don't blow your last reserves of energy.

Was? Schöne ruhige Walze für eine entspannte Spieleinlagen.
Wo? Bei Voss auf dem Vosso. Die Walze befindet sich an der E 16 genau 1,1 Kilometer hinter Bulken. Am Eingang zu einem kleinen Privatweg kann geparkt werden, dann zum Fluss durchschlagen. Achtung Privatgrund: Begrenzte Parkmöglichkeiten!
Wann? Eigentlich immer, oder? Auf *www.vosskajakkklubb.com* befindet sich ein Link: Vosso: 80-170 Kubik.
Besonderheit? Direkt hinter der Walze lauert ein unschöner Abfall, der im Spielboot nicht wirklich befahren werden möchte. Eine schnelle Rolle ist gefragt, also nicht die letzten Kraftreserven verballern.

Cheesy Robertson - Skjåk

Photo: DP

Arnd Schäftlein - Bulken

Andy Phillips - Skjåk

Photo: DP

8) SPEED CAMERA [VOSS]

What? Wave and hole, depending on the water level.
Where? On the Vosso about 6 kilometres before Evanger. The wave is on the left hand side after a blue iron bridge. Shortly after the bridge there is a permanently installed speed camera.
When? At low flow on the Vosso.
Special remarks: Don't get caught by the speed camera!

Was? Welle und Walze, je nach Wasserstand.
Wo? Auf dem Vosso etwa 6 Kilometer vor Evanger. Die Welle befindet sich linker Hand nach einer blauen Metallbrücke, kurz nach der Welle folgt ein fest-installierter Blitzer auf der Straße.
Wann? Bei Niedrigwasser des Vosso.
Besonderheit? Nicht blitzen lassen!

Arnd Schäftlein - Evanger

9) EVANGER BLUNTWAVE [VOSS]

What? Fast wave with a nice shoulder.
Where? Near Voss on the Vosso. The wave is about 500 metres before the Evangervatnet, 9.3 kilometres after Bulken. There is a parking bay on the left, just before a slight left hand bend, and the wave is just before this.
When? It is best when the Bulken wave has too much water. There is a link under www.vosskajakkklubb.com:
Vosso: 180-210 cumecs.

Was? Schnelle Welle mit schöner Schulter.
Wo? Bei Voss auf dem Vosso. Die Welle befindet sich etwa 500 Meter vor dem Evangervatnet, also genau 9,3 Kilometer hinter Bulken. Vor einer leichten Linkskurve befindet sich links eine Parkbucht, die Welle liegt knapp davor.
Wann? Am besten wenn die Bulkenwelle zu viel hat. Auf www.vosskajakkklubb.com befindet sich ein Link: Vosso: 180-210 Kubik.

At the bus stop

10) BUS-STOP-HOLE [VOSS]

What? Small hole which can be tuned with gates.
Where? About 13 kilometres before Voss on the Strondelvi. The hole is right beside the E 16 just upstream of a bus stop, about 200 metres before the bridge to Taulen camping ground.
When? At medium flows on the Strondelvi. There is a link under www.vosskajakkklubb.com: Strondelvi: around 20 cumecs.
Special remarks? The locals have made a wooden gate to channel the flow here. This should be dismounted at the end of each session. Please don't simply leave it hanging in the river as it can be destroyed by fluctuations in the water level.

Was? Kleine Walze, die mit Abweisern optimiert werden kann.
Wo? Bei Voss auf der Strondelvi, etwa 13 Kilometer vor Voss. Die Walze befindet sich direkt an der E 16 knapp oberhalb einer Bushaltestelle, etwa 200 Meter vor der Brücke zum Campingplatz Taulen.
Wann? Bei Mittelwasser der Strondelvi. Auf www.vosskajakkklubb.com befindet sich ein Link: Strondelvi: etwa 20 Kubik.
Besonderheit? Die Locals haben hier einen Abweiser aus Holz gebaut, der nach jeder Session wieder entnommen werden muss. Bitte nicht einfach im Fluss hängen lassen, da er bei Hochwasser weggerissen werden kann.

Photo: DP

Hurry up! - Skjåk

APPENDIX

Evening leisure, Rauma.

A BRIEF AID TO THE LANGUAGE _ EINE KLEINE SPRACHHILFE

Every Norwegian can speak English: the guy at the petrol station, the granny in the supermarket, the farmer at the fjord. The reason for this is quite simple: there are few films on TV which are in Norwegian, only the odd German ones but many English ones. It would be too costly to dub foreign films and therefore they only bear Norwegian subtitles. Every evening in front of the TV is like an English lesson. If the Norwegians did not speak English, communication with tourists would be almost impossible. With some fantasy it is possible to perhaps guess the meaning of the written language, but the spoken word is usually incomprehensible.

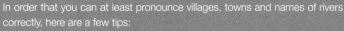

Alle Norweger können Englisch: der Typ an der Tankstelle, die Oma im Supermarkt, der Bauer am Fjord. Dies hat auch einen Grund, denn im norwegischen Fernsehen gibt es wenig norwegische, ein paar deutsche, und viele englische Filme. Die Synchronisation der ausländischen Produktionen wäre zu teuer, drum gibt es lediglich norwegische Untertitel – so gleicht jeder Filmabend einer Englischstunde. Ohne die Englischkenntnisse der Norweger wäre eine Kommunikation mit uns Touristen beinahe unmöglich, denn die Bedeutung von geschriebenem Norwegisch kann man vielleicht mit etwas Fantasie erraten, gesprochen ist es aber meist unverständlich.

In order that you can at least pronounce villages, towns and names of rivers correctly, here are a few tips:
- short Å pronounced similar to o in *lot*, long Å similar to oa in *boat*
- short U pronounced similar to oo in *foot*, long U similar to oo to *cool*
- short O pronounced similar to oo in *look*, long O similar to ow in *tow*
- short Ø pronounced similar to u in *trust*, long Ø similar to oo in *blood*
- short Æ pronounced similar to a in *lattice*, long Æ similar to a in *tap*
- SJ (skj) dipthong pronounced like sh in *shoe*

Damit man wenigstens Orts- und Flussnamen korrekt ausspricht, folgende Tipps:
- das kurze Å spricht man wie das o in *offen*, das lange Å wie das o in *Ofen*
- das U spricht man wie ein ü in *Südfrüchte*
- das O spricht man wie das u in *du*
- das kurze Ø spricht man wie das ö in *öffnen*, das lange Ø wie das ö in *böse*
- das kurze Æ spricht man ähnlich dem ä, sich dem a nähernd
- SJ spricht man wie sch in *schön*

When the consonant following the vowel is short (i.e. single), the vowel is usually long, and when the consonant following the vowel is long (i.e. double), the vowel is usually short. e.g. *lær* (leather), *lærd* (educated).

Vor zwei oder mehreren Konsonanten und vor Doppelkonsonanten sind alle Vokale kurz auszusprechen. Vor Vokalen, vor einfachen Konsonanten und im Auslaut sind die Vokale lang auszusprechen.

The following tables should help you become a little familiar with the language. After all, it is good etiquette to greet the locals in their native tongue.

Die folgenden Übersichtstafeln sollen helfen dem Norwegischen etwas vertrauter zu werden. Schließlich gehört es ein wenig zum guten Benehmen, die Einwohner eines Landes in ihrer Landessprache zu begrüßen.

... every day life / ... im Alltag

English	Deutsch	Norsk
Austria	Österreich	Østerrike
bridge	Brücke	bru
camp ground	Zeltplatz	camping plass
cheers!	Prost!	Skål!
church	(Stab)Kirche	stavkirke
France	Frankreich	Frankrike
Germany	Deutschland	Tyskland
Great Britain	Großbritannien	Storbritannia
glacier	Gletscher	bre(en)
good bye	Auf Wiedersehen	ha det bra, farvel
hello	Guten Tag, Hallo	god dag, hei
lake	See	vatn(et), (...sjø, ...joen)
left	links	venstre
mountains	Gebirge	fjell
peak, summit	Gipfel	topp
plateau	Hochebene	vidda, platå
please	bitte	vær så god
right	rechts	høyre
Santa Claus	Weihnachtsmann	Nissemann
sorry	Entschuldigung	unnskyld
Switzerland	Schweiz	Sveits
thanks, thank you	danke, dankeschön	takk, tusen takk
toll road	Mautstraße	bomveg
valley	Tal	dal(en)
yes / no	ja / nein	ja / nei

... about the river / ... am Fluss

English	Deutsch	Norsk
backwash	Rücklauf	tilbakestrømning
boat	Boot	båt
canyon, ravine	Klamm	juv(et)
confluence	Zusammenfluss	samløp, Åmot
creek	Bach	bekk
eddy	Kehrwasser	bakevje
eddyline	Kehrwasserlinie	strømskille
gorge, ravine	Schlucht	juv(et)
hole, breaking wave	Walze	valse
to portage, a portage point	umtragen, Umtragestelle	bøering, upadlebart strekning
rapid	Katarakt	stryk
river	Fluss	elvi, elva
waterfall	Wasserfall	foss
water level	Wasserstand	vannstander
weir	Wehr	kunstig valse
whitewater kayaking	Wildwasser paddeln	elvepadling

... at the supermarket /... im Supermarkt

English	Deutsch	Norsk
beer	Bier	øl
bread	Brot	brød
butter	Butter	smør
cheese	Käse	ost
cream	Sahne	fløte
fish	Fisch	fisk
ham	Schinken	skinke
meat	Fleisch	kjøtt
mussels	Muscheln	muslinger
milk	Milch	melk
onion	Zwiebel	løk
red wine	Rotwein	rødvin
salt	Salz	salt
strawberry	Erdbeere	jordbær

Why not read a book in Norwegian language?

GLOSSARY _ GLOSSAR

English:

action line	opposite of the chicken line
blocked	when a river's flow is blocked by obstacles, narrow passages are formed, making navigation more difficult, and increasing the risk of siphons
boil	upward flowing current which boils up to the surface like an air bubble
boof (v.)	a technique by which you run a drop or fall without breaking the surface and submerging in the water below; a necessity for overcoming big towbacks and other nasties
buffer	when current flows against an obstacle, forming a »pillow« of water, like a boily wave
canyon (box canyon)	cliff walls rise vertically from the river's edge; impossible or extremely difficult to move around the banks (sim. gorge)
cataract (more difficult rapid)	a series of drops and obstructions
chicken line	line through a rapid by which you can avoid the main difficulty
cliff start (seal launch)	method for getting on the river by which you sit in your kayak on a rock or cliff, and drop off into the water
creek	a mostly small, narrow river with steep gradient
creekboot	high volume boat fitted with safety equipment; special field of use: steep channels and waterfalls
cumecs	abbreviation for cubic metres per second (m³/s), the unit for the flow rate (water volume) of a river at a particular point
down time	time that you stay under water during a meltdown
drop	water falling vertically or at a steep angle, caused by an obstacle in the water which lies perpendicular or at an angle to the direction of the current; up to three metres in height
eddy	section of water which is still or flowing upstream, found behind obstructions or at the bank of the river
eddy line	area in which at least two currents meet
freewheel	freeride move over the edge of a waterfall
funcruiser	kayak with good play potential, but which is nonetheless well suited to paddling medium difficulty whitewater
gorge	banks rise steeply from the river's edge; it is usually possible to move around on the banks (sim. canyon)
high flow	describes when the water level of a river is significantly higher than normal; mostly after strong rainfall or as a result of snowmelt on hot days
hole (friendly)	water mass rolling perpendicular or at an angle to the current, flowing upstream on the surface; similar to the foam pile of a wave at the beach after it has broken
hole (nasty)	powerful hole (or towback), which loves to swallow kayaks, paddler and all
kagel (v.)	running a section which is actually unpaddleable, with total physical commitment; »this waterfall was first kagelled in 1998«; »he kagelled the monster waterfall«; orig. Nils Kagel
kicker	rock protrusion or stone which can be used to get air when boofing; beware of kickers on slides!
low flow	after cold or dry periods, low water level for a river
medium flow	the normal, ideal water flow for a river; the river bed seems to be formed to accommodate this level
meltdown, to melt	upon running a waterfall, when paddler and boat disappear completely underwater, this is termed a meltdown
must-run passage	section of a river which must be run because it is impossible or extremely difficult to portage
Park + Huck	bad habit in paddling: driving to the river to park up and just run the one spectacular section
Park + Play	bad habit in paddling: playboating at only one spot on the river, the car is parked within range of sight
potholes	cylindrical hollowing out of the river bed which causes the water to rotate and recirculate; mostly in connection with buffer walls and towbacks
rapid (easy)	series of waves, sometimes slightly blocked
siphon	a kind of underwater tunnel; forms when large boulders are stacked on top of each other; the gaps between the boulders can form deadly traps when the current flows through them
sneak (v.)	running the chicken line
tongue	clear passage of water flowing downstream through a hole or towback
towback	current flowing upstream behind drops and falls
undercut	hollowing out of the bank or of a rock below the surface of the water, caused by current flowing against it
waterfall	similar to a drop, but with no height limit
weir	man-made drop or fall which forms a regular, often dangerous towback

Deutsch:

Action Line	Gegenteil der Chicken Line
bekageln	das Befahren einer eigentlich unfahrbaren Stelle mit vollem Körpereinsatz; »Dieser Wasserfall wurde 1998 bekagelt«; »Er bekagelte den Monsterwasserfall«; Orig. Nils Kagel
boofen	Technik, mit der man Stufen und Abfälle überwindet ohne im Unterwasser einzutauchen; eine Notwendigkeit, nicht nur um große Rückläufe zu überwinden
Chicken Line	Linie durch einen Katarakt, auf der man die Höchstschwierigkeiten umgehen kann
Creek	meist kleiner und enger Fluss mit hohem Gefälle

Creekboot	hochvolumiges Boot mit Sicherheitsausstattung; Spezialgebiet: steile Rinnen und Wasserfälle
Down time	Zeit, die man bei einem Meltdown unter Wasser bleibt
Freewheel	Freeridefigur über die Kante eines Wasserfalls
Funcruiser	Kajak mit hohem Spielpotential, das sich trotzdem noch für mittelschweres Wildwasser eignet
Hochwasser	Wasserführung eines Flusses liegt deutlich über dem Normalwert; meist nach starken Regenfällen oder an heißen Tagen durch Schmelzwasser
Katarakt (rapid)	Folge von Stufen und Hindernissen
Kehrwasser (eddy)	die hinter Hindernissen oder am Ufer zurücklaufende (Ruhe-) Strömung
Kicker	Felsnase oder Stein, die beim boofen zum Absprung genutzt werden kann; Vorsicht jedoch auf Rutschen!
Klamm (box canyon)	Felswände steigen vom Flussufer senkrecht an; Ufer nicht begehbar (vgl. Schlucht)
Klippenstart (cliff start)	Methode des Einbootens, bei der man von einem Felsen im Kajak sitzend ins Wasser springt
Kolk (pothole)	zylindrische Aushöhlung des Flussbettes, die das Wasser kreisförmig rotieren lässt; meist in Verbindung mit Prallwänden und Rückläufen
Kubik (cumecs)	Abkürzung für Kubikmeter pro Sekunde (m³/s), als Angabe für die Durchflussmenge (Wasservolumen) an einem bestimmten Ort
Loch (hole)	kräftige Walze (o. Rücklauf), die mit Vorliebe Kajaks samt Paddler verschluckt
Meltdown, melten	verschwinden Fahrer und Boot bei der Befahrung eines Wasserfalles komplett im Unterwasser, spricht man von einem Meltdown
Mittelwasser	die (normale/ideale) Wasserführung eines Flusses, für die das Flussbett ausgelegt zu sein scheint
Niedrigwasser	nach Kälte- oder Trockenperiode geringe Wasserführung eines Flusses
Park + Huck	Perversion des Paddelns. Befahrung einer spektakulären Stellen eines Flusses, die mit dem Auto erreicht wird
Park + Play	Perversion des Paddelns: Spielbootfahren an nur einer Stelle des Flusses, das Auto steht in Sichtweite
Pilz (boil)	von unten nach oben gerichtete Strömung, die (wie Luftblasen) an die Wasseroberfläche empor kocht
sneaken	befahren der Chicken Line
Prallpolster, Presswasser	entsteht, wenn eine Strömung gegen ein Hindernis trifft
Rücklauf (towback)	hinter Stufen und Abfällen zurücklaufendes Wasser
Schlucht (gorge)	vom Flussufer ansteigende Steilhänge; Ufer meist begehbar (vgl. Klamm)
Siphon	eine Art Tunnel unter der Wasseroberfläche; entsteht, wenn große Felsen aufeinander liegen; die eventuell entstandenen Zwischenräume zwischen den Gesteinen können tödliche Fallen bilden, sobald sich die Strömung hindurch presst
Stromschnelle, Schwall	Wellenzug mit mehreren Wellen in Folge, teils mit leichter Verblockung
Stufe, Abfall (drop)	senkrecht oder schräg abfallendes Wasser, verursacht durch ein quer oder schräg zum Fluss verlaufendes Hindernis; bis 3 Meter Höhe
Unterspülung (undercut)	Aushöhlung des Uferbereichs oder eines Felshindernisses unter der Wasseroberfläche durch eine darauf gerichtete Strömung
Verblockung (blocked)	Hindernisse im Flusslauf ergeben eine hohe Verblockung; es entstehen enge Durchfahrten und die Gefahr von Siphonen erhöht sich
Verschneidung (eddy line)	Zone in der mindestens zwei Strömungen aufeinander treffen
Walze (hole)	quer oder schräg zum Fluss drehende Wassermassen, die an der Oberfläche zurücklaufen; ähnlich dem Schaumberg der Brandungswellen
Wasserfall (waterfall)	ähnlich der Stufe, allerdings ohne Höhenbegrenzung
Wehr (weir)	künstliche Stufe oder Abfall
Zunge (tongue)	ablaufende Oberflächenströmung in einer Walze oder einem Rücklauf
Zwangspassage (must-run)	Abschnitt eines Flusses der befahren werden muss, da ein Umtragen nicht oder nur unter enormem Aufwand möglich ist

For our friends from America: (make love, not war!)

Flow:		Gradient:	
Cumecs (cubic metres per second)	**Cfs** (cubic feet per second)	**Mpk** (metres per kilometre)	**Fpm** (feet per mile)
2	70	5	26
4	141	10	52
8	280	15	80
12	420	20	105
16	565	25	131
20	700	30	158
30	1060	35	184
50	1765	40	211
100	3530	45	237
200	7060	50	263

TABLE OF SEASONS FOR RIVERS _ SAISONTABELLE

RIVER	II-III	IV-VI	APR	MAY	JUN	JUL	AUG	SEP
Asbjørnsåe								
Austbygdåi, Upper								
Austbygdåi, Lower								
Åsta								
Atna, Upper								
Atna, Middle								
Atna, Lower								
Brandsetelvi								
Bua								
Bygdelva								
Bøvra, Upper								
Bøvra, Lower								
Driva, Upper								
Driva, Rafting Trip								
Driva, Gråura								
Driva, Romfo								
Eksingadalen								
Embla								
Ena								
Etna								
Finna								
Frya								
Folla								
Fora								
Forra								
Gaula								
Gøyst								
Grimsa								
Grøvu, Upper								
Grøvu, Lower								
Hemsil								
Horndøla								
Husevollelvi								
Imsa, Upper								
Imsa, Lower								
Jolstra								
Jordalselvi								
Jori, Upper								
Jori, Standard								
Jostedøla								
Langedalselva								
Lågen, Rosten								
Lågen, Hunderfoss								
Lora								
Mår, Upper								
Mår, Homerun								
Mår, Lower								
Mistra								
Mørkedøla								
Myrkdalselvi, Upper								
Myrkdalselvi, Lower								
Numlågen, Zambesi								

RIVER	II-III	IV-VI	APR	MAY	JUN	JUL	AUG	SEP
Numlågen, Laks run								
Ostri								
Otta, Pollfoss								
Otta, Big Gorge								
Otta, Family run								
Pyttåa								
Rauma, Upper								
Rauma, Lower								
Raundal, Upper								
Raundal, Full on								
Raundal, Train section								
Raundal, Playrun								
Raundal, Lower								
Setninga								
Sjoa, Steinholet								
Sjoa, Ridderspranget								
Sjoa, Åsengjuvet								
Sjoa, Playrun								
Sjoa, Åmot								
Skirva								
Skjerva, Upper								
Skjerva, Lower								
Skjoli								
Skogsåa, Upper								
Skogsåa, Lower								
Smeddalselvi, Upper								
Smeddalselvi, Road run								
Sogndalselva, Upper								
Sogndalselva, Lower								
Stordalselva								
Storeelva								
Store Ula								
Strondelvi								
Sumelvi								
Teigdalselvi								
Toåa								
Tora								
Tronda								
Trysilelva								
Tundra								
Tysselva								
Ula								
Ulvåa, Standard								
Ulvåa, Low water run								
Unsetåa								
Urdlandselvi								
Usteåni								
Valldøla, Upper								
Valldøla, Middle								
Valldøla, Family								
Veo								
Vinndøla								

NORWAY ON THE WORLD WIDE WEB _ NORWEGEN IM INTERNET

www.padling.no (Norges Padleforbund)
Norwegian Canoe Association (NCA)
Norwegischer Kanuverband

www.visitnorway.com
Norwegian Tourist Board
Norwegisches Fremdenverkehrsamt

www.nve.no (Norges Vassdrags- og Energidirektorat)
Norwegian Water Resources and Energy Directorate (NVE)
Norwegisches Wasser und Energie Direktorat (NVE)

www.odin.dep.no
Information from the Government and the Ministries.
Informationen von Regierung und Ministerien.

www.ssb.no (Statistisk Sentralbyrå)
Statistics Office Norway
Statistisches Zentralamt Norwegen

www.nafcamp.com (Norges Automobilforbund)
Camping guide of the Norwegian Automobile Federation (NAF)
Campingführer des Norwegischen Automobilverbandes (NAF)

www.visveg.no/norguide (National Road Database)
Official road guide for Norway, with route planner and maps
Offizieller Straßenführer für Norwegen, mit Routenplaner und Karten

www.nsb.no (Norwegian State Railway)
Local bus and train services in Norway
Nahverkehr in Norwegen

www.norwegen-shop.de
Alles rund um Norwegen

More internet portals:
Weitere Internetportale rund um Norwegen:
www.norway.no
www.norway.com
www.norwegen.no
www.norway.org

Kayak stores / Kajakläden:
www.vpg.no   (Vertical Playground, Oppdal, Driva)
www.striestrommer.no   (Heidal, Sjoa)
www.kajakksenteret.no   (Heidal, Sjoa - kayak school)
www.oppdalkajakklubb.com   (Oppdal)
www.vosskajakkklubb.com   (Voss)

BIBLIOGRAPHY _ LITERATURVERZEICHNIS

»Merian live: Norwegen« 1. Auflage, München: Gräfe und Unzer Verlag GmbH, 1998, ISBN 3–7742–0480–2

»Norwegen Süd/Mitte« 6. Auflage, München: Verlag Martin Velbinger, 1996, ISBN 3–88316–021–0

Dressler, Schneider »Norwegen« 1. Auflage, München: Verlag C.J. Bucher, 1993

Stikholmen, Granerud »Norwegen« 1. Auflage, Oslo: Normanns Kunstforlag AS, ISBN 82–7670–070–5

Flakstad, Ongstad »Elvepadling, Guide to Southern Norway«
Norges Kajakk- og Kanoforbund, 1987, ISBN 82–90674–00–7

Olli Grau »Besser Wildwasserfahren« (»White Water Kayaking«) 1. Auflage, Riedering: La Ola Verlag bei Blue and White GmbH, 2005, ISBN 3–9809315–0–1

»Langenscheidts Universal-Wörterbuch: Norwegisch« 11. Auflage, Berlin: Langenscheidts KG, 1992, ISBN 3–468–18241–4

»DKV Auslandsführer Band 4: Skandinavien« 4. Auflage, Duisburg: DKV Wirtschafts- und Verlags GmbH, 2001, ISBN 3–924580–85–5

KANUmagazin
edition 4/1995, 4/1998, 4/2001, 1/2003,
Stuttgart: Sport + Freizeit Verlag GmbH, www.kanumagazin.de

»Veiatlas Norge« Hønefoss: Statens Kartverk Norge, 2004, ISBN 82–7945–028–9

Internet:
www.visitnorway.com
www.ssb.no
www.padling.no

THE AUTHORS _ DIE AUTOREN

Whether it is a raging torrent or a millpond, water is the stuff dreams are made of. Big–O–Productions have made it their mission to record the fascination of canoeing. Olaf Obsommer and Jens Klatt have become slaves to whitewater just as much as they have to their cameras; they spend a lot of time on both activities.

The Foamboater video »Painkillers« was their first collaboration, »Young Fresh 'n New« followed at the beginning of 2002, »Sick Line 3« in 2004. »Painkiller 2« even won them first prize in the National Paddling Film Festival in the USA. This book brings to an end the first leg of their tour of Norway. They have toured the country year after year for almost a decade in order to add new rivers to their list.

Egal in welcher Form, ob reißend oder ruhend: Wasser ist der Stoff, aus dem die Träume sind. Die Faszination des Paddelns festzuhalten, ist die Mission von Big–O–Productions. Olaf Obsommer und Jens Klatt sind dem Wildwasser genauso verfallen wie ihren Kameras, und verbringen demnach viel Zeit mit beidem.

Das Foamboatervideo »Painkillers« war ihre erste Kollaboration, »Young Fresh 'n New« und »Painkiller 2« folgten Anfang 2002, »Sick Line 3« 2004. Mit der Erscheinung dieses Buches geht die erste Etappe ihrer Norwegenreise zu Ende. Fast zehn Jahre lang kamen sie jedes Jahr zurück, um immer neue Flüsse auf ihrer Liste einzutragen.

Jens Klatt (*1980) – www.jensklatt.com

Jens has had the travel fever ever since he took to the water in his native Federal State of Brandenburg. At first he was out and about with the canoe club on lakes and rivers in Germany but it was not long before whitewater enticed him further afield. He went on countless trips to the Alps, Turkey, Norway, New Zealand and Canada.

To canoe and take photos or to take photos and canoe? Getting to the bottom of this question can be confusing. A canoeist who takes photos does not have to be a photographer but there are very few photographers who canoe. Can you claim to be a photographer when people like your photographs or do you need a diploma in photography? One thing is for sure, Jens likes both canoeing and photography and in any case it was canoeing which took him on to photography. His second passion is to captivate the fascination of whitewater on paper and take the results home. What are a thousand words about a weekend spent canoeing when one photo says everything?

Seitdem Jens das erste Mal im heimischen Brandenburg auf dem Wasser war, lenkt ihn das Reisefieber. Anfangs mit dem Verein auf den Seen und Flüssen Deutschlands unterwegs, zog es ihn schon bald mehr und mehr aufs ferne Wildwasser. Es folgten etliche Trips quer durch die Alpen, in die Türkei, nach Norwegen, Neuseeland und Kanada.

Fotografierender Paddler oder paddelnder Fotograf? Dieser Frage auf den Grund zu gehen, kann verwirren: Ein Paddler, der fotografiert, muss kein Fotograf sein; Fotografen die paddeln, gibt es wenige. Kann man sich Fotograf nennen, wenn seine Bilder gemocht werden, oder braucht man da ein Zertifikat? Wie man es auch betrachten mag, eines steht fest: Jens liebt beides – paddeln und fotografieren. Schließlich war es auch das Paddeln, das ihn zum Fotografieren brachte. Die Faszination Wildwasser auf Papier zu bannen und nach Hause zu bringen, ist seine zweite Leidenschaft. Aus der ersten Kompaktkamera wurde eine Spiegelreflex, aus Papier wurden Dias. Denn was sind tausend Worte über ein Paddelwochenende, wenn man alles in einem einzigen Bild sagen kann?

Olaf Obsommer (*1970) – www.big-o-productions.com

Olaf's parents are to blame for everything. At an advanced stage of pregnancy Olaf's mother paddled him up and down the Rhine in her womb and in so doing infected him with the kayak virus. The virus spread during numerous collapsible boat tours which he went on with his parents. He became fully infected after getting his first GFK boat which took him slowly but surely in the direction of whitewater kayaking. Now absolutely incurable of the kayaking virus, he will no doubt some day be watching kayak videos in the old folk's home whilst going into raptures about waterfalls.

Although a fully trained machine fitter and geriatric nurse, he is now earning his living by producing kayaking videos – his second great passion after canoeing. He takes his camera absolutely everywhere, whether going to the lavatory or canoeing class VI. »With my videos I will perhaps succeed in seducing you into the wonderful world of canoeing« With such motivation he sits at his computer night after night in order to share his enthusiasm and films with others. Olaf is the father of the »Sick Line« film trilogy, which was filmed mostly in Norway.

An allem Schuld sind Olafs Eltern: Im Bauch seiner hochschwangeren Mutter schipperte Olaf den Rhein hinab und wurde so schon damals mit dem Kajakvirus infiziert. Den Rest seiner Prägung erfuhr er bei den zahlreichen Faltboottouren seiner Eltern, bis er es schließlich zum eigenen GFK-Kajak brachte, und langsam aber sicher in den Bann des Wildwassers gezogen wurde. Eine Heilung vom Kajakvirus ist völlig auszuschließen, er wird wahrscheinlich noch im Altersheim Kajakvideos schauen und von Wasserfällen schwärmen.

Als ausgebildeter Maschinenschlosser und examinierter Altenpfleger geht er beruflich nun seiner zweiten großen Leidenschaft neben dem Paddeln nach: er produziert Kajakvideos. Die Kamera hat er sowieso immer dabei – ob beim Stuhlgang oder auf WW VI. »Vielleicht gelingt es mir ja, euch mit meinen Videos in die wunderbare Welt des Paddelns zu entführen.« Mit dieser Motivation feilt er Nächtelang an seinem Computer, um seine Begeisterung zu vermitteln und Gefilmtes mit anderen zu teilen. Olaf ist der Vater der »Sick Line« Filmtrilogie, die größtenteils in Norwegen verfilmt wurde.

A FEW WORDS OF GRATITUDE
WORTE DES DANKES

Tusen Takk

Thanks to everybody who has purchased this book rather than simply copying the information – it took a great deal of work to complete. The fact that this book has finally been published is thanks to our many friends and partners. In particular, thanks are due to Hans Mayer from La Ola who supported every one of our crazy ideas and was a great source of motivation. To all those who I have forgotten: It is nearly three o'clock in the morning and the coffee has run out ... sorry!

Dank geht an alle, die sich dieses Buch gekauft und die Informationen nicht einfach kopiert haben – hier steckt viel Arbeit drin! Dass dieses Buch letztendlich zustande kam, ist unseren vielen Freunden und Partnern zu verdanken, denen diese Seite gewidmet ist. Danke insbesondere an Hans Mayer von La Ola, der alle unsere blöden Ideen unterstützt hat, was uns letztendlich auch die Motivation zu diesem Buch gab. An alle die ich vergessen hab: Es ist kurz vor drei in der Nacht und der Kaffee ist alle ... Schuldigung!

Jensen's corner:

Meine zwei Mädels: ihr seid mein Licht! Sorry, dass ich so wenig Zeit für euch hab. Mudder, Vadder - ihr gebt mir unendlich viel Kraft! Ich hoffe ich kann es irgendwann zurückgeben. Schwesterherz, hast du es schon bereut das du mich damals ins Bootshaus mitgenommen hast? August - nur die Besten sterben jung! LSK Jungs - wann kommt der zweite Teil? Michi, Sebbi, Debs - danke für die Bilder. Blaubär+Rumo - danke für die Unterhaltung. Jackson, Schniepe, Vroni+Flo. Cam, Richard - danke fürs Durchhalten. Aber vor allem Dank an die, die mir zeigten wie man den Stock richtig ins Wasser hält: mein Schwesterherz, Micha+der ganze WSV (Stahl Feuer!), Carsten, Bernd. Meine Nussdorf Leute: Olaf, Olli, Ingrid, Manuel, Phillis, Nico. Ohne euch alle wäre das nix geworden... I owe you something!

NEGATIVITY BRINGS FAILURE!

Jensen 2005

Allan Ellard, Almut Sohn, Andy Jackson, Anett Sjursheim, Antje Kahlheber, Arnd Schäftlein, Ben Brown, Benjamin Hjort, Bernie Mauracher, Bertrand Ragonneau-Flemming, Cameron Paul, Christian Neiger, Christof Langer, Daniel Jänsch, Dan Armstrong, Daniel Herzig, Deb Pinniger, Dunbar Hardy, Eric Martinsen, Flemming Schmidt and family, Florian Schulz, Fresko Vujkow, Gerd Kassel, Gerhard Esser, Gøran Langgård, Hartmut Moll, Heinz Zölzer, Holger Schröder, Horst Fürsattel, Ingrid Schlott, Jan Haluszca, Jan-Henning Wyen, Jeff Rivest, Johnny Kern, Jon Kristen Garmo, Kay-Arne Randen, Kate Donelly, Kelly Woolsey, Kjetil Hansen, Manni Eckert, Manuel Arnu, Mariann Sæther, Marine Chavanis, Markus Hummel, Markus Schmidt, Mathias Klötzler, Matze Brustmann, Michael Neumann, Mike Abbot, Morten Eilertsen, Motzens, Nick Wimsett, Nico Langner, Nils Kagel, Olli Grau, Pål Lindseth, Patrick Fitzgerald, Philippe Doux, Richard Popple, Roland Eggimann, Rune Kvalsnes, Sven Norby Andersson, Sebastian Gründler, Schorschi Schauf, Stephan Glocker, Team Painkiller, Thomas Hilger, Toll Torge, Tore Meirik, Tore Nossum, Trygve Sande, Udo Neumann, Ulrich Kittelberger, Werner Bauer, Wolfgang Haupt, Zicke, + das ganze Blueandwhite-Team

NORWAY
The Whitewater Guide

»Norway – The Whitewater Guide«
Jens Klatt • Olaf Obsommer

Travel Guide Norway: Jens Klatt
River Descriptions: Jens Klatt, Olaf Obsommer
Contributing Writers: Tore Meirik, Manni Eckert, Mariann Sæther, Michi Neumann, Olli Grau, Antje Kahlheber, Nick Wimsett, Fresko Vujkow, Nico Langner, Ben Brown, Ingrid Schlott, Sebastian Gründler
Main Photographer: Jens Klatt
Additional Photographers: Michi Neumann (MN), Sebastian Gründler (SG), Deborah Pinniger (DP), Olaf Obsommer (OO), Manuel Arnu (MA), Mariann Sæther (MS), Benjamin Hjort (BH), Ulrich Kittelberger (UK), Kay-Arne Randen (KAR), Rune Kvalsnes (RK), Tore Meirik (TM), Daniel Armstrong (DA), Kate Donelly (KD), Gerhard Esser (GE), Kjetil Hansen (KH), Gerd Kassel (GK), Ralf Schmitt (RS), Mathias Klötzler (MK), Daniel Herzig (DH)
Layout + Design: Jens Klatt
Translations: Travel guide and Appendix: Richard Popple, E-Mail: *richard.popple@t-online.de*
River descriptions: Cameron Paul
Stories: Almut Sohn

Contact: norway@jensklatt.com
Order: info@kajak.de / www.outdoorcenter.de
or at your local canoe store

The best paddler in the world is the one having the most fun!